Little Chapters in the Making

CHRISTOPHER R. ELLIOTT

Acknowledgements

It is a fact that, without the ready co-operation of hundreds of people here and abroad, a miscellany of this kind would not be possible. So, during the 50 years or so the book covers in the way of published material, the following people – some are no longer with us – deserve special mention fot their varied help:

Alan C. Phillips, Roger A. Freeman, Peter G. Wykeham, Christopher F. Currant, Hughie I. Edwards, VC, Michael Cornell, Jan J. Van der Veer, Patrick Hynes, Dennis Knight, Peter Foote, Robert J. Collis, Geoffrey Diaper, Daisy Tyler, Rosemary Fisher, Kitty Ranson, Ian McLachlan, Sam Cooke, Ian L. Hawkins, Charles Hall, Alfred Price, Owen Thetford, Christopher Cole, Bruce Robertson, Gerald Lawson, Kenneth Munson, Jack Leathley, Robert Malster, Harold P. Cooper, Ashley Cooper, Felix Bensley, John Gillies, Patrick Howarth, David Woodward, Kenneth Wakefield, Michael Skeels, Duncan Skeels, Jean Frazer, Maureen Skeels, Jeanne Frazer, Frank Trinder, Basil Brown, Guy Maynard, A.R. Edwardson, Martin C.H. Carver, Frank A. Tonkinson, Arnold W.L. Nayler, R.C. Shelley, John W. Archer, Norman Smedley, Brian Riddle, M.R. Hull, L.J. Wickes, Peter E.I. Lee, Donald Freeman, Steve Mockridge, George Worrall, Lynette Ramsay Silver, Richard A. Burn, H.R. Lingwood, A.G.S. Draycott, J.L. Drouilly, B.R. Wilson, B. G. Wilkins, Francis Simpson, Eric Fearnley, E.W. Pick, S.R. Grover, Henry Clarke, Leslie Mutum, Eugene C. Ulph, Derek Wood, A.J. Jackson, Geoffrey Sweatman, Alison Brand, Donald Smith, H.L. Oates, Alice M. Tomlinson, N.B. Livingstone Wallace, Diane Merrylees, L.A. Jackets, Marcia Thorp, Rainer Forster, Ian D. Mackersey, Robert B. McWhite, Percy Button, Edward Miller, Anne Haywood Gordon, Rose E.B. Coombs, R.A.N. Dixon, J.G.L. Spence, R.J. Rice, F. Fletcher, Ronald J. Elliott, John Elliott, A.W. Larke, Edmund G. Robbins, Stanley E. West, John R.A. Clark, Peter Elliott, R.W.A. Suddaby, John L. Hyde, Jessie Jones, K. Charteris, R. Pennells, Jack Stockdale, Hugh Snelling, Leslie Hunt, Donald Yates, Kenneth Blowers, Peter Flint, Sidney Freeborn and Norman Franks. Doubtless there are others, whose names have slipped my memory over the years, and for the oversight I am sorry.

The republished articles, in some cases, drew on written sources, for which credit is given in the text. The Appendix states, where traceable, the titles of the publications, and for permission to republish I am grateful to the editors and organisations concerned.

Not to be forgotten are the printers: D&P Bureau, Raynes Park, London SW20, whose staff (David Littler, Pauline Jenkins and James Jenkins) have from the start enthusiastically tackled the job of putting life back into the yellowing printed articles. It must be unusual for an author to be told: "We have enjoyed producing this book and, from time to time, having a good laugh at some of its sentiments".

Lastly, I have to thank my wife, Elizabeth, daughter Anne Wincott and her husband Keith, and sons Alister and William for being helpful in many ways during the making of this book.

C.R.E.

Published by

C. R. Elliott

Wimbledon • London • England

ISBN 0-9550969-0-1

Origination • Printing • Binding

D&P Bureau, Raynes Park, England

Foreword

By

RONALD BLYTHE FRSL, D.LITT

CHRISTOPHER ELLIOTT and I met during the early 1950s when he was a young journalist on the *East Anglian Daily Times* and I was a youthful poet at Colchester Public Library. The war hung around us, and especially for Christopher whose beloved brother had died in the Far East. I had founded a Literary Society to which, and to my amazement, some of the most distinguished authors of the period came to speak and read. Our mutual friend was the poet and novelist James Turner and his old house at Belchamp Walter became a meeting place in which to talk books and to think of our futures. What I noticed then was Christopher's unusual way of looking at things, at our native Suffolk, for example, and also the way in which he valued the small experiences which made up our lives at this time.

Little Chapters in the Making is the result of this art. It is full of remarkable views and conclusions, sights and opinions, which provide a striking commentary on an East Anglia seen from afar. There is the country man in town with a sturdy morality which stems from, in part, those great aerodromes which dominated the home scene during his boyhood, and in some ways this collection of essays could be described as a war book.

It awakens in the reader emotions and recollections which he may have long forgotten. Young people will know just what it felt like to be alive when the Americans came to Suffolk and Norfolk. The author reveals a huge interest in wartime flying and an expert knowledge of it. He is a collector, even a hoarder, of small telling happenings. Gathered together like this, they become important to our understanding of what has happened to us all these past fifty years. His book could be described as local history written from a distance, and made both the sharper and the more affectionate because of this. It shows an unwavering loyalty to a period and a place.

Dedication

Dedicated to my family, and especially to grand-daughter Hannah Wincott, a child of the 21st century, in the hope that she will encounter fewer demons and find, in her early years, lots of Little People to talk to at the bottom of her garden . . .

Cover Illustrations

Front-cover: Thomas Paine (1737-1809), the Thetford, Norfolk-born author of *Rights of Man;* the nose of the 8th USAAF's historical B-17 Flying Fortress named after him (Tom Paine – *Tyranny, like Hell, is not easily Conquered*), which made an emergency landing at Beccles airfield in 1944); the former wind-pump near Walberswick; old-time ploughing depicted on a 1907 calender under the title *The Harmony of Nature* (September-December) – it was bought for a shilling at Sudbury market on 29th April 1954).

Back-cover: an old wagon-wheel (noticed at Dennington in the 1960s) round which the pictures radiate. The hub shows Elisabeth Frink's statue of good St Edmund, cross held firmly, at Bury St Edmunds, where, some time before the historic signing of *Magna Carta* at Runnymede in 1215, earls and barons gathered at the local Abbey, holding St Edmund's remains, and solemnly swore that if King John refused the rights they claimed they would withdraw their support and make war upon him. Thus *Magna Carta*, the Great Charter of Liberties that established the rights of free men and the beginning of democracy, had Suffolk origins.

Around the hub in anti-clockwise sequence: the top oval picture shows animated ladies (28th August 1994) in a Lavenham carnival procession; harvesting the old way, near Brent Eleigh in the early 1990s; old wagon in the 1950s at Shadingfield, fresh from the fields; Saxtead post-mill; a remarkable ice-cloud stream over Suffolk in April 1987 (the fine elm tree in the foreground fell during the Great Gale, October 1987); looking out from old Lavenham churchyard after the tree screen had been felled; some of the affected wood-trunks.

Contents

Little Chapters in the Making

BEING a miscellany of some of the subject's journalistic contributions, photographs and occasional pen-and-ink sketches dating from the 1940s to the 1990s – about half-a-century. Shy of book authorship, like so many local newspaper-trained journalists of his generation and earlier, a newspaper or magazine page was, perhaps, the true mete for the work of this man, now in his mid-seventies.

INTRODUCTION

WHEN I started out in earnest in journalism in 1948, following a teenage ambition, I began as a very raw cub-reporter on an old-established weekly newspaper in the port of Grimsby, in Lincolnshire, and after a year moved on to a daily newspaper in Suffolk, my native area, which also published evening and weekly titles. Both newspapers had mentors of the old-school who, in those distant days, were always ready to assist and advise trainee reporters. But a nose for news, or the ability to delve, could not be taught.

So it was in those formative years into the mid-1950s, before I obtained other press posts in London, including Whitehall, Fleet Street and Pall Mall, that I started to casually contribute to a variety of publications – daily, weekly and monthly – on, more often than not, history subjects with an Eastern Counties' connection.

As the years went by, and the variety of articles, often illustrated with my own black-and-white photographs or occasional pen-and-ink drawings of inert subjects, proliferated, I was sometimes asked when I intended to turn some of this work into more permanent book form.

But there had been some early pointers: for Mr R.A.N. Dixon, editor of the *East Anglian Magazine,* one of England's most successful regional magazines, which he founded in 1935, publicly declared in 1952 that "Christopher Elliott has . . . an insatiable curiosity. Wherever he goes he finds things that other people miss. By writing about them and photographing them he has, at 23, already made a name for himself as a journalist."

And a well-known West Suffolk publican, Mr Edmund G. Robbins, who during the Second World War entertained such distinguished American journalists as Edward R. Murrow, the broadcaster, Allen A. Michie and Walter Graebner, joint editors of *Their Finest Hour* and *Lights of Freedom,* recited one evening over his pint and my orange juice: *When others around you are thoroughly pissed, you will tell them what they missed!* Well, that is what Mr Robbins believed.

Certainly, while in various London journalistic posts up to editor status, often taking in public relations as well, I assisted a number of authors with their books, but it was not until 1971 that a Suffolk publisher, Terence Delton, put out my *Aeronauts and Aviators,* now long out of print, which told of the progress in the air over the Eastern Counties between 1785 and 1939. It became a kind of pathfinder for a series of local aviation history books from the same publisher – but not by me.

Curiously, after that, the idea of books receded yet again. But in the 1990s, as more and more people from all kinds of back-grounds and professions, helped by smart new glossy printing techniques, started to publish books, I was again jolted into the realisation that it was high time I really did try to marshal a good cross-section of some of my widely-scattered articles and stories as I entered my seventies.

So that is how this first volume came to be published to be followed, who dares to predict, by a further round-up. Perhaps some of the pieces (vignettes(?)), for their content, stand up as potted book chapters. As I have already explained, I have dragged my feet over getting into permanent print, but it may be that, like so many journalists of my generation and earlier who were seeded in the provinces, a newspaper or magazine page – the crisp black and white effect – was our true mete!

Finally, as journalists often tend to recycle old details to help them with other articles, the reader must forgive the occasional repetition of facts between articles. Generally, the contributions, which often created readers' letters providing much new information, which often led to much-improved articles, appear in much the same form as they were published. An appendix at the back gives the sources.

Christopher R. Elliott
Wimbledon

Confessions of a Cub Reporter

THE arrangement, as far as I can remember, was that I should first of all be apprenticed to a weekly newspaper outside my native East Anglia for a year before joining a paper at Norwich. So I was sent up the east coast, to the port of Grimsby, Lincolnshire, in 1948, to be a cub reporter.

My lodgings were in a very poor area of dockland. Opposite my window fishing boats hooted their way to northern waters and, when the tide was low, propellers thrashed like the tails of dying whales. The weekly board took my tiny wage – just a pound or two – and for small pleasures I received a pound a week from my father.

I had not been on the staff very long before the sub-editor breezed in one morning at 8.45 and said: "Give it two columns and follow up". I never answered as I could not relate his instructions to anything I had done the night before. The sub-editor, who smoked a pipe, bent down over my desk, puffed smoke in my face, and said loudly: "Did you hear?" A mute "What do you mean?" gave him the answer: I'd overlooked on my doorstep – the place faced my lodgings across the river – the port's biggest factory fire since the war-time blitz!

Fogs, as dense as they were in Dickens's day in London, often shrouded the port and muffled the sea songs emanating from the rough taverns in dockland. Indeed, it was so dense on the night my pedal cycle was stripped of its wheels outside a church hall, where I was reporting a lecture, that I was taken into custody by two policemen for being a suspect as I walked home with the frame!

After about a year I came back to East Anglia, the plan being that I should go to a district office at Great Yarmouth, but on reflection I felt that would be too seasonal and that what I wanted was a start where the seasons would be clearly spring, summer, autumn and winter.

So I went instead to a newspaper in West Suffolk, and this is what I noted for my first day, Monday, 5 September 1949: "Arrived at Sudbury. Toured town. Examined All Saints' Church".

Being at a district office, away from head office, meant that one was largely on one's own. If you made a poor job of a story you could not, like they do in Fleet Street or the big cities, vanish into thin air leaving messages like "Just gone out", "Gone abroad" or "Day off" You had to face the music on the spot.

So it happened once – and it happens to lots of reporters – that I "buried" the wrong brother. That evening I was in a local pub, feeling on top of the

Author's Sudbury EADT office, January, 1953. The Imperial portable typewriter (left), acquired on entering journalism in 1948 is still in use!

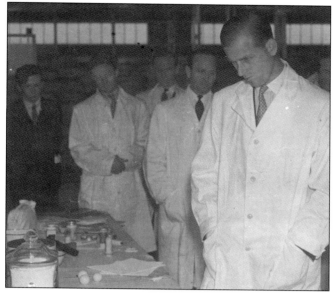

With the young Duke of Edinburgh inspecting industry at Grimsby, Lincolnshire, on July 13, 1949.
Photo: Courtesy Grimsby Evening Telegraph.

world, when a hand gripped my shoulder. I could see the white bony knuckles out of the corner of my eye. Then a voice, loud with indignation, declared: "You young . . . you've just buried Fred – that's me – and not my rotten brother Bill".

District reporters, at least in the late 1940s, often worked from any available office. My office was shared with a printing firm in old property overlooking the market place where the clock of St. Peter's church regularly marked the time of day.

Market Hill, Sudbury, Suffolk, on May 10, 1951.

My desk was old, with many pigeon holes, and some of the drawers contained printed matter and old negatives plates going back to the late 1800s. Soon I had my den fitted up so that it looked like a newspaper office.

There was even a gas-ring so that, if I felt hungry late at night, I could boil up a farm egg. Sometimes the law on its late rounds would pay me a friendly call. But more often my visitor was a mouse. It soon grew bold and ventured into one of the pigeon holes where, at every metallic click of my typewriter keys, its whiskers twitched!

When I went through Sudbury about 15 years ago I noticed that my second office had been demolished along with the old police station, but my first office on Market Hill, together with the entire north side, was unchanged. The afternoon sunshine, as of old, made the little shops look inviting.

Secrets? Well, yes, the place had a secret or two – at least, that was my impression. For there walked at night, when all was still, heavy feet on the stairs. They always paused, perhaps for rest, and then stamped on. I once asked the law to listen. But the feet never walked. Did they echo from another part of Market Hill? Perhaps they did. I could never tell.

Attending courts all over the area for every kind of rural crime took up much of my time. Chewing away one day in court, weary of the progress of justice, I received the following note from the extremely fair magistrates' clerk: "If the press require sustenance, and why shouldn't they, do they really think the court is the proper place for obvious refreshment?"

There was no telephone link with my lodgings (I lived with two old ladies) so the fire siren, wind permitting, was the only means I had of knowing about a fire at night. Thus it came about on the foggy and frosty night of Friday, 5 December 1952, that I went on a hazardous motor-cycle ride to report a dangerous fire in medieval Lavenham which, even

Ageing landladies' Stidolph and Strutt who looked after the writer at Sudbury, Suffolk, for several years. Sometimes they were rewarded with outings, one being boating on the River Alde with a jolly Slaughden fisherman at the helm!

EAST ANGLIAN
DAILY TIMES
INCORPORATING THE "IPSWICH EXPRESS" (EST. 1839)

EISENHOWER'S THREE-DAY VISIT TO KOREA
No Carrying of War Into China
MEETING WITH TROOPS OF MANY NATIONS

President-Elect Eisenhower, now on his way back to America after a secret three-day tour of the Korean front, declared at Seoul yesterday before he left:—

"There are many limitations on a war of this kind, but much can be done, in my opinion, to improve our position—much will be done, and help is going to come from outside for a very long time."

* news conference he str--- ----- was

£750,000 FUND TO FIGHT MAU MAU
Emergency Fund Announced

Police held, several thousand Africans in Nairobi yesterday for screening after receiving information of a steady drift back to the city from the Kikuyu Reserve.

Those who had come back include "spivs and thugs," they said.

The Finance Member of the Legislative Council, Mr. Matthews, announced that £750,000 was being allotted to a special emergency fund to meet expenditure arising from the abnormal situation.

Unless matters changed drastically, he hoped to avoid an interim Budget next year and extra taxation. The fund would be under strict Treasury control, he said.

The proposal gave unofficial members of the Council an opportunity to renew criticism of the Government's handling of the emergency.

The leader of the European Elected Members ... ... his col----- about---- --- --

LAVENHAM FIRE: Two houses in Lavenham High Street were destroyed by fire last night. Firemen fought for over two hours to save adjoining property.

Above: The night news editor of the East Anglian Daily Times ruled against a motor cycle ride from Lavenham to Ipswich on the icy night of December 5, 1952, but the writer made it and the front page of next day's edition! Because the negative was underexposed, it had to be touched up, and this is apparent in the fire picture.

Right: The story as published on the inside pages.

from over four miles away, lit up the tower of the local church. Space prevents me from relating what was done that night, against the night news editor's fatherly advice, and how my story and film finally reached Ipswich.

The result at dawn was very satisfying for a young reporter: my fire picture had made the front page of the *East Anglian Daily Times* and the story was inside.

That evening I went to the inn where Fred had given me a scare, feeling very pleased with the night's work, but no one spoke. I felt uneasy. Had I buried someone else's wrong brother? Then the customers started on me. First one asked: "How's the photography?". Another asked: "Do much night photography?". Yet another: "How do you stand, when you take a picture, at night?". "What's up?", I asked. "What's right?", came the chorus.

Then the pub took away – which was probably a good thing – the pride of my night's dangerous work. It seemed that the vivid photograph on the front page, made from an under-exposed and very thin negative, had at my tired and frozen instructions been printed the wrong way round and Sudbury readers who knew the scene, of course, had been trying to figure out the geography of the composition.

I suppose, apart from courts and councils, funerals were my third speciality. I remember one funeral on

DISASTROUS FIRES RAGE IN EAST ANGLIA
Lavenham Street Saved: Norfolk School Blaze

A fierce fire at Lavenham last night was the culmination of a series of disastrous outbreaks in East Anglia yesterday, including a school from which boys had to be evacuated in their nightclothes, and another at Wolterton Hall, the home of Lord Walpole, which was the most serious Norfolk firemen have had to deal with this year.

When a threatening blaze, the biggest for some time, broke out at Lavenham last night, four fire brigades battled with the flames for over two hours, and saved adjoining property, including an engineering factory.

Shortly before 6.30 p.m., R. H. Dawson's radio supply shop and Mrs. E. M. Snell's house, next door, caught fire.

Mr. I. W. Howlett, a butcher, of High Street, told an "East Anglian Daily Times" representative that when Mrs. Snell came and said she could smell smoke, he went to the window of the radio shop to look inside, and noticed that the windows were warm. He at once gave the alarm.

CRIMSON PALL SEEN MILES AWAY

At Great Waldingfield, over four miles away, a thick pall of white smoke, coloured crimson by the flames could be seen, and for some time the tower of Lavenham Church stood out clearly against the night sky.

Several hours later the shop and dwelling house had been gutted, but adjoining property, including Mr. James Cutts' small engineering factory, had been saved.

Mr. R. H. Dawson, of Red House, Pond Lane, Hadleigh Road, said when he left the shop shortly after 6 p.m. everything was in order. He had just reached home when he was told that his shop was on fire.

STREET CROWDED

Brigades from Sudbury, Long Melford, Hadleigh and Bury St.

Edmunds, under the direction of Station Officer C. Rogers (Bury) and Station Officer O. Webb (Melford) raced to the scene. A large crowd, estimated to be the biggest the town has seen for a long time, packed the street, but did not hinder the firemen.

By 7 p.m. the fire had got a firm hold, and soon all timbers of the building were exposed, while firemen, some on ladders and others on the ground, fought the blaze. Every now and then, as equipment in the shop exploded, showers of sparks rose.

GRATITUDE TO FIRE BRIGADES

By 9.15 p.m. the house and cottage had disappeared, and only a shell was left.

Flames at one time began to break through the roof of Mr. Cutts' private house, but firemen prevented the outbreak spreading.

An eye-witness told the "East Anglian Daily Times": "I don't know how to describe it. I could almost have wept to see it.

"If the firemen had not done such a good job in keep--- --- --- from Mr---- --- go---

the Suffolk/Essex border at a time when frost had made the ground rock-like. I arrived at the church twenty minutes before the funeral, in order to assess all the ways in, for I had to collect a big list of mourners single-handed as was local newspaper policy in those days.

Sudbury East Anglian Daily Times *district representative Jack Leathley and the author, his assistant, inspecting Farmer Harold Cooper's Roman excavations at Hill Farm, Gestingthorpe, Essex, on May 21, 1953.* Photo: Courtesy Bury Free Press.

Blizzards came and went and, from time to time, sky and earth seemed like one grey wall. What a day, I thought, to be buried. The bearers in their black macintoshes having delivered the coffin, lay huddled behind the tallest tombstone, their hands clasping hip-flasks, for, they told me, "Only such lubricant can keep us from joining him."

But that wasn't the end of the story: as the coffin was lowered into the frozen and flooded grave, there was a crash of breaking ice, and up popped the coffin, feet first, like the bow of a sinking liner!

For the first two or three years of my border reporting days I covered the ground on a pedal cycle in all weathers and at all times of the day and night. I experienced the four seasons as I had wished. I came to know in five or so years a great variety of people in all kinds of situations. I often wonder if some of them remember me as I most certainly remember many of them.

In trying to be honest with those I had dealings with, and insisting on nothing but the truth, I built up tremendous goodwill and, most important, the humble and the mighty had respect for one's newspaper. Thus the conduct, and performance, of youngsters new to the profession is a very important factor today.

Much later in his career – in the 1990s – C.R.E. was at a Beccles fete when he ran into Martin Bell, broadcaster and politician, the son of author Adrian Bell whose East Anglian-orientated books are well known.
Photo: Courtesy Anne Wincott.

Ambassador in Armour

WILLIAM MEADE LINDSLEY FISKE, of Chicago, entered Trinity Hall, Cambridge, in the Michaelmas Term of 1928. He studied economic history, but also found time to develop his sporting skills – golf and bobsleigh riding. Today he lies buried in Boxgrove churchyard, four miles from Vespasian's Chichester, and the head-stone to his grave reads: "Pilot Officer W.M.L. Fiske III, Born June 4th 1911 in Chicago. Killed in action August 17th 1940. He died for England."

How did Pilot Officer Fiske, the son of rich American parents, come to join the RAF so early in the last war and thus, by his death in the Battle of Britain 25 years ago, go down in history as the first American officer in the RAF to lose his life in action? His burial in Sussex on the day – 20 August – that Winston Churchill delivered his famous tribute to the RAF in the House of Commons caught the attention of the free world.

In this country astute political minds, even before his death, realised that in Billy Fiske, as he was known, they had an ambassador in armour. For he had given up a comfortable job in New York at only two hours' notice as the war clouds gathered in 1939. He was, in fact, the first of the many.

Now his diary, started in October, 1939, has been lent to me by the former Mrs Fiske, who today lives in France, and extracts are published for the first time.

Between his stay at Trinity Hall and his return to England in 1938 for a spell at the London office of Dillon, Read & Co., the New York bankers, Billy became well known on the Cresta Run at St. Moritz and for many years was the unbeaten champion.

He was a golfer, too, and at Cambridge and Mildenhall, just over the border in Suffolk, where he often played, he is still remembered by a few as the driver of a 4 1/2-litre Bentley. In this car he often covered the 19 miles separating the two places in 17 minutes, "never varying more than two or three inches in his road track", and sometimes reaching, on the long, straight stretches, 110mph.

Rose Bassett.
Photo: Courtesy Daily Telegraph

Pilot Officer Fiske on being commissioned in April, 1940.
Photo: Courtesy Rose Bassett

After many adventures – he even tried his hand at film-making in Tahiti – he learnt to fly at an aerodrome near London. He married Rose, the former Countess of Warwick, at Maidenhead in 1938. She remembers "the big day when he was allowed to take me in an open two-seater". Their planned short flight to Le Touquet on this occasion was marred by an oil leak that spattered over the windscreen and so hindered navigation that they landed at Deauville.

Early in 1939 Billy was recalled to his firm's New York office. What, then, led him, after only a few months, to embark for England shortly before war was declared on 3 September 1939? Apparently an English friend working in New York, Mr W.P. Clyde, an RAF reservist and a member of 601 (County of London) Aux. Air Force Squadron, talked him into sailing with him on the *Aquitania* on 30 August – a voyage that, because of precautionary evasive action, took eight days.

Opening his diary – the first page is dated 29 October – Billy says of his desire to record experiences and events: "There is really only one reason, other than my own amusement, why they may be worth recording, and that is the fact that I believe I can lay claim to being the first US citizen to join the RAF in England after the outbreak of hostilities.

"I don't say this with any particular pride, except perhaps in so far as my conscience is clear, but only because it probably has some bearing on the course of my career. My reasons for joining in the fray are my own. . . ."

But Billy knew at the time that, as the regulations stood then, "no person not a British citizen and a son of British citizens, could be eligible for any position whatsoever in the Air Force".

His plan, then, was this: he would have "to make a

very passable pretence at being a Canadian and of Canadian parentage". He appreciated, on the other hand, that with no identification papers other than an American passport, that was of no use at all, he would have 'to make up some very watertight answers for any questions they might be expected to ask me'.

Immediately, therefore, on landing in this country he set about joining the RAF. However, the going, he found, was even harder than he had anticipated. A London newspaper, soon after his arrival, referred to his presence in London, and Billy, on reading the report, felt that this spoilt any chance there was left of acceptance.

Luck was at hand. Billy was invited to lunch at the Savoy with Mr H.C.H. Bathurst, an Auxiliary Air Force pilot and the son of Lord Bledisloe. Mr Bathurst brought along an Air Ministry friend, and Billy was relieved to learn that, as a result of the newspaper publicity, the authorities were anxious to arrive at a swift decision in his case and subsequent cases arising from foreign volunteers.

A meeting, only briefly recorded in his diary, took place between Billy and a high ranking RAF officer. Before this meeting – it was on a Sunday – took place, however, a diligent check-up was made of Billy's background. One question, for example, checked if it was true that Mr Clarence Dillon, of Dillon, Read & Co., whose European partner was Billy Fiske's father, had once on behalf of a group of clients, signed a cheque for $150,000,000 for the purchase of an American motor works. Fiske III, with confidence, was able to reply in the affirmative.

We know from Billy's diary that, as the interview day approached, he made every effort to make himself acceptable because "it was largely a matter of pride and the terrific desire to be 'doing something'".

After a round of golf at Roehampton, for the purpose of acquiring "a healthy look", Billy Fiske

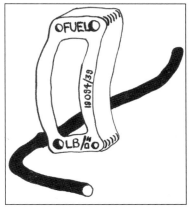

Fuel pressure gauge face and piping from Hurricane L1990 which crashed at Nyetimber, nr. Pagham, Sussex, on August 18, 1940. He had flown L1990 shortly before he died on August 17.

noted: "Needless to say, for once I had a quiet Saturday night – I didn't want to have eyes looking like blood-stained oysters the next day."

Anyway, whatever transpired at the interview, we know that Billy, full of the joys of life, went in October to No. 10 Elementary Flying Training School, Yatesbury, Wiltshire. He had won his first victory: he had fought his way into the R.A.F.

In his diary he describes the mixed company on the course and singles out a New Zealand shepherd who "gave himself confidence by whistling to it (the aircraft) the way they do to sheep in New Zealand".

Billy also noted how, on one occasion, he arranged to meet their French-Canadian pupil pilot at 4,000ft for "formation aerobatics" in Tiger Moths. "We met all right – nearly head-on. His idea apparently is that it doesn't matter how hard your wings hit each other as long as the motors themselves don't come into contact!"

After Yatesbury, Billy moved to the Flying Training School at Brize Norton, Oxfordshire, and with his wife took a small house at nearby Minster Lovell. At Brize Norton on 12 April, 1940, he became Acting Pilot Officer Fiske, and on 12 July – it could hardly have been by accident – he was posted to 601 (County of London) Aux. Air Force Squadron at Tangmere.

Now this squadron was variously known as the Legionnaires' and the Millionaires' Squadron, for it was at White's Club in 1924 that Lord Edward Grosvenor selected members of the club to serve under him in 601.

The former Mrs. Fiske recollects: "I found a house near Tangmere and, plus a van with all our bits and bobs and chickens, we moved in a body. . . . I remember the first time he went up in a Hawker Hurricane from Tangmere and how, on landing, he burst a tyre. One of the boys said it was very bad luck — which did not please me at all. It never entered my head that anything would happen to Billy."

But Billy had only a month to live. This was to be a month of intense activity, such as he had hardly contemplated, but undoubtedly it was what he wanted.

A 601 Squadron Hurricane in a hurry.
Photo: Courtesy Imperial War Museum

At Tangmere, however, with the Luftwaffe only just beginning its massive offensive, there was some apprehension in 601 about taking "this untried American adventurer" – at least, without careful nursing. But Billy had no pretensions or illusions about his flying skill and, having made this clear to everyone, he was soon accepted.

According to the operations record book of 601 Squadron, Billy, between 13-18 July, undertook considerable flying practice on the Hurricane. The log reads "type experience, circuits and landings, pip-squeak practice, formation and fighter attacks" and so on. Meanwhile, his friend, Mr Bathurst, had given him his well-worn pilot's "wings" so that he would not feel too much like a novice.

Then came the great day – 20 July – when Billy undertook two "operational take-offs" in quick succession on Hurricane L1951 late in the afternoon. This was just a month before his death. From this operational initiation, until his last flight, he threw himself into the fight with great spirit. An American radio commentator said in 1942 that Billy Fiske, during his fleeting service with 601, destroyed six enemy aircraft, the first being a Heinkel.

Then came his last fight. On 16 August Billy's aerodrome was singled out for attack by German dive-bombers. The operations record book of 601 Squadron records that he took off on Hurricane P3358 at 12.25pm. With him, as he rose over Boxgrove, were the rest of 601.

Squadron Leader Sir Archibald Hope, Bt, who now lives in Hampshire, led them and they were ordered to patrol Tangmere at about 12,000ft. The dive-bombers – Junkers 87s – were seen to cross the coast east of Selsey Bill. Permission for them to engage the dive-bombers was given, however, only when the Stukas started to dive on Tangmere. Several sharp individual combats then followed as the enemy – eight were definitely destroyed – were driven out over the coast around Pagham marshes.

Soon after 1pm the first Hurricanes started to land back at Tangmere, where damage had been caused, and some unofficial accounts have it that one – Billy Fiske's smoking Hurricane – was seen "to glide over the boundary and land on its belly".

The operations record book, however, says: "While the bombing was in progress, Pilot Officer Fiske was seen to land on the aerodrome, and his aircraft immediately caught fire. He was taken from the machine but sustained severe burns. . . ."

Sir Archibald Hope tells me: "When we had pursued them down to the sea, we returned to Tangmere and landed individually. I saw one Hurricane mildly burning on the runway. The ambulance was already there with the crew helping the pilot. I stopped to see if I could give any assistance and spoke to Billy Fiske . . . He was more or less conscious and told me that his aircraft had been damaged by the return fire from the rear-gunner

Pilot Officer Fiske's burial at Boxgrove, Sussex, on August 20, 1940, as Prime Minister Winston Churchill paid his famous tribute to the 'Few' in the House of Commons.
Photo: Courtesy Allan A. Michie

As Pilot Officer Fiske's headstone looked at Boxgrove, Sussex, on August 5, 1954.

Mrs. Rose Bassett's letter of 1965 on receiving a copy of the Sussex Life article on Pilot Officer Fiske

of a Junkers 87 which he was attacking somewhere near Bognor Regis.

I cannot remember whether he destroyed the aircraft, or even whether he was able to lower his undercarriage before landing. Billy Fiske had burns on his legs below the knee, on his hands and, to a lesser extent, on his face. He died 48 hours later from shock."

In *The Times* of 19 August, 1940, Billy Fiske was listed under "Fallen Officers". His obituary ran to the unusual length of 40 lines. The funeral took place on 20 August. As the coffin, covered with the Union Jack and the Stars and Stripes, was borne on a bier to the 800-year-old church at Boxgrove, only half a mile from the main entrance to Tangmere aerodrome, the Central Band of the RAF played funeral marches. Overhead the Battle of Britain continued with undiminished ferocity. . . . But Billy's comrades – some did not land back at Tangmere until 1.45pm on that day – came with him through the Sussex lanes to Boxgrove. The coffin was borne into the churchyard by six members of the ground staff. There was a wreath from Lord Beaverbrook, Minister of Aircraft Production.

Lt-Col. J.T.C. Moore-Brabazon (later Lord Brabazon of Tara), who was the first English pilot to fly and was well known on the Cresta Run like Billy Fiske, who had captained the US bobsleigh team in the 1932 Olympics, said of him in a newspaper tribute on 20 August: "We thank America for sending us the perfect sportsman. Many of us would have given our lives for Billy. . . ."

But that was not the end. The press next day reported that "on average 25 American airman a week are going to Canada to serve as instructors to the RCAF or enlist in the British RAF". The first American Eagle Squadron – No. 71 – was in the process of formation in this country. America, however, was still at peace.

Yet, almost a year after his death, Billy Fiske was still in people's memories. On the following Independence Day, by the bust of George Washing-ton, a tablet (with

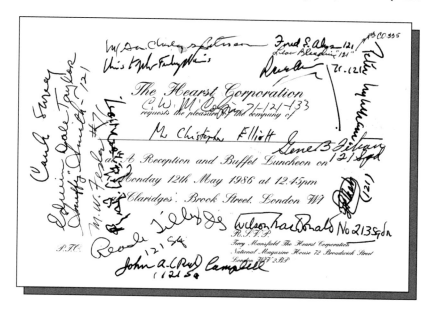

Historic gathering of surviving Eagles of Nos 71, 121 and 133 Squadrons at Claridges, London, on May 12, 1986, following Prime Minister Margaret Thatcher's unveiling of the Eagle Squadrons' memorial statue in Grosvenor Square. It was sculptured by Dame Elisabeth Frink of Suffolk.

his pilot's 'wings' framed below it) was unveiled in the crypt of St. Paul's Cathedral, bearing, beneath the name of William Meade Lindsley Fiske, the words: *"An American Citizen Who Died That England Might Live."*

At the unveiling Sir Archibald Sinclair, Secretary of State for Air, said: "Here was a young man for whom life held much. Under no kind of compulsion he came to fight for Britain. He came, and he fought, and he died."

Now, it is 25 years since Billy Fiske crash-landed his Hurricane at Tangmere and was laid to rest in nearby Boxgrove churchyard where today a stone, bearing the winged sword of 601's badge, marks his grave.

It is said that shortly before he died on 17 August (he had received first-aid at the Sussex Hospital, Chichester), he asked if his Hurricane was intact – if it would fight again. I have the face of the fuel pressure gauge and a broken piece of pipe line from one of Billy Fiske's Hurricanes. But these souvenirs were not taken from his Hurricane on 16 August. Hurricane P3358 – the one he was flying when he was hit – was, however, repaired, as he had hoped, and it flew again. Billy Fiske, in the course of his whirlwind partnership with 601, flew a number of Hurricanes. We know that, in addition to those already listed, he piloted several others from Tangmere, including L1990, N 2602, L2057, P3393 and P2920.

How did these souvenirs reach me? In 1953, a Bognor Regis resident, hearing of my collection, sent me the relics, saying they had come from a Hurricane – a special Hurricane – that had crashed at Pagham in the Battle of Britain. He understood at the time that the particular Hurricane had "at one time been flown by an American serving in the RAF who was the first American officer to be killed during the war".

What is interesting about these relics, I think, is that Billy Fiske, who was 29 when he died, should have been remembered and linked with them as late as 1953. Now I am passing on his memory. Truly, it can be said, he was an ambassador – an ambassador without portfolio – for this American set an example that led to a flood of volunteers when England needed them most.

Footnote: It was reported in the *East Anglian Daily Times* of 16 September, 2003, that preparations were being made for a film based on the true story about Pilot Officer Fiske, adapted from Alex Kershaw's historical biography *The Few*. Mr *Top Gun* star Tom Cruse was signed-up to play the part of Billy Fiske in the film, also named *The Few*. Interestingly, it was stated that Billy's "ancestors were from Suffolk, living in the villages of Dennington, Laxfield and Badingham."

How the US Navy came to Greenwich

CARVED on the floor of the Painted Hall of the Royal Naval College, Greenwich, are these words:

15th June 1941
On this day came three citizens of the
United States of America
The first of their countrymen
to become sea-officers of
the Royal Navy

The inscription and its association was unknown to me until recently when, while thumbing a pile of second-hand books, I came on a tome of 544 pages with 36 illustrations entitled "Yankee RN," the story of a Wall Street banker who volunteered for active duty in the Royal Navy before America came into the war, by Commander Alex Cherry, OBE, RNVR. The book was published in England in 1951.

This surprising volume, which at once took pride of place alongside my books on the American Eagles who started to join the RAF long before Pearl Harbor, told how Cherry was just packing his bags for Ottawa as another Eagle in April, 1941, when he received a letter from the British Consulate-General, in New York, asking him to "call at this office at your earliest convenience as a matter of personal interest."

By the spring of 1941 fifty American destroyers had been handed over to Britain under the Lease-Lend Act. The vital Atlantic supply line was being severed by German U-boats.

As Cherry knew how to fly, how to navigate a ship, and how to operate a ship's radio, he was divided over the course he should take, so he took a coin out of his pocket and spun it into the air.

"If Lincoln's head turned up," he recorded in his book, "the sea would claim me, if tails I would join the RAF. The coin hit the deck. There lay Lincoln, a good omen indeed. I wanted to shake his hand. It meant the sea and I was glad, for the sea was in my blood, and I realised at that very moment it was what I had really wanted."

Bound for Halifax, Nova Scotia, by then, Cherry was told to report aboard the Flagship, HMS *Seaborn*, for an interview with Rear-Admiral Stewart Bonham-Carter, flag-officer commanding Third Battle Squadron, which was at that time acting as North Atlantic Escort Force. Thus began Cherry's exciting wartime career as a Sea Eagle – in the British Royal Navy.

On reaching England he was sent to the Royal Naval College, Greenwich, and, in his words, "back to school." Soon other American volunteers joined him at Greenwich. On completion of their time there, Cherry and the others took part in the Battle of the Atlantic with many tales (as related in the book) to tell.

Finally, at the end of April 1945, as Germany's principal ports and dockyards came under scrutiny, Cherry was with the American 'Blue Jackets' on their entry into Bremen.

The Royal Navy Liaison Officer for Task Group 126, which had made a unique 400-mile trek through Belgium and Holland into Germany, Cherry said the entry was "a complete reversal of normal military procedure and for the first time in history the US Navy (Task Group 126) was carried overland by Army units to occupy an enemy port from the rear."

Cherry dedicated his book "To my friend, Lt. John Parker, RNVR, of Boston, Mass., the first American to be killed in action while serving under the White Ensign at sea – in a 'Four Stacker' in 1941."

In declaring that Parker was the first American on active duty to lose his life in a naval action in World War II, Cherry went on to add that he was "the first American volunteer, commissioned as a British Naval Officer, to be killed in action in all the Royal Navy's long history."

Vapour Trails
which would have delighted painter
JOHN CONSTABLE

AS National Aviation Heritage Week (27th September – 5th October 1997) looms ahead, marking the 30-year existence of the British Aviation Preservation Society, East Anglia's growing band of aviation buffs are getting ready to rev-up for some armchair flying.

Coincidentally, in Lambeth, London, a grand old-time balloon (tethered) is taking people aloft for a bird's-eye view of the city.

But there's more to the business of flying in peace and war, with its vast fall-out of bits and pieces, not forgetting the huge aircrew casualties of the two world wars, than many people realise.

For, while East Anglia's sky has steadily grown quieter with the contraction of RAF and USAF bases, a 'plane enthusiast in south-west London, who regularly rises between 3am and 4am in the summer and retires to bed at 8 o'clock, took startling coloured photographs of typical dawn air activity in early August, 1997, through his kitchen window using a 1920s Ensign box-camera!

The star picture – the one depicting the lower altitude zig-zag vapour trail due to lower wind conditions of a jet descending – appears to be a repeat of the description in 'Vapour Trails' from the Waveney Sonnets by the late A.E. Tomlinson, the Lowestoft poet, who was the first winner of the Crabbe Memorial Poetry Competition organised by the Suffolk Poetry Society in 1954.

The falling vapour trail was made by a decending air liner over south west London. This, in fact, was exactly like a World War I zeppelin looked when descending on fire. Zig-zag effect caused by air currents at lower level.

The sudden cloud manifestation over south west London for which there was no explanation at the time.

The poem runs:

> Someone takes a brush and paints a line
> Straight as a dagger through the empty sky
> Someone pours a flask of smoking wine
> Down from the tables of the gods on high
> And a vapour trail from a 'plane on the climb
> Is born in heaven in the evening light
> Joining today to the rest of time
> Like a song in the sky to the age of flight
> High in its own eternity
> Hand over hand it climbs up the world
> Climbing as high as the world can be
> Then rolls from the sky like an ensign furled
> Then someone takes a tin of scarlet dye
> And spills a sunset on the emptied sky!

But these extraordinary man-made cloud patterns – atmospheric conditions from time to time are conducive over the British Isles – are not the first to be taken by the south-west London spotter.

In the early 1950s, when he was a young reporter with the EADT at Sudbury, he photographed a variety of RAF and USAF vapour trails, including Wattishaw-based Meteor jets rounding on Stanton-based F-86 Sabre jets, viewed from Market Hill looking north. It was possible that the Meteors went

Above: Flying Fortresses at high altitude with lower formation not making vapour.

Below: Artist Paul Nash, who first painted war scenes in the Great War, painted in 1940 a number of pictures including Battle of Britain – an air battle in progress over the Thames.

Photo: Courtesy Imperial War Museum

American F-86 Sabre fighters 'fighting' RAF Meteors north of Sudbury, Suffolk, in the 1950s.

into a defensive ring an an attempt to throw off the much faster American jets.

Interestingly, two years ago, when the same spotter photographed a similar dawn manifestation approaching London from the south east, he took up the matter with the civil and military sides, asking about what was going on overhead, normally unheard, which only the evidence of vapour trails had revealed.

After many weeks, the Ministry of Defence, having checked their logs, declared that all the air traffic was civil – no movements by armed RAF or USAF jets ever took place over London, but military courier 'planes did sometimes join the London landing circuit.

Kart Badt, in his book *John Constable's Clouds* (Routledge & Kegan Paul, 1950), in which he dealt with the Suffolk artist's complicated attachment to clouds in his paintings, said: "Clouds were once the thrones of gods; on them angels knelt and the saints took their rest. It was a pillar of cloud in which the Lord went before the Jews to lead them out of Egypt to the land of Canaan and a cloud covered the tent of the congregation. . . ."

Curiously, August this year, also witnessed from the same south west London vantage point one

evening, the formation within minutes of a white nuclear-like plume, but a cloud, there being no ground disturbance – fire or chemical release – to cause it. This, too, was captured using the same old box-camera.

Footnote: While nothing much was said during the Second World War about the effect aircraft vapour trails have on earth, the *Daily Telegraph* of August 8th, 2002, stated that "vapour trails left by passenger jets reflect sunlight away from Earth during the day but trap heat at night". Scientists were given an unexpected chance to study the impact of contrails during the three days after September 11th when, because of the twin towers' terrorist attacks, aircraft in America were grounded. Aircraft typically produce contrails at cruising altitudes of 30,000 to 40,000 ft. Condensation trails do, in fact, often turn into cirrus clouds under the right atmospheric conditions.

The Lambeth, London, moored balloon under a lovely sky.

In Saintly Footsteps . . .

THE press reported in January 1985, that a boy, Ryan Williams, aged 10, had returned to school "after spending Christmas as a bishop".

His month as diocesan head of his local church, St. Nicholas's, at Bournemouth, Hampshire, it was pointed out, revived a medieval tradition among churches named after the 4th century patron saint of children.

As the Sutton Hoo research committee's 10 year or more investigation into the fascinating old Anglo-Saxon kingdom of East Anglia, awakened in 1939 by the discovery at Sutton Hoo, near Woodbridge, Suffolk, of the famous ship burial, develops, it is interesting to look at some of the area's saints with possible pointers to revelations on the horizon.

In cycle rides as a boy years ago I always found the Suffolk Ilketshalls and the South Elmhams – in the 1930s there were for certain four Ilketshalls forming parishes and about six or seven South Elhams – mysterious, lonely places with many old run-down dwellings, moated enclosures and forgotten farms. The area of the, Saints – St. Cross, St. Margaret, St. Nicholas, St. James, St. Lawrence, St. Michael, St. John, St. Andrew, St. Peter, St. Mary, etc. – owes its saintliness to the fact that the East Anglian bishopric was most likely there before moving to Thetford, Norfolk, about AD 1070 and to Norwich in AD 1091.

So all these parishes fall, in a manner of speaking, under the protection of these saints and the local churches, some so named, reflect many centuries of piety by those who lived round about and long ago gained their livelihood from the land and the sea.

With regard to the saintly parishes of this area of Suffolk, roughly situated in the oblong of Harleston, Bungay, Beccles and Halesworth, it is worth noting that none of the saints has specific East Anglian connections. On the other hand, with many other great and small saints, it is possible to pin them down to counties and places. But little reliable evidence exists of how they looked in mortal life.

Before dealing with East Anglia's many saints, it is important to remember that christianity existed in small pockets in Britain before East Anglia's growing band of seventh century missionaries began their evangelism.

St. Edmund – Warrior King. No. 1 in a series of postcard Stories of East Anglia and the Fens.

Christianity was certainly there during the Roman occupation, until about AD 406, when Constantine III began to strip Britain of troops for his conquest of Gaul and Spain.

Four years later Honorius told the civitates of Britain "to arrange for their own safety" as waves of Jutes, Saxons and Angles worshippers of Thor, Woden and other Nordic gods, pillaged the country for the next 150 years, driving Christians into out-of-the-way places.

That Christians existed in Britain was known because certain noted writers, living around the shores of the Mediterranean in the early part of the third century, mentioned the presence of "Christian communities in Britain". British bishops, too, were presented at the Christian councils (Arles and others) of the fourth century.

At Verulamium (St. Alban's, Herts) a Roman soldier was "martyred for sheltering a Christian priest after confessing that he, too, was a Christian."

Thus the foundations of Anglo-Saxon christianity, though not strong, had been laid for the saints who in the seventh century, especially in East Anglia, started to spread the gospel and, in some cases, persuaded local rulers and their armies to uphold the faith.

While many saints and bishops bore the name Felix, the one to whom several English churches are dedicated and who occasionally appears in medieval stained-glass, as at Blythburgh, Suffolk, is the gospel preacher sent to East Anglia who became the first bishop of nearby Dunwich in about AD 630, just a few years after the Sutton Hoo ship burial took place.

Another, St. Fursey, migrated to East Anglia in about AD 633 and, under the patronage of King Sigebert, settled at Burgh Castle, near Great Yarmouth, the abandoned Roman fort where today he is remembered in the form of a modern stained-glass window in the local church. While his mission work proved successful from that lonely site, the disturbances caused by the forays of King Penda of Mercia eventually caused him to seek refuge in Gaul.

At Iken, Suffolk, close by Snape where a seventh century Anglo-Saxon ship burial (c.AD 636-650), badly recorded, was unearthed by the *River Alde* in the 1860s, stands the church of St. Botolph where he is believed to have founded a Benedictine monastery in about AD 640, not many years after the death of King Raedwald (AD 624-425) whose possessions are associated with the Sutton Hoo burial ship.

As abbot of "Ikanhoe", now held by leading historians to be the Suffolk Iken, the local tie seems strong by the dedication to him in East Anglia of some sixty-five churches. Sometimes the saint is depicted holding a church.

Suffolk's renowned St. Edmund needs little introduction. King of East Anglia from AD 855 until he died (870) at the hands of the Danes, popularly at Hoxne but just as likely near Sutton Hoo, his popularity is attested by some sixty dedications and by his frequent appearance on screen-panes in churches.

Montague R. James, author of *Suffolk and Norfolk* (J.M. Dent, 1930), observed: "The area between *Deben* and *Alde,* bounded by the sea, contains some very attractive, breezy, heathy country, and some few sites of interest.

"On the road that leads south to the mouth of the *Deben* is Sutton, where we saw reason to think that St. Edmund was first buried after his martyrdom, and that the battle which he lost was on the tract called Staverton Forest or Park: there is no house, but the forest is said never to have been disturbed."

Interestingly, W.A. Dutt in *The Norfolk and Suffolk Coast* (T. Fisher Unwin, 1909) drew attention to a small stream, called *Butley River,* flowing into the *Ore* between Butley and Gedgrave. Near the junction of the two rivers was "a curious eminence", isolated on the border of the marshes and known as Burrow or Barrow Hill – a site of great antiquity. Human bones found there in such quantity and disarray at the turn of the century pointed to the site of an early battle often believed to have been that in which King Edmund, the martyr, was defeated and taken prisoner by the Danes.

Indeed, Staverton Forest, between Rendlesham and Butley Abbey, is sometimes said to have been the place of St. Edmund's stand as a Christian and the place, not Hoxne, of the fabled oak to which he was bound before being tortured.

The story goes that the Danes threw the king's head "into the undergrowth of a thick wood" so that it might corrupt in dishonour. Curiously, the head was preserved from other wild beasts by "a huge grey wolf, which accompanied the funeral cortege to Bury St. Edmunds and then quietly returned to the wood."

Is there any evidence, I wonder, of Hoxne ever having had such an ancient forest? What we do know is that, in the ninth century, dense oak forests existed in some areas of Suffolk and they harboured animals such as the wolf and the lynx. Thus Staverton Forest, still in evidence, could well have been the scene of his martyrdom in AD 870.

But these East Anglian saints I have mentioned represent only a few of a long list. Others, some women, would include St. Edwould (a brother of the martyred St. Edmund), St. Erkenwald, St. Ethelbert (not to be confused with the King of Kent who was converted by St. Augustine's mission in AD 597), St. Etheldreda (one of the four saintly daughters of Anna, king of the East Angles), St. Kyneburge, St. Sexburge, St. Wendreds, St. Werburge, St. Walstan, St. Withburga and so on.

What reputed powers have the saints displayed in East Anglia in modern times?

According to Arthur Mee in his 1941 edition of *Suffolk, Our Farthest East* (Hodder and Stoughton), which he edited, South Elmham St. Michael "has the memorable distinction of being among the 31 Thankful Villages where all the men came back from the Great War. Eleven went out, serving on mine-sweepers, and every one came back. It is the only village in Suffolk with this glowing memory."

St. Michael, this much-loved angelic patron to whom some 690 English churches were dedicated in the Middle Ages, was recognised as the leader of the spiritual forces contending for the church against the powers of darkness in the certainty of ultimate triumph.

So East Anglia's many saints, local and otherwise, show how, with increasing evidence of christianity from the seventh century onwards, the area became godly with many hospices for the sick and the poor. But the price was very high, even into the ninth century and much later, for did not St. Edmund die because he would not surrender to pagan demands?

One point about the majority of these Eastern England saints is that they grew out of the struggles of the seventh century, the time of the ship burials at Snape and Sutton Hoo, the latter reflecting a curious mixture of christian and pagan worship pointing to a gradual, almost tolerant, transition to St. Augustine's teachings.

To Hellesdon now Edmund fled
With the remnant of his army.
There Hingwar, warlord of the Danes,
Sent messengers to Edmund.
"Become my vassal, deny Christ
And live as King."
"You must accede, My Lord," cried
　　　　　　　Bishop Humbert.
But King Edmund would not deny
His Kingship or his God.

Then Hingwar flew into a rage.
"Capture insolent Edmund
And bring him here to me!"

Before Hingwar they brought
　　　　the virtuous King in chains.
Once more the Dane commanded him,
"Deny your God!"
Edmund, steadfast, refused.

They beat him.
Then they bound him to a tree
And Danish bow-men took their aim.
A score of cruel arrows pierced his side,
His chest, his arms, his legs,
His heart.
And so he died.
With Christ's name on his lips.

Words from postcard's open book .

Master's Tools and Goods

SOME years ago I was wandering around a stack yard in north east Suffolk when I heard a sledge hammer pounding on machinery. I crept round the corner of a stack and saw, back view, the farmer raining heavy blows on a broken-down tractor.

A little frightened, I withdrew, but back at the farm I learnt that Mr— had been like that, on and off, since his horses went.

But what about those of us who have no axe to grind and yet treat master's tools and goods like that? Indeed, as I go about London and the country, I find that man on the whole is unkind to tools and that, 50 years from now, tools that were once handed, proudly, from father to son will be a thing of the past. The reason? Simply that there will be nothing to hand on.

I have some hand-written notes in my possession – they were penned by great-grandfather William Elliott – which were written in the late 1800s and were the simple workshop rules for an engineering firm at Beccles.

One clause ruled: "For spoiling goods or tools – any one carelessly or wilfully spoiling anything, the firm shall take from wage sufficient to cover value of such and if there should not be enough to cover value it shall be recoverable as a common debt."

That seems to me to be a fair demand and still applicable today.

What is more unpleasant than having to take over a spade, say, which has been left standing in a trench over the weekend after a November fog?

Into the bargain, let's imagine, there has been frost, some rain, and before the spade was abandoned – at five minutes to five sharp – it fell in mud. Would you like to use it the following Monday?

Have you ever watched the embankments on a train journey – for stray tools and fittings which are, after all, our property. One sees shovels and picks by the dozen, all left to weather, but I am inclined to believe that this may be due to the disappearance of the cosy little gangers' huts that were once a feature of life on the permanent way in out-of-the-way places.

I can think of countless other examples of wanton handling of tools and goods. In London, costly alloy beer barrels, which have replaced the well-tailored resilient wooden barrels, are often delivered from lorry height without dropping mats such as were carried by draymen of the past. They fracture pavements, dent road surfaces, and are a danger to animals and small children as they roll, drunken-like, about roads and yards.

There is, to my way of thinking, great satisfaction to be earned from seeing a well-arranged workshop or toolshed with all the tools and implements hanging or standing in their allotted places, ready for instant use.

To be able to take up a well serviced tool or implement is surely one way of putting the best into the day's work. Could not this be a clue to some of today's factory-floor unrest – that workers are finding tools 'unfriendly?' for a clean or bright tool must appeal to the average holder.

For a 19th century view on this we must again turn to great-grandfather's notes. In the 1870s, we know, he was making at Beccles stationary steam power plants in three different sizes and three different qualities – "highly finished, as usually finished by good makers, and commonly called black engines."

He sensibly believed, from many years' experience, that "a bright engine, or one pleasing to the eye, lasts longer as a rule, than an ugly one, although the working parts may be the same in both cases."

There is, of course, a lighter side to all this. It is the thought of what archaeologists in a thousand years will make of lines of buried spades, all erect, in filled-in trenches all over the British Isles. Learned papers, as now, will be written by scholars, wrapping drama and mystery about every handle.

A sudden catastrophe, perhaps?

A sudden invasion from another planet, maybe?

As is so often the case, however, there will be no mystery: it will be simply because the tea-whistle blew on Friday afternoon, the rain came, work never restarted that day, and the trench caved in.

Radio – Ahead of His Time
A SUFFOLK PIONEER

THE FIFTIETH ANNIVERSARY of the BBC bought back many memories of pioneering days when the presentation of the human voice and music through wireless was still something of a novelty.

Sunday afternoons with the radio, certainly up to the mid-1930s, were a treat.

What is hard to appreciate today is that broadcasting was an innovation comparable in cultural importance to the introduction of printing. In fact, it found a responsive audience almost before the importance of the new medium was appreciated.

I was born into a family at Beccles, where wireless experiments, starting in 1918 (ten years before I was born), extended into the early 1930s. It was my father, who went to Woodbridge School, who was the interested party, but he was typical of hundreds of his generation who saw the great new possibilities of the various sciences while in the fighting services in the 1914-18 War.

However, as he has been dead some years and as my knowledge of the technical side of radio is rudimentary, we must therefore be content with a journey through his notebooks and papers with

The author, aged about 10, with his father, Maurice Elliott, who was from a line of inventive engineers.

which, like his Royal Flying Corps workshop notebooks, he kept with care.

Original research, quality of workmanship, and very high-quality sound reproduction were some of his hallmarks. In certain respects he was ahead of his time. He obtained patent after patent on new apparatus only to be beaten at each round by lack of adequate capital to sustain output and hold his patents.

What I have not been able to establish is the extent that other East Anglians were involved in wireless developments in the year which saw the BBC start broadcasting.

He appears to have started his wireless experiments in earnest at Shadingfield, near Beccles, and a General Post Office certificate dated 20 October 1922 gave him permission "to instal and use a station for receiving wireless signals for experimental purposes" at his council house overlooking the church. At a later date, he had workshops at different times at Kemps Lane, Gosford Road and Ravensmeer, Beccles.

Up until a few years ago, there lived in Gosford Road, close to my father's old workshop, Mr P. Button, his life-long friend, who continued to use some of the Beccles wireless apparatus right up to the time of his death.

It was at his Ravensmeer workshop, which is the only workshop I can remember as a very young child, that he "heard a wireless play after it was switched off," thus giving him the idea of electrically retarding

The Beccles experimenter used this local studio picture, by Leyneek, to advertise his automatic wireless set, tuned permanently to six stations. It was captioned: "What station shall we have now, Daddy?", and was posed in the late 1920s.

Cicely Courtneidge   Jack Hulbert

the tone so that a special kind of resonance, so much like today's reproduction, was possible.

He must, however, have regarded the experience, for which he recorded no written explanation, as unusual. This led him to contact Sir Oliver Lodge, who lived near Salisbury and was the author of such papers as *Signalling without Wires, Atoms and Rays* and *Ether and Reality,* the latter branch of study taking Sir Oliver into the anatomy of the ether of space.

This interesting twentieth-century figure, who died in 1940, tested some of my father's apparatus. My father believed that the secret of human existence was basically electrical in origin hence telepathy and so on, which incidentally, was one of Sir Oliver's interests.

Another willing adviser whose recreation was the encouragement of original research, was 'Professor' A.M. Low, of Bedford Park, London, whose range of inventions included a television system, an electrical rocket control, and radio-torpedo control gear. He died in 1956.

Having tested some of my father's apparatus, he told him in a letter on 19 April 1926: "Bearing these considerations in mind it would appear that the Tunometer advantages over ordinary coils are difficult to establish upon a direct 'electrical' basis but there are many other features where their utility from a practical standpoint is undoubted. I agree that the instruments are most interesting and genuinely useful." A.M. Low marked the report "Confidential".

My father, who was operating as an almost one-man outfit, won the attention of a wide field of journals and newspapers, including *Amateur Wireless, English Mechanics, The Electrical Review, Popular Wireless and Wireless Review, Modern Wireless, Experimental Wireless, The Wireless Dealer, The Wireless Trader, Wireless Magazine, The British Engineers, Export Journal,* not forgetting *John Bull, The Sphere, The Daily Mail,* the *Evening Chronicle, The Daily Express* and a generous local press which seemed to

enjoy following up the experimenter's activities around the country.

The list of wireless publications is, incidentally, only a sample of the large number of such papers which appeared in the 1920s.

The Radio Press in 1926 announced a backer for the Beccles experimenter. He was Mr Malcolm Lyon described as "a Suffolk squire", who lived for a time at Sudbourne Hall and, I imagine, was typical of that adventurous band of men and women of the 1920s who got a kick out of backing inventors on the ground and in the air.

The report, which noted that the radio industry was only four years old and that three million out of the 8,504,000 homes in the country were equipped with wireless receiving apparatus, went on to say that Mr Lyon weighed "24 stones", was "the jolliest looking man" at the National Radio Exhibition dinner in London, and expected great things from my father.

My father liked recalling the days he spent with Mr Lyon whose active mind appears not to have needed a full night's sleep, for my father was often alerted at night "to proceed to London on some wireless investigation or attend some business meeting involving a new piece of apparatus".

Fast cars were always available, my father sometimes acting as Mr Lyon's driver, and some fast runs, not without incident, were made.

One, I was told, involved a collision at night at Saxmundham, with a loaded baker's cart so that the poor horse, with only the shafts, dashed on for many frightened miles.

On another occasion, having raced to London by dawn, the car's fan flew off, penetrated the radiator, and under Big Ben "discharged a column of boiling water high into the air!"

However, his jet-set days, as they would be termed today, were easily out-numbered by days, weeks and months spent building a wide variety of apparatus. His output was supported by good publicity brochures, and he exhibited at Olympia in 1928, being one of only 25 named exhibitors.

He catered for novelty, too, for photographs among his records show a grandfather clock converted to contain one of his sets, the special Tunometer inductances, which he made by hand, being visible.

In a brochure dealing with the culmination of his developments, the 'Biafone', dated January 1931, he claimed that his Ravensmeer workshop was "able to supply the need for perfect reproduction of radio and/or gramophone records and moving pictures in the home."

He went on to say: "The latest development in Television definitely indicates that the Science can only be made profitable by an enlarged projection on to a screen, or alternatively by the employment of a multiple Light Screen. Here again your 'Biafone' will permit of its use in a compact and convenient manner."

He was ahead of his time when he combined sound and light on a screen so that "the sound moved with the object." This kind of system, I was interested to note, reached the public in 1952, when "Cinerama", described as an "American invention," was demonstrated at the Broadway Theatre, New York, it being stated that "a 'stereophonic' system of sound-recording reached the audience from the direction of the apparent source."

My father, as I have said, exhibited in London. He, went about East Anglia too, and showed the 'Biafone' at the Royal Norfolk Show at Great Yarmouth in June 1931. People who liked to have their drawing rooms "equipped for the best reception" were among his customers and he installed apparatus at, among other places, discerning Aldeburgh.

It was through Mr Lyon, who backed him for a time, that he met such stage figures as the Jack Hulbert, Cicely Courtneidge, Beatrice Lillie and others.

It is difficult, as I have said, to find out exactly why this early East Anglia experimenter, who caught the attention of Sir Oliver Lodge and A.M. Low, failed when he was so productive of new ideas and methods.

Certainly in the early 1930s, as he reached the peak of his wireless endeavours, there was the great business depression. But perhaps there were other more sinister reasons.

My father related, and I never forgot the details, two episodes that point to cut-throat competition. Once, while on a business trip to London, he woke to find a gas-tap turned on in his hotel bedroom.

At his Gosford Road workshop, where the windows were whitewashed well above normal head-height, a man on horseback one night looked at his workshop bench for several undetected minutes and, when disturbed, rode off at speed.

Perhaps his one-man drive irked the big interests who were then battling for the radio market.

As his wireless days came to an end, and the various companies were wound up, he noted: "The following are only a few of the patents and provisional patents abandoned due to lack of capital at different times, but are considered by the patentee as the more likely ones that natural progress must sooner or later overlap.

"Electrostatic sectional talkie-screen, film and record device for the screen, electrostatic output device, non-resonant and non-vibratory mountings, and improvements to inductance calibrating devices."

His notebooks, as I have said, were well kept documents. In some respects he must have worked by trial and error, for under "Particulars of Loud Speaker Construction" he made such quaint observations as: "It is of importance that the process of sticking the baffle to its frame should be carried on in a damp atmosphere."

By the mid-1930s, when he had returned to his family's old-established engineering business, his wireless days were over but other inventions, which are a separate story, were in the pipeline.

Certainly, for years after his wireless days, there was never a shortage of nuts and bolts and the like for our toys. The inductances, which I found in a workshop box after his death in the early 1960s, were those tested by Sir Oliver Lodge and A.M. Low and are preserved today.

Radio, there is no doubt, has come a long way since the 1920s when people everywhere went head-over-heels in pursuit of the new science.

A model of 'Professor' Archibald M. Low's guided-missile of 1917 – known for security reasons as the 'A.T.' (aerial target). Only in the middle 1920s were details released to the public.

Farewell Hazelwood Cottage

SUFFOLK-BORN Violet's reluctant departure from her old farm-house to a new dwelling, just across the aconite and strawberry beds, a matter of fifty yards, caught my attention some years ago.

Now I hear of another Suffolk departure, just across the road from Violet's plot, which turned out to be even more poignant because it meant the removal to another part of Suffolk – 25 miles or so – of two elderly neighbours who, over the years, Violet knew and drew strength from as infirmity touched her.

For close on 25 years the couple had lived in the same thatched dwelling with matching barn. The pair were my hosts, on and off, during that time and, when my children were young, they too came to the village in high summer.

First occupied by the couple in the early 1960s when antique furniture and property prices were a fraction of today's, Hazelwood Cottage (I call it that as I also hide Violet's real name), with its leaded windows and overhanging thatch, was soon tastefully furnished so that, as the years went by, what they acquired from Suffolk house sales and auctions became irrevocable parts of all their rooms.

For example, the great Flemish-dresser (well over six feet long) in the dining room, bought at Woodbridge, Suffolk, all those years back, claimed a genuine association with Edward FitzGerald's cloak and hat and the dinky child's country chair, *c*1675, had a ghostly connection with an old house at Yaxley, also in Suffolk.

Many domestic bits and pieces in the wonderfully cool pantry, including robust old wine or beer flagons, had sound Suffolk pedigrees – in one case, I was told, the household of a famous British Army general of the Battle of France, 1940

But the way the place was furnished was only part of the attraction of Hazelwood Cottage. Its cooking was another reason, for sometimes the animated cook thought nothing of baking largesse for half the village.

At dawn, when the sun rose over the Suffolk fields, it peered through a little upstairs window and through another in the dining room far better than any electric light beam could.

At sundown on a summer night the switching off of day was so gentle in the lounge that, sipping a sherry, one wasn't really conscious that night was falling – only that one's hosts, talking of olden times, were no longer discernible.

Always there was a deep silence after dark. There were, I felt, no unhappy ghosts in Hazelwood

As old pots hidden in chimneys often have superstitious meanings, particularly in East Anglia, it's just possible that this is not the last story emanating from Hazelwood Cottage.

Cottage for all, it seemed, were content with their warm 17th century abode.

Of outdoor visions, I retain thoughts of early morning fog in the vegetable garden, once a farmyard, of fruitful cornfields sloping gently uphill, of flitting bats at twilight between the cottage and its barn, and of ducks circling Violet's clay-line ponds so well buttressed with great elm boles, at dawn and sunset.

So, breaking that link with Hazelwood Cottage lasting a quarter of a century, the couple finally moved, as I have explained, to another part of the county.

I thought about them during the transition, as one of them had to go into hospital for a fairly big operation, and I sensed that the pulling up of those old roots hadn't been as painless as they tried to make out.

Around Christmas, 1984, I had to go to Norwich from London in a hurry, not having time to make any plans for calls, and during the late afternoon return in darkness. As I had a day to spare, I turned off the Norwich-Ipswich road for an area of haunting commons, thatched places and old farms, as winter twilight turned to deep darkness and rain.

From the high Suffolk common land, as it always seemed to me, I splashed down through narrow, lonely lanes to the village of so many stories where I knew two or three farewell packages had been left for me by the departed hosts of Hazelwood Cottage.

I collected them from a neighbour and, as I did so,

inform them that the alterations to the chimney had revealed a battery of fireplaces, including what sounded like a copper and a bread-oven. There was even a hook in the old chimney for bacon – or was it a pothook for a cauldron?

The surrounding brickwork was 17th century, or perhaps earlier and appeared to be part of a kind of central, see-through hearth which must have dominated the old place three-hundred or more years back. Just think, we had all sat round about, for close on 25 years, not realising so much was hidden.

As artefacts left in chimneys and fireplaces often have superstitious meanings, certainly in East Anglia, it's just possible that this is not the last story emanating from Hazelwood Cottage.

Early morning fog near the vegetable garden at Hazelwood Cottage.

I saw the thatched house of summer visits all aglow; every room was lit up as renovations were in place, for the new owners wanted the old interior quickly modernised and the oak beams shot-blasted.

As I loaded the packages into the car, I decided to go across the road to give Violet a surprise call, and strolling in the darkness and the rain past Hazelwood Cottage I glanced into the familiar lounge. I caught sight of the fairly modern brick fireplace, around which we had often sat, demolished to reveal a huge black hearth of indeterminate depth.

A day or two later, having told the old occupants of Hazelwood Cottage in a letter to their new home that I had collected the packages, as arranged, I declined to describe those intimate details of what I saw happening to the place.

However, I needn't have been so cautious, for back came a letter which, telling me that they were settling-in near Sudbury, went on to describe how a neighbour in their old village had telephoned to

Nelson – Not Forgotten

IN the United Kingdom there must be hundreds of streets and roads named after Norfolk's Lord Nelson.

Members of his different crews or household are also honoured, one of the latter, of course, being Lady Hamilton, of Merton Place, Surrey, now part of the old borough of Wimbledon, renamed Merton.

Indeed, when one goes over the territory most liked by Nelson, who was born at Burnham Thorpe on 29 September 1758, the conclusion is usually reached that, when ashore, he loved most of all Merton Place, long demolished, and its garden now swallowed up by 19th and 20th century buildings.

The area covered by the Merton property can be traced today in Nelson Road, Nelson Grove Road, Trafalgar Road, Victory Road, Hardy Road and Hamilton Road, all in London SW19. In those days Merton Place stood in open country – a retreat from the sea yet close enough to the *Thames* for Nelson to reach his command in a hurry.

Never rich, Nelson, who gave liberally to others, had difficulty in raising funds to buy Merton Place. Earlier he had written to Lady Hamilton: "It is . . . extraordinary, but true, that the man who is pushed forward to defend his country, has not from that country a place to lay his head . . ."

Apparently, Lady Hamilton's perseverance – Captain A.T. Mahan in his book *The Life of Nelson* said she was a better business-man than Nelson and went about his purchase with the deliberation of a women shopping – was such that by 20 August 1801, Nelson who was unable to get the Admiralty to let him leave his station for a few days, wrote: "You are to be, recollect Lady Paramount of all the territories and waters of Merton, and we are all to be your guests, and to obey all lawful commands".

In this way was conducted the purchase and preparation of the only home of his own on English soil that Nelson ever possessed, where it is said, he passed his happiest hours. and from which he set out to fight his last battle, the Battle of Trafalgar on 21 October 1805.

Merton Place was ideal, as I have said, and delighted Nelson. One of the walks in the garden he called the quarter-deck. Hyde Park was less than an hour's drive away. Moving-in, certainly for Lady Hamilton, was one big honeymoon, for Nelson, who was more often away on service, was told in a letter: 'It would make you laugh to see Emma and her mother fitting up pigsties and hencoops, and already the canal is enlivened with ducks, and the cock is strutting with his hens about the walks".

Horatio Nelson, born Sept. 29, 1758, died Oct. 21, 1805.

Lady Hamilton

When news came that Nelson was to leave to face the enemy, Lady Hamilton, according to Captain Mahan, spent the previous day in tears, could not eat, could hardly drink, and came near to swooning, and all at table.

On 13 September 1805, Nelson left Merton Place for Portsmouth. His last act before leaving the house, it is said, was to visit the the bed where his child, Horatia, then between four and five, was sleeping, and pray over her.

The solemn anticipation of death, which from this time onwards deepened more and more over his fearless spirit, as the hour of battle approached, is apparent in the record of his departure made in his private diary: "At half-past ten drove from dear dear

Merton, where I left all which I hold dear in this world, to go to serve my King and Country. May the great God whom I adore enable me to fulfill the expectations of my country. . . . If it is His good Providence to cut short my days upon earth, I bow with the greatest submission. . . .!

For some time after Nelson lay dying aboard HMS *Victory* his devoted friend Captain Thomas M. Hardy, who in the circumstances acted as commander-in-chief as well as Captain, could not leave his station to comfort the Admiral. But eventually this was possible – in fact, more than one visit to the death-bed was made by Hardy and that is why we have Hardy Road in Merton today.

What else is there round about Merton to remind us of Nelson? Well, there is the 'Nelson Arms' (renamed 'The Nelson') with coloured-tile plaques showing Nelson and *Victory*. Then there is the Trafalgar public house. By the church of St. John the old cannon, suitably inscribed. Not far from the Nelson Hospital, in the direction of Kingston, is the Emma Hamilton public house with a sign showing, as I remember, Lady Hamilton with her eyes on *Victory*.

Among the interesting items I have found in London in memory of Nelson is a fret-work plaque of *Victory* roughly inscribed 21 October 1805, with brass medallions of *Victory* and Nelson and the Admiral's famous signal "England expects . . ."

The wood used in the plaque – it was brought for 25p from a South Wimbledon bric-a-brac shop in the middle 1960s – was clearly part of an old tea-chest and my feeling is that it was made by an admirer to commemorate the centenary of Trafalgar in 1905.

Indeed, we know that Tower Tea Limited, then of 71 Eastcheap, published a colourful calender illustration of Trafalgar for 1905. Such an illustration, in excellent condition, was given to me in the 1950s on the death of a well-known Beccles fishmonger.

Among the best bargains in Nelson books I have picked up are the two volumes on the *The Life of Nelson: The Embodiment of the Sea Power of Great Britain* by Captain Mahan, United States Navy, dated 1897.

For my small investment of 75p in Charing Cross Road, London, I got nearly a thousand pages of text, many illustrations, maps and battle plans. But most outstanding, in my view, is the fact that both old volumes were inscribed 'Wardroom HMS *Revenge*'. Now *Revenge* fought in the Battle of Jutland on 31 May – 1 June 1916, which historians declare was in all respects as stirring as the Battle of Trafalgar. It's

HMS Victory, first rate, 104 guns, lying in Portsmouth Harbour. The Flag Ship of Lord Nelson, on board of which he was killed off Trafalgar, October 21, 1805.

Drawn by E. W. Cooke and engraved by W. J. Cooke

The Victory breaking the enemy's line at Traflagar.

possible that the two books heard the guns of that great naval battle in the North Sea.

Other Nelson books found in London second-hand bookshops since the early 1950s include two different editions of Robert Southey's *The Life of Nelson*, the book being first available in 1813. Both my copies are illustrated with line and colour drawings and I notice that in the same area as the Nelson roads at Merton is Southey Road. Perhaps it bears the author's name, for his Nelson study remains a classic to this day.

Then there is *Nelson and His Times* by Rear-Admiral Lord Charles Beresford and H.W. Wilson. Apparently the study was issued in ten fortnightly parts and is considered valuable as a source-book for illustrations, covering every aspect of the admiral's life from Burnham Thorpe to his burial in St. Paul's Cathedral.

Outside London, however, I have only found one useful publication on Nelson. That is *Nelson and East Anglia*, by Harold Simpson, which the *East Anglian Daily Times*, Ipswich, reprinted in 1905 for sixpence. It turned up in a Lowestoft junk-shop.

Last but not least the late Oliver Warner, of Haslemere, Surrey, the naval historian and author, who had a family connection with Beccles, gave me in 1974 a copy of his book *Lord Nelson: A Guide to Reading with a Note on Contemporary Portraits*. This is a most valuable little book, published in 1955, for anyone researching the life of the Norfolk hero.

Pictures taken from Life of Nelson *by Robert Southey. The book was published by Bell & Daldy, Covent Garden, in 1868*

Dunkirk: The East Coast Connection

SOME accounts of the evacuation of Dunkirk in May/June 1940, do not have the true facts of the contribution made by the Royal National Lifeboat Institution in providing lifeboats and crews to bring back the British Army.

What happened was that at 1.15 pm on 30th May 1940, the then Ministry of Shipping telephoned the RNLI and asked it to send at once to Dover as many lifeboats as possible. No other information was given.

As soon as the RNLI received that call it telephoned to 18 stations from Gorleston, 110 miles north of Dover, to Shoreham Harbour, in Sussex, eighty miles to the west. Each station was asked to send its lifeboat with a full crew, full fuel tanks, and "a grass warp for towing" .

While this urgent message was being sent to the lifeboats along those 190 miles of coast, two of them – the Ramsgate and Margate lifeboats – were already on their way to Dunkirk manned by their crews. Interestingly, in the light of what transpired as more lifeboats arrived at Dover, these two lifeboats had responded immediately to their local naval officers' requests without question.

Meanwhile, East Coast lifeboats were heading south. These included the *Louise Stephens* (Great Yarmouth and Gorleston), the *Michael Stephens* (Lowestoft), the *Mary Scott* (Southwold), the *Abdy Beauclerk* and the *Lucy Lavers* (Aldeburgh), the *E.M.E.D.* (Walton and Frinton) the *Edward Z. Dresden* (Clacton) the *Greater London (Civil Service No. 3)* (Southend) and others.

Of the 17 lifeboats that got away on the afternoon call on 30th May, 15 went to Dunkirk from Dover, and two, the Clacton boat and the boat from the Rowhedge Ironworks, Essex, went from Ramsgate.

An official account of the RNLI's contribution that day records that the first of these boats to leave their stations were the two from Aldeburgh. All but one of the 17 arrived at Dover within 29 hours of the summons.

However, the first three lifeboats that actually reached Dover on the evening of 30th May were from Hythe, Walmer and Dungeness, and the Hythe coxswain was the first to be told what was wanted of him.

The official report states: "He understood it to be that he was to run his lifeboat on the beach at Dunkirk, load her with troops and bring them out to ships. She was a boat weighing over 14 tons, and he said that it could not be done. He could never get her off without the help of winches, and he would never attempt at Dunkirk what he knew that he could not do at Hythe.

"The Walmer and Dungeness coxswains agreed with him. Their boats were of the same type as his but rather heavier.

All the RNLI boats sent to Dunkirk in 1940 came back very dirty and some, like this one, in an Essex boatyard for a refit, returned showing ramming, bullet and shell damage.

Photo: Courtesy RNLI

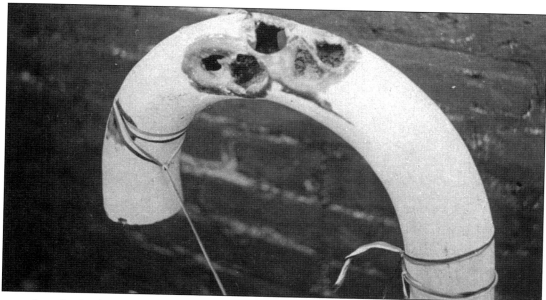

Lifeboat ventilating pipe
riddled at Dunkirk.
Photo: Courtesy RNLI

"Then the Hythe coxswain – he had served in the Navy in th 1914-18 war – asked other questions such as what pension would be given to their families should they be killed. When he was told, he asked to have it in writing That was refused, and he refused to go. His crew, and the Walmer and Dungeness coxswains and crews also refused. The Navy took the lifeboats . . ."

When the next seven lifeboats arrived off Dover in the morning, a naval launch went out to them, told their crews what they were wanted for, gave them their course to Dunkirk and sent them into the harbour to refuel.

The official report goes on: "As soon as they went in their boats were taken from them by naval men. Not knowing of the refusal of the first three crews, they were surprised and very indignant. Some, if not all, had guessed why they had come to Dover . . . They protested, but it was useless. The Navy had decided . . ."

When the harassed and overburdened naval officers at Dover announced that they would, on the other hand, take the motor mechanics of all the lifeboats the lifeboatmens' reply was a curt 'All or none". Thus, when the lifeboats provided by the RNLI headed for Dunkirk, they were mainly in the hands of sailors "who had never been aboard them before, and their engines put in charge of stokers, who had first to be taught how to start and stop them".

But even then the RNLI as a whole was hopeful of being given the chance to take its own boats into Dunkirk. For on the morning of 31st May Commander John Upton, the inspector of lifeboats for the East Coast, got wind of the difficulties and rushed to Dover. Unfortunately he was too late to attempt to put right what had gone wrong, although several of the RNLI's reserve mechanics were "ready to go anywhere and do anything".

Determined to take the next best course, Commander Upton and his mechanics became a repairing party for all the motor boats sailing out of Dover for Dunkirk.

It is known that the lifeboats from Lowestoft, Walton and Frinton and Clacton were among those that actually worked in Dunkirk harbour itself.

One of the lifeboat inspectors who was already in the Navy, Sub-Lieutenant Stephen Dickinson, found himself in command of the Southwold lifeboat. She was towed to Dunkirk by the paddle steamer *Emperor of India*. By all accounts, the Southwold lifeboat had a rough time waiting for men to embark under cover of darkness.

On one of her trips to the beach the Southwold lifeboat stuck fast, and later developed engine trouble. But she was seen by the Great Yarmouth and Gorleston lifeboat, just as they turned for England with troops on board, and they found room for a weary Lieutenant Dickinson.

At one time it seemed certain that several of the 19 RNLI lifeboats would never leave Dunkirk. Certainly three were seen ashore by one eyewitness but "by devious and mysterious ways" all except one returned. Oddly, this was the Hythe boat, the coxswain of which had refused to run her on the beaches because of her weight, saying that he would never get her off again.

Some weeks later, when an inquiry was held at Hythe, the coxswain who had been right about his lifeboat's handling, said: "I have a fishing boat and will not see a man drown if I can get her off." Two months later, as the Battle of Britain started, he made good that promise by rescuing two British airmen from a crashed bomber.

Hythe's motor mechanic said: "If the order had come from the RNLI to proceed to Dunkirk and do the best you can, there would have been no holding back."

Dunkirk Survivors – Tea & Cake

Soon after the retreat from Dunkirk 40 years' ago, there came to East Anglia weary soldiers to rest and regroup. They mostly occupied requisitioned houses and soon there were soldiers at the bottom of many gardens . . . The experiences which led to this story took place at Beccles in 1940

ARCHIE, a miner, came into my life when I was eleven. With other Dunkirk survivors he came to the quiet Suffolk town where I was born – to the house at the bottom of the garden where, probably to this day, the trunks of the old holly trees still bear their carved initials, like living totem poles. Soon they came over the wall to tea.

'Uncle' Charlie headed the survivors. He was an old soldier with a family in Liverpool. He, too, had stood in the sea at Dunkirk.

There were six of them at table that Saturday afternoon. I sat at the head on two cushions.

Hanging by its strap from 'Uncle' Charlie's chair was a German soldier's steel helmet, fresh from battle, bearing on one side the head of an eagle – a head with a hooked beak that recalled the Teuton devices I had seen in pictures of pagan longboats under sail. And 'Uncle' Charlie, just for fun, wore a tight-fitting German soldier's jacket stripped of insignia.

But I was not in a humourous mood. I was bitterly upset that my army had come home in little boats, mostly without its guns.

The maid brought in the teapot – a man's teapot – and slipped back to the kitchen without a word.

"Uncle Charlie, why did you retreat from Dunkirk?" I asked.

"We had no alternative, lad; but we will go back – some day when we are strong again."

"In my books," I said, "no one ever retreats."

'Uncle' Charlie looked embarrassed, the maid moved away from the net curtain over the kitchen door, and feelings overflowed.

"Take that jacket off," I demanded.

And 'Uncle' Charlie, obediently, took it off and sat in his braces and holy vest.

"Give me that helmet," I cried.

And 'Uncle' Charlie, obediently, gave me the helmet.

Into that helmet, which had lost its lining, I poured the boiling contents of the man's teapot. Into the dark mixture I flung the contents of the milk jug and a handful of sugar. My guests looked aghast.

The author in 1940, at the time of the Dunkirk soldiers' dressing-down by him, ready to give the German invaders a rough reception!

"Now you lot," I went on, "you're going to drink to – to the DAMNATION of the enemy that sent thousands of you fleeing like little girls."

'Uncle' Charlie took the first lick, without comment, and passed it down the table. But before it reached Archie a great sob filled the room. The miner's head was in his hands and 'Uncle' Charlie was by his side.

"Come, Archie, our host is talking to us all."

But Archie's sobs continued.

The others looked uneasy, and 'Uncle' Charlie, wise old soldier, thanked me for the unfinished tea, and silently they trooped out of the room, spoke to the maid, and went back over the wall.

The time was 4pm. Under my chair was the German jacket and on the table hardly sipped, was the Teuton teapot. I ate the rest of my tea slowly but was unrepentant. But later I felt tired and sorry.

I resolved next day to write Archie a note asking him to come to tea on the following Sunday.

The envelope, posted in the red pillar-box by the railway station that saw so many soldiers come and

Dunkirk Soldiers' Party – Uncle Charlie with author's youngest sister in 1940.

go, was addressed to 'Private Archie, Esq., The Kings Armie, The Billets, Station Road, Beccles'.

Archie got the note and replied, without using capital letters or full-stops, that he looked forward to " 'aving 'nother bite."

Tea was put out as before except that Archie sat at the head of the table and I on his right. A large chocolate cake inscribed "For Archie" stood where the Teuton teapot had stood.

I cut a slice for Archie. I also cut myself a piece but it was twice as big.

When I offered him a second piece he blurted out: "Not blinkin' likely if it's gorn to be like t'other piece. You're like blinkin' Hitler. You like tak'n big bits. You're a blinkin' little pig."

Rising, Archie shoved back his chair, stretched across the table, picked me up and, slinging me over his broad miner's back head first, carried me outside. A lidless dustbin lay in our path and it was into that dustbin that Archie, laughingly, plunged me.

Speechless from the messy ducking, I saw 'Uncle' Charlie, cap held high above his head, looking over the wall by the holly trees. Behind him stood the rest. Then there was a great cheer of "Good old Archie."

Archie and his mates, thank goodness, were in fighting trim again!

When Windmills Were Dashed to the Ground

EARLY in 1983 the biggest change for over a century in the care of old and historic buildings, including windmills, followed the second reading of the National Heritage Bill in the Commons.

The new Historic Buildings and Monuments Commission for England took over the funding, promotion and preservation of most old buildings, including Saxtead post-mill, near Framlingham, one of the country's best known examples.

Saxtead post-mill, however, has had a fortunate history: successive families of millers were always jealous for its upkeep and, finally, in 1951 the mill was placed under the care of the Ministry of Works. Between 1957 and 1960 the Ministry carried out a thorough overhaul of the 1796 structure.

In the prologue to his 1939 best-selling book *Suffolk Scene* (Blackie), Julian Tennyson, a great-grandson of the poet Tennyson – he was killed in World War II – declared of windmills: "I think I would rather have a good old Suffolk windmill than any other building in the length and breadth of England. I love it for its homeliness, its simplicity, the very plainness that is whole of its beauty . . ."

He went on to say, over forty years ago, that "there is in Suffolk a society for their preservation, and that there are still millers fond enough of the old order to stand by the superannuated devices of their forefathers".

Indeed, there was an active movement in East Anglia to save our windmills in the early 1930s, and being a windmill fan myself and acquainted with many that are no longer with us, I am able to refer to original accounts of their condition in the 1930s when only a handful of enthusiasts were interested.

Incredibly, age and decay have so shorn the English landscape of its windmills that of 10,000 which stood in their heyday to grind "by God's fair air" only the remains of probably fewer than 1500 survived in the early 1950s, and of those fewer than fifty were still working.

Today, however, the national windmill preservation lobby is huge and there's little likelihood of any more of the survivors being dashed to the ground as I often witnessed in East Anglia in the early post war years.

But when one considers what we could have saved at the time, even in the shape of large and small spares for better preserved windmills, one is forced to the conclusion that the post war years saw heritage philistines in numbers in just about every English county. What is also clear from the hundreds of windmill press cuttings in my hands – they mostly concern the Eastern Counties – is that there was a considerable cross-fire, some of it quite stupid, as to why this or that windmill should or should not be preserved.

I remember visiting Syleham post mill near Harleston, in about 1947 and meeting Mr Jesse Wightman, a Suffolk millwright. He told me that the windmill was built around 1823, and had been moved from Wingfield. He also wrote out for me, pointing out the types, a list of surviving Suffolk windmills and helped me to compile a list of windmill terms. Afterwards I photographed Mr Wightman at the top of the ladder in, I later discovered, the style of

It is unlikely that 'head-sick' (that's the technical term) windmills like this will ever be seen again. This is how Wrentham, Suffolk, post mill looked at the close of its life in the 1950s.

Gilbert Spencer's painting *The Miller* of between the wars.

In 1948 I cycled from Beccles to see the dashed remains of the little 150-year-old Wortham smock tower-mill, near Diss. When the reverberations of its demolition reached the London newspapers many people, too late, bemoaned its demise.

Like Julian Tennyson I knew, for example, the pretty 18th-century wind-pump on Westwood Marshes, between Walberswick and Dunwich, but was saddened to find after the war that misdirected artillery shells had ripped out the brickwork on the west side of the tower from top to bottom and that small arms fire had peppered much of the exposed woodwork.

When, in 1951, the late Sir Charles Tennyson, father of Julian Tennyson, who lived at Southwold, led a local appeal committee to raise £800 to do the repair work thoroughly, it was hoped that "the mill may be made available for bird-watchers if the platforms and window slits can be repaired".

Some of my early post-war photographs of Walberswick's much loved wind pump were used to help publicise the appeal which was backed by such names as Adrian Bell, Benjamin Britten, Allan Jobson, S.C. Seymour-Lucas, Ronald Jeans and Dr Martin Shaw.

But in 1956, after the wind-pump had been nicely restored, Sir Charles Tennyson told me: "The damage occurred during a violent gale in the spring and we have had to do the best we could to secure the surviving sail and repair the cap, at a total cost of £14.

"It would obviously not be worthwhile to make a general appeal – nor after this last one for money, do we feel disposed to make any attempt fully to restore the sails. This would be expensive and we have no guarantee that the new sails – which must be stationary – would stand the kind of weather to which they may be exposed.

Suffolk millwright Mr Jesse Wightman on the ladder of Syleham postmill, near Harleston, Norfolk, in 1947.

"It seems impossible now to get any reliable advice – the mill is remote and cannot be adequately looked after. It's all very difficult . . ."

Not long after Sir Charles wrote me that sad letter, fire finished off the wind-pump for, it seems, all time. So my photographs, taken on 17 May 1953, show the landmark at its best, closely resembling the wind-pump Julian Tennyson knew in the years before the last war.

Wrentham post-mill, near Southwold, which I saw pulled down in 1955 when it became dangerous, was in 1938 found by Mr H. Norman Collinson to be in a poor state, but the carcass (the body of the mill) was in a fair condition and the sails intact. Ex-policeman Mr J. Elmy, who lived next to the mill yard, was prepared to look after the mill if it were repaired and preserved.

Known as Carter's windmill and the only survivor of four or five, including two post- and trestle-types and a tower-mill, at Wrentham, the mill's demolition contractor gave me permission to search the fallen remains and I recovered two very interesting relics – a large and a small brass, as they are known in windmill language. These box-like objects, which could be renewed, acted as shaft bearings. Inside the

Fine brasses – shaft bearings which took the thrust – recovered from a demolished Suffolk postmill in 1955.

cup part of each is a channel into which tallow or grease was forced for lubrication purposes.

A year or two after the war ended, I had a pleasant encounter with a retired Wrentham farmer, Mr R.S. Girling, who in 1951 died in his 90th year.

Mr. Girling told me: "Although there were windmills in the village in the 18th century, Carter's mill dates from around the 1820s. The two-storey roundhouse, normally heightened only when growing trees took the wind, came about after the daughter of one of the millers was killed while playing under the moving sails."

Westhall post-mill, near Halesworth, which attracted many artists, including the Suffolk artist F.W. Baldwin, who now lives in London, was pulled down in 1957 after the county planning of officer of those days had commented: "It is amazing to me how it has stood up so long. A millwright has inspected it and has recommended that it should be demolished immediately as it has become dangerous."

A tablet on the roundhouse read: "Laid by C. Howes, Sept. 18th, 1879". However, the windmill as opposed to the roundhouse was built long before that – in 1781 – and Dorothy L. Miles, of The Mill, Westhall, told me in 1957: "The locality of the windmill is not Cox Green – Cox Green adjoins here, which is now called Mill Common, but in 1781 was called Westhall Great Common. In that year the miller, Matthew Swan, asked and was granted permission from the Lord of the Manor, Sir Robin Adair, to have land upon which to erect a mill".

Mrs E.R. Hayward, of Elm Tree Farm, Westhall, gave me these additional particulars in the year of the demolition: "I can remember the mill being struck by lightning in 1921, killing Mr I. Beans, who was standing in the doorway entrance to the roundhouse.

"My father, Mr Arthur Long, and Mr S. Felgate, were standing on the platform at the top of the mill by a chain which worked the sails. My father's clothing was scorched all down his left side, and Mr

Saxtead post-mill, Suffolk.

Felgate's left sock was scorched. They were, however, only slightly hurt. My father was 43 when this happened and sixty when he died."

Westhall windmill, according to an original report I have, was in poor condition in 1938 but the fan-tail, described as "a very large type", was still intact. It seemed to have been in use up to 1936. Mr Rex Wailes, the windmill authority, who called at the windmill in about 1940, noted "clasp-arm wheel very heavy with arms up to 11 inches deep".

This windmill, which I was allowed to look over and thoroughly photograph as it was pulled apart in 1957, gave up a number of relics, including its heavy flyball governors, a delicately shaped iron window hook, and a small iron wedge.

Somewhere about 1750, Thornham Magna post-mill, near Eye, which in May 1959, leaned quietly on its massive post, was built. By the end of the month, however, little remained of the friendly landmark apart from the cracked circular wall of the roundhouse and ashes.

What happened was quite wicked: three boys from an approved school, after stealing inside, fired some empty fertiliser bags in the roundhouse and in no time the whole structure was engulfed.

But in 1955, on a hot summer afternoon, I obtained permission from the Rose family to explore Thornham Magna windmill with the result that today, although all has vanished, I have a detailed report of what I found as I went over the interior inch by inch.

Here is an extract: "Noticed date 1750 on timber; while the two meal bins, which were decorated with two carvings of mill stones, bore, among other carvings, these names and dates – J. Webster 1851/3(?); 1(?). Wells(?) 1828; Thomas Tuft(?);

Few people would associate windmills of the post and trestle type with Australia. However, as early as 1797, such a mill was erected at Miller's Point, Sydney.

Eve(?); E(?). Ford; Bacon, Octo., 17 – (?) . . . On top floor . . . were . . . pencil inscriptions . . . on roof and compared with other examples, seemed authentic. The notes read – New cogs to head wheel, Oct., 1902; new hopper Oct., 1909(?), J. Wright(?). Other notes related to travels of a soldier, probably a miller or his son, in the 1914-18 war . . ."

In talking to the Rose family after my inspection, Miss F. Rose, one of three sisters then living at the Mill House nearby, where they were all born, said: "My grandfather, James Rose, who died in 1895, carried on the mill from one Webster (presumably the J. Webster of the inscription) and my late father, William Rose, who died in 1942 when the mill finally ceased working, was the last miller although, due to ill-health, he did not work it right up to the time of his death".

The Rose family gave me a relic from the windmill in the shape of a fine apple-wood pulley wheel, with a very worn iron spindle.

But windmills were not always landbound. As recently as 1910 the Norwegian timber-carrying barque *Ceres* mounted a windmill pump just forward of the mizzen mast. And in 1955 I saw what was reported to be the exposed wreckage of the Norwegian barque *Nina* – it founded in 1898 – between Walberswich and Dunwich.

Poking through the beach, it was said that the *Nina*, like the *Ceres*, carried a windmill for pumping-out purposes. The windmill, according to a Dunwich

authority, was rescued by a local farmer who tried to adapt it for grinding.

The enduring English post-mill seems to have been carried to far distant lands. In 1957 I was shown an old sketch of a post-mill completed in Sydney, Australia, in early 1797. The last was dismantled there as late as the 1880s.

Among other windmill souvenirs in my hands is a love-letter written by a village maiden to a Suffolk miller in, it is believed, the close of Victoria's reign. A fragment of the envelope, with the local postmark intact, is also preserved.

The passionate letter – I give an extract here – said: "They can all do and say what they like, there is no such thing as killing my love towards you. You, darling, are the only man on this earth that I have any love for. As things are I cannot have you – not at present anyhow . . ."

While easy access to the past is everyone's right, the privilege, I always think, requires consideration for the ghosts of those one disturbs in secret places. Thus no-one knows – except me – which Suffolk windmill on moonlit and stormy nights saw love among the cobwebs. All I will say is that the letter came from a secret place in a post-mill . . .

By God's fair air
I grind ye grain;
Make good prayer
When bread ye gain.

Wortham smock mill, near Diss, as the writer saw the demolished mill in 1948.

Digging Up Passmore

WHEN I lived a bachelor's life in South Kensington, London, in the late 1950s, my journey home at the end of the day was always from the underground station along Old Brompton Road to Cranley Gardens, Old Brompton Road being the home of several auction rooms and galleries over many years.

After sales – at least in those care-free times – most pavement dustbins overflowed with the 'rubbish' of the day's auctions, although I found them almost always worthy of inspection.

It was in Old Brompton Road on such an occasion that I came upon a spread of copies of the *Wiltshire Archeological and Natural History Magazine* for 1903 and the *Transactions of the Bristol and Gloucestershire Archeological Society* for the 1930s.

Star find, however was an old parchment notebook containing the local field jottings of an archaeologist whose hand, it seemed, was fairly old and scholarly. The owner's name, on the other hand, had been scratched out on the inside cover, but he appeared to like burial barrows.

At the same time, from associated dustbins, came a copy of the well-known HMSO publication *The Battle of Britain* – August/October, 1940, price 3d., which was published early in 1941 and became a best-seller, the historian author observing: "Nothing like it has ever been fought before in the history of mankind".

The cover of the HMSO publication was embossed "Callas House, Wanborough Wilts" and there was an ink monogram which, incorrectly, I read as "A.P.D. 15.4.41"– obviously the date when the booklet was acquired.

It struck me at the time that while the Battle of Britain booklet hadn't much of a link with the archeological proceedings the owner, whoever he was, had a certain feel for history and must have regarded his copy with some reverence.

Anyway, the weighty archeological proceedings and the Battle of Britain booklet were separated for preservation, one lot to the history bookshelf and the single publication to the aeronautical corner. But the circumstances of their being found at the same time were noted.

Curious about the monogram "A.P.D.", I wrote to the address at Wanborough, but on two or three occasions the letters were returned by the Post Office as "unknown". However eventually one of my letters was delivered to Callas Hill Farm, High Street, Wanborough, whose occupiers, Mr and Mrs A.P. Leitch, telephoned by return.

Yes, I had found the mark – but Callas House was gone. All Mrs Leitch could tell me at the time was that the house was lived in by "a famous archaeologist" and that, ironically, it was knocked down after his death by a builder although it was a scheduled property.

Not many days later came exciting news: Callas House had been the home of Arthur D. Passmore, (A.D.P. of the monogram), who had an association with the opening of King Tut-ankh-amun's tomb in the Valley of the Kings, Thebes, Egypt, in 1922. It was reasonable to suppose that the archeological proceedings and the field notebook were Mr Passmore's possessions.

Soon Mr and Mrs Leitch set Wanborough thinking and came up with more startling news: "Mr Passmore was the last surviving archaeologist that had entered Tut-ankh-amun's tomb. He was so convinced he also had the Tut-ankh-amun curse that he was too terrified to be alone at night. He did live to an old age but he went blind before he died." (Whatever may have been Mr Passmore's belief, the curse was of newspaper origin. As far as is known no one suffered ill from entering the tomb but one of the archaeologists, who was a diabetic, received a mosquito bite and complications.)

"His house was very big and full of archeological relics. Sadly, when he died, although the house was a listed building, it was pulled down . . . and all the contents sold."

With this knowledge of Mr Passmore's background the proceedings were examined for any signs of authorship. Interestingly, in the *Transactions of the Bristol and Gloucestershire Archeological Society* for 1934, Vol. 56, issued on July 22, 1935, which came from one of the dustbins, he contributed a solitary article on "A Beehive Chamber at Ablington, Gloucestershire".

Briefly, this was a kind of underground habitation, but to be fair to Mr Passmore his impression was that "we have here a beehive burial chamber in a mutilated mound which may be a barrow".

Close to this kind of thinking Christopher and Jacquetta Hawkes in their *Prehistoric Britain* (Pelican Books, 1949) observed: "Clearly the imaginative appeal of the pit-dwelling is very great: there is something of the romantic savage in the picture of our ancestors passing their lives crouched in holes 10ft below the ground.

"So great, indeed, is it that for long its supporters were blind to the evident truth that no human being could linger over a fire in such a pit and emerge alive.

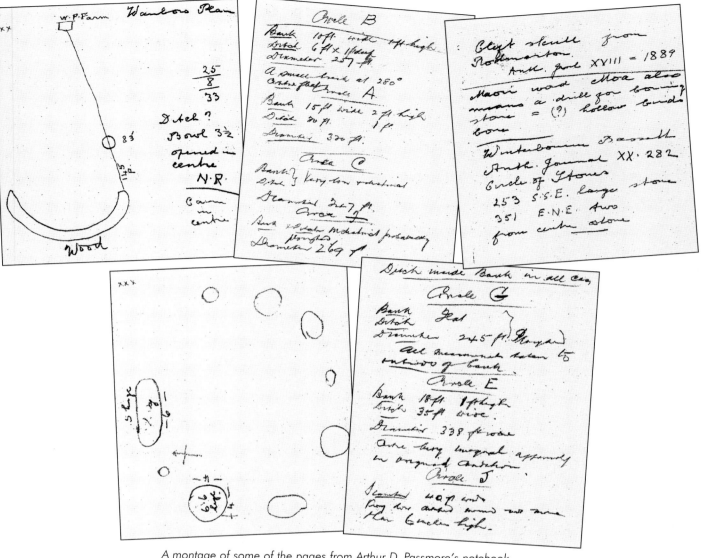

A montage of some of the pages from Arthur D. Passmore's notebook. The meaning of these mysterious archaeological notes were known only to him.

"Cold reason, however has been accepted in the end and banished the pit-dwellers from our history; instead it is recognised that these peasants had a practical means of storing the winter food necessary to support their increasing numbers."

As Mr Passmore explained in the 1934 proceedings: "Canon Samuel Lysons in *Our British Ancestors* records that about 1865 a small underground beehive chamber was found near the large long-barrow known as Lamborough Banks, north of Ablington. It was opened and described as having been furnished with stone seats. Then it was apparently lost sight of until the writer fell through a small hole in the roof which was concealed by rough herbage".

Bit by bit, then, I began to form a picture of Mr Passmore, but there were still details I wanted to know about. The Wiltshire Divisional Library at Swindon was approached.

Mr Passmore, born in 1890, was the son of a Swindon antique dealer, whose business he took over at 24 Wood Street. He died on 6th March, 1958, aged 85.

According to an obituary in the *Wiltshire Archeological and Natural History Magazine* for 1960, this connection gave Mr Passmore scope for the strong antiquarian bent which he acquired early in life and the opportunity "to amass the very large and varied collection which was to become his absorbing passion".

The collection he built up was particularly rich in porcelain, coins, "and archeological specimens which he either bought or discovered in north Wiltshire".

So his house at Wanborough – he succeeded two years before his death in getting Callas House scheduled for preservation on account of its great architectural interest – became a veritable museum until some years before his death when "the bulk of his collection was given to the Ashmolean Museum at Oxford".

In pointing out that for 56 years Mr Passmore was a frequent contributor to the *Wiltshire Archeological and Natural History Magazine,* the obituary noted that, while his contributions to local archaeology were outstanding, he remained a zealous collector and was probably "more intent to acquire a good specimen than to note its exact location and association". It was for this reason that his archeological collections lost much of their value as evidence though containing, of course, some unique items.

The obituary didn't identify him with any Tut-ankh-amun investigation but said that "he took part in excavations in Egypt". He was a keen aerial photographer in his part of England "which led, among other things, to the discovery of many of the unexplained ring ditches in the neighbourhood of Highworth".

From the same helpful library source came some additional anecdotes of special interest, because these rather confirmed the original conclusions I drew from the dustbin evidence of over 20 years ago.

A former editor of the *Evening Advertiser,* Swindon, Mr Hubert Harrison, put on record in the library that he knew Mr Passmore as a great friend and that the man "spent a long lifetime excavating not only in the vicinity of his home, but all over the country".

Mr Harrison associated his archaeologist friend, who must have provided him with some good local stories, with men like the Earl of Carnarvon, a patron of archaeology, Dr. Howard Carter, the eminent Egyptologist, Professor Flinders Petrie, Sir Mortimer Wheeler, and others "in excavations abroad in various countries, including Tut-ankh-amun's tomb in Egypt.".

Mr Harrison went on: "On one of my visits to his home my wife and I found Mr Passmore engrossed with a pile of Roman tiles and masonry littering a magnificent carpet on his drawing room floor.

"Even as a schoolboy he could gather his classmates from their play and assemble them round him while he discoursed on foreign stamps, coins, pottery, natural history, etc., for he was a born lecturer and loved to share his knowledge.

"Sad to relate, towards the close of his life . . . he imagined he was a Roman, dressing in a toga, sandals on his feet and wearing a sword. His beautiful house was demolished and not a trace of it remains".

Dr A.G. Sherratt, Assistant Keeper in the Department of Antiquities at the Ashmolean Museum, Oxford, lifted a bit more of the veil surrounding Mr Passmore: "He was a very eccentric and secretive figure . . . He loaned various items to us during his life, and on his death in the 1950s we acquired his collection of flintwork from the Avebury region, and one or two other antiquities. His notebooks, of which we have copies, are in the library of the Wiltshire Archeological Society at Devizes; though various other notebooks and photographs are known to be in private possession. My predecessor Mr Humphrey Case, who lives at Warborough, Oxfordshire, knew Mr Passmore in his later years and was particularly interested in his prehistoric antiquities".

Asked if Mr Passmore's house and grounds were searched after his death, Dr Sherratt said: "The grounds were not searched (he had an aviary in his back garden, and the vegetation was so tall it came up to the first floor); the house was left in the care of trustees of his will and it is unlikely that anyone searched the place thoroughly. Mr Case thinks he took most of the flints, save those kept by a Mr Banwood, who sprinkled them on his drive at his home in Aldbourne".

In an endeavour to pin-point just what came up for sale in London from Mr Passmore's old house, I checked with Bonhams, Christie's and Sotheby's. Sotheby's were able to confirm that they, in fact, handled some of his effects in 1959-1960 but no catalogue, as far as they could trace, was published.

Asked about next-of-kin, Dr Sherratt was able to say: "It is unlikely that Mr Passmore had any surviving relations. Mr Case and a geologist from the Geological Society, to whom Mr Passmore also donated material, were the only mourners at his funeral".

There is, in a sense, a lesson to be learned from the dustbins in Old Brompton Road: it is that, whereas collector Mr Passmore is on record as not being particularly precise in his archeological recording, the importance of related evidence, like the old HMSO booklet on the Battle of Britain, is a very good example of how important such detail is in arriving at the truth.

Primrose's Painful Transition

IT would never do for me to disclose exactly where Primrose lives in East Anglia for a number of reasons: for one thing, she lives within a stone's throw of one of my relations, and another thing she provides me with fresh eggs, including duck eggs, when I go back to London.

Apart from exchanging a few words when we meet, we have little contact, but Primrose does sometimes point out to my next of kin that she's seen something or other I've written in this or that paper – and that makes her even more guarded when she meets me!

What I can disclose, without giving the game away, is that Primrose (I've even hidden her real garden name) lives somewhere inside the oblong of country bounded by Garboldisham, Harleston, Framlingham and Stowmarket.

She's a country woman, through and through, with local roots going back several generations, and the same background applies to her hard-working farmer husband whose feet are also very earthbound.

When I first visited her village some twenty or so years ago, their timber-framed, pink-faced, L-shaped dwelling was already 300 years old, I'd estimate, and ivy was slowly smothering parts.

The farmhouse and surrounding buildings, grouped by a good duck-pond bordered by elms, had been managed by their families for several generations and the house, I believe, had seen three or four generations of Primrose's family hatched within.

It had, or did have, everything for rural comfort, including a freshwater pump and a quite extraordinary brick outhouse, standing alone, which contained an adult box-like commode with child's trainer-commode alongside. The whole structure, I thought, was a landmark and more than once I surreptitiously reported its existence to a higher authority, hoping a museum would take it.

"You should preserve that," I told Primrose, but I knew by the way she looked at me that she thought I was being downright rude.

As the years of my knowledge of Primrose went by, the farm house, so personal to her, fell into severe disrepair. But I was never invited inside, to look round, and only ever got a dim interior impression of a kitchen that seemed to extend into perpetual darkness. The half-door, around which her huge family of cats congregated to be fed on anything, gave the kitchen a friendly appearance. Yet some of the rooms, I felt sure, must have been too damp to live in.

Now the kitchen is vacant . . .

The story of Primrose's withdrawal from the place is a story of conflict between the old and the new. For several years ago, within sight of the old farmhouse, she had built to her requirements, a splendid new house – a dream house by London standards – with everything one could wish for in the way of services.

But, although the new house rose as planned not far from the old aconite and strawberry beds, watched over by certain trees, Primrose wanted left from the past, it was only recently that first one and then the other decided to inherit 'that new place'.

It came to my ear, more than once in the time leading up to their final surrender to the present, that all that happened for ages was that, although nicely furnished and beautifully heated, the new home was held at arm's length. Sometimes the couple walked round it, as if marking some ancient rites, looking in, but they ventured no nearer.

So it came as a great surprise recently to learn that the couple had at last switched from the past to the present and that someone was going to restore their old old home .

Other tales of Primrose's country life would fill a book, for she lives a good deal by old lore.

An amusing market story, I remember, is that after taking and selling ducks from her pond at a market town miles away, she had hardly got back with the cash before – well, the same ducks splashed back on the pond outside her old kitchen door!

"Aren't they stupid things," she's alleged to have remarked.

Certainly, while some things have changed for her. Primrose can still hear fox and owl calls from around the old buildings that are all very much part of her soul. For some, switching to the present is as disturbing as dying, but I expect Primrose will adapt.

'The Cat & Custard Pot'
THE HIGHEST PUB IN KENT FOR TALL STORIES?

'THE CAT & CUSTARD POT' free-house sign at Paddlesworth, up a narrow road from old RAF Hawkinge near Folkestone, Kent, depicts a cat-silhouette on top of the frame of a double-sided board picturing a cat pouring custard from a pot.

Even landlord Peter Wiggins' silver business-card, reminiscent of the silver-fabric 'planes that used the nearby airfield between the wars, shows a whiskered cat-face and a custard pot, confirming a connection with 'the highest pub in Kent'.

But the cat and pot association can be an embarrassment to some inquisitive customers who ask about the sign's origin, for when they re-tell the story elsewhere listeners, doubting it, sometimes leer.

Indeed, when I went to collect the photographs from my photographer, who has known me for years, he seemed to attribute my explanation for the pub's name to 'too much to drink'.

So, deeply disturbed, I wrote to Peter Wiggins and reminded him that, at lunch-time on 11 August 1992, I was the 'dashing young man' (I am 63) who, having given the very nice bar-lady the glad-eye, questioned him about the sign, asking at the same time for one of his silver business cards proving the existence at Paddleworth of 'The Cat and Custard Pot'.

Cheerful Peter Wiggins replied: "I'm not the least bit surprised you should ask. The yarn is unusual.

"In the years after World War II the pub, which was known as the 'Red Lion' in the Battle of Britain days, had its sign blown down. When an artist-signwriter was commissioned to redo the thing, he was allowed some license as, of course, we are a free-house . . .

"In the end, being a cat-lover, a cat appeared as the theme, but the yellow paint ran, and so in desperation, the clever fellow turned the trickle into custard pouring from – well, a custard pot.

"Naturally, on saving the day, he was awarded yet

The territory of The Cat & Custard Pot pub at Paddlesworth, near Folkestone, from a map drawn in April 1945 by Ernest Clegg, for a series commemorating England's counties at war.

another drink with, if he felt like it, the whole bar," added Peter Wiggins.

While 'The Cat and Custard Pot' pub, which serves traditional beer and food, contains many RAF photographs connecting the place with flying from Hawkinge from as far back as 1912, over 80 years ago, it is not so well known, even locally, that in April 1941, while attempting to make Hawkinge or nearby Lyminge in his badly shot-up Spitfire, Sergeant Jackie Mann, DFM (who in 1988 was held captive for 865 days by Lebanese kidnappers and not released until 1991), had to crash-land at Paddlesworth. He boldly photographed the sizzling pile before he walked away suffering from burns!

Standing as it does at ancient cross-roads, leading to deeply-banked Kent lanes of great beauty, the pub presides over a many-armed signpost pointing to Hawkinge, to Arpinge and Newington, to Acrise and Swingfield, and to Etchinghill and Lyminge, at whose airfield, it is thought by some historians, the RAF expected Hitler or Hess to arrive in early 1941!

The sign is a pointer to yet more airmen's tales, for it was at Newington in March 1941 that Sgt Mann

THE HIGHEST PUB IN KENT – FREE HOUSE
TRADITIONAL BEERS & FOOD

Peter and Jeane Wiggins

THE CAT & CUSTARD POT   TEL:
PADDLESWORTH   HAWKINGE
NR FOLKESTONE KENT   2205

Jackie Mann with his wife, from a TV programme frame, at the time of his release from prison.

Lt. Werner Schlather of II Lehrgeschwader LGII, shot down on 8th February 1941, by the Hawkinge gunners. Operating from Calais-Marck airfield on the French coast, Schlather's Messerschmitt 109 fighter dived into a field near the airfield.

Photo: Courtesy Roy S. Humphreys

who had half a dozen narrow escapes from death while with 421 Flight and 91 Squadron at Hawkinge, had another bumpy belly-landing in a badly damaged Spitfire.

The Luftwaffe, too, is remembered by the pointer to Arpinge. Flying from his Pas de Calais airfield on 8th February 1941, Messerschmitt 109 pilot Lt. Werner Schlather, briefed to give Hawkinge a low-level blasting, astonished RAF ground observers by giving a few minutes' aerobatic display over the centre of the grass airfield!

However, just as Schlather, who today lies buried in Hawkinge churchyard, was climbing into a loop a 40mm AA shell burst, damaging his port-wing causing the undercarriage leg to drop and his 'plane to 'skid'.

Unable to regain control or use his parachute because of his low altitude, Schlather's red-nosed Messerschmitt dived at speed into a field at Arpinge, burying itself 12 feet in the ground.

My late brother, who served as an engine-fitter at Hawkinge between November 1940 and May 1941, witnessed Schlather's antics over the airfield and rode on the fire-tender behind an ambulance to the blazing wreckage. "All that was left of the Messerschmitt," he said in a letter, "was part of a wing, the tail and a few odd bits."

Today I still hold part of the undercarriage leg responsible for the lop-sided dive, and part of Schlather's yellow-painted rudder with fabric still attached, as well as other items.

In the early 1970s, when the Brenzett Aeronautical Museum's aircraft recovery group investigated the site of Schlather's crash, all they found were "some small pieces of metal and a few cannon shells."

So 'The Cat and Custard Pot', if you believe all my stories, is clearly 'the highest pub in Kent' for – well, some of the tallest stories. Have you any better ones?

Jeanne Wiggins commented, as if to take the pub's story just another inch or two up the ladder: "Incidentally, Robert Neame, chairman of Shepherd Neame, sent Jackie Mann a barrel of their special Spitfire Ale on his release from the Lebanese. Spitfire Ale was brewed for the 50th anniversary of the Battle of Britain, which was marked in September 1990, with a great fly-past over London.

"To be quite honest, I am not completely sure we are the highest pub in Kent. Highest in East Kent, yes. Detling is higher, but I am not sure which pub there would qualify, if there is one. We are 650 feet above sea level. And, when the weather is bad, we sometimes 'float' in a kind of froth . . ."

Paddlesworth has a rhyme which runs:

> *The highest church,*
> *The lowest steeple,*
> *The poorest parish,*
> *The fewest people.*

Although the Brenzett Aeronautical Museum, Kent, investigated in the 1970s the crash site of Werner Schlather's Messerschmitt 109 at Arpinge, going down 15 feet, they found nothing worthwhile.

Photo: Courtesy Roy S. Humphreys

Digging for the Hidden Past

THIRTY-FIVE YEARS ago, I doubt if half-a-dozen people in any small English town cared much about archaeology. Those who did were often quietly ridiculed by neighbours as they strode in lonely places in search of Roman and Anglo-Saxon remains. Today there are plenty of well-informed volunteers for any archeological project.

As a young newspaper reporter in West Suffolk in the late 1940s and early 1950s, I used to keep my ears open for market-day gossip of farmers' discoveries. I built up good contacts with the farming community, and my reports were read by museum curators in Colchester, Ipswich, Bury St Edmunds and Norwich. They soon realised the advantages of an informal intelligence network, which often brought valued artifacts into their hands.

Not long after I arrived in Sudbury to cover the Suffolk/Essex border country, I got to know Harold P. Cooper. of Hill Farm, Gestingthorpe, who was then starting to investigate an extensive Roman site on his farm.

In those days Mr Cooper, who had found the site in 1948, was considered a bit odd by some of his fellow farmers. But he persisted with his digging and support snow-balled. Soon all his neighbours became interested.

When Jack Lindsay, author and classical scholar of Castle Hedingham, wrote *The Discovery of Britain* (The Merlin Press, 1958) he observed: 'Still, I needed a push to get going. It came when a young journalist named Elliott turned up one day from Sudbury on a motor-bike on a quest for news. He was interested in archaeology and air-photos, and introduced me to Harold Cooper . . . who was digging up a Roman site on his land'. In fact, Lindsay's book starts with 21 pages on Roman Gestingthorpe.

Above: *The Rodbridge, Suffolk, site from the air. It is now heavily wooded.*

Right: *Stages in the 1952 excavation of an assumed Anglo-Saxon hearth at Rodbridge, Suffolk.*

Above and below: *The following artifacts were found at Rodbridge, Suffolk, which included pottery rims, metal objects and animal remains.*

In September 1985, Mr Cooper's endeavours at Hill Farm received high praise from the Historic Buildings and Monuments Commission and Essex County Council's East Anglian Archaeology Report No 25 was entitled *Excavations by Mr H.P. Cooper on the Roman Site at Hill Farm, Gestingthorpe, Essex*.

Professor S.S. Frere, in the introduction, said: 'The great potential interest of the site gradually became more and more apparent through the wealth and quality of the finds unearthed. These were carefully preserved at Hill Farm, which virtually took on the character of a site museum. At length, in 1974, the site came up for scheduling by the Ancient Monuments Department.'

While Mr Cooper in the early 1950s probed Gestingthorpe with increasing results, I took on a Romano-British site not far away at Rodbridge, near Long Melford, which in 1951-52 produced a wealth of pottery and animal remains and some metal artifacts.

Curiously, when I started small test digs, I ran into difficulties with the old West Suffolk County Council and for a time work was suspended. Finally, obeying the county council, the finds were handed over to the old Sudbury Museum, but in 1985 I was astonished to learn that 'in a clear-out many years ago that sort of stuff was sold at Colchester'. And after all the care and trouble to which I'd gone to obey the county council!

The Rodbridge site taught me a good deal and improved my amateur status. Even the late Basil Brown, of Sutton Hoo fame, came over one day to inspect an assumed Anglo-Saxon hut hearth I had found. He drew it in my field notebook for posterity.

The Rodbridge collection of typical Romano-British refuse is now largely dispersed, but I was able to partly reconstruct some quite big pot rims and the bases of what had probably been small cups.

Now I am left with my field notes and photographs, and my memories of an aerial flight I made over the site in 1952.

Unlike Mr Cooper, I have no other evidence that my toiling at Rodbridge assisted local archaeology or was seriously noted – except by Basil Brown.

Footnote: It is only in recent years that Britain's leading archaeologists have come to accept that Basil Brown, in the end, had to be given public credit for sniffing out the Sutton Hoo treasure ship in league with Mrs Edith Pretty, the owner of the estate. In 2004 Christopher Durrant published *Basil Brown: Astronomer, Archaeologist, Enigma*, recalling his life (1888-1977), with a number of hitherto unpublished photographs.

Stages in the way the author 'nibbled' at the exposed edges of the old pit workings at Rodbridge.

Southwold Revisited
A WINTER'S TALE

MY AIM, that time I was in Suffolk, was a beach trek from Southwold to Minsmere and back by way of Dingle Walks – regardless of the cold and howling north-easterly wind.

Up at dawn at Beccles to make my own breakfast, I was away on the early bus for Lowestoft, with a transfer to the Southwold one, where the only other passenger declared "You must be daft, with travel companies crying out to take your hand to paradise."

Indeed, when I reached the Southwold I knew of summer days, I found the main street deserted. My only company was the tugging wind around me, squeaking shop-signs, and distantly the roar of the North Sea below the cliffs.

Anticipating a late return to Southwold, I quickly bought several pairs of kippers to take back to London, a pair of wool-gloves to warm my perished hands, and acquired free, for my collection, from Adnams corner-shop, an empty Rail Ale bottle, commemorating the Southwold Railway 1879-1929.

It never occurred to me at the time, that should some fatal misfortune have overtaken me on the lonely trek ahead, the coroner might well have adjourned the inquest to find out more about the uncooked kippers and the empty ale bottle in my water-logged knapsack.

Once across Southwold Green I descended by the coast-road to the harbour-mouth and then turned right for Blackshore and the *River Blyth* pedestrian bridge built on the old railway piers.

How the wind tore at me. I hardly dare look across the river to Walberswick for fear of finding Dunwich,

Storms at Dunwich, Suffolk, have caused the cliffs to fall in places. Here, in the remains of an old graveyard, human leg-bones are apparent.

my main goal, lost in flying spume and with it all my last resolve.

Once over the bridge, I crossed the heath where gorse clumps and hollows afford some protection from the fierce gusts, and entered Walberswick where, in passing, I spoke to an old friend, Mr Fisher, at his garage. He seemed surprised to see me.

As I left the village for the saltings, I passed a stern-faced woman who took it upon herself to remark that perhaps I had made a mistake by visiting her village in such weather.

When I turned down the beach way between the huts, saw the raging surf, flying spume and felt for the first time the stinging sand on my face, I cringed.

Looking north towards Southwold from Dunwich cliffs on a summer day, and (right), the boiling sea from the same vantage point during the storm.

Visibility was limited by a mixture of sand and salt-laden air and prospects under the sullen sky looked foreboding.

Would I get a quarter of the way along such a beach where, overnight, the pounding waves had played such havoc with the shingle? In some places. sheer shingle walls towered to head-height.

The north-easterly wind, once the bringer of amber and jet in quantity to the Suffolk shore, was instead casting ashore masses of North Sea flotsam and jetsam: timber beams, bottles, plastic containers, coloured rope, pieces of nylon, old clothing and oil-soaked sea-birds, fish and even the occasional ship's cat.

A spent shotgun cartridge, washed up from the shingle depths, brought a smile later on, for on close examination, I found it was stamped 'Style Mk.II (then a picture of a stile) Richardson Halesworth".

Only a short time before, I had been in touch with the Richardson family after a lapse of 35 years. And now, it seemed, the sea had sealed the reunion.

So the morning wore on . . . 11 o'clock . . . noon and, towards 2 o'clock, I got an uncertain view of Dunwich through my misty binoculars. Would I reach 'The Ship' Inn before closing time?

Well, I did, and passing between two rusty ships' anchors, testimony to the stress of past storms, I half fell into the warm, utterly quiet parlour.

Stiffly I sat down and scrutinised the menu-board, but decided on a tot of port – and another. I wondered if the landlady thought I was from a wreck.

Fortified, I left the inn to climb the cliff-top path to the ruins of Dunwich Monastery and from near the

Top: Looking south towards Minsmere on a summer day, and from the same spot during the storm walk.

grave of 19th-century John Brinkley Easey, aged 23, who like the rest of old Dunwich awaits the call of the deep, I had an aerial view of the zig-zag wind pressure marks on the boiling sea.

The roar of the breakers was tremendous – I had not heard anything like it for ages.

And as I watched the sea, taking the odd aerial snap from Dunwich and Minsmere cliffs, my thoughts turned to George Crabbe's poems about Aldeburgh, lower down the coast.

Then, by uneven cliff steps, I reached the beach below. There had been more cliff falls, and a warning notice told visitors not to probe the cliff face for relics of bygone Dunwich.

There was fresh boat wreckage on the tide-line, and I photographed the main piece, noting the bright red, blue and yellow/cream paintwork of the cap part. It looked very much like a hand-lever pump from a Dutch barge, was wood-encased, and quite old.

Mid-afternoon saw me back in Dunwich and following earlier directions given at 'The Ship' Inn, I

Once-upon-a-time Walberswick, Suffolk, had a post-mill. Since 1903, when this old postcard was posted, the village has been battered by winds and floods.

set out for Walberswick and Southwold by way of Dingle Walks.

I was glad to be walking a little inland this time as thickets and small woods provided some cover from the icy wind. But these warm places, so much used by coastal dwellers for all the ages of the old paths, made one linger – close to sleep.

It was while resting in such a place, which seemed so very old, that I thought I caught glimpses from time to time of beady eyes . . .

But no human beings were anywhere about, and the exertions of my walk, though quite exhausting, hadn't been sufficient to bring on hallucinations.

Perhaps, I thought, things of the past, human and animal, have a way of making themselves known to the living in lonely places in this peculiar, elusive fashion – but of course without malice or harm to the witness.

It seemed that the moment one's head turned to the left or to the right they were gone. Perhaps that's what the Little People of legend are all about.

As I trudged on, I picked up surviving cottages on a 1839 map borrowed from my first edition of Robert Wake's *Southwold and it's Vicinity,* and took the path to the east of Foxbarrow Walks.

Soon the derelict stump of the drainage mill on Westwood Marshes was sighted but, before reaching it, I ate my late snack below a dike wall, shielded from the wind.

Refreshed, I pressed on for Walberswick and the

A big roller builds up before crashing on the beach.

pedestrian bridge, just in time to catch the evening bus. I had been walking, I estimated, for about seven hours, much of the time in gale-force winds and rain.

I was so hungry that I could have eaten my parcel of uncooked kippers. But if I'd tried, I would have been without a drop of ale as, of course, the empty bottle in my knapsack was merely a souvenir of someone else's drink in the glory of some summer past.

But I prefer the cycle of our distinct English seasons with all their various moods.

So, when a writer like Josceline Dimbleby confesses "If I had to stay in England for a year without going away, I'd feel depressed and empty" . . . I'm quite dumbfounded. Our fair country, I'm sure, is worth getting to know in all weathers.

Strong winds at Dunwich, Suffolk, affect the cliffs. Here erosion is taking place as sand pours down.

52

Arthur H. Patterson

REMEMBERING when in Norwich recently that the art of taxidermy (preparing, stuffing and mounting the skins of animals with life-like effect) was once apparent in many a shop window there, I halted at a gunsmith's shop near Norwich Castle, as the museum to which I was bound had still to open its doors for the day, and noticed new aids I never knew existed for the modern shot: nitrogen-filled sights, sonic ear valves, target launchers, not, of course, forgetting much improved goose and crow calls.

Not far away, in a rather similar shop which was, however, more for the fisherman, I noticed a pipette advertised for obtaining 'sample of trout's stomach contents'. It was claimed that 'delicate insects are far less damaged than by a marrow-scoop, and often still alive'.

I wonder what Arthur H. Patterson, the Broadland naturalist, who had the inappropriate pseudonym 'John Knowlittle', would think of all these related aids if he could come back?

Actually, my visit to Norwich Castle Museum was to see the natural history exhibits with a view to finding out if Arthur Patterson was represented in any way. The dioramas of Norfolk animals and birds attracted me no end, but any link with the Broadland naturalist by name I could not find.

It was then that a keeper suggested I spoke to the natural history department on the internal telephone, which I did, but learned no more. The spokesman

THROUGH BROADLAND IN A BREYDON PUNT BY "JOHN KNOWLITTLE" (ARTHUR H PATTERSON)

WITH SKETCHES BY THE AUTHOR, AND PHOTOS.

A.H.PATTERSON 1920.

NORWICH:
H.J.VINCE, 19, BEDFORD STREET

Arthur H. Patterson aboard Moorhen on Beydon Water. It was this fine tidal lake, about five miles long and two-thirds of a mile wide, which gave the Norfolk naturalist the opportunity for continuous observation of nature subjects.
Photo: Courtesy 'Eastern Daily Press'

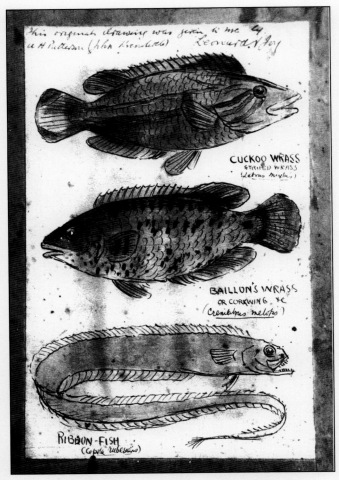

The three fish studies by Arthur Patterson, described in this article. They were executed for Mr Leonard Joy, a Norwich fishmonger, after a discussion with the naturalist.

Rough Notes on the Fish and Fisheries of East Suffolk. Published in 1910, one of only 111 copies, mine is number 30 and was autographed by the naturalist on 28th January 1910.

Born in poor surroundings at No. 8 Row 36, Great Yarmouth, on 19th October 1857, Arthur Patterson, who was a most prolific writer and contributed to the *Eastern Daily Press,* was the only survivor of nine children, all of whom died before they were 21. His famous old houseboat *Moorhen* was well known on the *Yare* and the *Bure* and on *Breydon Water.* He died in 1935 at the age of nearly 77.

As for my visit to Norwich Castle Museum, expressly to seek evidence of Arthur Patterson, I found on getting home that I had noted years ago that the naturalist generously presented his extremely valuable manuscript notebooks and copies of all his writings to Norwich Public Libraries. But there is no reason why the naturalist should not be shown, life size, in one of the natural history dioramas in the museum.

PREFATORY NOTE.

The following "Notes" and the "List" are the outcome of several days most interesting rambles and enquiries, made among the fisher-folk and others, during my Summer holidays of 1909.

I found very little literature on the subject. From Dr. Wake's short bare list of Southwold species, and the Notes on East Anglian Fishes which have been printed from time to time in the Transactions of the Norfolk and Norwich Naturalists' Society, some useful "dates" and "occurrences" have been gleaned, beyond which there seem to have been no other existent catalogues or references. My List is incomplete, of course, but it may serve as a basis for any future Local Naturalist Historian to work upon who may feel disposed to pursue the subject.

My thanks are due to several Suffolk gentlemen for information tendered, whose names will be a guarantee for the accuracy of their communications. I also wish to acknowledge the unfailing courtesy shewn me by the East Suffolk fishermen. The beautiful photographs of Fishing Boats are by Mr. YALLOP.

This reprint is limited to 111 copies.

No. *30*

Name...........................

*From A H Patterson
The Author
Jan 28 10*

ARTHUR H. PATTERSON,

GREAT YARMOUTH,

(*January 12th, 1910*).

Autographed page from *Rough Notes on the Fish and Fisheries of East Suffolk* in the writer's possession. Arthur H. Patterson signed the edition – one of only 111 copies – on 28th January 1910.

said he could recall nothing on display directly associated with Arthur Patterson but they probably had some papers covering his life's work.

One wonders, as Arthur Patterson was well known for his lightning sketches of natural history and other objects, what remains in private hands in Norfolk today? Apparently he would give a demonstration for '25p, or as may be agreed', with travelling expenses extra.

In addition to several of the naturalist's now much sought after books, I own a large original watercolour sketch of three fishes – cuckoo wrass, baillon's wrass and ribbon fish – which was given to me in the 1950s by a Halstead, Essex, man.

The original owner of the sketch, Mr Leonard Joy, a retired Norwich fishmonger, of Great Finborough, Suffolk, who gave me details in the 1950s when he was 82, said: "The reason 'John Knowlittle' drew these fish was owing to my having a cuckoo wrass on my slab. 'J.K.' was interested in it and said he would bring me a drawing of it. My man at Lowestoft used to send me extraordinary fish that he had caught, so that the naturalist could see them."

I see, too, that at Southwold in 1955 I found in a bookshop a secondhand copy of Arthur Patterson's

First Man to Fly the North Sea

JULY 27th 1909, is significant in aviation history, for on that day, in just over 37 minutes, Louis Bleriot, the French airman, flew the English Channel to Dover.

July 30th 1914 – 50 years ago this year – was also significant in aviation history but the accomplishment was overshadowed by the imminence of the Great War. Subsequently, chroniclers seemed to overlook the date.

That July day was the occasion of the flight made by Tryggve Gran, a Norwegian marine pilot, from Cruden Bay, Aberdeenshire, to Klep, south of Stavanger. He accomplished the flight – a distance of 320 miles – in a Bleriot monoplane with an open fuselage. He was airborne for four hours ten minutes and at the time his was the longest-ever flight over sea without sight of land. Certainly it was the first North Sea crossing by air.

Unlike Bleriot, Gran had no ships to escort him. However, he was, with his marine background, a nice blending of the air pilot and the sailing man, for the judgment needed for successful work in either sphere is of a similar order.

Gran had to wait a day or two at Cruden Bay before committing himself to the winds and the fogs. Eventually favourable weather showed up on 30th July, and at 0800 hours Gran rose into the sky in his frail machine. Twenty miles out over the sea he met fog and, wisely, decided to return to Cruden Bay. All that took him 40 minutes.

Gran's determination to accomplish the flight that day was so strong that, on receiving a telegram from Norway telling him that the weather was fairly favourable on that side, he took off again. The time was 1308 hours. He followed the Scottish coast for a little way, then struck a north-easterly course, duly allowing for 'drift' owing to the fresh north-westerly breeze that was blowing.

After three hours' flying, Gran encountered fog. Then he began to "experience the sufferings of air sickness". There was anxiety in his mind, too, about the petrol supply. He therefore flew in a slow climb to 6000 feet to give himself height should his engine fail. Then he saw the sun and – oh, joy – the distant, snow-capped mountains of his beloved Norway. Judicious Gran, master of the air currents, stopped the Bleriot's 80-hp engine, glided down through clouds, and landed on the shore of a lake 20 miles south of Stavanger. The time – 1718 hours.

Gran, who was the first Norwegian to win international fame as an aviator, immediately set out for Bergen and Christiania (now Oslo) in order to

Tryggre Gran in May 1914, by his trusted Bleriot. It had a 80hp Gnome engne, and carried an extra fuel tank for five hours' flying at a speed of about 78mph   Photo: Courtesy Norsk Teknisk Museum

deliver a copy of that day's *Daily Mail* that he had flown across to King Haakon and Queen Maud of Norway.

Norway, eager to acknowledge the flight, appointed Gran to the active list as a lieutenant in the Norwegian Army Flying Corps, and his faithful Bleriot was purchased by the Norwegian government and is still preserved in very good condition in the Norsk Teknisk Museum, Oslo.

But Gran's skill in the air owed something to British instructors. For, before 1914, he was a pupil at the Hall Flying School, Hendon, then he went to the Bleriot School at Buc, in France, "where he learned to loop."

In 1915, Gran, who later joined our own Royal Flying Corps and fought over London, used his flying ability to the full among the dangerous squalls and eddies that are a feature of the fiords of his homeland. With an observer, Gran hunted German submarines that were infringing Norwegian neutrality by creeping into lonely fiords and resting in their sheltered waters. Like an Arctic owl, Gran patrolled the fiords and,

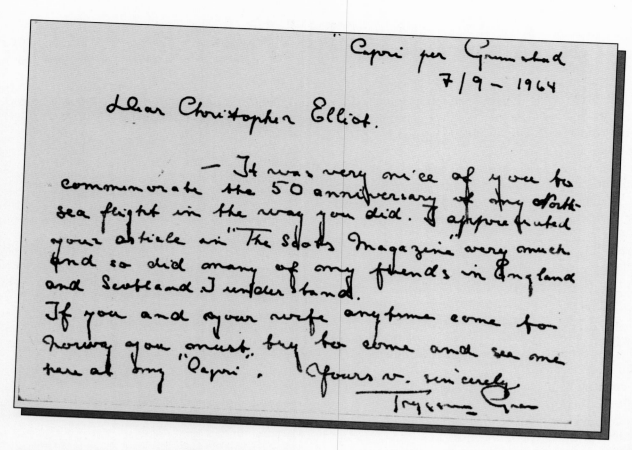

"Capri per Grimstad
7/9 - 1964

Dear Christopher Elliot.

— It was very nice of you to commemorate the 50 anniversary of my North-sea flight in the way you did. I appreciated your article in "The Scots Magazine" very much find so did many of my friends in England and Scotland I understand.
If you and your wife anytime come to Norway you must try to come and see me here at my "Capri". Yours v. sincerely,

Trygve Gran

whenever a submarine was sighted by his observer, flew down to within a few feet of the water and drove the intruder back into the North Sea.

Is anything being done in this country to celebrate the 50th anniversary of Gran's historic flight? If nothing is being done, it is not too late for the flying fraternity of Scotland to make some imaginative gesture. Scotland's maritime links with Scandinavia are surely strong enough to justify some kind of commemoration of this modern Norseman of the air.

An anniversary flight might be one idea – but few airmen today would care to follow Gran's route in an aircraft such as the Norwegian used in 1914. Gran's flight is no doubt in a class all on its own. But I fear, we have almost forgotten the airman who, in a full sense of the expression, may be said to be an *avant courier* for the air traffic later developed between Norway and this country. Happily, he is still with us, aged seventy-five, and living at Fevik in his native country.

Gran's Bleriot on Norwegian soil after his historic flight from Scotland on 30th July 1914.
Photo: Courtesy Norsk Teknisk Museum

In the Wake of East Anglia's Treasure Ships

While the forthcoming new excavations at Sutton Hoo, near Woodbridge, Suffolk, which gave up the renowned Anglo-Saxon treasure ship in 1939, are expected to create 'a wave of national and international support for archaeology in general', wonderful discoveries – some reported and some never reported – have been made in the country over the past century, between the *River Deben,* the river of Sutton Hoo, and the *River Alde,* which is tangled with the *Rivers Ore* and *Butley.*

In this connection I have always been intrigued by the Snape ship, which is of Anglo-Saxon origin, and discovered in the 1860s not far away, and of the uncatalogued finds which must have disappeared into private hands.

It was in 1862-63 that a pagan burial ground or an urn-field was partially excavated half a mile due east of Snape church and close to the Snape-Aldeburgh main road. In those days the site was marked by several large barrows about which little was known.

But at some other time, it appears, the site was explored 'by some gentlemen who were supposed by the inhabitants to have come from London'. It was rumoured that these men took away a 'waggon-load of vases and other things'.

The River Blyth, under storm clouds, looking to the Walberswick side.

What we do know is that the diggers of the early 1860s went below the level of the urn-field, where there was a barrow, and found traces of the Snape ship, 'the first of the Anglo-Saxon period to be recorded in England'.

The Snape ship AD 635 to 650, according to details published by RLS Bruce-Mitford, a leading authority on Sutton Hoo, in the 1952 *Proceedings of the Suffolk Institute of Archaelogy,* was from forty-six to forty-eight feet long and about nine feet nine inches or ten feet at midships. Traces of iron boat rivets and bolts and wooden ribs, as were found at Sutton Hoo, were noted at Snape.

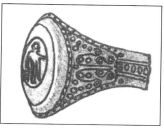

The Snape, Suffolk, gold ring.

It was 'on the wooden flooring in the centre of the boat'; in an area of bright yellow sand, that the famous Snape gold ring was found. But the man's ring, bearing on the flat central portion a nude male figure holding two ears of corn in his right hand and a libation bowl in his left, was lost to museum eyes until 1950 when, finally, it turned up in London.

In 1980, when I recalled the Snape and Sutton excavations in an article in another publication, it set people thinking.

One letter from an archaeologist, requested a sight of the photograph I had taken of the old Sutton Hoo boat-shaped excavation not long after the Second World War, when the historic site had been crossed, perhaps inadvertently, by military vehicles.

Most interesting of the letters, however, came from Mrs Winifred Christie, of Lower Addison Gardens, London, who wrote: 'The Snape ring was at no time lost but was lovingly treasured in my family. My grandfather, Septimus Davidson, owned the land where the ship burial was found.

As a keen amateur archaeologist he was asked to preside over the excavations, upon which he and others later reported, and the ring was his memento of these researches. The intaglio set in the centre of the ring is of Roman workmanship. I like to imagine the Snape man picking it up in a field a thousand years and more before the local digs.

'It is extremely unlikely that my father was at the excavations in 1862, as he was only three years old. On my grandfather's death the ring passed to him. He had become another enthusiastic amateur archaeologist. Realising that he was the guardian of a potential national treasure, he expressed a wish that it should be offered to the British Museum after his own death. He died in 1950, aged almost 91.

'As my mother's sight was failing I wrote on her behalf to the British Museum, who put me in touch with Mr Bruce-Mitford. He had just visited Suffolk in a fruitless endeavour to trace the ring and returned to find, by an amazing coincidence, that my letter was awaiting him'.

Mrs Christie, in further correspondence, told me: 'No, I can't recall ever having tried on the Snape ring until I was quite grown-up. It was enormous!'

'It was only after my parents came to live in this house in 1946 that I remembered seeing it – and this was the occasion when my father said he wished it to be given to the British Museum. He felt that the security there was likely to be first-class, and I feel he may have been guided to this conclusion by his realisation that the ring is unique'.

What of Sutton Hoo (AD 625) and now firmly associated with Raedwald, a King of the East Angles? It took years to sort out and classify the contents of the ship but Snape, unfortunately, was an opportunity lost simply because of the haphazard way the excavations there were tackled in the 19th century.

Many people are unaware that in 1980 the contents of the Sutton Hoo ship disappeared from England for nine months. What happened was they formed part of a major exhibition on boat-graves at the Statenshistoriska Museum, Stockholm, containing material from the princely burials of

Old Snape Bridge and River Alde.

Vendel and Valsgade, Uppland, Sweden, as well as from other major Scandinavian sites.

In 1981 the Government's Treasure Trove Committee, in reporting rewards paid for archaeological discoveries, said 'Hunters of buried treasure find the richest pickings in East Anglia'. But the only real fortune to compare with that of a winner of the football pools was an award of £135,000 for the discovery of 9th century Anglo-Saxon disc brooches at Pentney, near King's Lynn.

In 1982, during excavations at Coppergate, York, a superb Anglo-Saxon helmet of the 7th century closely resembling the famous Sutton Hoo helmet was recovered. Interestingly, this was a time when the city was known to have been a royal centre of the kingdom of Northumbria – a kingdom with which Raedwald was associated.

But while the majority of amateur archaeologists can never do much more than tell their local museums of things turned up or talked about, it is possible sometimes to actually meet long-boat skippers on the tide line.

When such a vessel named the *Hugin* was built and rowed across the North Sea from Denmark to commemorate the landing of Hengist and Horsa in England 1500 years ago, I asked Captain Peter Christian Jensen to sign my postcard of his Danish crew as they tumbled ashore at Broadstairs, Kent, on 28th July 1949.

The River Orwell at sunset.

East Anglian Ties with America

DISCUSSIONS in some sections of the media about the state of Anglo-American relations seem to take no account of the historical fact that from about 1942 into 1945 a large number of American service men and women – at peak period over 150,000 alone in the 8th and 9th USAAFs – were stationed in Suffolk, Norfolk and Essex.

Interestingly, a recent look at official papers in the Public Record Office at Kew, showed that the last return prior to D-Day in June 1944, when the USAAF in Great Britain was at its strongest, put American airmen in at least 10 counties with over 52,000 in Suffolk, over 55,000 in Norfolk and over 43,000 in Essex. Total strength of the USAAF in Europe at that time was over 404,000 personnel.

Which reminds me that in 1980, while shopping one Saturday in London, I discovered in a bric-a-brac shop, since destroyed by fire, an unusual wartime link with the United States which is now, I fear, very much forgotten history.

The link, which appears to have an old association with Suffolk, took the form of a stone book-end with a lead medallion embedded in it, inscribed with a picture of Big Ben and the towers of Westminster, surrounded by the words 'Houses of Parliament – London 1941'.

Believing the book-end to be one of a pair, I asked the bric-a-brac lady to find the other, and after a search it turned up in a drawer. Embedded in the second one was a medallion showing St. Paul's Cathedral and the old city in flames with the inscription 'London 1941 – Bombed – Burned – But Unbeatable'.

Closer examination away from the bric-a-brac shop revealed a small printed stamp on one of the ends which read: "This stone came from the Houses of Parliament. Processed in England by London Stonecraft Ltd. – No. 920'.

The House of Commons public information office told me: "The Houses of Parliament were bombed on 26th September and 8th December 1940; and again on 10th May 1941. The most destruction was wrought by the May 1941, raid, when the Commons' Chamber was entirely devastated by fire caused by incendiaries.

"We have no records of London Stonecraft Limited or the making of book-ends from the stone of the Palace. We would imagine that the then Ministry of Works, who were then responsible for the fabric of the Palace of Westminster, sold the waste materials, and that London Stonecraft bought some stone either from the ministry or through the concern to which the ministry sold it."

It seems that the wartime assault on Parliament had a far-reaching and beneficial effect on Anglo-American relations. For when Northamptonshire author and lecturer Mr Eric Underwood, whose wife came of the old Thurlow family of Bloomville Hall, Suffolk, paid a visit to the United States, he took with him 'stones from the war-destroyed House of Commons for presentation to Congress in Washington and to each of the 48 states'.

What's more, Mr Underwood, whose recreations

The lead bookend medallions commemorating St. Paul's Cathedral and Big Ben under fire.

59

included the promotion of Anglo-American understanding, had the rare experience of having articles written by him read on seven occasions in the US Senate and House of Representatives and "unanimously ordered to be reprinted in Congressional Record".

In trying to identify Bloomville Hall, I was directed to Blomvyle Hall, Hacheston, near Wickham Market, where Mr Colin Walker told me early last year: "There have been many spellings of the house . . . so it may be the one you wish to trace. There have been Thurlows in the area and it is possible they lived here at some stage but I do not actually have evidence of it. It is a Suffolk family which is wide spread . . ."

Inquiries elsewhere to do with the fashioning of articles from rubble taken from the Houses of Parliament revealed that the defunct magazine *Illustrated* of 6th March 1943, had written that, following the enemy attack on 10th May 1941, "the Minister of Works and Buildings handed over to Sir Vincent Baddeley, on behalf of the Red Cross and St John Fund, damaged stone and timber salvaged from the shattered buildings of the Palace of Westminster".

Pieces of stone, timber and glass were thus "cunningly fashioned into various shapes to the design of Fellows and Associates of the Royal Society of British Sculptors".

Each article was accompanied by a signed and numbered certificate of authenticity (my book-ends were numbered 920) and the proceeds from their sale went to the Red Cross and St. John War Organisation.

Finally, Mr J. A. Rundle, writing from Headington, Oxfordshire, told me that his father owned Stonecraft in the 1940s and that "various household articles were made" from the debris of the fire of 10th May 1941 – the moonlit night, incidentally, that brought Deputy Fuhrer Rudolf Hess to Scotland in a Messerschmitt on a supposed peace mission and imprisonment in Spandau Prison, West Germany.

But Parliament seems to have shared bigger pieces from the May 1941 assault for, while on a visit to south east London early last year, I spotted a gargoyle staring down at me from Millstream House in Jamaica Road. A stone plaque at ground level explained:

"The north west corner of this building was destroyed by bombs on 14th October 1940; and rebuilt in 1947. This stone and the gargoyle above were taken from a part of the Houses of Parliament also damaged in the air raids."

Thus, it seems, this fragmented story of Parliament, here and in the United States, is as complete as it can be. It would, however, be satisfying to know if Mr Underwood's Suffolk Bloomville Hall is the Bloomvyle Hall we know exists today near Wickham Market.

Wartime stone relics from the Houses of Parliament were given numbered certificates.

Churchill – The Aviator

IT was announced in March that a film is to be made about Sir Winston Churchill, Britain's wartime Prime Minister, and from the proposed title, 'Young Winston,' one gathers that it will cover his early years only. But will it stick merely to the first 40 years or so? For Winston Churchill, right to the end of his amazing life, enjoyed being puckish.

One aspect of his early years, I imagine, will be exploited – the great man's early interest in aviation and the 'accidents', some recorded and others ignored, which befell him when aeroplanes were then quite unreliable.

In looking at references for a history of the growth of aviation in East Anglia I have learned a little more about Winston Churchill's flying experiences along the East Coast.

A newspaper appeal for information about a reported descent in the sea of the statesman when he was First Lord of the Admiralty before the 1914/18 War revealed little. The rumour of an 'accident' in Harwich harbour as early as 1913, while he was flying as a passenger in a Borel monoplane, could not be positively confirmed.

The reason for the lack of information about this 'ducking' (and other spills) is that right from the start of Winston Churchill's interest in flying, there was a feeling in official circles that he was running

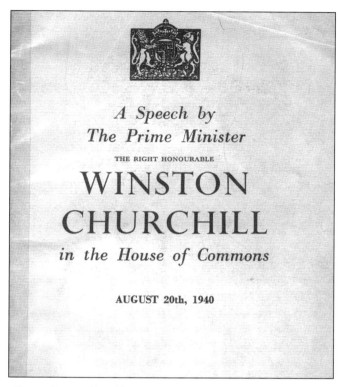

A Speech by
The Prime Minister
THE RIGHT HONOURABLE
WINSTON CHURCHILL
in the House of Commons

AUGUST 20th, 1940

Above: Cover of booklet reporting Churchill's first principal wartime speech at the height of the Battle of Britain.

Below: The skywards look: Mr Churchill at RAF Biggin Hill, Kent, in 1947, with (insets) a Spitfire salute and one being welcomed back by a mechanic.

unnecessary risks. In fact, he wrote fairly dull letters about his early flying experiences, but kept off forced landings, which is no doubt the reason why the Borel story is difficult to pin down. However, what must have been his second local 'escape' was reported in the Press.

It happened on 24th April 1914, when the First Lord of the Admiralty, who wanted seaplane bases at a number of points along the East Coast, was being flown from the Isle of Grain to inspect Felixstowe, which eventually became a famous base. Something went wrong with the engine of seaplane No. 79 and Lieutenant J.W. Seddon, RN, his pilot, had to land in the sea off Clacton jetty.

While the lieutenant sent for another seaplane, Winston Churchill, perhaps impatient of the delay, walked to the Royal Hotel, Clacton, where he remained unrecognised until a local journalist, who had been out in the Boer War, recognised him. Afterwards word spread quickly that he was in Clacton.

It was while he was on the jetty before starting in the replacement seaplane – it was No. 19 – that he was approached by 'the local militant suffragists'. Replying to a question, Winston Churchill said he considered it "part of his duty to understand flying and to visit the great naval air stations". Suffragist propaganda circulated freely and some was found in seaplane No. 79!

A Felixstowe woman, whose uncle was the first commanding officer at Felixstowe in 1913, showed me Winston Churchill's autograph collected on 24th April 1914. The CO and his officers at the time had their headquarters in a local hotel, which in those days was run by my informant's parents. Apparently her uncle brought Winston Churchill to the hotel to 'dry off and have tea'. Then the First Lord of the Admiralty returned to London in borrowed underwear!

Exactly how many times Winston Churchill visited East Anglia on official business is not clear. On 20th June 1939, we know he visited the radar laboratories at Bawdsey on the Suffolk coast, landing at Woodbridge 'in a rather disreputable aeroplane'.

I have a scarce set of cigarette cards – they were issued in the 1920s, are coloured, and measure 5 x 2½in – called 'Famous Escapes'. They describe escapes by such characters as William Tell (c.1307), William Seymour (Early Stuart period), Jack Sheppard (the 1720s) and, of course, Winston Churchill who escaped from Pretoria on 12th December 1899, the card showing him slipping out from under sacks of wool in a railway truck.

I saw Winston Churchill in the flesh at close quarters once in my life. That was on 20th September 1947, at RAF Biggin Hill. I was about to enter journalism but got an introduction to the CO, and was the only outsider present when the great man as Honorary Air Commodore of 615 Auxiliary Air Force Squadron, met a handful of pilots. My impression of him, as he spread himself on the mess couch, cigar in position, was that of a wily but likeable business man who seemed detached from the proceedings. Or was it his restless mind at work?

My last animated memory of Winston Churchill came when he was dead. Like thousands of other grateful citizens, I went to the City of London on the eve of his state funeral – 29th January 1965 – to make sure of a place at dawn. I settled without thought in a shop doorway – it turned out to be No. 1 in the city's address system – facing the steps of St. Paul's Cathedral. What transpired that morning has already been well chronicled and nothing quite like it will ever occur again.

Finally, on 19th September 1965, I watched the unveiling, in Westminster Abbey by the Queen, of a commemorative tablet to Sir Winston Churchill. The Dean said at the bidding: "We have . . . come to honour . . . one man . . . whose very words were actions as he walked with destiny and got for himself a perpetual name."

Familiar figures: Mr and Mrs Churchill at the Kent air show in 1947.

East Anglian 'Magpie'

THERE must be many people around who are stirred at the sound of the huntsman's horn. However, in my case, the cry of 'Any old lumber', followed by a chat with some rough old dealer, who looks like the late Sir Alfred Munnings dressed for a country walk, is more likely to stir me. Then, of course, junk shops (the more untidy the better) have the same appeal.

For the acquisition of oddments of olden times, particularly with East Anglian associations, is one of my main hobbies and it leads me into many unusual channels of research and, I don't mind admitting, provides me with a good few free teas and an occasional dinner.

However, the casual collector today will never get the bargains which were common 15 or 20 years ago. For television, for good or ill, has stampeded nation into collectors of countless objects, often without any real justification. These ephemeral collectors, in turn, unable to appreciate values, tend to push up prices to the detriment of serious amateurs who for years past have enjoyed a comparatively cheap hobby untainted by commercialism.

Incredibly, I don't suppose in 25 years I have spent more than £20 on all my hundreds of objects – less than £1 a year. I am, therefore, glad that I had a chance of collecting in the easy years when so much was about which one connoisseur, on seeing my

An American vintage car expert, Mr. Greg Shipley, of Wisconsin, USA, with associations with the Experimental Aircraft Association Aviation Center at Oshkosh, Wisconsin, who at present has the Wangford-made fretwork model on temporary loan in his private museum, believes that the model – the glass case was damaged 50 years ago – once had front mudguards. Once-upon-a-time, too, the model rested on a padded white silk base, the whole arrangement being very regal.

humble collection, declared was 'the rubbish of civilisation'. I wonder? Did his collection of rare paperweights, three-quarters inherited, without exerting effort, from his father, tell my story – the story of civilisation from the dawn of man to the present day? I doubt it.

What use, one may ask, is this hobby to the outside world – a world which might, if one suddenly departed, be left with boxes of unmarked objects (for I am 15 years behind in getting things marked) which not even a qualified archaeologist could sort out? Often it is the story surrounding an object which makes it a worthy acquisition.

Well, I can claim at least, to have brought East Anglia to London. Schools are always on the lookout for real items and my small son has made a contribution to his school programme by taking a variety of objects.

He has taken my case of stuffed kingfishers which were salvaged at Dedham when about to be broken up with other cases of animals and birds. This colourful exhibit was the work of John Pettitt, naturalist, ornithologist and taxidermist, of the Colchester area, who in his day was one of the best Essex shots. His taxidermy – the case bears his name and address – was so good that the British Museum accepted work from him at the turn of the century. Apparently the children had a nature lesson on kingfishers and finished up by drawing them. For many of these Londoners, I dare say, it was their first sight of this beautiful bird.

On another occasion I let the school have on loan a set of Stone-Age weapons and tools from Grime's Graves, Weeting, which is still one of the most

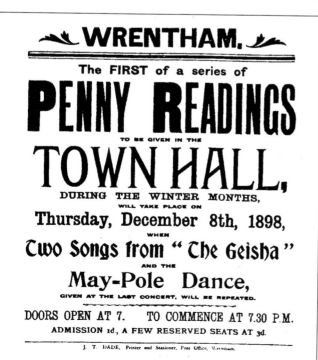

At Wrentham, Suffolk in 1898 there were winter Penny Readings.

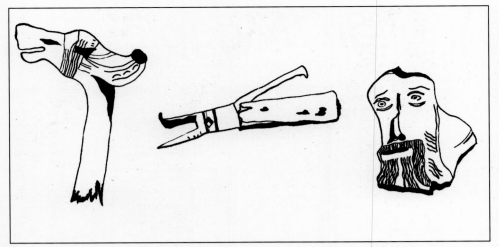

fascinating ancient sites in England – the 'Sheffield of the early Stone Age'. These tools and weapons were given to me in return for lay help over another archaeological matter.

Digging for Roman remains in old gravel pits at Rodbridge, near Long Melford, kept me occupied in my spare time for a period of two years in the early 1950s. The finds, turned up with the knowledge of a local museum, produced positive evidence of a long occupation of the site. Furthermore the experts took an interest in my lay archaeology.

In his book, *Rivers of East Anglia,* James Turner writer and poet, who now lives in Cornwall, referred to this dig: 'The river twists and turns in the meadows behind the rectory and comes to the gravel pits at Rodbridge. Here . . . it is possible, from his finds, to suppose the Romans had a settlement here

and he has unearthed the remains of a Saxon hearth . . .'.

The Saxon hearth – it was also referred to by Jack Lindsay, author and historian, in his book *The Discovery of Britain* – was, of course, a most interesting find, together with a large fragment of associated pottery. As always, expert advice was called for, and in this case Basil Brown, of Rickinghall, who figured in the discovery of the famous Sutton Hoo £250,000 treasure ship near Woodbridge in 1939, came over one afternoon on his cycle.

Over the years I have collected some early copies of local newspapers. One edition – that of the *Suffolk Chronicle; Or, Ipswich General Advertiser, and County Express* for 15 May, 1824 – devoted space to Parliamentary news and one paragraph could be from today's press:

'During the week both Houses of Parliament have been busily engaged. Besides the debate on the Assessed Taxes, in our last page, and that on the Salt Tax, which follows, both of which we have selected as most likely to interest generally our readers, the affairs of Ireland have engaged the time and attention of the House of Commons, and given rise to long and spirited debates.'

At a fairly early age I was given books by Arthur H. Patterson, the Broadland naturalist, better known to East Anglians by his inappropriate pseudonym 'John Knowlittle'. Many years later – in 1954 – Mr F.C. Edwards, of Halstead, gave me three original drawings of fish by Great Yarmouth's famous son. The naturalist of many sides died on 27 October 1935, at the age of 78.

One of the earliest items in my collection was a fretwork model car, known as 'The Century' motor car, which my grandfather, Mr Alexander Elliott, ran in East Suffolk at the turn of the century. My father told me in 1952: "The model, I believe, was made by a Mr Hughes, barber, of High Street, Wangford, who had a business facing the 'White Lion' in the early 1900s".

It seems likely that the model represents the Benz, index number BJ 192, which had a blue and black

At Henham, Suffolk, the Cavalier Baronet, Sir John Rous, may have been hidden in a hollow oak when Roundheads hunted him. Such a happening was depicted in this painting by Sir John Everett Millais.

All that remained of the Henham, Suffolk, oak of Civil War days in the early 1950s, the last living bough being blown down in 1903.

dog-cart body and which weighed, unladen, eight hundredweight. It had a 3 1/2hp engine. It was registered on 1 June, 1904, at County Hall Ipswich.' It's a fine model – about 18 inches long in a glass case.

Not long ago I was given an interesting pocket hoof knife which had been in a family at Thornham Magna since the 1770s. The knife, I learnt, was used 'for picking out stones and scraping packed ice and mud from hoofs'. The diamond-shaped aperture on the knife was used 'for putting in cleats on icy roads'. What tales that knife could tell.

Eighteenth-century pocket or clasp knife found during restoration work at Sudbury in 1950.

However, the most interesting domestic knife I have in my collection was found in 15th-century property in Friars Street, Sudbury in 1949. Moyse's Hall Museum, Bury St. Edmunds, had this to say about it:

> 'The knife which you sent for inspection and opinion as to a likely date is a very interesting specimen, and a type used by the better-class people during the 18th century. I am inclined to date it anywhere from 1750 to 1800, judging by the decorated handle and its workmanship generally. The pocket or clasp knife came into use in England about 1650. The idea spread from Flanders.'

In early 1940 on the seashore at Benacre I found a small medallion. Said the National Maritime Museum, Greenwich:

> 'We see no reason to doubt that a merchant seaman could have worn this medallion . . . We would not have thought it older than about 100 years . . . It is suggested that as reference is made to St. Paul's Epistles, and as that reference is made in French, that a likely place of origin

would be one of the bi-lingual parts of the Empire such as Mauritius, the Seychelles, French Canada or Newfoundland. It is likely that the medallion was intended as a religious keepsake and that the ring at the top was added subsequently. The obverse design is orthodox and possibly taken from a church ornament; the reverse side may have a similar origin.'

Some years ago my friend, Mr H. Sawyer, of Wrentham, gave me a poster recalling that in 1898, for one penny, one could enjoy an evening's entertainment at the Town Hall, Wrentham.

During renovation work at Green Farm, Hales, in the 1950s a silver shilling of Charles I was found. It was passed to me, and the Castle Museum, Norwich, commented:

> 'The Roman twelve (XII) indicates this denomination. The (R) is the mint mark and shows that it was a Parliamentary issue in 1644 or 1645.'

It was, then, a coin of the Civil War (1642-1644) which broke out after Charles I had ruled England without a Parliament from 1629 to 1640. In 1644 – around the date of the coin – the Parliamentary Army, under Cromwell, defeated the Royalists at the Battle of Marston Moor, and the same Ironsides, as they were called, beat the King at the Battle of Naseby, Northamptonshire, a year later.

I wonder what the Hales coin could tell of those tragic days? E. Thornhill, in *Historical Rambles in East Anglia,* whispered: 'There . . . are few written records of Hales . . .'.

I see, too, that I have in a bottle a fragment of the Henham Oak, which legend said Sir John Rous was hidden in when a party of Cromwell's men went to Henham with a warrant for his arrest.

The Earl of Stradbroke told me in a letter in 1953:

> 'In reply to your enquiry about the Henham Oak, to which certain legends attach, I believe the last living bough of this tree was blown down in 1903, since when the remaining trunk has gradually mouldered away until many years ago it became merely a heap of rotten wood held together by iron stays, evidently emplaced at some time when the tree was alive and grown over with ivy and roses. For a long time no particle of sound wood has remained, and there is therefore now no possibility of preserving the tree.'

Well, having started by referring to Sir Alfred Munnings, that 'champion painter' of the past and one-time president of the Royal Academy, we might as well finish with him. I see that I have a diatribe in his own hand, written from Castle House, Dedham, in the early 1950s. But it was not addressed to me. It came into my hands from a Great Cornard woman artist, who had sent Sir Alfred some of her artistic works for advice, and it said:

> 'Why send me a parcel which I have to do up again. Never, since I was a boy, did I ever send such things to artists. These are good efforts and no doubt you enjoy doing such honest work, but I can give no advice. Remember that I have scores of letters which are impossible to answer – that I have work to do also –
> Sorry.
> *Alfred Munnings*

Breath of the Jets

IN the autumn of 1943 the RAF and the USAAF learnt of the development of German jet aircraft. Then, in late 1944, the USAAF reported the first encounters with enemy jets. Intermittent encounters, mostly lasting only a matter of seconds, continued, and then, curiously, on the day that our contributor was privileged to spend a day with the 357th Fighter Group, 8th USAAF, at Leiston, the biggest ever force of jet and rocket fighters was sighted.

The possibility of the German Air Force suddenly regaining aerial supremacy became a very real challenge. Some of the Leiston Mustang pilots, fighting far above their normal speeds, were showing the strain. The enemy jets were equipped with weapons which were 10 years ahead of anything which the Allies had.

It was the dawn of a new era in aerial fighting. And for the Allies, the only answer to the rocket and jet fighters was to catch them taking-off, landing and on the ground.

I never got much sleep in the small hours of Saturday, 3rd March 1945, for the previous day a message had been received that I should report – I was 16 at the time – at Leiston airfield early the following day. I had been pressing to be allowed to see the start and finish of a typical USAAF fighter escort mission and to meet the pilots. But naturally, I could never be informed in advance of a mission – I could only expect to be invited to see whatever they had to offer.

The almost empty train was away on time, and as it pulled out of Beccles for Brampton, I scanned the brightening eastern sky for the first signs of the bombers forming up. They showed up, like tiny silver fish, as the dawn sun caught them. Halesworth was reached, then Darsham and finally Saxmund-ham.

Captain Emil Maldea (left) was the author's guide on 3rd March 1945.
Photo: Courtesy USAAF

My host, Capt. Emil Moldea, of the crack 357th Fighter Group, 8th USAAF, had promised that I would be collected at Saxmundham.

"Say, kid, you wouldn't by chance be the fella' I've been sent to collect for transportation to Cap'ain Moldea?" asked a waiting Jeep driver.

I showed him my letter of introduction.

"Guess," he said, "I couldn't quite figure out exactly where you came into the picture – you see, we usually get guys visiting from London city and not from up country. Wherever you're from, brother, you're mighty welcome."

With that the driver moved off, and we headed, as far as I can recall, for Knodishall Green and the airfield which lay west of Leiston Abbey, taking in Hill Farm, Bush Grove and Moat Farm. At the airfield check-point my identity card was examined and a pass, which I still have, was made out.

Already the P-51 Mustangs, in pairs, were lifting off from Leiston, drop tanks imposition, for the day's mission. In the distance, for miles, the Mustangs could be seen climbing, and already the first squadron of the 357th was taking shape in the form of three or four pairs. A 1100-strong bomber assault, with an escort of 700 fighters, was slowly blooming in the East Anglian sky. Targets, I later learnt from press reports, were Magdeburg, Misburg, Dollbergen and Brunswick.

Tall Capt. Moldea came to meet me from his office which had outside a notice "Gymnasium – Special Service Office". I took coffee inside as he went about urgent desk duties.

VISITORS PASS
AAF STATION F-373

NAME OF VISITOR C. Elliott
IDENTITY CARD NO. OF VISITOR
NAME OF ESCORT
TIME IN 10.57 TIME OUT ___ DATE 3-4
NAME OF GUARD
NO. OF PASS 1 GATE NO. 1
CO. SIGNED Emil Moldea TIME 15/5

The author's pass that took him into the 357th base at Leiston on 3rd March 1945.

Sometimes said to be the Suffolk 16-year-old questioning 357th pilots at Leiston on 3rd March 1945.

"I'm going to show you what I can of our outfit," explained the Captain, "but you must bear in mind that a mission is on and you won't be meeting everyone. We hope you'll stay for lunch, and by 15.30 hours, I guess you'll have seen the whole show."

As I was to learn on the spot that day and years later, as official records were made available, the 357th Fighter Group, made up of the 362nd 363rd and 364th Fighter Squadrons, with a total potential strength of 75 fighters, was a famous unit. It was, in fact, the first Mustang group in the Eighth Air Force to become operational and, when it did on 11th February 1944, it helped to alter the outcome of the daylight aerial war over Germany, for it meant that for the first time bombers could be taken to the heart of enemy territory and brought back under escort. It was Capt. Calvert L. Williams who got their first victory – a Messerschmitt 109 – on 20th February 1944.

On 6th March 1944 the 357th participated in the first successful daylight raid on Berlin, 33 of its Mustangs destroying 20 enemy aircraft and damaging others for no loss. On 14th January 1945, the Group reached its fighting peak when, led by Col. Irwin H. Dregne, it took part in one of the most

vicious air-battles of the war. On that day the Leiston Mustangs destroyed at least 58 enemy aircraft for the loss of three pilots out of a strength of 56. They were outnumbered by at least three to one.

On the day of my visit half the group were resting from the previous day's fighting so I was, therefore, able to meet some of the pilots as they relaxed in their comfortable rest-rooms. I found them immensely friendly and in no time I had two pages of autographs. I think of the smiling face of Capt. Robert P. Winks, who brought down five German aircraft, and of the wiry Lt. Otto D. Jenkins, destroyer of at least 10 enemy aircraft, when just three weeks after my visit, while 'buzzing' the operations room of the 362nd squadron on 24th March 1945, hit a tree and crashed blazing into stacks near Harrow Lane Farm, Leiston, with fatal results. A machine-gun from his Mustang was driven through a tree trunk and was still embedded five months later.

After lunch in the officers' mess, Capt. Moldea said: "I've a very special guy to show you. He's the pride of the outfit." I immediately thought of a Group mascot – perhaps a goat or a monkey – for over at Framlingham, where the 390th Bombardment Group was based with B-17 Flying Fortresses, they had a live bear as a mascot.

But it was to be nothing of the kind. I was shepherded into the base hospital. As we approached a line of beds, the majority of which were unoccupied, my guide pointed to a figure in a dressing gown, legs drawn up, who was, to my astonishment, snipping away at what I took to be a paper cut-out book.

"Tell me, Captain, what on earth is he doing and who is he?" I asked.

"This," said Capt. Moldea, "is Capt. Leonard K. Carson, our leading ace."

Captain Calvert L. Williams downed the 357th's first enemy 'plane on 20th February 1944.
Photo: Courtesy USAAF

On 3rd March 1945 the writer met 2nd-Lt Otto D. Jenkins, credited with 10½ German 'planes, shown in the cockpit of his 357th Fighter Group P-51 Mustang. On 24th March, while buzzing his squadron HQ to celebrate his last mission, he crashed by the airfield at Leiston and was killed.
Photo: Courtesy USAAF

The author on 22nd March 1953, finds evidence of Lt Otto D. Jenkins' crash site at Harrow Lane Farm, Leiston, Suffolk.

Photo: Courtesy Roger A. Freeman

Captain Lee K. Carson, the 357th's top-scorer with 22 victories, was resting in the base hospital.

Photo: Courtesy USAAF

Capt Carson, who was quick to sense my surprise, said: "I'm pleased to meet you. Yes, I'm a little tired. We've all been going very fast lately. We all have to rest once in a while."

Capt., later Major Carson, finished the war with a score of 22 enemy aircraft. According to a list of USAF names I saw in April 1967, this officer was still on active duty. His allusion to "going very fast lately" is interesting. He was undoubtedly referring to the encounters they were having with German jet and rocket fighters – a critical period in the final bid by the Allies for aerial supremacy.

In the early afternoon we went to the control tower to watch the final phase of the day's mission – the return of the fighters. As the ETA (estimated time of arrival) approached all windows in the control tower were opened, staff came on to the balcony with binoculars, to scan the fighters for battle damage, and

an air of expectancy permeated the gathering A visiting 8th Air Force officer of high rank, probably from the 66th Fighter Wing which controlled the 357th, was among those who waited on the balcony.

Suddenly the first pair of Mustangs dived home out of the haze over Sizewell. They hurtled over the control tower and, as they banked, there were sharp reports, like a sail flapping, as they pulled round sharply for the landing. Wheels popped out in this crazy attitude, which struck me as being rather risky because of unknown battle damage. Yet all landed safely, their landings barely taking up half the length of the runway. In the distance, slowly over the tree tops at Great Glemham. the Flying Fortresses of the 390th Bombardment Group were coming to earth.

Did I see bouncing, joyous youth sitting in the cockpits as the Leiston Mustangs taxied to their parking bays? I did not. They simply switched off and sat still while their engines clicked to cool down. I saw no finger gestures for a victory, such as the film-makers love to introduce. Ground-crews, as the film-makers would have us believe, did not all bound up on to wings, asking for the latest score. Mostly they waited patiently nearby for master to rise from his cockpit, stretch, and perhaps climb down to sit for a

In American artist, William S. Phillips' "A bandit goes down", a pair of P-51 Mustangs from the 357th Fighter Group flash by. "Old Crow" was Captain Clarence E. Anderson's.

Photo: Courtesy RAF Museum

P-51 Mustang fighter ace, Captain Charles E. Weaver, who shot down eight German planes while flying with the 357th Fighter Group, included a Messerschmitt 262 jet fighter capable of 500 mph plus.
Photo: Courtesy USAAF

Lt Robert G. Schmanski with his pet duck at Leiston.
Photo: Courtesy USAAF

Captain Charles E. Yeager, who claimed 12 victories with the 357th, made the world's first true supersonic flight – in a climb – in the revolutionary Bell X-1 research aircraft in 1947

Against a backcloth of highly-polished P-51s, in a blister hangar at Leiston, ground-crews celebrate the 357th's 500-plus victories score on Christmas Eve 1944.
Photo: Courtesy USAAF

P-51 Mustang camera-gun shots of the demise of a Messerschmitt 262 jet fighter.

Photo: Courtesy USAAF

minute or two on an undercarriage wheel, drawing on a cigarette or chewing a piece of gum. The process of letting pilots unwind was worked out with dignity. All popular conceptions were dashed that afternoon.

What was the outcome of the mission? Naturally no information on the day's work was given to me. However, the importance of that day in the history of the 8th Air Force, faced with the growing threat of the German jets, which were seen in the largest number to date, can be appreciated from *The Army Air Forces In World War II*, Vol III: "The opposition on 3rd March, came from the dreaded jets. More than fifty Messerschmitt 262s and Messerschmitt 163s playfully encircled the slower P-51s, making a few attacks and eluding the Mustangs without apparent difficulty. Finally, the jets shot down six American fighters and three bombers before allowing themselves to be driven off by the P-51s. The Germans seemed to be experimenting with formations and tactics . . ."

Roger A. Freeman, of Dedham, who was then writing a history of the 8th Air Force, was able to give me a snippet relating to the 357th. On that day – apparently the group "claimed two Messerschmitts 262s damaged".

So ended my day with the 357th Fighter Group, the USAAF fighter unit which finished the war with a record score of nearly 700 enemy aircraft destroyed in a mere 15 months' aerial fighting and with a record of no fewer than 47 fighter aces (pilots who shot down more than five enemy aircraft). Some of its pilots were little more than boys – like Lt. Dale E. Karger who was credited with five victories before reaching his 19th birthday in February 1945.

Before I left the airfield, not to return again until the place was derelict in 1953, Capt. Moldea took me to the base photo-shop – a veritable Aladdin's Cave – and allowed me to select pictures for my aeronautical collection.

A couple of years after the war – on 14th October 1947 – Major Charles E. Yeager, who claimed 12 enemy aircraft while fighting with the 357th, made the world's first true supersonic flight – in a climb – in the then revolutionary Bell X-1 research aircraft.

Afterwards he pioneered further high-speed flights, and so his risky journeyings into the unknown had a direct bearing on subsequent American Space flights.

Another 357th champion, Major John B. England, who destroyed 18 enemy aircraft, was killed in a flying accident in France on 17th November 1954, and today England Air Force Base, La., USA is named in his memory.

Thus the fliers, who found their feet at Leiston nearly 25 years ago, will long be remembered in the history of aerial fighting. Their techniques after all these years were, of course, Victorian in relation to today's requirements, but their spirit – well, that is something which time cannot erase.

357th pilots' signatures obtained on March 3, 1945.

Footnote: Interestingly, at a special gathering of Allied and German fighter pilots at Duxford Imperial War Museum, on 11th July 2003, I was able to meet a number of American fighter pilots I had met in 1945, including Captain Charles E. Weaver of the 357th. Another fighter pilot present from the 357th was Col. Clarence E. Anderson, who in 2004, was revealed as co-author with M.Sgt. Merle C. Olmsted of a massive volume, *To War with the Yoxford Boys: The Complete Story of the 357th Fighter Group* (ISBN: 0-97210600-6-5 standard edition; ISBN: 0-9721060-7-3 de-luxe, autographed, limited edition). The standard edition makes 376 pages and measures 9 x 11½ins.

A spread of aces of the 357th Fighter Group, Leiston, Suffolk, as the scores stood in early 1945.

Photo: Courtesy 'Escort' March 1945

Literary Days at Colchester

LITERARY SOCIETIES were once a feature of local life and they must have proliferated in Victorian times.

If they weren't always able to introduce people to authors in the flesh for the first time, they made up for it by getting someone else to introduce their works.

Such bodies, mostly organised and run by literary-enthusiasts, performed an educational role in society, but today they are few and far between.

I knew the Colchester Public Library Literary Society, founded in 1949 by Ronald Blythe, later the successful author of *Akenfield* and *From The Headlands*, in the early 1950s.

Surprisingly, with only one small time of decline, the society flourished until 1980, having, in its period, been addressed by many eminent literary figures. Declining membership brought about the society's closure.

So when Ronald Blythe, who was born at Acton, near Sudbury, Suffolk, in 1922 and during my days in West Suffolk was on the staff of the old Colchester Public Library, talked on "East Anglia and its Writers" at the 1984 history festival at the Museum of East Anglian Life, Stowmarket, it revived memories of many happy literary evenings at Colchester.

In fact, when I was certain I could attend, I had a good look at my stored papers and found that almost all the artistic-looking invitations for the first half of the 1950s lectures were preserved. Ronald Blythe, on seeing some examples, thought they were scarce reminders of a golden age.

"Yes", he declared,"we did attract some eminent literary figures, and we must have been taken seriously to have drawn so many valued speakers from the world of letters.

"I remember the Sudbury days, too, when you used to visit James Turner, poet, novelist and broadcaster, and his wife at The Mill House, Belchamp Walter, in Essex.

"Remember the snap you took of us all one afternoon in April, 1951, standing by the garden roller after we had returned from a walk with a large bunch of sticky buds? That's some 33 years ago – but it only seems like yesterday."

A haphazard look at the old literary society invitations, which must have gone to many people in the Essex/Suffolk border country in those early days, reveal the variety of speakers (non-members were charged one-shilling) Colchester heard.

They included Sir Osbert Sitwell (reading from his own work), Sir Francis Meynell (on his mother Alice Meynell, 1847-1922, English poet and essayist), C.P. Snow (on the modern novel), R.H. Mottram (on English literature in the first-half of the 20th century), Basil Blackwell (on book publishing) and A.E. Coppard (reading from his own work combined with a discussion on the art of the short story).

There was also Elizabeth Jenkins (on Jane Austen), Wallace Evennett (giving a dramatic reading of Bernard Shaw's *Heartbreak House*), Dr C. Willett Cunnington (on the traditional customs and superstitions associated with childbirth and infancy), R.N. Currey (on modern poetry), Lt.Col H.B.T. Wakelam (on the microphone and the pen in sport), Dr S.C. Roberts (on James Boswell), Dr Laurence Lockhart (on Persian literature), John B ensusan-Butt (on the writings and sayings of painters), William Addison (on the character of Essex), Robert Gittings (on John Keats), Canon E. Rich (on the sources of European Civilisation), W.R. Rodgers (on life and letters), R. Ketton-Cremer (on Thomas Gray and Horace Walpole), Patric Dickinson (on writing poetry), Sir Ronald Storrs (on the Bible, Homer, Dante and Shakespeare), Laurence Brander (on George Orwell), James Turner (on George Crabbe), Philip Toynbee (on the problems of the modern writer), Dr Marie Stopes (on the sonnet), Lt.Col. R. Appleby (on King Coel), Edmund Blunden (on glances at great writings), S.L. Bensusan (reading two of his short stories and talking about the Essex marshlands) and so on.

On one occasion, I see from the old invitations, seven speakers discussed the work of a number of first world war writers and poets under the title "Youth and War". Members' work was read on several occasions. And in December 1953, there was a Dickens evening with readings from his work and from ballads.

In checking up with what is now the North East Division, Central Library, Colchester, I learned that the old Colchester Public Library Literary Society, whose founder himself became a literary figure, also attracted such personalities as Hammond Innes, Christina Foyle, Norah Lofts and Jack Lindsay, the Australian-born author of general history, biography, historical and contemporary novels, and auto-biography who was known to me in my Suffolk/Essex border reporting days in the 1950s.

When I went to interview Jack Lindsay at his home near Castle Hedingham, where I saw artefacts from his probings into archaeology, I was greatly impressed with his enormous library.

Vintage Model Planes
RARER THAN THE REAL THING

OLD flying-model aeroplanes, like old real ones, fetch high prices, but their fragile construction has prevented their mass preservation. Indeed, such models could in some instances be outnumbered by real examples.

Cecil H. Bullivant in *Every Boy's Book of Hobbies* (T.C. & E.C. Jack), published as far back as 1911, devoted a chapter to model aircraft. Bleriot had crossed the English Channel in his monoplane two years before.

'The charm pertaining to flying machines – be they actual or model – is undoubtedly real, and exists quite apart from any of that sense of exhibition which belongs to actual flight. Perhaps this is because they convey the idea of the frustration of nature's law of gravitation, by which man has always felt himself curbed, and which today frequently gains the upper-hand with calamitous results', observed Bullivant.

Bullivant went on to say that 'the earliest type of flying machine (model) consisted of a two-bladed tin propeller spun on a frame by unwinding string, as with a top, and suddenly released'. It made its appearance under the name of 'Maxim's Flying Wonder'. Purchasers, however, soon discovered that a milk tin-lid could be cut into a similar shape and made to revolve rapidly on a string.

It seems that the first model aeroplane to fly under its own power and on its own was made by John Stringfellow (1799-1883), a designer of lace-making machinery who was interested in flying. In 1848 he made a model which flew inside the length of the lace factory, a distance of 22 yards, in the little town of Chard, in Somerset.

With Bleriot's Channel crossing vivid in very nearly every household, the model aircraft industry really started in Britain round about 1909. But it is believed that the country's first model aircraft firm

Action picture taken on 5th October 1929, showing Mr A. Willis and son Anthony, flying 'fuselage' and 'stick' models respectively in a 30-mile-an-hour wind on Wimbledon Common.

was T.W.K. Clarke & Co., Crown Works, High Street, Kingston-on-Thames, Surrey, founded in 1906. Another pioneer firm was Weston Hurlin & Co., who sponsored the first model aeroplane journal called *The Amateur Aviator*, which failed after just three issues.

The start of World War I in 1914, and the increasing recognition of the aeroplane as a weapon, led to a huge increase of interest in model flying and more and more people bought and flew the 'A' shaped and 'stick' type models. The former type had the apex of the A at the front and two propellers at the back, while the latter usually had the propeller at the front. Construction was normally of wood or piano wire covered with paper or oiled silk. Such early models must be very rare although early model propellers, undoubtedly from these early types, do turn up from time to time.

Among other famous early names who mass produced model aeroplanes were Bragg Smith, Mann and Grimmer, the latter claiming to be 'the first to mass produce models' and export them 'to every country in the world by 1913'. What is certain is that the 'stick' type, such a popular and easy flier, amused thousands of boys (and men) between 1914 and the early 1930s.

Then, in 1932, came a true toy aeroplane capable of being flown by a child without adult supervision. It was the famous F.R.O.G. (Flies right off ground) of metal and celluloid, costing 10s. 6d. (52p). The model came in a box fitted with a patent starter which stopped over hand-winding. It was advertised as

Trophies and medals won by the Willis family in the field of model aeroplane development in the 1920s and 1930s.

Picnics with the Willis family and friends seemed to have consisted of – well, largely model aeroplanes!

being capable of a high performance and each model was accompanied by a certificate of airworthiness signed by Hamley's head ground engineer.

Improvements followed and by 1934 the F.R.O.G. type was being sold round the world, bearing international markings. Lines Brothers, whose famous Triang Works were located at Merton, in south west London, marketed the model.

So, while preserved examples of some model aeroplanes could be less common today than real vintage types, photographs do turn up more frequently recalling the early days of endeavour in the model field.

In this connection *Everything* . . . has examined an album of the 1920s and 1930s which recently turned up among possessions acquired by a dealer in south west London who handles antiques and bric-a-brac. The album recorded in pictures and documents the exceptional record of the Willis family of Wimbledon with model aeroplanes between the wars.

Containing over 80 photographs, the album shows such rare models as float-planes on, presumably, Wimbledon Common, with a variety of flying models in flight and models taking-off and landing. Some skeleton models (probably prototypes before acceptance as kits), an unusual model of the ill-fated R101 airship and a display of trophies and medals won by the Willis family. Pages torn from old magazines preserved in the album showed Mr A.T. Willis 'with his parachute-dropping machine' (*The Model Engineer & Practical/Electrician.* September 10, 1931), Mr Willis' high-wing monoplane, fitted with an 'Atom Minor' engine, described as 'a magnificent piece of design and workmanship' (*The Model Engineer,* July 25 1935), and the Willis 9-ft. span petrol model, winner of the Sir John Shelley Cup at Fairey's Great West Road aerodrome, in cutaway form (*Flight,* November 7, 1935).

The *Flight* report noted: 'The clockwork ignition relay can be set to give any desired length of flight, and the other clockwork mechanism is set to throttle back the 15cc two-stroke engine to cruising speed after the take-off, thus securing steady, level flight'.

The album also contained six treasured certificates awarded by the Model Aircraft Club to Messrs. A.T. and A.M. Willis, father and son, for achievements with their models. All were awarded between April and July 1932, and one was for a record flight of 18 minutes two seconds.

As so often follows with creative minds, their sketches appear on the back of several documents, one depicting a breakaway from aeroplanes – a small speed-boat (more like a hydroplane).

Strong winds didn't seem to bother the family, for an agency photograph taken on 5 October 1929, showed Mr A. Willis and son Anthony 'model aircraft-flying in a 30 mile wind on Wimbledon Common', while another taken on the same occasion showed a party of interested Boy Scouts watching one of the Willis planes take-off from ground level. A car and figures in the background all help to place the pictures as being late 1920s.

Serious model aeroplane enthusiasts in the 1930s were, it seems, well on the way to the jet age although they probably didn't appreciate it. Thus 'a compressed air-driven machine was observed, and also one flash steam-machine', at a power-driven model aircraft contest in 1935.

What were these early models constructed of? The *Flight* report for 1935 on the giant Willis monoplane described earlier, said 'the spars were of spruce, centre and end ribs of birch three-ply, other ribs of balsa, the wing tips of steel wire, and the covering was of jap-silk clear and silver doped. The wheels were made 'by fitting two three-penny Woolworth balls with valves, discs and an axle'.

So it looks as if model planes from those far off days are likely to be very rare on account of their delicate construction and, in some cases, their size. Some intricate models must have taken a year or two to build only to be dashed to pieces on their first test flight.

One of the six certificates found in the album issued by the Model Aircraft Club: this was awarded in 1932 to Mr A.M. Willis for a record flight of 18 minutes two seconds.

Billingshurst to Billingsgate

WHEN one gets an invitation from eighteenth-century Sotheby's of London, to attend one of their *posh* sales – in this case historic 'planes, aeronautica and medals – at their Country House Sale-room, Billingshurst, West Sussex, decent men for certain, would not dream of going in anything briefer than a suit and waistcoat, carrying an umbrella. Naturally I cannot speak for the ladies.

Anyway, on the Saturday in question, I was up like a lark and away on the breakfast train to Billingshurst where, just before it got there, it halted at Christ's Hospital Station (apparently named after the famous London boys' school, removed there in 1902) although, when I poked my head out for an explanation, I got little help.

"Don't know", grumbled a huddled figure as it passed my window.

However, there was 'someone' waiting for me at Billingshurst, not anyone I had ever met, and that was lovely Toni Scammell, one of the country's few station-mistresses, in the form of a coloured poster giving me her telephone number and other particulars!

"I'm here," she seemed to scream, "to help the weary wayfarer all hours, whether you're walking or rolling on my lines."

After buying a packet of wine-gums, I learned that Sotheby's Country House was "a mile or two up the road, turn right, and keep walking . . .".

On turning right, I found myself in Billingshurst proper, and in checking my progress, a middle-aged lady had only a word of woe for me.

"It's a long way, all up-hill," she mused, "and you will find it far too much for your legs."

I was so angered by her superficial medical assessment of me – I'm a natural walker and talker – that the wine-gum poised on the tip of my tongue shot out of my mouth like a bullet and landed at her feet. It could not have been better aimed!

So, seething that she had dared to undress me like that, I went, uphill, out of the village under a bright but overcast autumn sky. There was no wind. The air was good.

As I walked, changing road sides for pavement protection from the endless rush of cars, I saw a sign that pointed, right, to Friskey's Wood.

Friskey's Wood? Just as my thoughts dallied, a lady on a cycle, seeing my wonderment, stopped and commented: "It's like the Garden of Eden up there – they've fruit to sell of every description, including damsons".

Damsels? So I journeyed on under fruitful

'So the roads and lanes I had trod that day were theirs and, in their day, they must have been tranquil walks.'

chestnuts and oaks that seemed to salute my every step with bouncing nuts and husks. My great concern, as this fertility demonstration continued, was that a prickly chestnut-case might cratch the tip of my nose and bloody me!

Approaching Sotheby's stately sale-room, which I later learned had been a farm and then a girls' convent, I saluted their 1744 house flag and found myself in a fine drive flanked by great trees shedding autumn leaves, Half-a-dozen Shetland ponies grazed to my right.

Once in the great house, I went about my business, and even had time to explore rooms devoted to things other than aeronautica.

Other people were around, too, and two ladies, who quickly opened and closed an old work box, left in a hurry. Why?

Later I twigged them talking to a member of the staff so, when I saw them strolling in the great garden, I had the cheek to ask them what was so odd about the box.

Said the younger one: "I'm a nurse. I spotted a syringe. Can't be too careful these days".

As the sale time for the aeronautica approached, a list of late lots included 'a Luftwaffe scarf fragment and other items, various dates, the triangular fragment in off-white silk with black eagle'.

When I asked to see the item, I knew at once that

the triangular piece matched the one I have in my aviation collection taken by a policeman from a German Air Force prisoner at Croydon in August 1940.

Amusingly, I pointed out to an official, the souvenir on sale was no part of, let's imagine, a bonny *fraulein's* silk scarf, perhaps waved to her departing boy-friend hero, but part of a sweaty Nazi airman's PT vest – the kind of swastika-dangling eagle British captors always removed!

As the sale progressed, even at a pace, still half remained to be sold at 4 o'clock. So my thoughts drifted to Toni Scammell and what she might be able to do for me at her little station – that is, in the way of getting me back to London.

Away I went, on foot, along the route I had come, but this time downhill.

With a little time to spare, I found the town full of interesting names that set me smiling.

In one cottage window I spotted a card that advertised 'Mrs Buddock's bed-and-breakfast'. Her trademark appeared to be a pair of rosy apples and a honey pot!

Roman Way, to my left, jogged me into remembering that Roman Stane Street, first traceable

from Chichester, closer to the Sussex coast, passed through Billingshurst on its ancient way to London. Goodness knows how many pairs of feet in war and peace had tramped that path.

Yet more local services caught my attention: Felicity Thorpe offered 'decorative accessories', Sam's Frying Machine provided fish-and-chips, Quercus were furniture-makers, Crickmay advised on property, Claudia offered mixed workouts, Daphne's parlour cream teas, Jack-in-the-Box (No. 90 next door) revealed no trade sign, the Elite Centre no clue either, Badger's Bistro billed good food, and so on.

What a lovely lot of jolly occupations!

But suddenly, as I walked on, I lost my grin when I saw the spire of the Church of St. Mary-the-Virgin guarding the war memorial. Even as I climbed the steps to it, a slow bell-chime marked the passing of time.

Casualties for the two world wars were revealing: nine local men failed to return during 1939-45, while over 50, including two Trueloves, did not come back between 1914-18. What sad gaps were left in that town which, even by the late 1940s, had a population of under 3000.

So the roads and lanes I had trod that day were theirs and, in their day, they must have been tranquil walks.

Thirsty, yes, I was after my hikes uphill and downhill. There were, I found, three pubs to try – King's Head, King's Arms and Ye Olde Six Bells – and being close together they seemed to hold each other up! I visited the first one.

Onwards I went to the railway station, ever mindful of Toni Scammel, and well I kept her in my thoughts for, being a Saturday, there was just a chance that trains would be so thin to London that she would have to put me up at her station!

As I waited, I potted up and down the platform finally discovering that Billingshurst, like Christ's Hospital, still retains a manned signal box with levers

Said the signalman: "I've been in the box for 14 years".

When my train finally arrived, bound for London I left it at East Croydon for Streatham Common in order to collect some books I had left with relatives.

Returning to Streatham Common at almost 9 o'clock, I found the station nearly unmanned. In the shadows, however, lurked ladies of the night whose faces were hard to discern, and for over an hour, as I waited for the Clapham train, I twirled my umbrella to keep them at bay!

All very *fishy*, you may think, this journey to Billingshurst, but just about every word is true. Small English towns, when seen through new eyes, are fascinating places. May they long remain so.

How Bomb-Disposal Sergeant Proved He Was Loved

"I SEE you by these billets almost every evening and most Saturdays all day", she said as she dismounted from her cycle. "Do you really think *their* language is *your* language?"

"Don't know, Miss. All I know is that, in their game, they're here today and gone tomorrow. Coming to think of it, Miss, I can hear the same language at the cattle market on Fridays. Ever been there on a Friday, Miss?"

Miss Davenport, remounting her cycle, replied that she was unfamiliar with the market.

"And who the 'ell is that chicken?", cried a Cockney-soldier's voice.

"She's my mistress" I innocently responded.

And so did the soldiers at the window! For the full significance of my remark never registered with me at the time.

My friends at the billets in Hungate, Beccles, Suffolk, belonged to a detachment of No. 4 Bomb-Disposal Company, Royal Engineers, who were responsible for that area. Their risky occupation: dealing with unexploded bombs and the like by day and night and often in dangerous under-ground situations.

Although I did not get to know them until, I think, 1942, one of their number, Major H.J.L. Barefoot, who had Ipswich connections, had been awarded the George Cross in early 1941 'for numerous incidents and for continuous investigation of many types of bombs and fuses'. Here, I quickly realised, was a really exciting branch of the Army. The element of danger (dare?) attached to their work, which made the chance of survival touch and go, caught my fancy.

Their local headquarters was in a commandeered house adjoining a butcher's shop. Slowly, from

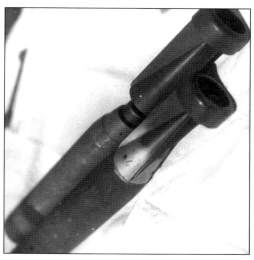

Early German explosive-type incendiary-bomb (tail withdrawn to show hidden charge), and ordinary type.

pavement chats with the men, I graduated into the front-room and into their strange world of fuses and wires and puzzle gadgets. To this room, after a bombing incident, were brought the latest fuses to be reported on to London.

My best friend was the sergeant – a quiet man who smoked a lot and who was, I believe, a butcher in civilian life. He must have touched death many times. I wonder if he survived the war?

I got to know nearly all the men in the detachment, except the officer in charge, who was sometimes present in the room when I was with the sergeant at the "laboratory" table. He never once acknowledged me but, on reflection, I concluded it meant that he was prepared to turn a blind eye.

"You are not doing enough field-work", said the sergeant one day. "You had better come with us one Saturday – to the bomb cemetery".

The long-awaited Saturday dawned badly with low clouds and drizzle. An air raid alert at breakfast time heralded a day of sneak raids by lone Dorniers and Heinkels which, on swooping low, sometimes machine-gunned civilian targets, including passenger trains.

"Very far to go?" I asked the sergeant as he helped me aboard the truck with BD (bomb disposal) signs front and back. "To the cemetery down Cucumber Lane", he replied.

Cucumber Lane, 60 years ago, had a working sandpit on the left-hand side going from Beccles towards Weston, and it was in this area during the war that German ironmongery of every description was deposited: high explosive bombs, unexploded

incendiary bombs by the thousand, faulty parachute flares and so on. A 12ft-high barbed-wire fence surrounded the entire pit and the gates were padlocked. It was a dangerous place for the uninformed and wasn't, in fact, very well known to my school pals.

Our work that Saturday, made so miserable by the drizzle from the North Sea, was to burn-up dozens of incendiary bombs. Care had to be taken however, to separate the explosive-type from the ordinary ones – the type we were destroying. For easy handling purposes, the Germans hand-painted the nose-caps of the explosive type with a red 'A'. Soon, with hundreds burning, it was impossible to approach the magnesium inferno.

"What about some tea?" suggested the sergeant.

"Corporal, take two 500-pounders, melt-out the explosive, and brew a can of tea on the end-product", ordered the sergeant.

Thus I was initiated, heart beating fast, into bomb-disposal. The 500-pounders, their green fins and base-plates removed, were then rolled into position and a fire kindled. Soon a yellow polish-like substance began to spread out on the ground around the fire. And over the flames our tea-can swung on the bent rod from an incendiary-bomb container. We were certainly the tinkers of Cucumber Lane!

"Sergeant, I know the fuses have been removed but – but just supposing they are fitted with hidden heat-sensitive fuses", I suggested with a look of terror in my eyes.

"Too bad", said the sergeant. "You won't know anything about it if this lot goes up. Besides, it's too cold to wonder. Huddle closer and enjoy the enemy's warmth."

Tea was made and dished out in chipped enamel cups rather like those I had seen tramps carrying, then five steaming cups were placed on one of the warm bomb-cases. I was terrified.

"When we've melted out the explosive", explained

...COLLECT SOUVENIRS.

WHEN WORKING ON A (17) FUZE, LISTEN AT FREQUENT INTERVALS (SAY 5 MINS.) TO THE CLOCK.

...TRY TO TAKE ANYTHING APART UNLESS YOU KNOW EXACTLY WHAT YOU ARE DOING.

The late Colonel Kenneth Merrylees, of Lavenham, Suffolk, designed for the Royal Engineers in the Second World War a light-hearted Do's and Don'ts poster for bomb-disposal staff. Here three details are depicted.

the sergeant, "the empty cases will go for scrap – and then back to Hitler via RAF bombers".

Meanwhile the melting process went on. Drizzle continued to fall, as it had done since dawn, and down between the two 500-pounders on a groundsheet two of the squad snoozed at the enemy's expense!

Other members of the squad wandered out of the pit to talk to some girls on cycles. Then the sergeant disappeared into a disused pit across the water-splash that ran in those days at the Weston end of Cucumber Lane.

Five minutes later there was a sharp explosion from the sergeant's direction, a piercing scream of

Inert German No. 17 type fuse, stamped 1940, in the author's collection.

pain, and high over the trees, flailing its arms, soared a body in a greatcoat – an unidentified body.

"Quick, it's the sergeant", the men cried as they dashed towards the spinney into which the body, as it looked to us, had crashed like a winged pheasant.

Then, suddenly, we became aware of the truth, the base truth. A voice from nowhere addressed us thus: "I know you all love me", it said. And there, standing on the green bank, arms outstretched and all smiles, was the sergeant pleased that his little prank had worked and that the body – a potato-sack filled with wet cabbages and dressed in a scarecrow's wet greatcoat – had soared heaven-wards as planned!

Thus, for better or for worse, I was initiated, against my English mistress's wishes, into the secrets – and the horseplay – of bomb-disposal.

A German magnetic-mine parachute cone, still bearing its green paint, which was netted by fishermen between Sizewell and Southwold, Suffolk, in the 1970s.

8th June, 1946

TO-DAY, AS WE CELEBRATE VICTORY, I send this personal message to you and all other boys and girls at school. For you have shared in the hardships and dangers of a total war and you have shared no less in the triumph of the Allied Nations.

I know you will always feel proud to belong to a country which was capable of such supreme effort; proud, too, of parents and elder brothers and sisters who by their courage, endurance and enterprise brought victory. May these qualities be yours as you grow up and join in the common effort to establish among the nations of the world unity and peace.

George R.I.

Country Diaries

Gilbert White (1720-1793), author of *The Natural History of Selborne*, who was a naturalist from childhood, told a friend in a letter: "Faunists . . . are apt to acquiesce in bare descriptions and a few synonyms: the reason is plain; because all that may be done at home in a man's study, but the investigation of the life and conversation of animals is a concern of much more trouble and difficulty, and is not to be attained but by the active and inquisitive, and by those that reside much in the country".

PUBLICATION of country diaries kept by ladies is on the increase and it was marked in June, 1977, by *The Country Diary of an Edwardian Lady*, a facsimile reproduction of a naturalist's diary for the year 1906, by Edith Holden. It recorded words and paintings the flora and fauna of the British countryside through the changing seasons of the year.

My edition is the twelfth impression printed in November, 1979, which goes to show that there is money in diaries. More recently the same publishers – Michael Joseph – put out *Murial Foster's Fishing Diary* kept by a "perfectly splendid, large and tweedy lady" for the years 1913 to 1949.

A spokesman for Michael Joseph, the publishers, said in May that they were going to press with the thirteenth impression of Edith Holden's diary and that would take the printing run so far to "over one and a half million copies".

Asked if they had received, as a result of the success of the Holden diary, other diaries worthy of publication, the spokesman said they had been offered "about 20" but there was nothing to match the Holden draughtsmanship.

Was there any advice to give the nature diarist of the future who had ambitions to publish?

Draughtmanship and layout, if the diary is to be produced as a facsimile like Edith Holden's, are essential. What the company is sure of is that the Holden diary will be just as interesting to readers in a hundred years time as it is today.

In June Christie's handled for sale in London the final, hand-written draft of 339 pages of Gilbert White's *The Natural History of Selborne* which had been lying for more than 40 years on the shelves of a private library in America. It was bought for £100,000 on behalf of the Gilbert White Museum at Selborne.

A country parson, White set down his observations on the wildlife which filled the fields about his native Hampshire village. Since his death in 1793 at the age of 73, the book has seen more than 200 editions, many translations and large sales.

While Holden and Foster diaries are not, of course, likely to turn up very frequently, it is amazing how many people – particularly girls and women – kept nature diaries between the wars but cannot remember where they are today. Mostly, I dare say, they went to younger brothers and sisters and, tattered, were eventually discarded .

Typical of the between-the-wars generation that kept such diaries is Mrs Jean Frazer, of Caterham, Surrey, who grew up in north east Suffolk with an older brother who adored the countryside as she did. In the early 1930s, as she entered her teens, she started diaries with him although his were more scrap-books of nature cuttings and birds' feathers plus a large egg collection.

One of her diaries, *My Nature Book for 1937-1938*, survives, illustrated with a number of her miniature water-colours. So does a snap of her as a young girl holding a bouquet of dandelions.

The 40-page exercise book of five chapters covers such subjects as 'The Rookery', 'The Coronation Thrushes', 'Flowers', 'Our Owl' and 'Black and White Blackbird'.

Her ability as a nature observer, with her friend Peternel, is reflected in the diary.

During the week 18 April 1937, she had rooks under observation in Bungay Road, Beccles, noting: "Later that week . . . we returned to watch them again, and this time a different scene met our eager eyes. On one of the tall oaks . . . sat 14 rooks. In the midst of all these noisy birds sat one silent, cringing one. Suddenly, four important looking rooks, which were perched near this one, began to caw loudly and quickly. The rest of the birds added a caw now and then.

"All at once the silent bird flapped his wings, and without further warning, flew away. Immediately the others rose as one and followed him, cawing loudly. When the birds were out of sight, Peternel told me that she had read that birds have their own way of punishing wrong-doers. We then decided that we had watched the poor bird's trial, which had been strange, but very interesting".

'The Coronation Thrushes' was a fairly long study from 27 March to 12 May 1937, illustrated with four little water-colours and two feathers, and concerned observations kept at her home, then in Kemps Lane, Beccles.

The diary noted: "Then, two minutes before the King was crowned on 12 May, the fully-fledged thrushes hopped out of their nest. I think I was very lucky to be able to watch their first experience of the outside world . . .

"The baby thrushes had a very exciting time in their first day out . . . Soon after they came out of the nest my little brother discovered them. Being very anxious to show Mummy and Daddy, who were out, his new find, he took a cardboard Easter-egg box. It was fashioned as a miniature bird cage and it opened at the top. One by one the mischiefivious (sic) lad captured the scared little birds. Into the box he put them all. That was how he proudly displayed them to me, ten minutes afterwards.

"Of course, I immediately set them free, and I am glad to say that they were none the worse for their strange adventure. They grew into strong, healthy birds, and eventually . . . left our garden . . . to seek further adventures".

'Our Owl' tells of the experiences with one kept for a time in 1938 when she lived in Fair Close, Beccles.

Her diary explains: "One evening, as my brother was cycling home from the country, he saw a young owl lying in the road. By looking closely at it he found that it had hit some wires and hurt its wing. He had seen owls flying about in this special farm before, and knew there was a nest somewhere. Anyhow, he picked the wounded youngster up, put it on his arm, and brought it home.

"For the first two days we kept it in the shed and fed it on meat . . . When we first opened the door,

and went to pick him up, he made a funny little knocking noise with his mouth, but at last we managed to get him outside. He fluttered up a tree and sat there on a bough, motionless and solemn, for about an hour. We tried getting him down by putting food underneath the tree, but no! he would not move.

"Every time we walked round the tree, his head followed us, but his body didn't. It looked just as if his head was fixed on a wheel, for he was able to turn it very nearly round. At last we managed to bring him down on the end of a prop and put him in his shed once more.

"Then, the next morning, we woke up to a chorus of excited chirpings coming from dozens of little sparrows in a tree . . . There sat our owl, silent and still. The little sparrows kept flying round him on all sides and chirping as if to say 'Who's this newcomer, invading our trees?' What made it funnier still was the fact that the poor owl was fast asleep and not taking the slightest notice of his tormentors.

"Suddenly, something happened. Our owl woke up, fluttered his wings, and flew into the next tree. This showed how brave the little sparrows really were. Like leaves blown by the wind, they raced into the next garden, and never returned again that morning".

Interestingly, in support of the nature diary, is a snap from the family album of the owl.

Also for 1938 she noted: "A few yards away in the same field we saw a blackbird with white dashes in its wings and tail. My brother says he has seen it there several times before, and knows where its nest is. The eggs are the same as an ordinary blackbird's" .

While the girl, in her nature diary, recorded heron habits, her brother made an attractive wooden fire-screen at school showing a motionless heron, one leg drawn up, waiting for fish by a dike (see above). In the back-ground is a windpump. The fire-screen, made in 1937, exists to this day with a duplicate at Ipswich.

So there you are: what have you got in the way of forgotten nature diaries that your friends, if not a much bigger public, should also enjoy? They may not find a London publisher but they may, somewhere, find a sympathetic local publisher whose vision may put some town or village on the map to make – well, another Selborne .

'The White Mouse'
– WORKED HERE . . .

A PUBLIC INQUIRY is at present going on at Church House, Westminster, for the redesigning of London SW1, including Whitehall. A nominee from the Ministry of Public Building and Works has said that, as Georgian Richmond Terrace and late Victorian New Scotland Yard are unsuitable for the accommodation of our enlarged race of civil servants, they should therefore be pulled down. There is, of course, strong resistance to this plan to demolish these interesting buildings.

Richmond Terrace, which stands on the opposite side of Whitehall from Downing Street, is a building I know, as in the 1950s I worked there as a civilian on a RAF magazine. It was during that time that I was asked to compile an historical note about the building as few people working there knew anything about the place.

I did my research in the lunch-hour and found the first building on the site – Richmond House – was demolished between 1792 and 1820 and that by 1825 there "were eight residences of the first-class, and appropriate domestic and stable offices thereto . . . which were called Richmond Terrace.

Naturally, in looking at the history of the building, I was interested to find out who had lived there before the premises were turned into government offices. I found that over 85 families and individuals had resided there between 1826 and 1930.

What isn't so well known today is who has worked at Richmond Terrace in the succeeding years. I know that 'The White Mouse' worked there for a period during my association with the place. Who was 'The White Mouse?' Well, I hadn't been at Richmond Terrace very long before I learnt that we had under our roof the famous Nancy Wake, GM, who in the Second World War became one of the creators of the escape route to Spain which fed back to freedom more than a thousand trapped men and women.

By the time the Germans had occupied Marseille she was already known as 'The White Mouse', and the South of France became too dangerous for her – at least for the time being. She got to England by her own escape route and started training for work as a saboteur in France.

Nancy Wake as remembered at old Richmond Terrace, Whitehall, in the 1950s.
Photo: Courtesy Nancy Wake

On 1st March 1944 she parachuted into the Auvergne "with a million francs in her handbag" and instructions to organise all the Maquis in the area. In a short time she had more than 7000 men behind her. Pitched battles were fought, and eventually 22,000 enemy troops with artillery, mortars and dive-bombers were thrown against Nancy Wake's army.

Russell Braddon told the story of this remarkable woman in *Nancy Wake*, which appeared in 1956.

My recollection of her at Richmond Terrace, where she worked for the old Air Ministry, is wrapped around chocolate. For Nancy Wake's work then involved, as far as I can remember, escape and survival. This meant that from time to time she had special chocolate pass through her hands, rather like chunky cooking-chocolate, and it wasn't long before we made it known to her that surplus pieces would be welcome with our tea. Pieces arrived on our desks with the compliments of the famous freedom-fighter. I even got a note one day which said: "This will build you up."

Not long before I left Richmond Terrace Nancy Wake went elsewhere. Before she left she gave me a handy metal box, which had accompanied her for some years, for my gramophone records. She also signed for my collection – she used the names Nancy Wake, Nancy Fiocca, Andree Joubert and Helene – a reproduction of her membership card of the Federation Nationale des Anciens des Maquis.

And when I finally left Richmond Terrace I took a picture of the old Air Ministry plaque at the entrance with, on the right, a vague outline of the building with Greek details and Ionic columns.

Perhaps some day a commemorative tablet will be erected saying: *Nancy Wake Worked Here . . .*

Footnote: The *Daily Telegraph* of 29th January 2004, reported that Nancy Wake (91), was living at the Royal Star and Garter home for disabled sailors, soldiers and airmen in west London, after previously living at the Stafford Hotel in Piccadilly. Her life story is understood to have inspired the novel and film *Charlotte Gray.*

*'The White Mouse' had a number of names:
Nancy Wake, Nancy Fiocca, Andrée Joubert and Hélène.*

Suffolk Farm Accounts

IN THE late 1940s, while exploring the derelict post mill at Wrentham, I met the late Mr R.S. Girling, retired farmer, then approaching his 90s.

After his death in 1951 his daughter, Miss Brenda Girling, remembered the meeting and gave me for safe keeping some fascinating local farm labour accounts for the period 1896-1914.

Once a farmer at nearby Uggeshall on part of Lord Stradbroke's estate, Mr Girling, who told me about the heyday of Wrentham's several windmills, later worked Field Farm, Covehithe, nearer the coast, which was the source of the handwritten accounts I received.

These labour accounts, written in ink and pencil, starting on 11th October 1896, show payments like 2s.6d each to the boys Hammond and Muddit for seven days' toil, and payments of 8s.4d to men like Napthine for five days and 6s.10 1/2d to a Bloomfield for five and a half days.

So, taking the first two pages of the accounts (11th October to 6th November 1896), we find the farmer's labour costs totalled £9 17s.6 1/2d for about half-a-dozen men and boys!

For Christmas Day 1896, the following payments were recorded: "Bloomfield and boy six days – 18s.6d; Napthine seven days – 11s.6d; Reeve six days 10s; Hammond boy seven days – 2s.6d".

Labour costs for the 1914 harvest, which must have been completed as World War I was declared in August, and scores of Suffolk men joined up never to return, totalled £51 11s.6 1/2d. The figure-work covered three pages.

By that time the farmer was paying insurance of 1s. per man and the harvest entries included eight separate payments of 1s. cover for employees so engaged. But a year earlier (1913) the insurance per head for harvest work was a bit more – 1s.4d.

It's interesting to compare these wages of over eighty years ago with those of a 17th-century farm labourer (about 6d a day) and those of a modern general farm worker (about £19 a day or £95 for a basic week).

By about 1837 a farm labourer's wage, according to G.E. Fussell in his book *The English Rural Labourer* (Batchworth Press, 1949), was "7s. to 9s. a week". Thus the late 19th-century accounts for the Wrentham area – sixty years on – appear to reflect a static situation.

The first page of the Wrentham farm-labour accounts for 1896 showed labour costs between 11th and 23rd October as a modest £4 14s. 8½d.

The second page of the accounts to November 1896, put the farmer's labour costs, carried forward, to a total of £9 17s. 6½d. for about half-a-dozen men and boys.

Indeed, it wasn't until just before World War I that the average wage of a farm labourer "rose slowly, with fluctuations, to between 12s. and 14s. a week", according to G.E. Fussell, but there was clearly no uniformity county by county.

The average minimum agricultural wage just before the start of World War II was "about 34s. a week". Interestingly, the price in 1938-39 of a 4-lb loaf of bread was 9d, 1-lb of butter cost about 1s.2d to 1s.6d, and 1lb of margarine could be bought for 4d to 8d.

Always, it seems, the wages of the agricultural labourer for hundreds of years were largely spent on food in the midst of food. Grain and bread was by far the most important purchase, taking, even in prosperous times, "between 30 per cent. and 70 per cent. of the total wage". Meat, another commodity often close at hand, was mostly outside the purchasing power of the average labourer.

Classing the early Wrentham area farm accounts as of the Victorian Age (1837-1901), it is surprising to think that the population of England in 1821 was a mere 13 million, in 1871 getting on for 23 million, in 1901 36 million and in 1931, when farming became very depressed, 40 million. Today, the mouths to be fed in the whole of the United Kingdom number over 55 million.

George Ewart Evans in his book *Ask The Fellows Who Cut The Hay* (Faber, 1956), which was a study of the agricultural side of the Suffolk village of Blaxhall, near Wickham Market, discussed the difference between a boy (as mentioned in the Wrentham accounts) and a lad. The lad, to begin with, got more money than the boys as he was, in fact, older and would not be called a lad until he had left school.

At the time of the contract a boy left school when he was between 10 and 12 years of age. From that time until he was 17 or 18 he would be called a lad.

Assuming, for example, that the Wrentham area boys Hammond and Muddit of 1896, who toiled seven days a week for just 2s.6d each, must have been quite young, it is interesting to find G.E. Evans saying that "boys and girls who were still at school were often taken on at fixed wages".

Boys and girls, we learn, had various jobs: they helped with the turnip hoeing; they carried the elevenses and fourses – the men's snacks at 11 in the morning and four in the afternoon – into the fields; some of the boys would lead the wagon-horses, and both boys and girls would be employed as bind- (or band) pullers with the tier-ups who followed the reapers, their duty being to pull out three or four ears of corn from a bunch lying somewhere near to hand to the tier when he was ready to make his knot.

"One of the reasons why lads and boys were included in the contract", explained G.E. Evans in his book, "is that they were taken on to make up the harvest – to bring the company up to the requisite strength. For, necessarily, two men on the farm the stockman and the horseman – would not be included in the contract; and boys were taken on to avoid bringing a stranger into the team and possibly hindering its smooth-working. Boys, moreover, meant a lower wage-bill".

But as Dr. E.J.T. Collins, director of the Institute of Agricultural History and Museum of English Rural Life at Reading University, told me in 1983: "I'm afraid very little has been published on the interpretation of old farm accounts".

Boys and girls of school age played an important part on farms in olden times.

Apprentice to Battle

The time will come when thou shalt lift thine eyes
To watch a long-drawn battle in the skies,
While aged peasants, too amazed for words,
Stare at the Flying Fleets of wondrous birds.
England, so long mistress of the sea
Where winds and waves confess her sovereignty,
Her ancient triumph yet on high shall bear
And reign sovereign of the conquered air.

A prediction by THOMAS GRAY in 1737

THIS YEAR WILL SEE the release of the long awaited £5m film *The Battle of Britain* – the battle which future historians may compare with Marathon, Trafalgar and the Marne. Some of the Spitfires and Hurricanes which were used in making the film came from the Battle of Britain Memorial Flight at RAF Coltishall, Norfolk. Some famous RAF fighter pilots of those days will tell their stories, perhaps for the last time, for nearly 30 years have gone by since they were young men. But memory tends to play tricks; and contemporary written sources will be the most reliable.

I had a brother in the Battle of Britain who in 1938 went to No. 1 School of Technical Training, Halton, Bucks, as a boy-entrant from the Sir John Leman School, Beccles, Suffolk. He took the trade of engine-fitter. At Halton good manners, and the ability to get to work quickly, were impressed on the boys. Discipline was rigorous: boots were kept polished, long hair was forbidden, and boys were given three days' 'jankers' for laughing at the warrant officer's voice. Pep pills and 'pot' were unknown.

It was at Halton that my brother, who was 16, started to write informative weekly letters on RAF life. Suffice to say that in one of several official workshop notebooks from his Halton days in my

LAC Donald V. Elliott in 1940.

possession he wrote an essay on 17 July 1939, on 'My Idea of Dealing with Aggression'. He said:

'*The task of dealing with the European situation at the present time is extremely difficult, especially for one to talk or write about who is lacking in experience of politics and has not the slightest interest in affairs of this kind. If the countryside of England herself was to be invaded by an aggressor I might take a graver view of things of this nature . . . She (Germany) would probably make one massed air attack in co-operation with Italy. . . .*'

He jumped, as he had predicted, at the opportunity of joining one of the first Spitfire squadrons, No. 66. Yet, pressed from dawn until late into the night with demands far beyond his years – he had not completed his full apprenticeship at Halton before being sent, just after his 18th birthday, to an operational squadron in June 1940 – he still wrote his weekly letters which were preserved and now give us, well, a worm's-eye view of how the Battle of Britain looked to a country boy. Altogether, with his Halton output, there are about 100 letters and documents with, it seems, little break in continuity.

His first posting was on his own doorstep:

'*We got our new stations last night. I am posted to 66(F) Squadron, Coltishall. It's on the main road between Norwich and Mundesley. It's eight miles from Norwich so I shall be about 28 miles from Beccles altogether . . . It's a five minute flight from there to Beccles so I may be seeing you sometime.*'

Action, with Dunkirk just over, came quickly:

'*We lost one of our Spitfires over the sea on Wednesday afternoon. His engine seized up and he had to jump . . . Every little job you do, however small, is done perfectly . . . The other morning, when that German machine raided Norwich, it could be seen from this aerodrome by our pilots but, as usual, another muddle and they were not allowed to take-off . . . We have managed to get one or two Jerries in the last day or two . . . Yes, of course, I have worked on some of the machines that have shot down Nazis. I expect I have been on all of them; there's not many of us for the engines of the whole squadron.*

'*I am still as busy as ever. We start at eight in the mornings now, and every night it's either been eight or nine before we have packed up. Sunday is exactly the*

The station badge for RAF Coltishall, Norfolk

Worked in coloured silks, the badge of 66 Squadron was the work of the apprentice's eldest sister.

same as any other day up here, so we don't know one day from another now. . . .'

When historically did the Battle of Britain start? Once-upon-a-time 8 August 1940 was taken as the date. However, the Ministry of Defence, some time ago, settled on 10 July. In 1968, I briefly referred to the Coltishall dawn engagement in which three Spitfires from 66 Squadron fired the opening shots – the opening round in which the Suffolk apprentice played a small part, for the three pilots concerned, P/O C.A. Cooke, P/O J. Mather and Sgt. F.W. Robertson, all depended on him at different times when far out over the North Sea. Exactly what happened that day has never been related in detail.

The three pilots – the apprentice was at dispersal to see them leave – took-off on patrol at 4.40am over Stalham, Norfolk, and intercepted a Dornier 17 bomber at 15,000 feet. They made a climbing astern attack and met accurate machine-gun fire from under the raider.

'My machine,' P/O Cooke noted in his combat report, 'was hit in five places, one bullet striking the windscreen causing me to break off the engagement as I could no longer see through it.' (The apprentice, incidentally, found six bullet holes to the pilot officer's five.)

Out over the sea off Winterton the crippled Dornier, flying low, was finally 'downed' by Sgt. Robertson who pressed home his attacks to within 50 yards. Three of the crew were afterwards seen swimming separately in the sea but, as other Dorniers were operating in the area, local shipping could not aid them. Sgt. Robertson, mindful of their plight,

circled the German airmen as long as his fuel would allow.

Meantime P/O Cooke had returned to Coltishall. Said the apprentice in a letter written that very day:

'The German's burst of gun-fire went straight through the revolving airscrew and into his bullet proof windscreen – it's a piece of glass about three times the size of this paper and is an inch thick. It was like looking at snow to look through it. It's been fitted since war started. If it hadn't, the pilot would have got it in the head. As it was, he said that he said his prayers when the windscreen splintered. I have got a piece of it.'

Next day – 11 July – 66 and 242 Squadrons (the latter squadron had come from France in low spirits and had been reformed at Coltishall by S/Ldr. Douglas Bader, the legless fighter pilot) got their first concrete evidence of what the champion was like as a leader. Bader went off at 7.50am to intercept a Dornier 17 half a mile off Cromer. The weather at the time was particularly bad and Bader did not think that it was fit enough for his pilots. Nevertheless he found the enemy aircraft and shot it down.

From Coltishall on 19 August the apprentice reported:

'Out of the blue about 3 o'clock this afternoon came one of those . . . Nazi things. He let go six or eight over the next hangar . . . I am sorry to say there were about a hundred workmen working on and around it . . . a few were killed and a good many injured. It shook us up a good bit – some of the boys couldn't remember where they were and what they were doing before the bombs dropped . . . The air raid siren went after all the bombs had been dropped.'

My brother, in addition to his letters, kept a diary going, and we read for 20 August: '66 Sqdn. shot down 3 Nazis – Sgt. Cameron 1 – 1 Spitfire lost – 1 Hurricane 242.'

What lay behind these diary references? Well, we know that P/O C. Bodie, P/O H.C. Kennard and Sgt. M. Cameron from 66 Squadron spotted three

Sometimes the apprentice's Spitfires came back shot-up and on fire.

Messerschmitt 110s five-miles south of Lowestoft flying in a wide vic-formation at 11,000 feet. All six dived vertically at about 400mph and, just before one of the Messerschmitts dived into the sea on fire, one of the crew baled out at about 1000 feet and landed in the sea a few hundred yards from the burning wreck. He was last seen swimming for, one imagines, the Suffolk coast.

On that day as well 242 Squadron lost Midshipman P.J. Patterson over the sea (he was one of three Fleet Air Arm pilots who, because of the shortage of RAF pilots, had joined 242 on 1 July).

That day – Tuesday, 20 August – in a wider sense has a permanent place in history, for the matchless fighting spirit of the RAF drew forth from Mr Winston Churchill at 3.52pm in the House of Commons this stirring sentence: 'Never in the field of human conflict was so much owed by so many to so few.'

From Coltishall on 22 August the apprentice wrote:

'Jerry came again yesterday dinner time, only our fighters were ready for him. It was like disturbing a hornet's nest when he came over. Both squadrons – 66 and 242 – shot up after him and then began a lovely game of hide-and-seek in and out of the clouds over the camp. Presently one of our Hurricanes came back full-out, dived down low over the drome and shot up into the air again, doing a complete roll. That's the sign they all give if they have scored a victory.'

What became of the raider? Apparently it was a Dornier 17 and it crashed '20 miles south of Norwich' within sight of Harleston, Norfolk, the spot being in a wood at the back of Conifer Hill, the home of Major A. Lombe Taylor, who was then the company commander of Harleston Home Guard. Among the 242 Squadron pilots who claimed it was another Fleet Air Arm pilot, Sub/Lt. R.E. Gardner.

During his last month in Norfolk the apprentice requested his older sister to work for him in coloured silks (he rightly felt like an English baron) the badge of 66 Squadron – a rattle-snake and the motto *Cavete: Praemonui* (Beware! I have given Warning). However, when the framed badge was sent to him through the post, the glass got cracked.

As the days wore on, and RAF Fighter Command began to feel the strain, the battle developed into a slogging match. Invasion was expected in early September. On 3 September – by all accounts it was a fine day – 66 Squadron and the apprentice were called south to RAF Kenley, Surrey. Twenty-four hours later enemy agents landed on the Kent coast but were almost immediately detected. They had landed with the 'object of gaining information regarding coastal defences and the morale of the British people'. The moment of greatest peril had come.

Footnote: The lad's prediction at RAF Halton that Germany would probably make one massed air attack in co-operation with Italy, was borne out when, on 11th November 1940, a force of Fiat BR20 bombers, escorted by Fiat CR42 bi-plane fighters, tried a coastal raid. Three of their number were brought down in Suffolk – a bomber at Bromeswell, near Woodbridge, and two fighters at Orfordness and Corton respectively. The Orfordness machine is in the RAF Museum, Hendon.

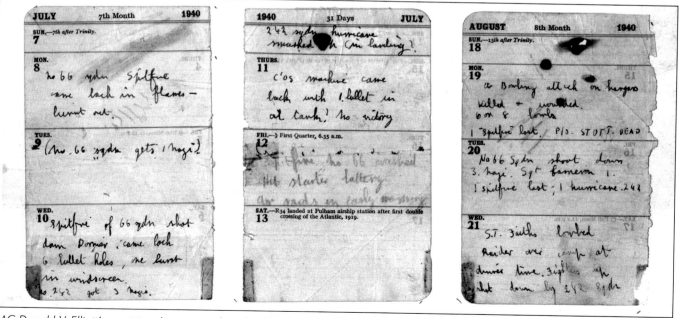

LAC Donald V. Elliott's surviving diary pages from his 1940 stay at RAF Coltishall, Norfolk.

Norfolk House & D-Day
MISSING ARTEFACTS

FORTY YEARS ago Norfolk House, St. James's Square, London, was probably the most secret place in the United Kingdom. In the building, which was gutted during a rebuild- during the late 70s, the D-Day invasion and the earlier North Africa invasion had been planned by an Anglo-American team.

For years, apparently, the artifacts of the rooms where those historic invasions had been organised were marked and stored for posterity. But now they are no longer there – apparently they have gone to private collectors.

Towards the end of December 1943, a number of very important military appointments were announced and the public, for the first time, realised that the Allies intended to deliver Europe from the Nazis in a matter of months.

The fact that the greatest invasion operation in history was planned in Norfolk House is no secret – a plaque outside tells of the historic link.

However, it wasn't until the late 1970s that my curiosity over Norfolk House led me to make some inquiries as to exactly what the connection entailed and what, if anything, remained inside which was associated with the secret gatherings.

Seeing the gutting of the interior of Norfolk House in 1978, I obtained permission from the builders to go inside. Site staff, who went to a lot of trouble on my behalf, took me to what they called "The Eisenhower Room" – but it by then had been stripped. I wasn't convinced that I was seeing all.

Allowed to wander through all the floors, I finished up in the basement which seemed the right place for secrets, and saw a bunker-like structure with steel doors which the site foreman said was an old safe vault "as big as a big room".

On leaving the building I made further inquiries, and eventually received confirmation that the Eisenhower room I had been shown in good faith was only part of the story. The bunker-like structure far below, they admitted, contained "artifacts from the Eisenhower room".

Further ritual, which involved a lot of pressing on my behalf, produced two keys and so, in the end, I was escorted into the secret chamber.

The artifacts, which had all heard the secrets between 1942 and 1944 of Operations "Torch" (North Africa) and "Overlord" (D-Day), consisted of a big array of panelling, including a magnificent wooden mantelpiece, all carefully numbered and ticketed for possible re-erection. The extensive range of pieces – there were hundreds with items as small as nails and screws preserved in trays – were all arranged in perfect order round the vault walls.

The temperature and air reminded me very much of derelict but sealed USAAF airfield combat wing bunkers from the war years I had been in East Anglia. The conditions were ideal for preservation purposes.

In 1978, when I was shown the Eisenhower artefacts, there was no plan, as far as I could ascertain, to do anything with the Norfolk House pieces except preserve and safeguard them.

A chance remark about important framed letters having been a feature of the Eisenhower Room after the war led me to check with the British Aluminium Co. (now British Alcan Aluminium Ltd.) who on 1st September 1939, 48-hours before war was declared, acquired the lease and then had Norfolk House taken over by the government until handed back to them in 1951.

Eisenhower's short letter (typewritten) was dated 12th July 1945, and stated: "The Board Room of the British Aluminium Co. Ltd., in Norfolk House, will always occupy a place in British and American history."

Montgomery's quite long letter (handwritten) was dated January 1969, from his home at Alton, Hampshire, and stated: "The planning for the invasion of Normandy began in Norfolk House late in 1942, and when General Eisenhower arrived in London in January 1944, he set up his headquarters there . . . The final inter-Services, and inter-Allied plan was approved by General Eisenhower at a conference in Norfolk House early in February 1944".

But my curiosity about Norfolk House didn't end with these letters. Why was the building selected out of all the places available London?

When the building was erected in the late 1930s and it incorporated advanced use of steel and concrete, as such, was no doubt considered to be fairly bomb-proof. At the same time it was within reach of Whitehall and the seat of government. What was certainly true was that it was also within easy reach of fashionable London.

However, while the secrets of D-Day were contained within Norfolk House during the vital period leading up to the Normandy landings, the artifacts I have describe were in January this year found to have been dispersed into private hands although, it is understood, attempts were made to keep the items together for display in one of our national museums. Thus the historical continuity I detected in 1978 was in the end broken. What a pity!

The Gypsies

IT IS several years since I roamed East Anglia as a journalist. During that time I got to know several gypsies and, once, when I attended a village court in West Suffolk, the defendant – a gypsy – came over to the press table and greeted me before the case. We had met six years before near Ipswich, when I wished to photograph his large family round their fire, and he had not forgotten the meeting. Afterwards, out of sight of the sergeant, I paid the gypsy's fine. And then I gave my newspaper the story for next day's edition.

Much has happened to the gypsies of this country since the early 1950s. In March this year, in fact, a government census of Britain's gypsies, didicoys and other itinerants, the latest figure for whom, based on the 1961 census, was 17,516, was undertaken for the Minister of Housing and Local Government. Eventually, I understand, the Prime Minister will see a report on the survey.

The survey was staged following the submission to the Minister of a paper on the problems by the late Norman Dodds, Labour MP for Erith and Crayford, who was an acknowledged authority on gypsies. In it, I understand, he urged the establishment of rehabilitation centres, and emphasised that 'experience has shown the great importance of providing facilities for television and radio'.

Obviously there are problems in fitting the genuine gypsy into our modern society. Frequently in recent years there have been outcries, in one part of the country or another, against the Romany over camping sites. Again, his slow perambulation by horse-drawn caravan along our modern highways, reserved for the 'with it' citizen, has its dangers. But because the gypsy is in the minority we must guard against being too harsh in our judgment of him and his way of life.

I wonder what the great gypsy supporter George Borrow, who was born at East Dereham in 1803 and so much enjoyed meeting them at the horse and cattle market on Castle Hill, Norwich, would think of today's scheme to 'nationalise' – I can think of no better word – the Romany? My feeling is that he would have rebelled – as, indeed, I do – at the thought that soon there may be a Ministry of Gypsies with an office in Whitehall to peg them down. (Talking of pegs, reminds me that my wife has abandoned the modern plastic clothes-peg for the good old wooden clothes-peg and that, for the time being, a regular supply is promised from a gypsy living near Diss.)

How many gypsies, for instance, are there in Norfolk? The exact figure, it seems, will never be

A gypsy family group near Nacton, Ipswich, in 1947

known, for no one at the moment, thank goodness, can tie gypsies, lovers of oriental display, down to one county. Tomorrow it may be Suffolk. Next day it may be Essex. A superstitious point, in fact, has been known to drive them to another county overnight.

I do know, however, that in 1948 Gypsy Petulengro, King of the Romanies, told a Beccles journalist that he had 300 'subjects' – real gypsies – in Norfolk, Suffolk and Essex. Altogether, in the British Isles, there were about 3500 real Romanies 16 years ago. But it seems likely that the overall figure has diminished since then.

The number of true Romanies in any county, please note, is a small percentage of all the travellers or nomads. The chief problem, surely, is that created by families occupying certain camps who are not really nomadic. Romanies – the real ones whom we should do our best to preserve – are a race apart. Could it be, then, that the genuine Romany is the unfortunate nigger in the woodpile – that he may not require television?

Is the average gypsy child in need of care and attention? Well, 12 years ago the National Society for the Prevention of Cruelty to Children stated that gypsy children are in the main physically in as good a

Using a 1929 small plate camera, the author in the 1950s, having obtained special permission to enter the camp while the men folk were out working, captured the series of pictures of Romany families at Horley, Surrey, April 8, 1956. Their head was Sharlotte Smith; they made pegs and sold flowers. The 20 gypsies included many children. They had four caravans and nine horses. Surrey and Kent was their home.

condition as children of the rest of the community and that their parents keep them as clean and feed them as well as do the parents of children living a more settled form of life.

What, then, are we trying to give them? Mr Dodds, as I say, believed they want, among other things, television. But my children, who live a settled life in London, do not have television because I want them to see other things. Now the gypsies of the 1970s, if Whitehall has anything to do with it, will no longer believe that 'the souls of all gypsies go into the bodies of cuckoos'. But my children, who, as I say, live a settled life in London, believe in 'the Little People' and, for the time being, are to be encouraged to believe in them.

It is said that the average gypsy family, over the past century, has shown no great desire to change its way of life. So as recently as 1953 the burning took place of all the belongings of a dead gypsy woman – her caravan included – 'so that the spirit of the dead person shall not return'. What a splendid way to stop family squabbles.

My feeling is that there is a danger that the real gypsy, who was first noted in a written record as far back as 1505 and whose ultimate origin was Northern India, will disappear from our midst because he is in the minority. Whitehall may obliterate the genuine wanderer – and his beliefs – in an endeavour to settle those more numerous folk who are not true nomads.

Aeronautical Archaeologist

LAST summer (1966), while on other business in Scotland, I was able to locate the crash site of a fairly early Heinkel 111 in Berwickshire and, by accident, stumbled on an amusing story in the same area of the "capture" by Eyemouth fishermen of a Heinkel 115 seaplane. In both instances, despite a lapse of over 25 years, I was able to obtain relics from both aircraft – a number-plate from the first giving the exact type, and several instruments from the seaplane in good condition.

This kind of luck is typical, I should say, of hundreds of similar journeys I have made all over the country over the past quarter of a century interviewing people and studying local and central records in my quest for original story material and relics for my private aeronautical collection. At the same time hundreds of letters inquiring about this and that have been written to people all over the world.

My field of study has always been broad and covers the growth of aviation from the early 1900s right up to the present. But man's earlier endeavours to fly are not, of course, overlooked either. After all these years – I had a father in the RFC and a brother in the RAF – the number of relics, photographs, books and documents must run into several thousand and, in fact, I have not yet completed the histories of many aeronautical items collected during World War II. I wonder how many other readers, on being drawn to the subject, have progressed and grown up in this way'?

When did my interest in aircraft and airmen (please remember that, even today, the human factor is still as important as ever), really start? Perhaps at Martlesham Heath, Suffolk, during the Empire Air-Day displays of the 1930s. Certainly the arrival, upside-down, near my home of a Hawker Hind in May 1937, increased the interest.

In 1953 I visited with my friend, Roger A. Freeman, the British 8th USAAF historian, a number of ex-American bomber and fighter bases to see what was left of group paintings and the like in derelict Nissen huts and control-towers.

At Leiston, Suffolk, where the 357th Fighter Group, flying P-51 Mustangs, was based (I was given a special facility as a boy to spend a day with this group on 3rd March 1945, when Messerschmitt 262s and Messerschmitt 163s gave battle), we found a painting in the decaying control-tower of a 357th Mustang with chequered red and yellow nose.

The painting now, of course, is no more but we have a photograph of it.

At the old airfield used by B-17 Flying Fortresses

Youngsters of the 1950s intently examining WWII aircraft relics at one of several Battle of Britain exhibitions the writer organised for the local branch of the RAFA at Sudbury, Suffolk.

Photo: Courtesy Bury Free Press

of the 390th Bombardment Group at Framlingham, Suffolk, not far from Leiston, we found one of the finest surviving 8th USAAF murals – a mural covering the entire centre wall of the 569th Bombardment Squadron's operations room. It was a unique pictorial history of the group's many actions. A few years later the Air Ministry demolished the structure. However, photographs were taken during our visit and now a four-foot square photograph has been prepared and mounted on varnished hardboard as an interior decoration for a wall in my house. A two-foot square photograph of the Leiston P-51 has been similarly processed.

Colonel F. Curry, Director, Air Force Museum, Wright-Patterson Air Force Base, Ohio, is to send a member of the British-based USAF to examine the murals and take more photographs with a view to the Parham mural being exhibited perhaps full-scale, in the American Air Force museum.

In 1954 I was shown further paintings at Great Ashfield, Suffolk, which was the home of the 385th Bombardment Group, equipped with B-17 Flying Fortresses, by Anne Haywood-Gordon who, as a local young artist during the war, painted the pet names on many of the group's aircraft – 'Back To The Sack', 'Mr. Lucky', 'Powerful Katrinka' and 'Dragon Lady'.

But I began my airfield pilgrimages much earlier – in 1946. In 1943, when the 56th Fighter Group, equipped with P-47 Thunderbolts, settled at Halesworth, Suffolk, I spent some Saturday mornings helping to wax-polish the wings for extra speed (another 20 mph, they used to say), and got to know the airfield well. When, therefore, the airfield was closed after the war, I visited the derelict buildings

The up-side-down Heinkel 115 float-plane which Eyemouth, Scotland, fishermen towed in in September, 1940.

Relics taken from Bodie's Spitfire after it was burned out at RAF Coltishall, Norfolk, on July 8, 1940: l to r scorched altimeter, melted parachute strap buckle, boost pressure gauge face, and artificial horizon face.

When the then Air Vice Marshal H. J. Maguire made what was officially to be the last appearance over London of 1940 fighters, his Spitfire SL574 of the Battle of Britain Memorial Flight had to be crash-landed on September 20, 1959, on the Oxo Sports Ground, Bromley, Kent, in the midst of a cricket match. Afterwards the badly dented spinner was passed to the writer for his collection. In 1989 at RAF Halton, Bucks, SL574 was presented to the San Diego Air and Space museum in memory of the Eagle Squadrons who flew with the RAF before transferring to the 8th Air Force at the end of 1942. In return the RAF received the P-51 Mustang now resident in the RAF Museum, Hendon.

Impression of crashing Messerschmitt 110 at Washington, Sussex, on 4th September, 1940, with (in valley) the site under excavation in 1965. Airman's belt buckle and English half-crown from this wreck.

The Heinkel III brought down on February 22, 1940, near St. Abb's Head, Scotland.

Bromley Spitfire spinner after crash.

before it was too late and was able to salvage from the briefing room of one of the squadrons – the place was constructed from packing cases – an original drawing of a Walt Disney character. This drawing, which I have in my collection, must have seen Robert Johnson, Walker Mahurin, Francis Gabreski and the late David Schilling who were among the original fighter pilots of the 56th.

Now, like the rest, all these buildings have vanished.

Living in East Anglia during the war, of course, gave me opportunities as a boy of seeing the return of crippled aircraft. On 11th April 1944, I was with other boys at Beccles emergency airfield, Suffolk, when the historically famous B-17F Flying Fortress 'Tom Paine' (No. 230793) of the 562nd Bombardment Squadron, 388th Bombardment Group, Knettishall, Suffolk, returned in a damaged state from a maximum penetration mission to Posen, Poland. Many years later an official USAAF picture of 'Tom Paine' at Beccles was traced by Mr Freeman and he, remembering my encounter with the stricken bomber which almost killed us as it ground-looped, arranged for me to have a copy. Eventually all the crew were traced and in 1963 I received a most interesting letter from the captain that day giving full details of how, with wounded aboard, they found their way back to England and decided not to belly land in view of the critical condition of the co-pilot.

So the business of research, if it is to be done properly, may often extend over many years.

The Heinkel 111, mentioned in the introduction, was the one which F/Lt. A.D. Farquhar, of 602 (City of Glasgow) Fighter Squadron, brought down near St. Abbs Head on 22nd February 1940. As the crippled aircraft flopped down on its belly in lonely country, Farquhar, anxious to capture the Heinkel intact, landed his Spitfire alongside but overturned. From this undignified position, hanging head-down in his harness, he saw the crew take a wounded man to a safe position and then return and fire the Heinkel. Afterwards one of the German airmen walked over to the Spitfire and released Farquhar. Then the mixed party made their way to a distant farm house where the wounded gunner was placed on the kitchen table.

The number-plate, giving the type as a Heinkel 111P2, was given to me by the farmer's wife. Its Werk Nr. – the number appeared on several other plates – was 1594.

The story of the Heinkel 115, which I learnt about while visiting the farm near St. Abbs Head, is particularly interesting. "Round about 16th September 1940", my fisherman eyewitness told me, the crew of the seaplane – it had been forced down – were found in their dinghy. Subsequently their seaplane, upside-down, was spotted by the same Eyemouth fishermen and towed in. How did it end up inverted? It seems that the crew fired their pistols into the float tips, hoping to sink the seaplane, but all that happened was that the seaplane stood on its nose and finally went over when a tail wind got up! From a description of the unit badge I was able to establish that the seaplane had come from List, Sylt. Soon after it was beached at Eyemouth a storm got up and the seaplane broke up.

The instruments had been kept all these years by an Eyemouth man.

When No. 57 Squadron at RAF Marham, Norfolk, converted to Victor tankers in early 1966 after their Valiants were scrapped, a big quantity of items and documents concerning the Valiant turned up in a scrap dump near Beccles, Suffolk. The pear-shaped piece of plywood numbered 377 was used to protect that Valiant's bomb aimer's side window when on the ground.

Some fine wood items made from WWI planes. The small four-bladed propellor generated electricity for the great Handley Page 0/400, Britain's first true heavy bomber.

There is, as I have indicated, great satisfaction to be had by those who care to do original research. But the most authoritative sources are not always correct with their information. I am thinking in particular of a case back in the 1950s when I wanted the official angle on the dropping of 4000 caltrops – small spiked, steel pyramids – by the Luftwaffe near Lowestoft, Suffolk, on the night of 23rd October 1943. Caltrops, in earlier times, were used on battlefields for laming horses. The caltrops dropped in 1943 – I have an example and it is rare – were, however, intended for the tyres of RAF bombers. But the Air Ministry, in their reply, thought that caltrops were last used in World War I! I wonder how many RAF bombers, after that curious raid, burst their tyres on landing or take off?

Here is a typical selection of items I have acquired over the years

- Hand-made wooden wing rib from the second powered aircraft flown between 1905-1910 by J.E. Humphreys, of Wivenhoe, Essex, which was "well in advance of its British contemporaries".

- Rare piece of original music c.1909-1914 dedicated to "Colonel" Samuel F. Cody who was the inventor of the first practical British flying machine. When told of the find — the piece of music turned up in 1966 among old papers in London — the librarian of the Royal Aeronautical Society, Mr F.H. Smith, said: "I congratulate you on your find which is unknown to us . . . It is quite amazing that this should still be available and I am surprised that the RAF have not done something with it".

- Compass from SE5a together with original diagram of compass from cadet's 1918 notebook.

- Original diagram of cockpit layout of BE2 — the BE2 was the first aircraft to be officially adopted by the RFC — from cadet's 1918 notebook. Diagram was exhibited at the RFC Golden Jubilee Exhibition at the Imperial War Museum in 1962.

- Propeller from Avro 504 — this was the first bomber in the world to be fitted with a mechanical bomb release — recalling the bombing mission flown by three Avro 504s to the German zeppelin sheds on Lake Constance on 21st November,1914.

- Original water-colour (12 x 20in) made by Cockney artist near St. Paul's Cathedral, London, on 7th July 1917, when 21 twin-engined Gotha bombers caused fires in the area. Details of formation shown in pencil.

- Instruments from Spitfire of 66 Squadron, Coltishall, Norfolk, which came back in flames on 8th July 1940, after a dawn engagement with a Heinkel 111 off the East Coast. The pilot was P/O C.A.W. Bodie.

- Nearly complete 20mm H.E. Oerlikon cannon-shell fired by a Messerschmitt 109 and picked from the fuselage of a 66 Squadron Spitfire in 1940 — several dozen fragments.

- Relics from Dornier 17Z (markings F1-HT) of 1/KG76 which was brought down on 18th August 1940, when Kenley airfield, Surrey, was attacked at very low level. The Dornier, which struck a bungalow, was helped down by a PAC (parachute and cable) anti-aircraft device.

- Drogue parachute from secret British aerial mine used in 1940-1941 against night raiders. Apparently balloons were released, each with an explosive charge attached to 2000 ft of piano wire, and when an aircraft flew into the wire the bomb (on paper) was supposed to be drawn up with fatal results.

- Part of wing trailing-edge from the Fiat BR 20 bomber of the 43° Stormo based at Chievres, Belgium, which 257 Squadron, Martlesham, Suffolk, brought down at nearby Bromeswell on 11th November 1940, when the Italian Air Force launched its attack on this country from bases in the Low Countries.

- Airman's belt buckle, decorated with eagle, and English half-crown, dated 1939, from Messerschmitt 110CI (markings 2N + DP (?)) of III/ZG76(?) which fell at Washington, Sussex, when 15 Messerschmitt 110s were brought down on 4th September 1940. Relics were dug up at site in 1965.

- Panel showing swastika victories from Spitfire IIA (markings DL-M (P7735)) of 91 Squadron, Hawkinge, Kent, which was destroyed on the ground by attacking Messerschmitt 109 on 4th February 1941. The Spitfire belonged to the late F/Lt. D.A.S. McKay who, it will be remembered, did so much for Air-Britain in the early post war years.

- Luftwaffe target maps, photographs and briefs found near Mons, Belgium, in September, 1944. Some relate to reconnaissance flights made over England as far back as 1938.

- Number-plate from brand new Messerschmitt 109 (markings 22DG+NR) which was flown to Herringfleet, Suffolk, on 15th May 1944, by an Austrian deserter. The Air Ministry, after the war, said that the aircraft had come from Zerbst between Magdeburg and Dessau — an important jet-training establishment at the time. The pilot, according to eye-witnesses, gave us important information.

- Pilot's goggles, instrument and fabric showing Rising Sun insignia from Japanese Zero fighter brought down in 1944 at Imphal, Mampur, Burma, by 28 Squadron and ground-fire. Pilot was wearing ceremonial sword.

- Spinner from Spitfire Mk16 (SL574), flown by then Air Vice-Marshal H.J. Maguire, which crash-landed near Bromley, Kent, on 20th September 1959, after Battle of Britain fly-past. Was supposed to be the last Spitfire to fly over London. SL574 was among batch SL541-579 completed at Castle Bromwich in August/September 1945. Spinner presented by RAF.

- Stiffening bracket for the airbrake compartment of a TSR-2 — the cancelled £750m project for 180 such aircraft (a neighbour, by the way, has a pair of wheels from the first TSR-2 which flew — XR219)! Bracket given by BAC.

Suffolk Names in Stone

WHEN you stumble on an English churchyard with tombstones inscribed with christian names like Priscilla, Joseph, Jane, Henry, Eliza, Thomas, Sarah, Robert, Emma, Samuel, Eleanor, William, Harriet, Jessie, Annie and others, you know it's an old resting place of the dead. These names were all spotted at Beccles.

In the course of wandering about the country I have visited a good few graveyards, the majority in East Anglia, but I have explored others as far apart as Surrey, Lincolnshire and Yorkshire.

It was during my early journalistic days in the once great fishing port of Grimsby, on the Humber, that I knew by heart the local gravestone inscription to the memory of Edward Ward, watchmaker, who died on December 12, 1847, aged 54 years:

Here lies one who strove to equal time:
A task too hard, each power too sublime.
Time stopt his motion, o'erthrew his balance wheel,
Wore off his pivots, though made of harden'd steel;
Broke all his springs, the verge of life decay'd.
And now he is as though he'd ne'er been made.
Not for the want of oiling—that he tried,
If that had done – why then he ne'er had died.

At Carshalton, Surrey, where I worked for a local newspaper in the early 1960s, I had a thorough look at All Saints' churchyard, finding many hidden aspects of local history, but most remarkable was the children's corner.

Selected many years before for that specific purpose, the graves lay beneath a great beech tree. Presiding over them was the grave of one, Nurse Ellen Nash, the only adult in their midst. Now Nurse Nash was a much respected local midwife in her day so, when she died, it was decided to bury her with some of the children she had brought into the world.

Then, in 1982, I was surprised to find that the people of Worlingham, near Beccles, on the discovery in 1980 of human bones during trenching work opposite the 'Three Horseshoes' public house, believed to be the site of the village's first burial ground going back many centuries, had re-interred the remains and erected a tombstone with these words:

Here Lie The Mortal Remains
Of 23 Parishioners
Of St. Peter's Parish
Worlingham Parva
Re-interred
1981

So it's clear that, for centuries, English people have remembered their dead so that, in villages at least,

Sight of the local church in olden times took villagers' thoughts to the churchyard.

the living were always in touch with the dead through the sight of the local churchyard and the simple, regular ceremony of putting flowers on the graves.

Certainly, when I was a child at Beccles in the 1930s, I can remember visiting Beccles cemetery, off the London Road, almost every week, summer and winter, to mind the graves of my grandparents.

Incredibly, the simple ritual of filling up the watering can, and climbing the stepped bank to one of the graves, was an agreeable duty. Afterwards, as my mother chatted to other visitors, there was the endless exploration of the paths and the silent yews . . . But the widespread ritual of attending graves ceased in the mid-1940s as world-war two ended with, of course, so many local lads dead and buried in far-off lands. My RAF brother, who survived as a prisoner-of-war of the Japanese in distant Borneo until a month or two before the war ended in the Far East, has no known grave. Perhaps, in a wider context, this goes some way to explain why by the mid-1940s so many graveyards were neglected because families could no longer bring themselves to centre their remembrance on mere local branches who in any case had died in peaceful, familiar surroundings.

In newspaper cuttings I have collected over the years, churchyard neglect shows a steady increase – let's start in the 1970s.

At Harwell, in Berkshire, a reader stated that "the neglect into which many old churchyards have fallen has lately been dealt with, in some cases rather controversially, by taking up old gravestones and either removing or re-siting them". He instanced "an

Members of the Elliott family buried in Haddiscoe Churchyard		
Names	Date of Death	Age
John Elliott	Nov 6 · 1742	47
Wife of above	Oct 10 · 1743	—
Susan Mayhew daughter of John and Susan Elliott	Aug 7 · 1780	28
Elizabeth Elliott	Aug 9 1782	80
John Elliott	March 23 · 1791	61
Susannah Elliott	Aug 16 · 1816	96
Martha Chalker daughter of above	March 8 1794	4
Robert Mayhew	Aug 26 · 1829	49
John Elliott	Feb 9 · 1856	73
Elizabeth Elliott	Aug 26 · 1844	82
William Elliott	Aug 16 · 1837	81
Mary Elliott	Sept 3 · 1844	85
Jacob Elliott	Dec 8 · 1845	89
Jacob Elliott	Jan 20 · 1896	86

The continuity of burial is well illustrated in this old list of members of the writer's family buried round the Saxon-towered church at Haddiscoe, Norfolk, for the years 1742 to 1896 with John Elliott having been born in 1695.

excellent compromise" at Harwell: the stones were cleverly positioned on either side of the main path, upright, and graded in height. For safety reasons, they were made to lean slightly backwards.

In 1982 a Hornchurch, Essex, funeral director recalled that, in 1829, the cost of an "economic adult funeral was £2 plus church dues, preparation of grave, and so on". This represented "over five weeks' money for the man in the street".

Then, early last year, a Leeds man referred to "the draconian regulations governing the material and shape of grave-stones and the hefty 10 per cent increase in churchyard fees for 1983.

"In the guise of protecting the aesthetic beauty of the 'country churchyard'," commented the Leeds writer, "restrictions on gravestones have become intolerable . . ."

Also early last year, the Rev. Maurice Rhodes, vicar of Walsall Wood, West Midlands, advertised in his parish magazine for a manufacturer to develop a prototype plastic gravestone to cut "the rising cost of burials."

Then there was the High Court case of a widow, who put wreaths and vases of flowers on her husband's grave in her local cemetery, who was ordered with three other people to stop the ritual.

A representative for the North Bedfordshire Council, whose burial regulations were alleged to have been broken, declared: "The purpose is to facilitate maintenance of the cemetery and render it more economic".

In June 1983, it was reported that "saboteurs tried to halt a funeral for the third time . . . by filling in the grave dug by mourners . . . because council workmen were on strike."

Amusingly – but not for the bereaved family – the strike, involving 500 council workers, began "after a row over the appointment of a council leisure-centre barmaid."

If grave-diggers can find reason to strike over a barmaid, I think it is time the General Synod of the Church of England, who have an interest in burial matters, let a bit more light into our churchyards by encouraging, not hindering, families to honour their dead.

Epitaphs, too, should be allowed to be more expressive of those they honour. The following one for a sailor is most apt:

His Anchor was the Holy Word
His Rudder Blooming Hope
The love of God his Mainstops'll
And Faith his Sailing Rope.

Pakenham, Suffolk, cemetery at dawn.

Southwold Fishermen
BY-GONE DAYS

IT IS said that the instruments used in this country for the capture of fish proper and shell-fish are many and various, and there survive, to the present day, methods and gear which are probably relics of primitive times.

As for the earliest method of taking fish in quantity, it was undoubtedly the stopping-up of the mouths of narrow tidal creeks with brushwood or stones, through which the water would run-off on the ebb tide leaving the fish inside the barrier high and dry.

The British industry is not what it was. For anyone born on the east coast and alive in the 1930s, these were the last years of the steam fleets of Lowestoft, Great Yarmouth and Grimsby.

After the second world war, the decline of the well-known fleets became marked, and the last time I sailed as a passenger on a big fishing boat was in 1949 from Lowestoft – and that, of course, was a diesel boat.

In the early 1950s, when I knew the Southwold/Walberswick area quite well, I often went out with the Southwold inshore fishermen, one being William 'Rory' Tooke, skipper of *Felix,* named no doubt after Dunwich's St Felix of the 7th century. Usually a willing skipper could be found in The Harbour Inn, Blackshore, on the Southwold side of the *River Blyth,* where in those days their little fleet tied-up.

According to old notes, such a fishing trip was arranged on 4th August 1953, and away we went into a steady so'-wester.

Standing at the tiller, etched against a high mackerel sky, his Nordic nose and forehead glistening with the salt-laden spray which whipped over the gunwale as high as the quivering mizzen mast, 'Rory' Tooke, cap askew. seemed to know what he was doing.

When I asked him why he wore no lifejacket, although I did, he said a solo fisherman had little chance if overwhelmed and might as well drown quickly . . .!

Felix's 12-hp car engine, bolted to the boat's 15ft-long hull, pitched and rolled with us as we chugged to Sole Bay where, on 28th May 1672, Dutch Admiral De Ruyter fought a famous battle with the English, some cannon-balls falling on land between Southwold and Dunwich.

As terns, gulls and swifts flew by, and a lone pigeon raced low in a southerly, 'Rory' Tooke reminded me: 'We are now over the lost town of Dunwich. Listen

William 'Rory' Tooke testing the warp as he trawled off Dunwich.

for the bells from the engulfed churches. If you can't hear 'em then you're a pagan!"

Constantly taking bearings from distant landmarks, 'Rory' Tooke eventually reached the sacred fishing spot known, it seemed, only to him. He then made preparations to drop the 18-ft. trawl which in those days cost 'anything between £20 to £25'. The engine speed was accordingly reduced, the tiller handle was removed (a rudder is useless during a trawl), and the trawl beam carrying the net was lowered over the starboard side. The warp, which was coiled amidships, was then paid out over the same side. The trawl started at the rate of three knots an hour.

'Rory' Tooke sat in the stern holding the warp to check the behaviour of the beam on the sea-bed eight fathoms (48-ft.) below. In this way he identified obstructions, like wreckage, on the sea-bed, but on this trawl he found only a sandy, ideal floor.

As *Felix* bobbed about I spotted a dozen or so blocks of cement heaped in the stern as ballast and wondered if they'd punch a hole in her old bottom if we got into rough water. 'Rory' Tooke said the blocks were taken from a demolished first world-war pill-box which guarded Southwold beach in 1914-18.

Fisherman William 'Rory' Tooke working Felix off the Suffolk coast on 4th August 1953.

When 'Rory' Tooke wanted to turn the boat to starboard, he pulled on the warp, and the rudderless *Felix* responded. Later, after the warp had been partly pulled in by means of a small capstan geared to the engine, he turned the boat using a long oar.

Seeing him so engaged reminded me of the story he had told me on another occasion, of how at the age of nine, he worked for Alfred, his father, for a halfpenny a week when things were prosperous, and how his father made him a small oar so that he could "learn the trade early".

With our catch of Southwold sole and roker (skate) safely aboard, and with some of the fish already gutted by 'Rory' Tooke, *Felix* turned for home with a following sea rising and falling – dangerously it seemed to me – just below the boat's transom.

Asked if he had ever caught anything unusual in his nets, dead or alive, 'Rory' Tooke listed 'a rare crab covered with hair', which was preserved. He remembered that Frank 'Workie' Upcraft, back in 1946, while shrimping in *Integrity* only 30 yards from the shore between Dunwich and Walberswick, picked up one of the front leg bones of a dinosaur, 42-inches long and barnacle-covered, which weighed so much that it damaged the net.

When 'Rory' Tooke was a lad of 16 "at least 60 inshore boats plied out of the *Blyth* but this year (1953) they number less than a dozen", William 'Stork' Mayhew, aged 76, was the oldest working fisherman at Southwold in the early 1950s.

What of fishermen's names – especially their

An early morning scene at Lowestoft, Suffolk, in the last days of the East Coast fishing fleets. Photo: Courtesy Elizabeth Gregor

christian or nicknames? 'Rory' Tooke over 30 years ago reeled off a long local list, some most-fitting, but it was my other fisherman friend on the Walberswick bank of the *Blyth*, 'Dinks' Cooper, who told me his mother named him Robert Henry George Charles "to make up for lost brothers".

Southwold fishermen of my youth told me many tales mixed with much lore.

For example, the fathom (abandoned for the metre) was "the distance between a man's finger-tips with arms outstretched", and was a way of measuring rope. In the 18th century the fathom was loosely specified in three kinds: the first, which was that of men-o-war, contained six-feet; the moulding or that of merchant ships, five-and-half-feet; and the smallest, used in different kinds of small boats, only five-feet.

Although the fathom later became six feet by common agreement, it was never legally defined, which presumably meant that the relative physical statures of men in the Royal Navy, the merchant service and fishing fleets measured by the length of their arms, set the unofficial seal on ocean depths!

A fisherman's weather-vane at Walberswick, Suffolk.

BRIG. GENERAL FREDERICK W. CASTLE
'The Last Flight'

A GOOD few years ago I was surprised to receive from some old Suffolk friends various personal effects, including a large framed portrait and citation, associated with the late Brig. General Frederick W. Castle, Congressional Medal of Honour, famous 8th USAAF. Flying Fortress leader, who on Christmas Eve, 1944, forty year's ago this year, died in an air battle near Liege Belgium.

His achievement – he was an outstanding worker for Anglo-American relations and is remembered today in the annual 'Castle Award' administered by USAF Lakenheath, Suffolk – came sharply to my attention in the summer (1984) when I received a copy of *Castles In The Air: The story of the B-17 Flying Fortress crews of the US 8th Air Force*, by Norwich author Martin W. Bowman.

One of the most revealing books ever written about daylight aerial warfare, it touched on the beginnings of the 8th Air Force in England in early 1942 and mentioned that Castle was one of General Ira C. Eaker's original staff.

Martin Bowman, in his well-illustrated Fortress history of 205-odd pages, recalled that on Christmas Eve, 1944, in the worst winter weather in England for 54 years, a maximum effort was called for to attack the Luftwaffe fighter airfields supporting the strong German land forces in the Ardennes.

Thus, in the face of atrocious winter conditions on the ground and in the air, the 8th Air Force mounted "its largest single attack in history with 2034 heavies participating" with an added five-hundred RAF and 9th USAAF bombers in "the greatest single aerial armada the world has ever seen."

Up front, as their leader, and running the risk of being picked-off because he was the brains of the mission, was General Castle.

Mr. E. G. 'Robbie' Robbins, who managed The Swan Hotel, Lavenham, during the war encouraged his service visitors to sign wall panels, which are still in position today.

Brig. Gen. Frederick W. Castle dressed for battle.

Photo: Courtesy USAAF

Let Martin Bowman continue the tale: "General Castle, former CO. of the 94th Group, Bury St. Edmunds, and now commander of the 4th Wing, drove to Lavenham airfield and elected to fly in the 487th formation, even though he carried a thirty-day leave order in his pocket, and led the 3rd Air Division on what was his 30th mission.

"Soon, Castle was in the air, and all went well until over Belgium, about 35 miles from Liege, his right outboard engine burst into flames and the propeller had to be feathered. The deputy leader took over and Castle dropped down to 20,000 ft. At this height the aircraft began vibrating badly and he was forced to take it down another three thousand feet before levelling out.

The Fortress was now down to 180mph indicated air-speed and being pursued by seven Messerschmitt 109s. They attacked and wounded the tail-gunner and left the radar navigator nursing bad wounds in his neck and shoulders.

"Castle could not carry out any evasive manoeuvres with the full-bomb load still aboard and

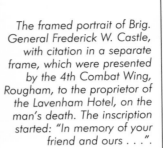

The framed portrait of Brig. General Frederick W. Castle, with citation in a separate frame, which were presented by the 4th Combat Wing, Rougham, to the proprietor of the Lavenham Hotel, on the man's death. The inscription started: "In memory of your friend and ours . . .".

Some of the many war time signatures, mostly left by RAF and USAAF visitors, on one of the panels at Lavenham, Suffolk. This was how the signatures looked in 1953.

he could not salvo them for fear of hitting Allied troops on the ground.

"Successive attacks by the fighters put another two engines out of action and the B-17 lost altitude. As Castle fought the controls in a vain effort to keep the stricken bomber level, he ordered the crew to bale out. Part of the crew baled out and then the bomber was hit in the fuel tanks and oxygen systems, which set the aircraft on fire. Castle (and 1st-Lt. Robert W. Harriman) attempted to land the flaming bomber in an open field close to the Allied lines, but nearing the ground, it went into a spin and exploded on impact."

The crash spot was near the Chateau d'Englebermont, Hody/Liege, Belgium.

General Castle was posthumously awarded the Congressional Medal of Honour – the highest ranking officer in the 8th Air Force to receive the

award – and in later years Castle Air Force Base was dedicated in his memory in America.

Interestingly, Roger Freeman, the British historian on 8th Air Force matters, who lives in Essex, sent me for a Christmas card in the early 1950s, when we were both young enthusiasts, his own water-colour impression of Castle's Fortress rising over Lavenham church to head the world's greatest air armada.

Subsequently, in his *Mighty Eighth War Diary* Freeman gave Castle four pages, concluding: "Frederick Walker Castle seemed to many to be a strange man because he did not conform to the general pattern of social behaviour among fighting men. He was the antithesis of the tough, hard-talking leader that tended to dominate the combat commands in the 8th Air Force.

"Yet he gave his life to leadership and had a combat record few other men of his rank could equal.

Once incorporating a cigarette lighter under the tail, this model B-17 Flying Fortress stood on Brig. General Frederick W. Castle's desk at 4th Combat Wing HQ, Rougham, near Bury St. Edmunds. After his death in action it was presented to the late Mr. E. G. 'Robbie' Robbins, war time proprietor of The Swan Hotel, Lavenham, and in later years came into the writer's possession after being a child's garden toy!

Above: On December 24, 1944, the 8th USAAF mounted its largest single attack in history with 2034 heavy bombers with an added 500 RAF and 9th USAAF bombers. It was the greatest single air armada the world had ever seen.

Photo: Courtesy USAAF

Below: Frank E. Beresford's painting of 94th Bomb Group Flying Fortresses, led by Brig. General Frederick W. Castle, descending through cloud near Bury St. Edmunds in June 1944.

As a man to whom duty was paramount he would have wanted nothing better than to be remembered as the only general in his country's history to die in a direct act to try and save the lives of his subordinates."

So it is at Lavenham and round about Bury St. Edmunds that Castle's name is remembered today. In the Swan Hotel, Lavenham, where Castle was a close friend of the war-time proprietor, the late Mr E.G. "Robbie" Robbins, there is a picture of the general, but all the original Castle relics, once the personal property of Mr Robbins, were passed to me for safe keeping many years ago. With them were a number of famous RAF squadron badges associated with RAF Wattisham, Suffolk, as Castle believed in Britain and America sticking together to keep the peace.

Footnote: The terrible air-fighting conditions, and the cost in American and German lives, is well illustrated in *Six Months to Oblivion: The Eclipse of the Luftwaffe Fighter Force* (Ian Allan, 1973/75).

Werner Girbig, in describing the great air-battle on Sunday, 24th December 1944, in which Brigadier-General Castle lost his life, noted:

"IV Squadron spotted the leading bombers just in front of Liege. The American fighter escort was not yet in position . . . Right across the board, *3 Jagdgeschwader* (fighter group/wing of 80 to 90 aircraft) had the largest number reported missing that day. However, one of the flying Fortresses shot down was flown by Brigadier-General Castle, one of the ablest commanders in the US 8th Air Force . . . fierce in-fighting developed over the High Venn. More and more vapour trails sliced across the blue sky; the tragic beauty of their curves, rings, wave-patterns and whorls bearing witness to watchers on the ground of the progress of the fierce battle. At 13,000 feet it was bitterly cold, and thus another hazard lay in wait for the young pilots – icing. No one knows how many pilots succumbed to icing, but it may well be that some of those reported missing were not in fact killed in action and that their remains lie hidden for ever in the wild heathland and bogs of the Venn . . . The destruction of 44 four-engined bombers bears witness to the intensity of the fighting . . . A few hours later, as the darkness closed in on Christmas Eve . . . nobody knew the terrible price that the day's operations had really cost the German fighter force . . . only much later did it become clear that 24th December fighter-pilot casualties amounted . . . to 85 killed or missing".

ETERNAL WINTER

At 35,000 feet the temperature is 67 degrees below zero. The air is so thin it does no good to breathe it. Without oxygen, a man will lose consciousness in half a minute. This is the beginning of the true stratosphere, the region where the air does not get colder, no matter how high you go. In the Second World War, as aircraft flew to new heights, but not always protected against that eternal winter, oil became gum, metal shrunk, grease froze, and bullets were liable to shatter tyres like clay pigeons.

Once displayed in the bar of The Swan Hotel, Lavenham, these RAF badges represent (left to right) No. 18 (motto 'With courage and faith'), No. 107 (We shall be there). RAF Station Wattisham ('Above the sea and above the land') and No. 110 (I neither fear nor despise')

Night Under a Wold Sky
OR 'SLEEPING IN A HAWTHORN LAIR'

WHEN I went on a press freelance assignment to Lincolnshire on a fine day in July 1989, I had every intention, that evening, of finding accommodation in order to be presentable for the following day's work. But something went wrong.

At Louth, between the city of Lincoln and the port of Grimsby where I had been dropped, I was assured of a bed in one or other of the pubs in the old market town of Binbrook, ten miles away, which still protects its 13th-century cross, while another sports a crusader's sword remembering the dead of the two great wars.

Finding transport, I sped westwards to Binbrook against a dazzling setting sun but found it deserted with pub beds a thing of the past. Three miles outside Binbrook, however, a helpful farmer dropped me by an isolated country hotel – that turned out to be full!

The time, by then, was coming up for 9 o'clock and as no one seemed to respond to my 'lift' signals from the roadside, I started walking through magnificent rolling harvest country along the road curving gently back to Binbrook.

The cloudless sky – it had been like it for days – was a deep violet and westwards, all the distant field contours – trees, hedges, gates, wood fences and farm buildings – stood out as faultless silhouettes. What a lovely day to be walking, I thought, if one hadn't to worry about finding a bed.

Near the next day's place of appointment the security guards, responsible for the property, told me that the staff I wanted to see had left for hotels as far distant as Lincoln and Grimsby.

"If you keep walking," said one of them, "you're bound to find a bed-and-breakfast place.

Well, I kept walking, but by 11 o'clock knew my luck had run out. I'd have to sleep rough for the night!

Having, by that time, retraced my steps to Binbrook's outskirts, I found myself looking down into a small valley with, distantly on the other side, the fading village lights. By walking down into the valley I felt I'd be able to find a warm, overhanging hedge.

I came to a spot where the road forked and I settled for a gnarled, old hawthorn hedge on a dry bank whose projecting canopy of foliage spread out over sloping pasture land. The lair, I felt certain, would afford protection should a thunderstorm blow up during the night.

As I struggled into the heart of the lair with my hold-all and cameras, the time was now 11.30pm. In front of me, across the pasture, a great, full, harvest-moon was ascending, but not yet in its fullest glory.

By the moonlight I was able to pick out the extent of the pasture and concluded its worn edges suggested cattle – but none were to be seen. I was separated from their pad by a short barbed-wire fence tacked to old posts.

It was 11.35pm and I was astonished at the swiftness with which the night's interludes unfolded and ended – the golden moon, riding like a huge orange in the sky, revealed a distant Lincolnshire Wolds' skyline of soft hills and scattered, dark clumps of trees.

At midnight I tucked my hands into the top of my jacket for warmth and began to doze. Binbrook's church-bell tolled. Then a calm seemed to settle over the sleeping countryside broken only by spasmodic animal and bird cries.

Oddly to begin with, and it persisted until the early hours of the morning, a solitary sheep's bleating, sometimes near and sometimes distant, suggesting a big field somewhere in the darkness, over which I now presided.

With the moon at its fullest and as beautiful as I had ever seen it from any point in England, slivers of cloud, like airships, slid over it and their edges turned to quicksilver. Minutes later the moon burst through again.

As the night wore on I heard foxes, owls and other creatures and, rather puzzling, the heavy plops of big fish leaping from water and splashing back.

While these lawful denizens of the countryside went about their nightly rituals, it transpired I was not the only human-being with his eyes open, for distantly I made out in the moonlight, a dog walking well ahead of a hunched figure by, it appeared, a beck or small river. Soon they faded from view.

Between two and three in the early morning the temperature dropped and I tucked my hands deeper into my jacket. Pungent marsh mist started to form above the beck, slow-moving, claw-like fronds crept up to my hawthorn shelter, and then, because of the bank, rolled backwards and returned to the river.

Night progressed and a big airforce 'plane of some kind passed low overhead and I remembered RAF Binbrook high up behind me, whose old airfield was a famous bomber station for nine squadrons in the 1940s. Doubtless, I thought, many of their crews down in enemy territory must have hidden like me.

Around 4 o'clock, before I could be clearly seen, I changed my shirt and socks and cleaned my dusty black shoes with a handful of dry grass. I shaved and brushed my hair using a pool of water as a rough mirror.

I had survived the night and didn't, I reckon, look too untidy for the day's business.

A day or two later, when I worked out from an ordnance map exactly where I had gone to earth that night near Binbrook, I found that I had settled down near the earthworks of an old priory. Nearby Hoe Hill Farm sheltered a long barrow and another long barrow existed on Ash Hill. Towards Tealby, not far away, snaked the Viking Way. I had slept with good company. . . .

I doubted if I would ever establish the identity of the man and dog who passed me in the night but I remembered the ballad:

'The Lincolnshire Poacher'

When I was bound apprentice, in
famous Lincolnsheer,
Full well I served my master
for more than seven year.
'Till I took up poaching, as
you shall quickly hear.
Oh, 'tis my delight of a shiny night,
in the seasons of the year.

Last of the Puffers

Having worked for three years hauling truckloads of un-fuzed bombs to Earsham bomb dump for Liberator bomber airfields in Norfolk, the old steam puffers of the L.N.E.R., kept at Beccles, Suffolk, were almost worn out by 1945. As the Waveney Valley line was single track, there was always the handing over of the right-of-way key (as shown), after which steam was got up. These pictures were taken by the author, soon after the war ended, when he boarded No. 5400 for a ride on the foot-plate to Harleston and back.

Glider 'Bashers' 1945

AFTER my American cousin, 15340767 Cpl Edward 'Bud' Miller, of Columbus Ohio, had worked with Section 9 Squadron 'C' Base, Air Depot 2, Warton, near Preston, Lancashire, on USAAF engineering work from 1944 into 1945, he moved to Germany where he was involved in helping to dispose of surplus American aircraft, particularly fighters, and sorting captured enemy planes and equipment for shipment to experimental establishments in Britain and America.

The latter work meant that he came on a variety of enemy 'planes, including many German gliders, some of which had been used by the NSFK (National Sozialistisch Flieger Korps) trainees destined to fly such advanced Luftwaffe jets as the Messerschmitt 163 and 262 and the compact little Heinkel 162 which resembled a V-l flying-bomb in appearance.

While the Allies picked carefully for the enemy's secrets, hundreds of intact German aircraft and gliders were deliberately broken up or burnt, and it was in the course of this work that my cousin sent me, in regular letters, a variety of interesting glider plates recovered from cockpits before the wrecking started.

Before looking at some of the glider plates, which I think must be quite rare acquisitions, it is interesting to reflect that soon after World War I ended, when Germany was restricted in powered-aircraft development, pioneer work on gliding was done in Germany on the 3000ft Wasserkuppe mountain in the hilly Rhoen district between Cassel and Frankfurt.

Cpl. Edward Miller by windlass at Gorleston.

There, for certain, early aerodynamic advances in sailplane design were investigated so that, by the mid-1930s, the Germans were designing stream-lined cantilever-winged gliders with enclosed cockpits and long tapered wings.

The gliding school on the Wasserkuppe was very important: pupils were trained from scratch so that by the end of 1929 alone, something like 400 pilots had gained their 'C' soaring certificates. As the Luftwaffe expanded in the middle 1930s, more and more glider men (and women) went through the school to fly bigger things.

Among the items salvaged by my cousin when he

A somewhat battered snap of Cpl. Edward Miller by an abandoned Heinkel 162 jet fighter at Cassel, Germany, bearing an operational number (4) and possibly the boar's head with white flash on shield insignia of J.G.84.

Photo: Courtesy USAAF

While abandoned enemy planes occupied some of the Cassel base, during the time the writer's cousin was stationed there, dozens of P-47 Thunderbolts, mostly for scrapping, took up even more space. The P-47 nearest the camera was a 'D' type serial number 44-2022G with two German victories. The crew chief was S/Sergeant Charles Snyder but the pilot's name was erased.

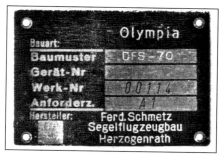

Plate from DFS 70 Olympia (Meise) glider.

Plate from Minimoa glider stamped 1939.

Plate from Kranich 2 glider stamped June 30, 1943.

Believed taken from a Heinkel 162 Salamander jet at Cassel, and associated with the pilot's seat, the cloth patch is thought to refer to 'shoulder quick release harness'.

was with the 10th Depot Repair Squadron, Cassel, in 1945-6 was a transfer silhouette of a glider superimposed with the letters ESG cut from very light ply-wood.

Today, of course, we know that these letters stood for Edmund Schneider Grunau, a famous German glider factory situated in Grunau, Silesia, which in the early 1930s was responsible for the Grunau Baby series of sailplanes.

Interestingly, the family emigrated to Australia in the 1950s and re-established the business at Gawler, near Adelaide, with help from the Gliding Federation of Australia.

Other items sent included plates from such types as the advanced Argus-powered DFS 40 Delta V which featured a prone position for the pilot. In connection with prone pilot positioning, it is interesting to note that the DFS (Deutsche Forschungsanstalt fur Segelflug (German Research Institute for Sailplanes) development programme of November 1944, provided for five Kranich ls to be so modified for research purposes by Edmund Schneider.

Of course, the DFS attracted some advanced thinkers, William Green in *The Warplanes of the Third Reich* (Macdonald and Jane's, 1970) observing: "From some aspects the title of DFS was to appear in retrospect a misnomer, for the organisation to which it was applied concerned itself with aspects of aeronautic research and development seemingly remote from the glider and gliding. The Me.163 Komet rocket-driven interceptor owed its existence to work originally undertaken at the DFS . . ."

Cousin Edward's offerings from the Luftwaffe's

Betätigung der Bremsklappen

1.) **Langsam** und **gleichmäßig** öffnen !

2.) **Möglichst vor** 150 km/h Geschwindigkeit!

3.) **Zur Verhinderung von Wolkenflügen,** im **Gefahrenfall** bei abnormalen Fluglagen und Landung, bei **Vereisungsgefahr** in den Wolken (mehrfach betätigen).

4.) **Vorsichtig abfangen** bei geöffneten Klappen!

Cockpit instruction placard for airbrakes operation – probably the Olympia or Govier.

Interesting transfer silhouette of glider with letters ESG cut from very light ply-wood of captured German glider. The letters stood for Edmund Schneider Grunau, a famous German glider factory once situated in Grunau, Silesia.

Apart from gliders, my cousin, who after the war worked with old USAAF colleagues in Ohio making and selling 100mph harnessed model planes (they made over 1500 at an early count), came on a variety of German powered aircraft, including some Heinkel 162s, the prototype of which flew for the first time on 6 December 1944, having progressed from drawing board to initial flight tests in the fantastically short period of 69 days. The machine was intended to be operated by unskilled youngsters as a last stand, which meant crashing into enemy bombers if other forms of attack failed.

Looking, as was said earlier, like the more common V-1 flying-bomb sent against this country from June 1944 until March 1945, my cousin was photographed alongside one fairly intact example bearing an operational number: 4. The unclear badge on the He.162's nose reminds me very much of the boar's head with white flash on shield carried by J.G. 84, the first operational unit to fly the type.

Cousin Edward, who sent one or two cockpit souvenirs from this He.162, captioned the picture: "Me and my rocket – Y-96 (the base number) Kassel (Cassel)."

However, only 116 pre-production and production He.162s were actually completed by the end of the war. As for those found by the Allied forces in 1945, the number was quite small –only 31, of which ten were broken up and 12 were brought to the United Kingdom for examination and tests.

In 1945, when schoolboys were still forbidden to wander around the Royal Aircraft Establishment, Farnborough, Hampshire, packed with captured

abandoned hideouts in Germany went on to include a Minimoa plate (stamped 1939), a Kassel 12 plate, a Kranich 2 plate (stamped June 30, 1943), a DFS 70 Olympia (Meise) plate and several cockpit placards, including one for airbrakes operation. In 1966 an expert source in Germany examined the relics.

As hundreds of Luftwaffe and German civilian gliders, so useful for youth training, were rounded up, mostly for burning, the late Philip Wills, who was the leading British glider pilot for nearly 30 years of his career, protested and saved many examples.

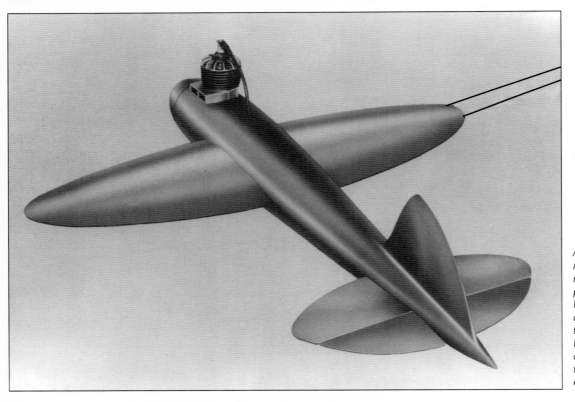

After the war, 'Bud' Miller and buddies made and sold this plane in kit form in the USA. It was capable of speeds of more than 100 m.p.h. It flew in a circle attached to two wires that controlled the elevators.

R.A.E. Pass for Entry and Exit.

TWB D i64/4

This Pass must be given up to the Warder at the gate on exit in order that the visitor may be allowed to leave the R.A.E.

Name *Christopher R Elliott*
(Signature)

Business *Snelling & Payment*
(Nature of)

To see Mr. *Passmore.*

.... Passed in by authority of Director, R.A.E.

R.A.F. Form 1371.   (*15370—13549) Wt. 31812—4268   400 Pads   10/44   T.S. **700**

Date and Time of Entry.
15. 9. 45.
0824

Date and Time of Exit.

In 1945, when schoolboys were still forbidden to wander around the Royal Aircraft Establishment, Farnborough, Hampshire, packed with captured enemy 'planes of every type, the author got into the place as 'an apprentice on trial'.

enemy planes of every type, an uncle of mine, who worked for a London builder, got me a pass into the place as "an apprentice on trial!" (see above).

In the course of that memorable day, which started as early as 6am, I was sent around the establishment on concocted errands. In a blister hangar, near a huge pile of dumped 'planes, I caught a glimpse of some small German gliders of different types. It was just possible, I thought, that cousin Edward had had a part in boxing them for us As to whether all the cockpits still had their plates I didn't dare inquire . . .!

P47's for salvage at Cassel.

German junk – mainly engines.

Junk pile – more Thunderbolts.

Me and my rocket'.

A P-38 Lightning fighter.

A B-24 Liberator, Warton.

A P-61 Black Widow night fighter bogged down.

In Praise of Trees

IN April 1985 Queen Elizabeth the Queen Mother planted a mulberry tree at Anne Hathaway's cottage at Stratfordon-Avon to inaugurate the Shakespeare Tree Garden.

The garden, which is being developed jointly by the Tree Council and the Shakespeare Birthplace Trust (Anne Hathaway was the daughter of a yeoman farmer of Shottery and married Shakespeare in 1582), is to have specimens of all the trees mentioned in Shakespeare's works. By each tree a quotation which refers to it will be displayed.

Soon after the tree-planting act by the Queen Mother, the Tree Council reported a long list of trees linked to the poet and dramatist's works, including almond, apple, ash, bay, birch, box, cedar, cherry, chestnut, crab, cypress, elder, fig, hawthorn, holly, laurel, medlar, mulberry, myrtle, oak, peach, pear, pine, plane, plum, pomegranate, quince, sycamore, walnut, willow and yew.

This revival of interest in trees reminds me that, years ago, a shipwright gave me a sweet-smelling box full of marked wood samples of all his hardwoods and that a carpenter, coming to the end of his days, passed on some highly interesting reference books on timbers for woodwork.

The carpenter's old books tell, for example, about the hardwoods of the United Kingdom – about the oak, ash, elm, beech, sycamore, walnut, poplar, the willows, plane, the chestnuts, lime, alder and other native hardwoods.

It is interesting to thumb through the old works and find out how some of the woods were being used sixty years ago.

Massive hornbeam at Worlingham, Suffolk, in 1948.

A very old chestnut at Snaresbrook, London.

British Oak – barge- and boat-building required planks in varying thicknesses and long lengths. The same trades also used the many crooked limbs for what were known as 'knees', which formed part of the framework of wooden boats. Wheelwrights and coach-builders were also large consumers of oak for the framework of heavy and other vehicles. The railway wagon and carriage construction firms were at one time heavy consumers of oak for the building of the frames of rolling stock. The building trade, too, took fair supplies for use in the making of sills, frames, newels, stair-treads and similar work. Oak was also used for quality coffin-work, posts and gates for farms use, ladder-rungs, spokes and many other miscellaneous needs where a tenacious and durable material was required.

British Walnut – long occupied a recognised position for its fruit-bearing qualities apart from the timber it provided, thriving fairly well in the southern counties, and as far as the north Midlands. However, the uses of English walnut, when it could be procured, was limited. Formerly, when it was plentiful, it was utilised in the making of furniture. Then it became the chief material in the making of gun-stocks and remains so to this day.

Ash – in the estimation of many "the finest, most useful and valuable wood that is grown in the country." It was the timber that took first place in the estimation of the wheelwright and carriage-builder for the framework of vehicles, for the shafts and for

When old wooden vessels were broken up, crooked oak limbs used in their construction, known as 'knees', were sometimes embodied in barns as in this case at Gislingham, Suffolk.

the felloes of the wheels. It was the wood for tool handles – spades, forks and shovels and formed the woodwork of agricultural machines. In the First World War, the forest and straightest grown timber was used in the construction of aeroplanes, high prices being paid over seventy years ago for selected ash. Propellers in 1914-18 took much native timber, Boulton and Paul, of Norwich, who also made aeroplanes, making a record number of propellers for East Anglia – 7835.

Space considerations prevent a further listing of the usefulness of woods in everyday life.

At Henham Park, near Wangford, Suffolk, shortly before the 18th-century hall was demolished in the early 1950s, I was allowed to examine and 'bottle' in a jar a fragment of the Henham Oak – a venerable tree to which an interesting story of loyalty and wifely affection is attached.

Agnes Strickland recorded: "One of the village chroniclers told me many years ago that there was a brave gentleman of the Rous family in the great rebellion, whose life was preserved, when a party of the rebels came down to Henham with a warrant for his arrest, by his lady concealing him in the hollow trunk of that venerable old oak beneath the windows of the hall.

"This tree, being used by the family as a summer-house, was luckily provided with a door faced with bark, and which closed so artificially that strangers, not aware of the circumstance, would never suspect that the tree was otherwise sound.

"The hero of the tales was, I presume, the Cavalier baronet, Sir John Rous, to whom Charles II wrote an autographed letter thanking him for his loyal services.

"According to the story, the Roundhead authorities used threatening language to the lady to make her declare her husband's retreat, but she courageously withstood all their menaces.

All that remained of the Henham, Suffolk, oak of Civil War days, in the early 1950s, the last living bough being blown down in 1903.

A magnificent cedar prepared for felling at Assington, Suffolk, in May 1952.

The English countryside, in ancient times, was heavily wooded.

This elephant-legged tree was a feature of Wimbledon Common, London, in the 1970s.

The Henham, Suffolk, estate was once noted for its old trees.

"They remained there for two or three days, during which time, she, not daring to trust anyone with the secret, stole softly out at night to supply her lord with food and to assure herself of his safety.

"I fancy this conjugal heroine must have been the beautiful Elizabeth Knevitt, whose portrait is preserved at Henham. The oak was afterwards a noted resort for select Jacobite meetings of a convivial nature, when Sir Robert Rous, and two or three staunch adherents of the exiled house of Stuart, were accustomed to drink deep healths 'to the king over the water', on bended knees".

The late Lord Stradbroke, in giving me permission to look round the hall and grounds, told me in May 1953: "I believe the last living bough of this tree was blown down in 1903, since when the remaining trunk has gradually mouldered away until many years ago it became merely a heap of rotten wood held together by iron stays, evidently emplaced at some time when the tree was alive, and grown over with ivy and roses. For a long time no particle of sound-wood has remained, and there is therefore, now no possibility of preserving the tree."

This fine elm tree at Lavenham, Suffolk, fell during the Great Gale of October 1987.

110

Walberswick's Patriotic Film-Maker

WRITING in 1954, Lindsay Anderson described Humphrey Jennings as "the only real poet the British cinema has yet produced". Equally, he was "a major contributor to modern ideas of art".

Frank Humphrey Sinkler Jennings was born on 19th August 1907, at The Gazebo, Walberswick, and when he was a little boy he was carried in the basket of his mother's bicycle to picnic on the common between Walberswick and Blythburgh. In the summer there was the bright yellow gorse: and sometimes a spark from the famous Southwold/Halesworth railway, which closed in 1929, set the dry bushes on fire . . . .

As a young boy Jennings, who in the Second World War was to give England some of the best film documentaries, saw the soldiers of 1914-1918 by the ferry 'testing horses for France' while men on the banks of the *Blyth* 'hallooed and shot-off guns in the air' . . . .

At Walberswick, as he grew up, Jennings was a witness of the ceaseless struggle between Man and the Sea. But what struck him especially was the unwritten story of the people's resistance, 'uncelebrated in words their struggle and labour' against whatever threatened . . . .

These three aspects – fires on the common, preparations for war and the sufferings of ordinary people – must have had some impact on Jennings' character, later reflected in his films, and I take them from a number of his experiences in early life because I feel they are naturally important.

In 1916 Jennings went to the Perse School, Cambridge, and in 1926 won a scholarship to Pembroke College, Cambridge, to read English. He became deeply involved in amateur dramatics, and started to design sets and costumes.

By 1934 – and this is what this article is about – he had joined the GPO Film Unit and was living at Blackheath, London, near the film studios, working under the celebrated Alberto Cavalcanti.

In February 1938, Jennings, for some reason, gave a talk on the BBC on 'The Disappearance of Ghosts'. Taking the title literally, I wonder if it had anything to do with George Orwell, the literary pseudonym of Eric Arthur Blair of *Animal Farm and 1984* fame, who sometimes lived I at Southwold and who, I recall, once claimed he saw a ghost in Walberswick churchyard.

In the early part of 1940 Jennings worked on

Humphrey Jennings c.1933.   Photo: Courtesy of Mary-Lou Jennings

Spring Offensive, Welfare of the Workers and *London Can Take It* – all films demonstrating Britain's ability to survive during the blitz and, after the fall of France, in Europe alone. *London Can Take It* was aimed specifically at the Empire and American market.

As the Battle of Britain developed, and the need for co-ordination became necessary in all things, the GPO Film Unit was transferred to the Ministry of Information and the Crown Film Unit.

After his family left for America in September 1940, Jennings started work on *Heart of Britain*, a complement to the city-based *London Can Take It*, which reflected the country and towns of Britain at war.

Jennings, in a letter at that time to his wife in America, said that while the blitz was consuming, and would go on consuming, so many London lives and her precious, old buildings, 'a curious kind of unselfishness is developing which can stand all that and more'.

Early in 1941 – by then London had suffered several major fire-raids – Jennings began *Words for Battle* which juxtaposed words and pictures to show what Britain was fighting for. By the early summer he was working on *Listen to Britain*, filming on location in London, Manchester, Blackpool and the Lake District.

In October, as autumn came, he began writing the first treatment of a film on the work of the recently

On the night of the blitz on London, 7th September 1940, Reginald Mills, a professional illustrator, who was a member of a fire-fighting unit, made this painting of a furniture factory blaze. On 29th December 1940, W. Marvyn Wright (top right) saw firemen on a roof nearSt Paul's Cathedral. Unable to obtain a canvas, he painted this picture on a ping-pong table-top!

formed National Fire Service, another vital piece of co-ordination which unified the mixed fire brigades of the country, to become *Fires Were Started*. Location shooting on the Fire Service film started in February 1942 and continued through to April.

Meanwhile, the Germans massacred the citizens of the mining village of Lidice, Czechoslovakia, and the Ministry of Information decided to commemorate the obliterated village in the form of a film. To make it, Jennings went to Wales and settled on the mining village of Cwmgiedd. The film was called *The Silent Village*.

But *Fires Were Started*, undoubtedly one of the most dramatic Home Front films ever made, led to a major row over cuts in order to conform with the demands of the commercial distributors.

I remember seeing *Fires Were Started*, as a boy during the war, and it was interesting many years later when I became editor of one of the leading Fire Service magazines, to recognise some of the natural players in senior post-war positions.

Bearing in mind that the preservation of St. Paul's Cathedral, London, during the main serial on-slaughts of 1940-1941 lay very much in the hands of firemen and firewatchers (firewatchers came from all over the country to do their stint), Jennings in one of his 'war poems' wrote:

> I see London
> I see the dome of Saint Paul's like the forehead of Darwin.

In July, 1944, Jennings was filming on location in the South of England on a film about the new German V-1 flying bomb, the first of which landed here a few days after the Allied armies got a grip on the Normandy beaches on 6th June.

Jennings continued to work on a variety of films, all portraying the land and life he loved so much, and although he went on after the war making films until his death in 1950, I think it is appropriate to remember that one of his last war films was *A Diary for Timothy* – the story of a boy born as peace came in 1945 who had never tasted the blackout nor seen Londoners sheltering from the terror from the air.

No doubt, as Jennings put the ordinary man and woman on film in the Second World War, his thoughts went back sometimes – to picnics long ago near Walberswick when the gorse was so yellow and, when sparks flew from the local train, the flames were so fierce and hot. But, as his later films illustrated so often, the spirit of new life strove to poke through the ashes to make the world green again.

The Lady with Unseeing Eyes

IN THE EARLY 1930s, when I lived on the southern outskirts of Beccles, we used to play in Sandy Lane, which led up to the London Road level-crossing. Not far from the level-crossing, on the left going towards Weston, there was a cottage which had in its little garden the wooden effigy of a woman. Her head, as far as I can remember, tilted skywards, and the folds of her full-length skirt made her look as if she was on an errand of some moment.

Her features, being etched in black paint, made her a staring figure whose unseeing eyes were disturbing. Sometimes on a dull day, when I was alone, the silent figure on the garden bank made me quicken my pace, and I never looked over the hedge to meet her wooden-gaze if I could avoid it.

Who was she? Well, it wasn't until I sat down to write this article that it dawned on me, after all these years, that the figure, if it was not something from a fairground, must have been a ship's figurehead from, perhaps, a wreck at Pakefield or Kessingland.

I wonder how many people remember the set of cigarette-cards put out by John Player & Sons in 1912, depicting 25 ships' figureheads? Such a set was given to me years ago and is now, I believe, quite valuable. The set has some East Anglian associations.

Take, for example, the figurehead from HMS *Royal William* (No. 1 in the picture). The first *Royal William* was launched in Charles II's reign as the *Royal Prince*, her name having been changed to the *Royal William* by order of William III. She fought with distinction at, among other scenes, Sole Bay.

According to a report I have, entitled "A Note on the Drawings . . . illustrating The Battle of Sole Bay, May 28, 1672, and The Battle of Texel, August 11,

An old Devon salt eyes a pretty young figurehead attached to a building near the harbour at Salcombe.

1673," by Julian S. Corbett (it was published in 1908), the vessel came in for some rough treatment off the Suffolk coast. "About the same hour," the report says, "De Ruyter's concentration on the *Royal Prince* had so cut-up her masts that she was unmanageable, and the Duke was persuaded to shift his flag to the *St. Michael*, leaving Narbrough in charge of the *Royal Prince*, for Cox had been killed early in the action. Almost immediately he had to

Three cards from the set of ships' figureheads issued in 1912. All three have East Anglian associations.

The figurehead from the sailing ship Princess Augusta, which was driven ashore at Southwold on 28th October 1838.

tack to avoid the bank off Lowestoft."

The next cigarette card (2) shows the figurehead from HMS *Seahorse*. It was in 1774 that Nelson, of Burnham Thorpe, then 16 years of age, was appointed midshipman on-board the *Seahorse*.

The last card (3) shows the figurehead from the *Sybille*, which was built in 1847. It is especially interesting as having been carved from a portrait of Lady Hamilton, Nelson's mistress, as a Sibyl.

One wonders, after recollections of so many old ships' figureheads in odd places years ago, what has become of the majority. What is clear is that long ago carpenters worked in shipyards as sculptors in wood, oak and elm being the most popular woods in British yards. They chipped and carved gigantic figureheads for, it was said, a ship in olden times without a figurehead was inconceivable. Grinling Gibbons, the English wood-carver, who was born in 1648, put some of his skill into figureheads for men-of-war.

I have heard it said that in the heyday of figureheads, when as much as £7000 alone was spent on carving and gilding a vessel, they were thought so highly of that when danger threatened they were

An old ship's figurehead seen at Southwold, Suffolk, in the 1950s.

An artist painting the figurehead of the old schooner-yacht Wild Flower by the River Blyth in 1950.

unshipped. Arms, legs – and even heads – were sometimes made to unscrew for safe stowage!

And the chances are, if you find a figurehead of a woman without a pedigree, it most likely portrays the wife of some forgotten sea-captain. For the plump little ladies in early Victorian dress – the effigies of captains' wives – were once upon a time common on the prows of colliers and the like.

Southwold fishermen, in the 1950s, told a good few tales of the Suffolk coast, one of which concerned 'a bobbing woman' they rowed hard to rescue. But she turned out to be 'a deadpan wooden effigy of some old sea-captain's wife or port mistress!'

But the custom of decorating a vessel apparently began way back in the dim past – in ancient Egypt and India, where an eye was painted on either side of the prow.

I wonder how many figureheads are left in East Anglia today?

But ships are not the only vehicles of travel that have carried decorated prows. Beginning in the Great War (1914-1918), airmen started to paint the noses of their aircraft vivid colours. In the last World War (1939-1945), American airmen – particularly fighter pilots – were in the habit of painting the noses of their planes to represent the head of a beast or bird. The fashion spread to bigger aircraft – bombers – so that by 1944 B-24 Liberators of the Norfolk 2nd Air Division could look quite fearsome.

Beowulf
COULD HE HAVE KNOWN DEEPING FEN?

AS THE Sutton Hoo research committee's 10-year look at the implications of the 7th century Anglo-Saxon ship burials at Snape, near Aldeburgh, and Sutton Hoo, near Woodbridge, Suffolk, enters its third year, the subject of *Beowulf*, the first great Anglo-Saxon poem, is bound to interest a growing audience for both ships, excavated in the 1860s and the 1930s respectively, echo passages in the saga.

In an article last year, I touched on the possibility of Beowulf, the hero of the poem, having a connection with the silted port of Uggeshall/Frostenden, now inland from Covehithe, Suffolk, but the pundits ruled it out.

Likewise, when I sent *Beowulf* up the Suffolk coast into the then wide estuary covering much of Norfolk in order to deal with the Grendel monster in Fritton Lake, near where in the 1830s an Anglo-Saxon boat was unearthed, there was silence . . .

With *Beowulf*, however the story is viewed, one gets the impression that the principal Grendel monster was a marsh or fen creature and that such beasts – prehistoric left-overs I suggest – could have been driven to fresh-water (like Fritton Lake) due to severe weather upheavals of biblical proportions.

As the dragon-like beasts of Beowulf's time all had fiery qualities, could not this appearance have arisen because the creatures were nauseated by sulphurous fumes in the water from earthquake openings or a massive meteorite blasting the soft fen country around the *Wash* without any noticeable traces today?

Also, could not their glowing forms have been due to phosphorous on their bodies from rotting food in their fishy lairs – the kind of condition which has led to herons and owls, as an example, sometimes being mistaken for ghosts?

So much for *Beowulf* v. the Grendel family of monsters. But an examination of all the saints of Eastern England is most revealing, since several of them in the 7th century undoubtedly helped to shape the English character. I wonder if another clue to the origin of *Beowulf* lies in St. Guthlac (AD673-714) who is associated with Crowland Abbey, lying on the edge of *Deeping Fen*, close to the meeting place of Lincolnshire, Northamptonshire and Cambridgeshire?

Belonging to the royal family of Mercia, Guthlac, like Beowulf, was "born to do daring deeds", many as an outlaw. Then, repentant, he turned to religion,

Left: Could the demons described by St Guthlac have been ferocious-looking Danish raiders from the Wash?

Above: Fragment from the 6th-8th century Beowulf, the first great Anglo-Saxon poem.

finally rowing to "a sort of island, as much infested by demons as the deserts of Egypt."

As for the demons, they were "in countenance horrible, and they had great heads, and a long neck, and a lean visage; they were filthy and squalid in their beards, and they had rough ears, and crooked nebs, and fierce eyes, and foul mouths; and their teeth were like horses' tusks, and their throats were filled with flame. . . ."

Faced by the horde, Guthlac, the brave, did not quail and stuck to his island cell in the fens. Anyway, unlike Beowulf, he wasn't killed but, aided by his patron saint, Bartholomew, destroyer of idols, who in the *Beowulf* tradition faced a thousand armed men before suffering a cruel death, Guthlac triumphed after a struggle in muddy waters laced with brambles. Thus the "Crulande (Crowland) devils" were driven into the sea.

However, before Guthlac achieved this victory, it is interesting to note that "they beat him with iron whips (maces or clubs I suggest), and after that they brought him on their creaking wings (an allusion to the flexible wings on their helmets I fancy) between the cold region of the air." Could the demons have been Danish raiders?

For 15 years, says the old record, St Guthlac dwelt in the fen country, which must have been near the *Wash*, and when he died the monks founded Crowland Abbey to mark his piety.

The abbey, by all accounts, was extremely rich in the kind of possessions Beowulf seems to have known in the poem, "its twelve altars rich with the gifts of Danish vikings and princes" won over to christianity.

Jets & East Anglia

40 YEARS AGO

I T is impossible, in the 1980s, to think of the US 3rd-Air Force bases in East Anglia without also thinking of jet aircraft. Yet 40 years ago this week, the thought of jet aircraft in that part of the world was linked with the most serious threat to Allied air superiority since the Battle of Britain.

As the end of World War II neared in the European theatre, the 8th US Army Air Force, based in the UK, faced a little-publicised crisis as advanced German jet and rocket fighters, equipped with sophisticated weaponry, challenged them in large packs.

For some weeks, beginning in March 40 years ago and continuing into April, the situation facing the American fliers, who had been given the role of daylight sorties, was menacing.

Vulnerable only to the Allies' hottest fighter, the P-51 Mustang (top speed around 440 mph) and then only at take-off and landing, the Messerschmitt 262 jet (530 mph plus) and the Messerschmitt 163 rocket (590 mph plus) fighters forced the American escort pilots to fly their piston-engined 'planes to their

In 1960 ex-Corporal E. 'Bud' Miller, of Columbus, Ohio, sent this picture to England of the Messerschmitt 262 on display in Dayton Air Force Museum. Interestingly, the 20ft wing-span high-wing-loading DFS Stummel-Habicht (Hawk) glider, which first flew in May 1943, and was at the the Royal Aircraft Establishment, Farnborough, in 1945, was used by trainee-pilots destined to fly such jets as the Messerschmitt 262. In June 1994, a Texas engineer was reported to be building a batch of replica 262s from scratch.

Colonel Johannes Steinhoff was the first man in history to command a regular formation of jet fighters. This portrait of him, given to the writer not long after the war by the German ace, shows him before he suffered terrible burns to his face in a Messerschmitt 262 jet crash in 1945. In 1967 he underwent a plastic surgery operation on his eyelids at Princess Mary's Hospital, RAF Halton, Buckinghamshire.

endurance limits as a kind of second Battle of Britain situation arose.

While the 8th Air Force at that time was the strongest bomber and fighter force ever assembled in war, and the RAF possessed a handful of operational Gloster Meteor jet (410 mph plus) fighters, the viper-like jet thrusts of the dying Luftwaffe posed a real threat to the Allies. No American operational jet fighter was contemplated before the autumn of 1945.

But the German jet threat was not unexpected. As far back as 29 July 1944, P-38 Lightning pilot Capt. Arthur Jeffrey, 479th Fighter Group, Wattisham, Suffolk, attacked and photographed with its camera guns an Me.163 rocket-fighter, which he believed he shot down.

In daylight after that, the USAAF, and the RAF to some extent, continued to have spasmodic encounters, mostly very fleeting, and between November and December 1944, the Luftwaffe lost 11 jets.

Meanwhile, what were thought to be German jet test establishments and production plants were heavily attacked, but the scientists and craftsmen simply retired to underground hide-outs to continue work. Thus the visual destruction of what seemed to be the heart of the Luftwaffe's jet production was misleading.

Still, a few astute Allied air force commanders believed "it was entirely possible that jets could upset the balance of air power in Europe".

ME. 163 AND ME. 262 AIRFIELDS

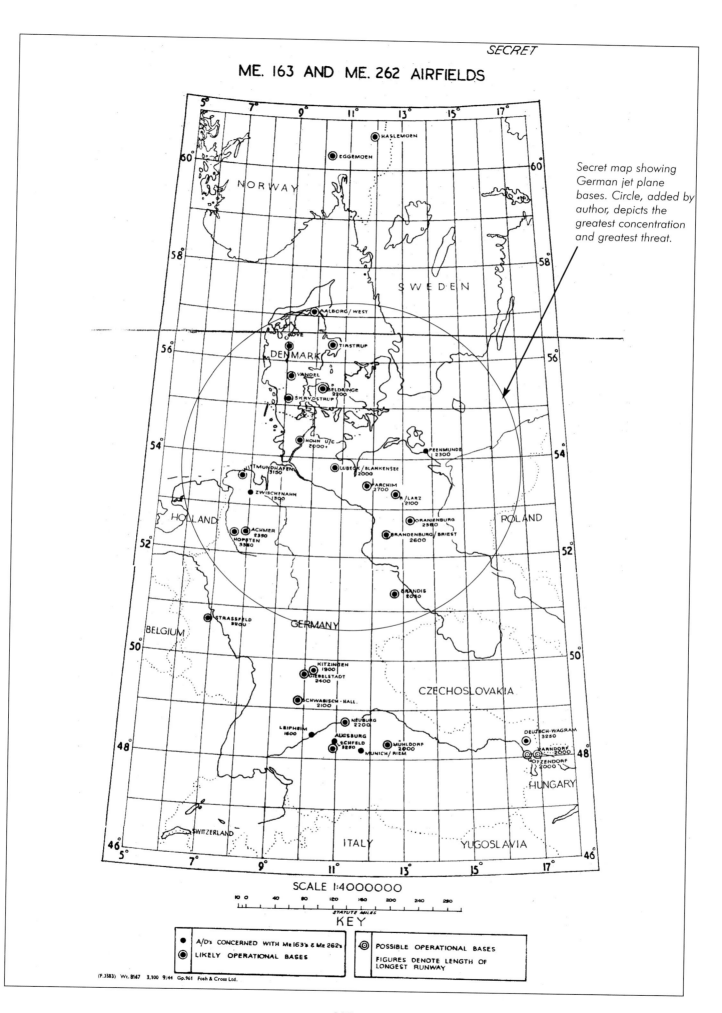

Secret map showing German jet plane bases. Circle, added by author, depicts the greatest concentration and greatest threat.

SCALE 1:4000000

KEY

● A/D's CONCERNED WITH Me 163's & Me 262's	◉	POSSIBLE OPERATIONAL BASES
◉ LIKELY OPERATIONAL BASES		FIGURES DENOTE LENGTH OF LONGEST RUNWAY

(F.3383) Wt. 8167 3,100 9/44 Gp.961 Fosh & Cross Ltd.

General Adolf Galland formed the famous JV44 wing flying the Messerschmitt 262 jet fighters. He had 104 victories.

Boy's sketch of a damaged B17 bomber, with a big hole blown in its starboard wing-root, returning over Beccles, Suffolk, on 18th March 1945, when German jets rose in force.

Things came to a head on 3 March 1945 when, as a young British visitor authorised to watch the 357th Fighter Group in a day's action at Leiston, Suffolk, I was the innocent spectator of Mustangs returning from a historic brush with German jets, in which two 357th pilots, Capt. John L. Sublett and Capt. Ivan McGuire, hit and claimed as damaged a pair of Me.262s.

Also, when peace came, I learned that Capt. Donald H. Bochkay, who did two tours with the 357th totalling 123 missions, was one of the few American pilots in the war to destroy two Me.262s. American Air Force historians declared five years later:

"The opposition on 3 March 1945, came from the dreaded jets. More than 50 Me.262s and Me.163s playfully encircled the slower P-51s, making a few attacks and eluding the Mustangs without apparent difficulty.

"Finally, the jets shot down six American fighters and three bombers before allowing themselves to be driven off by the P-51s. The Germans seemed to be experimenting with formations and tactics and were not prepared for another two weeks to challenge the Allies again."

After the two weeks in which the Allied air forces had encountered practically no German air opposition, the biggest daylight raid ever mounted on Berlin – 1250 American bombers shielded by 14 Mustang groups – on 18 March "revealed that the long-hovering menace of a jet air force had materialised".

German air and ground opposition that day was surprising for a country nearly defeated. Twenty-four bombers and five fighters were lost, mainly to jet fighters which attacked in formations as large as 36 aircraft and displayed, as American Air Force historians later noted, "a range of interception greater than the Americans expected".

One of the Royal Aircraft Establishment, Farnborough, Heinkel 162 Salamander jet fighters, often seen flying in the area in 1945/46.

Another advanced German 'plane seen at the Royal Aircraft Establishment, Farnborough, in 1945, was this Messerschmitt 163 rocket-propelled type. It is known that at least 29 Komets, as they were named, came out of Germany at various times, 25 were in England, five in America, four in France, two in Canada and one in Australia. At least 10 of these Komets in the 1970s were in museums around the world, a good example being the one in the Imperial War Museum collection at Duxford. On using up its highly volatile fuel, the Komet had to be glided home, as potential pilots were first tutored on gliders for fast, deadstick landings.

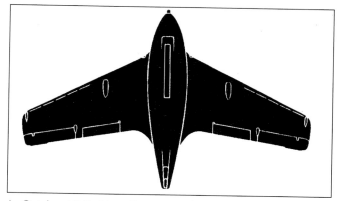

In October 1941, Heini Dittmar reached 624mph in experimental version of the Messerschmitt 163.

On that day I was in the garden of my home in Beccles, Suffolk, a town well-known to the 8th Air Force as a check point, when the battered B-17 Fortress formations returned, and it was then that I made a sketch of one of the cripples, a huge hole blown in its starboard wing, and dated it.

On 30 March 1945, as the war progressed, a brand new Me.262 jet was flown into American hands at Frankfurt, Germany, by a German test pilot deserter.

An important prisoner, whom the Allies could have done with a year earlier, the pilot who was on his way to London for interrogation was first taken to Leiston airfield in Suffolk, for a question and answer session on jet aircraft. Interestingly the 357th, whose pilots had tasted the hot breath of the new German jets on such unequal terms, was the only 8th Air Force operational unit to have him as its guest, with some air battles still to be fought.

So advanced were the German jet designs of early 1945 that aspects appear to this day in American, British and Russian supersonic aircraft. Otherwise, for the Allies, it was a close shave at a time of apparent air supremacy.

Forty years after the jet war crisis the lesson is: never under-estimate a foe, even in his death throes.

Footnote: The Bell P-59 Aeracomet jet-fighter design, which was ordered on 5th September 1941, took the British Whittle thermal jet propulsion unit. In October 1941, a Whittle engine, a set of manufacturing drawings and a number of engineers from Power Jets Ltd, were flown to America to assist their development programme.

It is said that the reason why the Americans seemed to drag their heels over jet development was because their aircraft industry, geared in a massive way to conventional aircraft construction, believed with the USAAF, that they could beat Germany and Japan in the air with propeller-driven 'planes through sheer numbers. The prediction nearly proved incorrect. Similar British help to Russia on jet engine development helped the enemy in the Korean War in the early 1950s.

It was reported in 2003 that the first flyable replica-Messerschmitt 262 had been damaged in a landing accident at the end of its second test-flight in America. Authentic in most respects, its engines are, however, General Electric J85 turbo-jets in place of the German Jumo 004s. Five replica machines were in stages of completion, priced around $2-million apiece. One of the five went to the Messerschmitt Foundation in Munich, Germany. Of the 1400-odd Messerschmitt 262s built for the Luftwaffe only eight survive, but only as ground exhibits.

Artist's License

Modern artists, often short of ideas, are in the habit of consulting others' photographs. Here a cosy farm shed at Sotherton, near Halesworth, photographed by the author in the 1950s, with water butt, hollyhocks, swinging half-doors and cat dish apparent, was years later converted into a pencil sketch by artist 'J/F'.

Sir Alfred's Letter

THERE'S a good deal of similarity in the work of two great East Anglian painters, now dead, Sir Alfred Munnings, of Dedham Essex, and Edward Seago, of Ludham Norfolk. But in some other respects they were quite different.

Liking both artists' work because they did such magnificent paintings of the East Anglian scene, I have their various books, and in *Tideline: The Ebb and Flow of Memory and Experience* (Collins, 1948) Edward Seago describes how a stranger, Florence M. Pennymore, wrote in praise of one of his books and his artistry.

Anyway, to cut a long story short, he didn't just brush her off but took the trouble to answer her letter. Then, one day, he went to Devon to see her and the window-view she kept talking about

But Sir Alfred Munnings, by all accounts, was a different person altogether and the following story is testimony of what I mean.

Sir Alfred's 'other side' came to light in 1953 when, one day, an artist acquaintance of mine, the late Miss Jo Furbank, of Great Cornard, near Sudbury Suffolk, wrote that she'd received "a shocking letter from someone of importance in the art world" and that she was "terribly upset."

Being a keen young reporter, my ears pricked up at the news, and I was soon at her door.

The offended artist, Miss Jo Furbank.

She thrust into my hand a piece of notepaper headed "From Sir Alfred Munnings, KCVO, PPRA, LL.D, Castle House, Dedham, Colchester . . ." with the following message in rough pencil scrawl:

"Why send me a parcel which I have to do up again? Never, since I was a boy, did I ever send such things to artists.

"These are good efforts and no doubt you enjoy doing such honest work, but I can give no advice. Remember that I have scores of letters which are impossible to answer – that I have work to do also – Sorry! *Alfred Munnings*"

What had Miss Furbank done to upset this ex-president of the Royal Academy (1944-1949) and world-famous painter of horses, one of whose paintings, *The Start at Newmarket,* was sold at Christie's in London in March, 1984, for a record £220,000?

All she did was to send Sir Alfred two of her artistic works for criticism – a painting of St. Andrew's Church, Great Cornard, and a 1951 Festival of Britain card she had designed. She felt that the artist's autobiography (contained in three volumes, *An Artist's Life, The Second Burst* and *The Finish*) was a reflection of a man who would be slowing down a bit and would have time to enjoy his fan mail.

In that doorstep encounter with Miss Furbank in 1953 she said: "Just look at this – this little piece of Munnings at his worst. I don't think I want his letter. Take it away. Burn it. He's not a bit like his autobiography – not a bit."

Well, I didn't burn the letter. Sir Alfred, on the other hand, lost a supporter in Miss Furbank.

Then, on 17th July 1959, Sir Alfred, who was born at Mendham Mill, on the *Waveney,* and left Framlington College, Suffolk, at the age of 14 to be apprenticed to a firm of lithographers in Norwich, died at the age of eighty after a remarkable career achieved in spite of a very serious handicap.

At the age of twenty, not long after he set up his first studio in a former carpenter's shop at Mendham, he was pushing through a hedge with some dogs when a thorn snapped back and totally blinded his right eye.

Sir Alfred Munnings by Sir Alfred Munnings – the great artist at his easel.

Thus the major output of this great artist was produced with the use of only one eye. Perhaps his one eye made him a bit testy? Appropriately, he ended his career in John Constable's country by the Stour.

On 2nd July 1959, a few days after his death, the following tribute from poet John Masefield, For Alfred Munnings, appeared in, I believe, The Times.

The shadows lengthen in the summer eve;
The rooks draw towards roost on flagging wings;
O friend how very lovely are the things,
The English things, you helped us to perceive.

FROM SIR ALFRED MUNNINGS, K.C.V.O., P.P.R.A., LL.D., CASTLE HOUSE, DEDHAM, COLCHESTER.
Telephone DEDHAM 2127

Why send me a parcel which I have to do up again ` Never—since I was a boy — did I ever send any things to artists .

There are good efforts & no doubt for anyone doing such honest work, but I can give no advice. Remember that I have scores of letters which are impossible to answer. — that I have work to do also ———

Sorry. Alfred M

Built of English Oak

WOOD, like water, is an essential ingredient of life and has been since the beginnings of man as an artificer. Both these necessities of life are, however, taken very much for granted and most people seldom give a thought to wood and water in this context. Take, for example, wood. The following is a translation of an inscription which appears in Portugal wherever timber trees are growing:

'Ye who pass by and would raise your hand against me, hearken ere you harm me. I am the heat of your hearth on the cold winer nights, the friendly shade screening you from the summer sun, and my fruits are refreshing draughts quenching your thirst as you journey on. I am the beam that holds your house, the board of your table, the bed on which you lie and the timber that builds your boat. I am the handle of your hoe, the door of your homestead, the wood of your cradle and the shell of your coffin. I am the bread of kindness and the flower of beauty. Ye who pass by, listen to my prayer – harm me not'.

An idea of the home timber position in the two great wars can be got from Frank House's *Timber at War*, published by Ernest Benn in 1963: 'At the outbreak of the first Great War in 1914 no official organisation existed in this country in connection with timber supplies or forestry. No reliable information was available as to the country's timber resources, except that Ordnance Survey maps showed approximately 3,000,000 acres as woodlands. Approximately 80 per cent of our total consumption of hardwoods was imported and more than 95 per cent of softwoods. As the war progressed the demand for timber increased, while, with the opening of the German submarine campaign, imports became increasingly difficult. A large increase in home production became vitally necessary. This was sponsored in turn by one or two Government Departments, until finally vested in the Board of Trade. The Canadian Forestry Corps was then

formed to assist in production, both in this country and in France.

'At the outbreak of war in 1939 more precise knowledge of the actual position existed. The Board of Trade had already obtained a census of production from all home timber merchants and more information was available as to our resources of growing timber from the census of woodlands which had been undertaken by the Forestry Commission. Returns of stocks of all sawn timber were almost immediately called for. The general supply position disclosed was far from satisfactory, owing to the extremely heavy demands for all classes of timber in the early part of the war. A large portion of our total imports normally came from the Baltic, whence supplies were precarious and, in fact, before long ceased entirely. It soon became only too apparent that a large bulk of our timber requirements would have to be met from home-grown sources. What was the position?

'A great quantity of the best of our mature timber had been cut during the 1914-18 war, and while, through the combined efforts of the Forestry Commission and private owners a considerable quantity had been replanted only that planted in the first few years after the war had reached pitwood size and could be of any value. The volume of increase in standing timber due to annual increment would have been more than offset by the amount cut during the last twenty years, so that, taking it as a whole, we were considerably worse off for standing timber than in 1914.'

Yes, the tree is certainly one of man's best friends, despite the coming of synthetic materials, and it is true that until quite recently the RNLI, for its main building material, depended on a variety of woods. A box of wood samples, recently turned out of an office

Various woods being seasoned.

122

at the RNLI headquarters at 42 Grosvenor Gardens, and now reserved for the day when the life-boat service has its own museum, pointed to some of the following woods: English oak, Honduras mahogany, teak, elm, pitch pine, silver spruce, larch, cedar, walnut and beach.

Further evidence of wood in the raw can be got from old photographs preserved by the RNLI.

For example, there are photographs of an elephant hauling a teak log in Burma in the early 1930s 'for building of English lifeboats'. There are photographs of RNLI timber converters, also taken in the 1930s, using their templets for selecting the best natural curves, just as navy converters did in the days of Elizabeth I when selected standing trees were logged to provide essential parts for man-o-wars for many years ahead.

One 1 3/4-ton oak crook, for instance, taken from the Haddiscoe Hall Estate, Norfolk three years before, was in May, 1932, taken via Darby Brothers, timber merchants, of Beccles, Suffolk, to Beccles railway station for conveyance by rail to a yard building RNLI boats. Another picture shows the butt-end of a 200 year-old oak crook, weighing five

tons, in position over a saw pit with two hand-sawers in position. The crook was brought to Totnes, Devon, for life-boat stems in the mid-1930s.

It is a sobering thought that not so long ago all planks used in building were sawn up by this slow and laborious method. The sawyers worked in pairs – a top sawyer and a bottom sawyer – and it would be likely to take a young man many years before he worked his way out of the pit into the superior (and much less dusty) position of top sawyer.

The toughness of English oak was demonstrated to the full in May, 1942, when a boat-yard at Cowes, IoW, which was doing contract work for the RNLI, was gutted by fire-bombs. Apparently some of the incendiary bombs fell among oak crooks, from which stem and stern posts are made, but the crooks, it was pointed out, 'are of English oak – they were charred but not destroyed'.

In the specification for building a 52-foot twin-screw Barnett type motor life-boat dated July 1957, it was stated: 'All timber will be supplied by the Institution. In converting the wood generally, considerable margin is necessary to allow for subsequent shrinkage. On receipt of the order to build immediate steps are to be taken to convert as far as possible all the wood that will be required, and it is to be placed where and as it will best season and harden-off naturally and not artificially. Contractors are warned against working wood into the boat before

it is properly seasoned, or has had time to develop any latent shakes or defects'.

The same specification went on to state that the wood keel was to be of 'selected East Indian teak or approved alternative timber'. The stem was to be of English oak. So were the stem apron, fore deadwood, stern post, stern apron, stern knee, gunwale and bilge keels.

In connection with the hull planking, this was given as 'mild tough and clean mahogany, not grain cut'. Planks had to be worked cold where possible and steamed only at the most acute bends. And the 52ft Barnett's rudder too was of wood. The specification ordered mahogany.

Thus it will be seen how important wood has been in the history of the life-boats of the RNLI. Today,

however, steel and GRP (glass-reinforced plastic) life-boats are increasingly in service.

But wood for some years yet, it is thought, will form part of the life-boat building programme as, indeed, it will of other kinds of boats. If wood is finally abandoned as a boat-building material it will only be because the special skill required to work wood is no longer available.

This year (1973) is important in the history of English trees. For the government has launched a campaign to plant trees on a massive scale and try to rebuild the country's once-famous woods and forests. Thanks to the State scheme perhaps, even after the year AD2000, there will still be many ships built of English oak. Let's hope so.

Old Cannon Bollards

Left: Old cannon bollards in London, often erected years before the end of the 19th century, sometimes varied in size with, in the background, what looks like a howitzer barrel. Sometimes the barrel was stuffed with a cannon ball set in concrete.

Below: A cannon ball was sometimes embedded in the barrel.

While I have not been able to stop to see exactly what is going on in the re-jigging of the walk-ways on London's Tower Hill, I have the impression from bus-rides that important cannon bollards, which I wrote about in November 1980, have been removed. Some of the barrels, where the muzzle had not been filled with cement, had a cannon-ball plug.

Bollard cannon, because they were often scrapped from wooden naval vessels, may very well be as historic as those lifted from known wrecks such as the *Mary Rose*. Some cannon were specially inscribed with the ship's name.

What had to be remembered about cannon bollards was that many dated well before the 1870s, were iron and were very likely so used because of a trunnion break which couldn't be repaired in those days. Bronze cannon were far too valuable, even when scrapped, to be used for bollards.

Most if not all cannon bollards still around are iron and being iron there is little chance of any breach inscriptions being readable because of corrosion due to being embedded in the ground.

Cannon bollards are normally old six, nine or 12-pounders with an occasional piece of larger calibre such as a howitzer.

It is generally difficult to give bollard cannon any precise date for identification without actually excavating them, since so much of the evidence – inscriptions and so on – lies underground, as must have applied in the case of some examples I saw on Tower Hill in 1980.

Incidentally, cast-iron imitation cannon are still around in numbers as they quickly became standard London street furniture from 1812 onwards.

I have the impression from dockland walks that cannon bollards – those from actual ships and imitation ones – have in recent years been whisked away by developers. It would be interesting to know if the heritage people involved in all dockland and port schemes up and down the country have the cannon business under proper control.

War Poets with Suffolk Links – Abbey Honour

WITH the news that 16 Great War poets are to be honoured for their testament to the horror and pity of the Western Front, with a memorial in Poets' Corner, Westminster Abbey, comes the recollection that East Anglia had at least two of them – one for long periods – live within the area.

The two soldier-poets were Edmund Blunden, who died in 1974, and Edward Thomas, who was killed in action near Arras in 1917.

In January 1985, the Dean of Westminster, Dr Edward Carpenter, told me: "I am not in a position at this stage to let you know when the date of the unveiling will be.

"We have to raise at the Abbey some £7000 for this memorial and until we have this sum of money we cannot have the memorial made. As soon as subscriptions reach this target then the matter will be plain sailing. We are not quite half way at the moment."

Edward Thomas' connection with East Anglia is nebulous but intriguing and came about when, at the end of 1907, he went to stay in a coastguard cottage near Dunwich, Suffolk, in order to complete a 90,000-word book on the life of Richard Jefferies (1848-1887) another mystic, who also loved the English countryside and its people.

Being interested in Edward Thomas' connection – he adored Minsmere and the wild marshes – I went to Dunwich in early 1953 seeking impressions of his stay.

It didn't take me long to discover that, when he was there in 1907-08 for some weeks, Mr Edwin J. Clark (77) could remember that shortly after the coastguard station at Minsmere was closed down in 1906, one of the cottages was taken over by Mr and Mrs Frederick W. Aldis and Mr and Mrs William T. Webb.

When Mr William Dix (82), a retired farm worker, was shown a photograph of Edward Thomas, he remembered the face after some 47 years. He explained that he had known both families at the coastguard cottage well, the connection being that he had acted as carrier for them.

"If Edward Thomas travelled to Suffolk via Liverpool Street, he said, "I would have picked him up from Darsham railway station. I know the face but like Mr. Clark, I can't remember his name."

In the course of the poet's stay at Minsmere, during which he finished the book on Jefferies, he fell

Buried at Long Melford, Suffolk, there is a plaque on the garden wall of this house recording that Edmond Blunden lived in the village for a time.

half in love with a girl of 17 who, to his particular way of thinking, looked like a sea-nymph, "with two long plaits of dark brown hair, and the richest grey eyes, very wild and shy".

When, in 1967, I referred to the girl in an article, Myfanwy Thomas, of Eastbury, Newbury, Berkshire, the poet's younger daughter, wrote that she and her sister, Bronwen, were appreciative of the "delightful article" linking their father with Dunwich.

Myfanway Thomas explained: "My mother had some girlhood friends called Aldis – a brilliant family – who came from Minsmere. One of the brothers of her particular friend Janet, who married Harry Hooton, and who is still living at Cambridge, was a brilliant mathematician who invented the Aldis sight on fighting aircraft, and who lived in a mystic world of figures.

"The Webbs, I think, must have been the family whose beautiful girls mother was nursery governess to, before her marriage, and it was one of the Webb girls who so enchanted my father.

"Mother often told us how lovely the girls were with their long hair and Rosetti-ish features, and wearing the Liberty loose dresses of flowered silk or lawn. But I cannot be absolutely sure if this child was a Webb or a relative who was staying there. How one wishes one had made notes as mother's memory was

Of the Great War poets, some of whom lost spirit because of the carnage they saw, Edmund Blunden stood out strongly in his belief that in any future conflict, British youth would face the challenge.
Photo: Courtesy Imperial War Museum

Restored today, the old coastguard cottages at Dunwich, Suffolk, where Edward Thomas stayed in 1907-08 while writing his book on Richard Jefferies.

clear and shrewd up to the time of her death this year."

Not long after I heard from Myfanway Thomas, I received the following note from Dr Phillis Cunnington, of York: "I was one of the Webbs who lived for a time at Minsmere and my sister Hope, was the girl of 17 – 'the unattainable dryad' of the story.

"Helen Thomas *nee* Noble, as a young woman, was my mother's help' and we as children adored her and wept buckets when she left to be married to Edward.

"Mrs Aldis, of Minsmere, was my father's sister and her son, Cyril, was the inventor of the Aldis lamp for the Navy.

"I have very happy memories of Minsmere, and thank you very much for your Minsmere recollections, which I am tempted now to take in," added Dr. Cunnington.

Edmund Blunden, whose celebrated book *Undertones of War,* published in 1928, became a best-seller, lived at various times at Stowlangtoft, Stansfield and Cowlinge, in Suffolk, and for a short time at Cheveley, just over the border in Cambridgeshire.

In 1964, when I heard that he was retiring to Long Melford, Suffolk, from the post of Professor of English at Hong Kong University, I asked him if he would give me an idea of what he was going to do when he settled back in Suffolk. He complied, and the results were published in 1964.

Of the Great War poets, some of whom lost spirit because of the carnage they saw, Edmund Blunden stood out strongly in his belief that in any future conflicts British youth would face the challenge.

In fact, when I asked him in 1964 how he thought today's young men would shape up under Flanders' conditions, he told me: "I believe today's young people would have all the courage needed, and would also have wits enough not to let a war in mudholes and high explosive concentrations drag on four years."

I see from old letters that, when I had to visit France on business in the 1960s, I sent Edmund Blunden a postcard from one of his haunts.

Edmund Blunden replied: "Now comes your card from Arras battlefield, and though it is perhaps a little draughty on the Bapaume road or by the river at Peronne, I envy you the journey."

Poppies, always associated with remembrance after the first Great War because of their prolific growth in Flanders' shattered countryside, making a colourful display by the roadside at Snetterton Heath, Norfolk, in June, 1990

Flying Moles – Beware!

DURING harvest time, at the end of August, I was in the Great Waldingfield area around eight one Sunday morning when I decided to explore the winding, hedged road leading to Edwardstone, last visited by me in the middle 1950s when I was a young newspaper reporter in the area.

In the course of the drive I passed a couple carrying bags, one of which for certain contained pottery pieces, but they would not tell me if the artefacts – Roman, Saxon and medieval I thought – belonged to one site.

But in my drive to Edwardstone I had noted, on my right, extensive gravel workings with sheer cliffs varying between 20 and 40 feet. Were the excavations related to their finds?

Curious to see more of the site, I climbed into the workings to scan the cliffs with binoculars for archaeological and geological remains, as going too close would have been dangerous with some of the overhang and signs of landslides. Certainly there was plenty of geological scree to be seen.

Scree? Well – yes, and the shower from above of pebbles, fortunately the size of peanuts, made me run as they ping-ponged all around me. Arriving with them, with a light thump, was a small furry creature which plummeted into sandy mire at my feet. I put my hand into the squelch and fished it out. It turned out to be a middle-aged mole, winded, but alive.

By then the early morning was finding its way into the pit, and taking a piece of scrap board as domestic refuse was being used to replace the gravel, I put the panting animal on it to dry out. It stayed on the board, glad of a firm surface, for 15 minutes.

On returning to it, I put the mole in my handkerchief and climbing out of the workings, let it run free in a neighbouring harvest field.

"For goodness sake, mole, be careful in future," I muttered as it shuffled out of sight along a stubble furrow.

What, I thought, did the mole think of its attempt to fly and, finally, the plonk from 40 feet?

It was clear to me what had happened: the mole, madly boring at dawn, had gone out through the side of the sand pit in error – and sailed into space! Lucky I was there on impact for the pit slurry would have

Arriving with them, with a light thump, was a small furry creature which plummeted into sandy mire at my feet . . . It turned out to be a middle-aged mole, winded, but alive.

enveloped the poor old thing. At the same time it was lucky the mole hadn't brought down the cliff face on top of me with, possibly, death for us both.

May I make a plea? Mole, I am sure, would be grateful if you would let him take a change in the cycle of the countryside without, thank you, the formation of, say, the British Mole Preservation Society with a set of rules for our already harassed farmers.

At the same time, when the owner of the pit workings reads that I was down there, I hope he won't have me prosecuted for trespass. I didn't discover, until I returned to Great Waldingfield, that the huge hole I'd been in was an organised business. Just think: it could have been a tomb for mole and me. Obviously it's no place for casual Man or Mole.

Sutton Hoo and Beowulf

THE 7th century Sutton Hoo Anglo-Saxon ship burial site of 1939, which is now being reinvestigated at a cost of £500,000, is probably as well known as the discovery in 1922 of King Tutankhamun's tomb.

Found in a barrow group overlooking Woodbridge, on Suffolk's *River Deben*, the Sutton Hoo treasure ship – a cenotaph, as no body was found – is now thought to honour King Raedwald, whose death occurred in AD 624 or 625 and whose family was torn between christian and pagan living.

What, however, always puzzles me in connection with ship burials is why so few have been unearthed in this country since the 19th century when, for good or ill, inquisitive antiquarians with time on their hands started their investigations.

It was in 1861 that Dr Daniel H. Haigh, sometimes described as an East Anglian scholar, published two books through John Russell Smith, London: *The Conquest of Britain by the Saxons*, the narratives of early chroniclers collected to throw light on the foundations of 5th century history; and *The Anglo-Saxon Sagas*, an examination of their value as aids to history. I have studied both copies in the British Museum Library, London.

It was the latter volume, I suggest, which could have sparked off the 19th century treasure ship hunters, for county records show that in the 1860s nearly two bushels of iron screw-bolts were found in Roman barrows by the *Deben* and converted into horse shoes by a local blacksmith! These rivets came from the Sutton Hoo group of barrows and point to mutilation of a ship without, curiously, any reported trace of treasure.

But Sutton Hoo, it is interesting to reflect, had a much earlier treasure legend – of treasure found or still be be found.

At the same time two separate groups of people in 1860-63 dug into what was most certainly an Anglo-Saxon ship burial (AD. 635-650) at Snape, near Aldeburgh, with some rudimentary recording being made.

Surprisingly, one of the most important relics – a massive gold finger ring of Roman work-manship – did not reach the British Museum until the early 1950s. As the 19th century discovery of iron screw bolts at Sutton Hoo suggested, it seems highly likely that the Snape boat, if it had not been robbed in earlier times, contained much more valuable items than we are led to believe.

Exclusive? In presenting this outstanding photograph of the 1939 Sutton Hoo ship burial to the writer, Mr Ronald W.T. Meehan, of Trimley St Martin, Suffolk, told him he took it in July 1939, when he first had 'Amateurish connections with the site'. A lady (left background) was also photographing at the time.

As the writer saw the Anglo-Saxon ship burial site at Sutton Hoo, nr. Woodbridge, Suffolk, in 1949, just 10 years after the treasure was found.

In fact, the first unidentified party at Snape, said to have come from London, were rumoured to have taken away a waggon-load of vases and other things from an extensive urn field on the site.

The second party (1862-63), to give them their due, appeared to be dedicated antiquarians and drew up a plan of the Snape boat, iron rivets and all, on the lines followed at Sutton Hoo in 1938-39 by the highly professional archaeologists.

Yet, apart from Sutton Hoo and Snape (and some evidence from the banks of the *River Chelmer,* near Chelmsford), all well-documented but with some gaps, I know of only two other possible Anglo-Saxon hulls, or parts of complete hulls, which may be revealed because the facts have appeared in public archeological pro-ceedings. These were found in 1830 at Ashby Dell, near Fritton Lake, over thirty years before Dr. Haigh's saga book, and in the 1950s at Caister-on-Sea, north of Yarmouth, where parts of a ship were found laid over 7th century burials.

With regard to the Caister-on-Sea evidence, Miss Barbara Green, keeper of archaeology at the Castle Museum, Norwich, told me: "The precise significance of the pieces of boat found over the burials . . . is still a matter of conjecture. Although my father dug the site in 1951-54, he did not live to publish it. The report on the site is being written at the moment . . ."

In order to get an appreciation of what the pre- and post-Anglo-Saxon coastline was like between, say, the 6th and 9th centuries, it is necessary to appreciate that in Roman times (55BC to AD450) Norfolk and Suffolk – the former especially – were covered by waters extending well inland. Naturally, all high, dry ground became living sites and it is the plotting of such sites today which gives a clue as to the old shores.

As time progressed and the Anglo-Saxon phase developed, the North Sea waters receded in many places, and it is this uncertain coastline which we are left with today when we try to imagine – sometimes from the origin of place names – where the Anglo-Saxons and the Danes had their strongholds and burial places.

E.M. Ward in *English Coastline Evolution* (Metheun, 1922), noting that much land was lost in the historic past, observed: "Easton Bavents – between Lowestoft and Southwold – was once a projecting cape. It now forms part of a straight length of shore and lies perhaps two or three miles westward of its position in the time of the Romans".

It is this local description of a piece of the Suffolk coast which brings me back to Dr. Haigh of 1861, who in daring to link the fabled Beowulf of the first great Anglo-Saxon poem, suggested that the mysterious figure could have sailed from, and returned to, the now silted port of Uggeshall/Frostenden, now inland from Covehithe, on his expedition against the Grendel family of fen monsters.

Dr Haigh declared in 1861: "From these two descriptions, of Beowulf's outward and homeward voyage, it appears that he started from and arrived at the same point; but whereas at starting he had some distance to travel before he reached the sea, on his return he found King Hygelac of the Geats resident near the shore.

"This residence was perhaps Uggeshall, and the point of embarkation some place on the neigh-bouring coast. Covehithe is the nearest point to Uggeshall; its name indicates an ancient harbour, and it answers the description in the poem very well".

Thus, when one considers E.M. Ward's descrip-tion of the lost territory north of Southwold, Dr

Haigh's view that Beowulf's men on their homeward voyage saw "the well known cliffs of the Geats, the high lands between Lowestoft and Southwold", is convincing.

While, I admit, scholars place the substance of Beowulf in Northumbria, which had important links with East Anglia, but see the geography of the poem as the land of the Swedes, the Geats, the Danes, the Frisians and the Franks, translators like Michael Alexander in *Beowulf* (Penguin Classics, 1983) say that "as a finished literary work it is almost universally held to be the product of a relatively sophisticated and Christian Anglian court – though one that had evidently not yet repudiated its ancestral links with the Germanic peoples across the North Sea".

So I am driven on, like Dr Haigh, to develop the Uggeshal/Frostenden theory. The land contours between these two places and Covehithe are interesting and suggest that Beowulf, away "about one hour of another day" in order to deal with the Grendel problem, simply sailed up the coast and into the great estuary which in those days could have taken him round to Fritton Lake, which is not to be confused with the evolution of the Broads.

Indeed, the antiquity of wooded Fritton Lake, whose length gives the impression of a northern landscape, was confirmed by historian B. Granville Baker in his *Blithe Waters* (Heath Cranton, 1931): "The traditional associations of Fritton Lake are . . . lovely; it was known in past ages as Gunhilde's Mere, after Gunhilda, a christian, the beautiful sister of Sweyne, the Danish pirate and father of Canute".

What reality can be attached to the fen monsters of the Beowulf era? Well, bearing in mind that the ancient poem is in various ways concerned with the subtle ebb and flow of paganism and Christianity, factors which must have grated in King Raedwald's time, could not Beowulf have gone forth as a kind of hunter/gamekeeper to quell fen monsters – prehistoric leftovers – which had been driven to seek the fresh water of Fritton Lake as a result of some natural upheaval, say an earthquake?

As for the happenings in *Beowulf* being a reflection of the disturbed times following the departure of the Romans, there's some evidence in East Anglia that weapons and jewellery could have been so deposited in order to appease the gods. Whether the votive deposits were made as a result of wars or severe weather upheavals isn't important – something awesome led people to offer up their possessions.

While Dr Haigh may, of course, have been way out in 1861 when he tied up the silted port of Uggeshall/Frostenden with the mighty Beowulf, I have in my possession – it was found in an Ipswich secondhand bookshop in the 1950s – a copy of the second edition of James Bird's poem *The Vale of Slaughden*, first printed at Halesworth in 1819, telling of Danish/Saxon strife in the 9th century along the coast from Dunwich to Snape, Sutton Hoo and elsewhere. It was, explained the Earl Stonham poet in the preface, a blending of "fiction with truth".

Inscribed in the front cover in two places – in 1826 and 1828 – were the names of the Gibson family of Uggeshall. I wonder why the Gibsons in their day were attracted to James Bird's 9th century description of a changed Suffolk coast which, two miles east of Dunwich, was then "exceedingly steep and rocky" – just like the coast described in *Beowulf?*

Splashing up the River Deben in the 7th century . . .

130

IN THE BI-CENTENARY FOOTSTEPS OF
George Crabbe

AS ONE who very much enjoyed the East Anglian-orientated exhibitions and lectures of the first half-dozen Aldeburgh Festivals, beginning in 1948, I noted last year there was a good deal of reflection by key music writers on the shape of things to come, finance being a major factor.

Lowestoft-born composer Benjamin Britten died some years ago, Imogen Holst, conductor, music lecturer and writer daughter of composer Gustav Holst, passed away fairly recently, and last April, it was announced that Lord Harewood, the musical administrator, whose name, like the others, will always be linked with the foundation years of the Aldeburgh Festival, was standing down as managing director of English National Opera in order to devote more time to his estate in Yorkshire.

However, the point of this article is to look back to 1954 when, I recall, the George Crabbe (1754-1832) bi-centenary celebrations were held.

Mostly self-taught, the son of the collector of salt duties at Aldeburgh, Crabbe had a deep understanding of the rural life of the late 18th century. He knew the life of the country poor by his personal experience, and his studies in botany and other branches of natural science enabled him to substitute for the graceful vagueness of the pastoral poets a background drawn with minute exactness.

So it was on 16th June 1954, that the 'Crabbe celebrations' were inaugurated at the East Suffolk Hotel, Aldeburgh, when a luncheon was held and the speakers were E.M. Forster, the novelist. and William Plomer, the writer.

After the luncheon, there was a special excursion to Crabbe country – Parham Hall (erected in 1851 on the site of Parham Lodge, the home of Sarah Elmy, Crabbe's wife, where Crabbe and his family lived from 1791 to 1797).

After Parham, those making the Crabbe pilgrimage went on to Rendham, where a plaque placed on Rendham Grove by the Blyth Rural District Council was unveiled by the late Earl of Stradbroke, Lord Lieutenant of Suffolk.

Apparently Rendham Grove is the only house now standing in Suffolk which is known to have been occupied by Crabbe, who lived there from 1801 to 1804.

Next port of call was Great Glemham House, where William Plomer read selections from the works of Crabbe. Then, as I remember, we all had tea, and

Distinguished group at Snape garden fete in 1954, including Benjamin Britten, the tenor Peter Pears , Lord Harewood and his former wife, Maria Donata Stein.

I took one or two informal snaps, including one showing Benjamin Britten, E.M. Forster and William Plomer who all signed my grandfather's 1846 edition of *Crabbe's Poems* (John James Chidley) which he obtained from a Mr H. Turner in 1929.

Crabbe lived at Great Glemham House, then the property of Dudley North of Little Glemham, from 1797 to 1801. In the latter year, the estate was sold, which is why Crabbe moved to Rendham. The poet's old house stood at the bottom of the park but was pulled down by the purchaser who built the present house in 1811 on a different spot. For the benefit of the 1954 pilgrims, the old site was given a heavy application of nitro-chalk to bring out the buried foundations.

About the time of the June, 1954, Aldeburgh Festival, I went to a garden fete at Snape in aid of the festival where author W.G. Arnott, who wrote *Alde Estuary: The Story of a Suffolk River* (Norman Adlard, 1952), signed copies of his book. It was there that I took some more pictures, including a group which included Lord Harewood and his former wife, Maria Donata Stein, Benjamin Britten and Peter Pears, the tenor singer.

Interestingly, *Kobbe's Complete Opera Book* (Putman, 1976), edited and revised by Lord Harewood, states: "The idea of Peter Grimes came to Britten in America in 1941, after reading an article in *The Listener* by E.M. Forster on the subject of George Crabbe, the poet of England and, more particularly, of East Anglia.

"Shortly afterwards, Koussevitzky, the conductor, offered to commission him to write an opera and,

Benjamin Britten (holding jug) with others, including E.M. Forster, the novelist, and William Plomer, the writer, at Great Glemham House in 1954.

immediately on his return to England (in the spring of 1942), he went to work with Montagu Slater to hammer out the libretto".

However, I have a note that the partnership between Britten and E.M. Forster really started way back in 1936 when W.H. Auden, the poet, introduced his composer friend.

Thus the article by E.M. Forster in 1941 not only clinched Britten's decision to return from America and indeed to settle in Aldeburgh, Crabbe's native town, but to write an opera on the Peter Grimes of the local poet's poem *The Borough*.

> Old Peter Grimes made fishing his employ
>   His wife he cabin'd with him and his boy,
> To town came quiet Peter with his fish,
>   And had of all a civil word and wish.
> He left his trade upon the Sabbeth-day
>   And took young Peter in his hand to pray:
> But soon the stubborn boy from care broke loose,
>   At first refused, then added his abuse:
> His father's love he scorn'd his power defied,
>   But being drunk wept sorely when he died.

When Vessels Founder

Left: The vague shape of a sunken barge by the quayside as Hull's famous berths were neglected as the fishing port declined in the 1960s.

Above: The remains of the barge Castanet, built in 1897, which was disposed of by fire in 1955 at Levington, Suffolk, by the River Orwell.

High Jinks at Hawkinge

TWENTY-EIGHT years ago on 29th November 1940, at Hawkinge RAF Station, Kent, LAC John Amer, aged 18, a rigger in 421 Flight, climbed into the cockpit of a 360mph Spitfire IIA, started the engine, and – well, tried to take-off in an attempt to earn his RAF wings just like that!

What are the facts behind this amusing but costly skylark that took place when the Duke of Kent was visiting?

My late brother, LAC Donald Elliott, aged 18, who was also a member of 421 Flight which in early 1941 expanded into 91 Squadron at Hawkinge, sent me three souvenirs from the bent metal propeller of LAC Amer's Spitfire. I hung on to the fragments, as to this day I have a collection of Battle of Britain relics, and finally in 1965, after many inquiries, Mr Amer was traced in London. He even executed a drawing for my scrapbook showing how he ended up.

Mr Amer's desire to fly started when he was a boy apprentice – he was then 15 – at No. 1 School of Technical Training, Halton, Bucks. When the Battle of Britain got going and he tasted action at RAF Hornchurch, Essex, the urge to fly grew stronger.

Subsequently, while his first squadron (65) was resting at RAF Turnhouse, Scotland, he almost succeeded in his plan but ran into last minute complications. The Spitfires there still had battery starters, requiring an assistant, the machine he had his eye on was parked too close to the squadron office, and there would have been at least one spectator of his death-or-glory attempt.

Later in 1940 he transferred to 421 Flight, which undertook special duties for Fighter Command and had a most active time operating from Hawkinge. In November Mr Amer, who by then had 'scrambled' dozens of pilots into battle, got his chance.

It was about 3.15pm on 29th November. Spitfire P7319 with the code letters LZ-H (a machine, incidentally, flown by a pilot who had destroyed 14 enemy aircraft), stood at instant readiness. This Spitfire had a cartridge starter operated by the pilot from the cockpit without external help.

At about 3.27pm my brother, who had just checked the engine as it was a cold day, walked into the dispersal tent and said: "There's one you can take – I've just warmed it up." Mr Amer replied: "OK, I'll have a look at it."

Then, and no one took much notice at the time, Mr Amer removed the Spitfire's chocks, pushed the tail round to the direction of take-off and

Ex-LAC John R. Amer, of 421 Flight, on 29th November 1940, when the Duke of Kent was visiting RAF Hawkinge, tried to take-off in a Spitfire to prove that he was fit for a pilot's course. Here he meditates on a 1966 visit to the author's home.

climbed into the cockpit. He was wearing his 'erk's' overalls and wellingtons. Still no one paid much attention. Someone in the tent growled: "He's at it again!"

Suddenly the cartridge starter cracked into action . . . smoke belched from the exhausts . . . and Mr Amer was moving off in a west to east direction – and into RAF history. The time was 3.30pm. Ahead of him lay the English Channel and Galland's Messerschmitts. He had plans to call up his CO on the R/T and state his case for going on a pilot's course.

But something went wrong. Just at the moment of 'unsticking', the starboard wing of the Spitfire touched the ground, was torn off cleanly at 85mph, and the rest of the machine, with its nose tearing into the turf, ploughed on for some distance. Perhaps the powerful engine-torque or the rigger's muddy wellingtons on the rudder pedals caused the starboard wing to drop at the critical moment.

The crash alarm sounded. At the same time many running figures closed around the wreck – in fact, there were so many people round the bent fuselage that the would-be-pilot could, in his opinion, have mingled with them and denied all knowledge because of his attire. As things turned out he had a hard job convincing an officer that he was *the pilot*.

"Your brother", Mr Amer told me, "was furious. All he kept saying as we stood by the wreck was: 'You damn fool, you damn fool'!"

Mr Amer was court-martialled for attempting to take-off and so negligently controlling the Spitfire that it crashed and caused damage of not less than £20."

He was placed under close-arrest for six weeks at Hawkinge. On the morning he was leaving for a

ULTIMATUM BY BOY IN SPITFIRE

Tries to fly off after warning:
'Let me be pilot or I crash'

Daily Express Staff Reporter O. D. GALLAGHER

SOMEWHERE IN THE SOUTH-EAST, Tuesday.

JEFF AMER, eighteen-year-old Londoner, is both the hero and the villain of a ten-minute drama that took place at one of our fighter stations.

He is a rigger in the R.A.F. He joined up when he was fourteen and a half, and was made a boy apprentice.

That was the first step to achieve the one ambition of his life—to wear wings, to be a fighter pilot. Since the blitz began he has hopped into hundreds of fighter cockpits, tested the aileron wires, the "stick," oxygen mask and all the rest of a pilot's gear.

As many hundreds of times he has had to force himself out of the plane again to make room for the men he envied so—the pilots. The boy who wanted to fly was

→ BACK PAGE. COL. FOUR

TRIED TO FLY SPITFIRE

→ FROM PAGE ONE

always left on the ground, until

This boy said 'If I only had wings'
Crashed in ace's plane—and kit

Daily Express Staff Reporter O. D. GALLAGHER

EVERY dance band's favourite song, "If I Only Had Wings," came true yesterday, when Jeff Amer, boy rigger at an R.A.F. station, was court-martialled for trying to fly a Spitfire because he wanted to be a fighter pilot.

Not only was the plane he borrowed that of a D.S.O. ace who has shot down fourteen Nazis, Jeff wore the ace's flying suit and oxygen and radio mask as well.

JEFF AMER "You'd see my picture in the papers," says the song.

— IF I ON LY HAD WINGS.

The boy is only eighteen years ten months old, but he stands

'If I only had wings' R.A.F. boy is jailed

Daily Express Staff Reporter

JEFF ("If I only had wings") AMER, 6ft. 2in. boy rigger who crashed a Spitfire when he tried to take it up without authority in November has been found guilty by the court-martial that tried him on January 9.

RE BOY DISPLEASES MOTHER
ff should take nishment,' she says

Daily Express Staff Reporter

AMER, mother of eighteen-year-old I only had wings") Jeff, the R.A.F. rt-martialled for trying to fly a Spit-not approve of her spectacular son.

prised at his behaving like this," she said erday at her home in Alvaston-avenue Kenton, Middlesex.

She had just heard that Jeff had escaped from police custody at a airfield and been rearrested i London. He was on his way to serv three months in an R.A.F. jail.

"He has always been mad to fly said Mrs. Amer, "and I suppose h thought his progress towards bein a pilot was too slow.

"But I did not think he would t to escape after the court-martial

---

JEFF AMER
('if I only had wings') ESCAPES

JEFF ("If I only had wings") AMER, R.A.F. rigger who tried to fly a Spitfire, escaped from R.A.F. police custody yesterday morning.

He got clean away from the airfield and was not caught until an assistant provost marshal spotted him—in London.

Eighteen-year-old Jeff was due to be taken to the "Glasshouse" yesterday to serve his six months' ser (half of it remitted). e escaped while being taken fr iardroom to the cookhouse fast.

SPITFIRE BOY IS FREE

Jeff ("If I only had wings") Amer, boy rigger of the R.A.F., has been released after serving only three weeks of his six-months' court-martial sentence.

Jeff tried to take off in a Spitfire last November, without either the necessary qualifications or permission. He crashed before he could leave the ground, doing £20 worth of damage.

Court-martial followed, and he revealed his ambition to be a pilot instead of an A.C.1.

It had been his intention to drop a note from

JEFF AMER

the Spitfire saying if his commanding officer did not promise to send him for training as a pilot it would be "good-bye to this aircraft and this laddie."

"If I only had wings"
Another 27 days for Jeff, R.A.F.

Jeff ("If I ohly had wings") Amer, R.A.F. boy rigger who escaped from R.A.F. custody in the south of England last Friday and was rearrested in London the following day has been sentenced to an extra twenty-seven days' imprisonment.

Originally he was given six months' imprisonment with a remission of ninety-one days for trying to take off in a Spitfire without authority and the necessary qualifications, thereby crashing it and causing damage of not less than £20.

At his court-martial this eighteen-year-old, 6ft. 2in. boy who wanted to fly said his life's ambition was to be an R.A.F. pilot.

134

detention camp – he had been given a six months' sentence of which half had been remitted – he escaped over the railings of Hawkinge churchyard at around 7am.

Near Bexhill a soldier on guard duty asked him: "Are you on the run? If you are, I haven't seen you." Finally, after being given a meal by a Bexhill publican, whose other guest was a local police constable, Mr Amer was put on a train for Victoria. At Marble Arch, however, he was picked up by RAF policemen.

What would have happened to Mr Amer if he had got airborne? What if he had run into Messerschmitts over Folkestone? The RAF generally regarded the escapade lightly – "youthful ebullience" was how one officer passed it off. In fact, Mr Amer stayed on in the RAF for many more years and did air-traffic control duties.

Footnote: Tracking down Mr Amer took some time. I found his home address (Kenton, Middlesex) and when I visited that part of London on business I went to his road and asked a group of neighbours if anyone knew Mr Amer. They all said they did and spoke warmly of the boy who wanted to be a pilot. But Mr Amer's mother was dead, his sister had moved elsewhere, and no one knew what had become of the rigger. However, a neighbour said that Mr Amer was in the habit of returning to see them, probably once a year, and on his last visit he had left his telephone number – a Hyde Park number. I contacted this number and was told that Mr Amer had since moved on to another job. I was able to obtain his last known address – it was in Croydon – and closed in to find him. But I was further confounded. I found the road but could not locate the number I had been given. I resorted to the police at Croydon and they soon solved the riddle. The house where Mr Amer had been living had been demolished to make way for a new development.

Eventually the word got round Croydon and Mr Amer turned up with a box of chocolates for my wife and a bottle of wine for me!

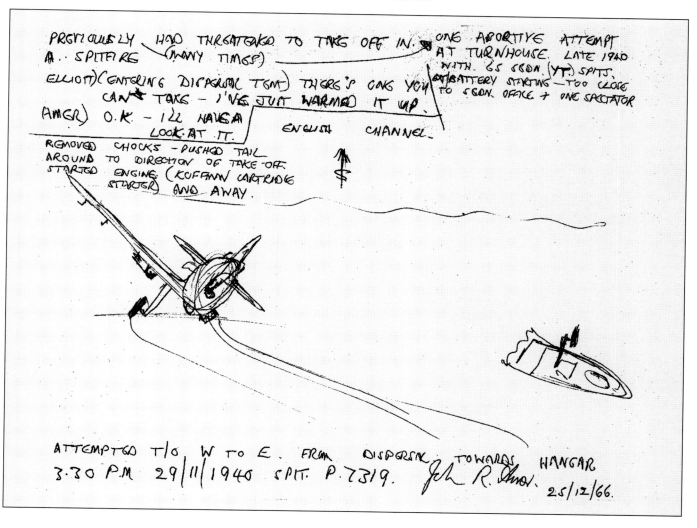

Mr Prickles

A LONDON HEDGEHOG IN THE ROLE OF ROAD-SAFETY OFFICER FOR TWO SMALL CHILDREN

OUR Mr Prickles, sometimes known as Urchin or Hedgepig, is dead . . . But the hedgehog's death the other Sunday – he was knocked down by a car – has left a profound impression in the minds of my two children, Alister. aged five, and Anne, aged three, that subsequent road-safety lessons may never succeed in imparting in later years.

Now the 'little hedgehogger' as they continue to call it, lies buried at their request in the tiny garden behind our flat in Wimbledon.

How did Mr Prickles take on the role of road-safety officer so successfully – when he was stone-dead?

Little Mr Prickles' flattened-form by the cross-roads near their home caught their attention as they went to Sunday school. At first they were merely curious to know why he was "so flat and still." I explained that wheels did that – well, to anything.

Returning, Alister once again halted the pram at the accident spot. He then requested that the 'little hedehogger' be lifted and buried in his garden.

"It's the wheels – the thought of more wheels going over him when he's 'deaded'," Alister explained with obvious feeling. "Please daddy, pick him up. I'll carry him . . ."

The appeal was too sincere to brush aside so, returning home, we found an old strawberry basket with a handle, some brown paper, and the garden trowel. They stood on the pavement, hand-in-hand while I dealt with Mr Prickles.

Back home they eagerly told their mother that the 'little hedgehogger' was safe. A hole was dug by last year's Christmas tree and the brown paper unwrapped from around Mr Prickles. They looked on in silence at the still, broken form with its single,

A shy hedgehog pictured at night with a flashlight.

tiny outstretched claw. Doubtless, too, they noticed other features about Mr Prickles but did not say.

When the burial was over they found a jam-jar and some water. Their mother gave them two asters from the dining room vase and from their garden they picked sweet lavender.

Later that day, when they were indoors, they relived on the carpet the hedgehog's last moments. It was shown shuffling along, nose to the ground, and then crumpled on its side. One solitary arm – Mr Prickles' last gesture – protruded from both bundles on the floor. With more and more practice the message became ever more poignant. We wondered, in fact, when our Sunday road-safety lesson would end!

Mr Prickles' death, quite clearly, had left its mark. Alister, remembering my many warnings about crossing at a road junction where four streams of traffic could converge at one time reiterated the warning and showed that he knew that Mr Prickles was at fault although, of course, he did not know that it was very likely Mr Prickles' shuffling 1 to 2mph that had 'deaded' him.

That evening we saw Alister standing on his bed looking at the hedgehog's grave below.

"When will we see him again?" he asked.

"You'll see him." I quickly replied, "when you see your next hedgehog."

With that Alister lay down and went to sleep. The day's road tragedy on his doorstep had kept him thinking most of the day and he was tired.

Anne and Alister of the story a year or two before the death of the hedgehog in a road accident.

The Tennyson Brothers

A MEMORIAL WINDOW donated by the grandson of the poet Alfred, Lord Tennyson, at St Edmund's Church, Southwold, Suffolk, which was dedicated in 1971, came about when the late Sir Charles Tennyson's surviving son, Hallam, suggested that friends and relatives should give his father money gifts for his 90th birthday on 8 November 1969.

Over £1000 was raised, and Sir Charles decided to dedicate the window portraying East Anglia's St Edmund to his wife, Ivy (1880-1858) and to his sons Penrose (1912-1941) and Julian (1915-1945).

It was Julian Tennyson who, in 1939, published *Suffolk Scene* (Blackie), a book of description and adventure, dedicated "To my parents in gratitude for an upbringing which made possible my early adventures", which was reprinted throughout the war years and subsequently, testimony of its appeal.

But the author, one of the most gifted and sensitive writers of his time about the English scene, hardly lived long enough to enjoy the congratulations of his many readers as Captain Tennyson, of the Oxford and Bucks Light Infantry, was killed in action in Burma in March, 1945.

His *Suffolk Scene,* which followed his *Rough Shooting For The Owner Keeper Month By Month* (Adam and Charles Black) of 1938, has always

Julian Tennyson
Photos: Courtesy Sir Charles Tennyson

Penrose Tennyson

enjoyed a special place on my East Anglian bookshelf and has led me over the years to gather impressions of the brothers' wanderings.

Rough Shooting . . . whose chapters covered everything from partridges to poachers, was written at The Ancient House, Peasenhall, Suffolk. With his brother, Penrose, who was a very promising film director and was killed in a Fleet Air Arm 'plane crash in July, 1941, Julian Tennyson there spent many hours discussing the plan of the book.

Apparently Penrose Tennyson, with the help of Mr T.C. Bland of Thomas Bland Sons, the London gunsmiths, undertook (anonymously) the chapter on guns.

Julian Tennyson, in the preparation of *Rough Shooting.* . . . was also aided by Mr Alec Bloomfield. According to Sir Charles Tennyson in his *Life's All A Fragment* (Cassell, 1953), many were the afternoons and evenings which the two spent walking about the woods and heaths of Scott's Hall, near Dunwich, Suffolk, where Mr Bloomfield was gamekeeper, or discussing fine points of practice and natural history in Alec's little cottage or at The Eel's Foot at nearby East Bridge.

In the preface to *Rough Shooting* . . . Julian Tennyson observed: "No sportsman, and certainly no gamekeeper, can know too much of the habits of game and vermin. For this reason I have laid continual stress on natural history, which is the keynote to success in all shooting."

In the chapter on vermin, Julian Tennyson expressed a balanced view: "If game and rabbits thrive on your land, there the vermin will come for a certainty, but if your stock is poor, both winged and ground marauders will express their contempt by passing hastily to more fruitful hunting grounds. So, since you cannot have the one without the other, I hope for your sake that you are plagued with vermin in plenty".

Dawn by the River Blyth near Blythburgh, Suffolk.

This is how Julian Tennyson, author of Suffolk Scene, saw Walberswick wind pump in the 1930s. The picture, however, was taken on May 17, 1953, following extensive repairs.

A close up of the Walberswick wind pump taken on May 17, 1953.

Telling many forgotten secrets in the chapter on poachers – it is worth remembering that Julian Tennyson was writing in the 1930's – he added prophetically: "It seems that a motor-poacher can belong to any walk of life. Company directors, under-graduates, bank clerks, factory hands, small provincial townsmen – all of these have been caught in the last 15 years. Perhaps the day will come when poaching will be done by machine-gun from an aeroplane."

It was while the opportunity to write *Rough Shooting* . . . came in sight that Julian Tennyson met again, and fell in love with, Margerie Yvonne le Cornu, a native of the Channel Islands, whose acquaintance he had first made in the Isle of Wight a year or two earlier.

In 1955 the author's widow, who later remarried and lived at Walberswick, Suffolk, let me borrow her copy of *Rough Shooting* . . . while guiding me onto a scarce second-hand copy for retention.

Inscribed in her copy was the following cheerful salutation from the author "To Yve – So I'm not allowed to keep the last copy of my own book, eh? I surrender it to you, my dear, with love and pleasure, and I can only hope (a) that you will be able to read it all through, and (b) that you will he kind enough to lend it to your old man occasionally. Bless you. March 1938."

The return of the Tennyson household to Suffolk in 1935 also enabled the Tennyson boys to renew old coastal friendships, as their Peasenhall home was only 12 miles from dear Aldeburgh of their youth.

One old friend was Alfred George Henry "Jerry" Wood, fisherman, wild fowler and yachtsman, of Aldeburgh and Slaughden Quay, whom their father noted in the limited edition of *Penrose Tennyson* (A.S. Atkinson, 1943). The river. of course. was the *Alde.*

Said Sir Charles Tennyson: "That was the beginning of wonderful experiences for Pen: river picnics at Iken, Orford and Havergate Island . . . Wildfowling with Jerry and, later on, Dooley (Julian

Tennyson) . . . Dooly has described those magical days and nights . . . in pages which I think those who love youth and England will not easily allow to be forgotten. . . .

"Pen grew to love not only the river, but the sailors and fishermen who made their living from it – Jerry Wood and his his half-brother 'Spider' . . . and the countless Wards and Cables who . . . trawled their nets or pritched for eels. . . .

And Jerry was the best of teachers. He . . . taught the boys to work and think for themselves . . . All thanks to Jerry Wood the schoolmaster and the windy river *Alde,* his classroom."

Determined to speak with Jerry Wood, if still alive, I found and photographed him on Slaughden Quay in the 1950s, showing him at the same time my old copy of *Penrose Tennyson* personally inscribed "For Alice McGrath – from Pen's parents."

In the 1950s at Sudbury, Suffolk, I remember Mr and Mrs Clement Sillitoe, who ran 'The Ship and Star' in Friars Street, telling me that in 1936 Julian Tennyson was a visitor. Five times after that he went back to the 400-year-old hostelry – an inn with which the Sillitoes had a 200 years' connection – and wrote in a bed-sitting room upstairs on returning from daily hikes of 25 miles or more.

Interestingly, when there was an exhibition of Suffolk books and maps at the 1951 Aldeburgh Festival, a manuscript of Julian Tennyson's "of an account of a walk he made from London to Peasenhall about 1936" was on view.

Then, in January, 1958, in connection with a survey of Suffolk county records, it was reported that Sir Charles and Lady Tennyson had presented "a brief manuscript account of a four-day walk undertaken by . . . Julian Tennyson from London to Peasenhall in 1937."

While Julian Tennyson no doubt used Sudbury as a base when he was gathering West Suffolk material for his *Suffolk Scene,* it seems likely that in his walk from London to Peasenhall he would have followed fragmentary Roman roads to Sudhury and Long Melford, then across country to Baylham, Framlingham and home.

In the chapter he did on rivers in *Suffolk Scene*, Julian Tennyson said "The loveliest part of the whole river is at Iken . . . When I was a child, I decided that here was the place for me to be buried. I have not altered my mind.

"Everyone wants to lie in his own country: this is mine. I shall feel safe if I have the screams of the birds and the moan of the wind and the lapping of the water all round me, and the lonely woods and marshes that I know so well. How can anyone say

what he will feel when he is dead? What I mean is that I shall feel secure in dying."

Penrose, his brother, who was his companion on the many expeditions on the *Alde*, left the following lines among his papers signed with his initials: "The advent of death is like the coming of a great wind: no man knows whence it is nor where it goes. Its visitation is often without reason and its action without intent the understanding may perceive."

Suffolk Scene, in a way, turned out to be Julian Tennyson's memorial. Alfred, Lord Tennyson (1809-1892), son of the rector of Somershy, Lincolnshire, his illustrious ancestor, ended his poem "The Brook" with these lines:

And out again I curve and flow
To join the brimming river,
For men may come and men may go,
But I go on for ever.

So, although the Tennyson boys, Penrose and Julian, had their promising lives terminated by war, the *Alde*, true to the poem, still follows its ancient course to the sea and all the other seas.

A harvest evening at Henham, Suffolk, in September, 1954, when an owl was seen perched on a broken gate against a most glorious sky.

Once an East Coast fishing smack with Grimsby, Great Yarmouth and Lowestoft associations, the Ionia ended up as a beached 'house' on the north bank of the River Alde between the wars. A shack was built on her bows and a tumbledown apartment in her stern. Long since demolioshed, the vessel is as it looked in 1948.

Face to Face with Tom Paine

'THE most restless and unruly of Norfolk-born writers was unquestionably Thomas Paine, born at Thetford in 1737.' So says W.G. Waters in his book *Norfolk in Literature*.

Son of a stay-maker, Tom, after several jobs, developed a passionate indignation over many social problems of the period. He soon became a champion of the peasant classes, both here and abroad, and in 1791 published *Rights of Man*. Tom, however, was handicapped by an inability to see any validity in the arguments of an adversary – in some respects a serious defect in his character. Finally, Tom died in New York on 8 June 1809. The whereabouts of his bones, brought by William Cobbett, author and politician, to England, remain, however, a mystery to this day. But the spirit of Tom, there is no doubt, lives on.

This, I think, is where I should confess that I have met Tom Paine – the second Tom Paine – and that a friend, who remembered my encounter with Tom in 1944, last year sent me an official United States Army Air Force photograph of the Flying Fortress named Tom Paine (No. 230793) parked on Beccles airfield, Suffolk, just as he was left after making an emergency landing there in 1944 – nearly 20 years ago. And we were present to see Tom do it.

The second Tom Paine, in addition to having the political fighter's name painted on the port side of its nose, also bore these words from the writings of the Norfolk lover of democracy:

The naming ceremony at Knettishall airfield in 1943 (centre) Professor J. Frank Dobie, visiting professor of American history at Cambridge, and (left) Tom Paine's original pilot, 2nd-Lt James E. Zenerle. *Photo: Courtesy USAAF*

'Tyranny, like Hell,
is not easily Conquered!'

What is the story behind the Tom Paine of 1944 – the Tom Paine that turned up in an album of photographs in America'? Tom, we now know, belonged to the 562nd Squadron of the 388th Bombardment Group, 8th USAAF, and operated from Knettishall airfield, Suffolk, only a few miles from the first Tom's birthplace at Thetford.

Let co-Pilot T.R. Copeland, who was recently traced in America, continue the story:

McWhite's B-17 Fortress was attacked head-on by Focke-Wulf 190 fighters, rather on the lines of this illustration from Target Germany (HMSO, 1944).

Smoking Tom Paine, or a B-17 like it, crosses the North Sea with its wounded.
Photo: Courtesy Target Germany.

'On 11 April 1944 I was a crew member on USAAF aircraft No. 230793 named Tom Paine. Our mission that day was to Posen, Poland, but because of cloud we returned to Rostock and dropped our bombs on a railyard. As our group reformed for the trip back we were attacked by nine Focke-Wulf fighters. Group by group they knocked our planes on each pass. Then our group – the 388th – was the target. Crew members later told me our group lost three planes, including ours. Damaged and with three crew-members wounded (navigator, bombardier and me), Tom dropped out of formation. It was only through the valiant efforts of the 1st Pilot and Engineer we made it back to England'.

It was long after the main American bomber force had come home that we spotted Tom flying high and approaching from the north-east. With him, wing-tip

American stamp of Thomas Paine.

to wing-tip, were two Thunderbolt fighters. As Tom grew larger in the sky we could see smoke streaming from one engine. Word quickly went round among the children, who were playing in the burnt-out fuselage of a Horham, Suffolk, Fortress, that a straggler had been sighted.

Suddenly there was no engine noise and the green shape of Tom loomed big in our frightened eyes. With brakes hard on and engines throttled back, Tom was doing his best to pull up before running over us and blundering off the airfield, as other crippled planes had done, into Farmer Dodd's field. We ran for our lives, but the rough ground of the new airfield – the nearest to Germany –was too much for our legs.

But behind us the frantic efforts of the crew to hold the bomber on the runway had proved successful, Tom had gone through an unusual manoeuvre for an aeroplane with a wide wing span of 103 feet and a weight of more than 20 tons: he had spun on his wheels in a perfect circle – two or three complete revolutions – and had finished up, eager-like, facing

Still smiling: three of the youngsters at the author's birthday party on 14th April 1944, who had to run for their lives three days before when the B-17 Fortress named 'Tom Paine' was ground-looped. They were Michael Dodd (right), Maureen Elliott (right) and (seated) the author.

in the opposite direction and ready for take-off. He had run off the concrete but was still on the airfield. He would fight another day.

We looked round and there, just as in the photograph, stood grimy Tom. The air smelt of burnt rubber. An American in a jaunty field cap and headphones looked down from the cockpit and called for an ambulance. We answered that we could hear it coming. Then the Thunderbolts reappeared, flying very low, and they dipped their wings over Tom. Thankful hands waved back.

So ended Tom's Easter mission to Germany.

I was unable to ascertain anything else about Tom that day, except to note Tom's name and the quotation from his writings, but now, thanks to a friend, I know a little more about Tom Paine of the 388th.

From a London news agency – and proof positive that we have got the right Tom is borne out by the serial number 230793 in inch-high lettering just below the cockpit – has come a photograph of Tom Paine's nose before it was shattered and the information that, when the photograph was taken at Knettishall, those in the picture included 2nd Lieutenant J.E. Zengerle (and an unnamed man in a broad brimmed hat). Zengerle, who was also recently traced in America, belonged to the 388th and was able to tell me that he took Tom on his maiden raid some weeks before the Posen mission.

On this first raid Tom drew 'considerable flak' and was 'so full of rents and tears that the ship was taken out of service after this one mission to determine if any stress had made the plane unsafe to fly'. That was the last Zengerle saw of Tom and the further exploits of this famous Fortress were a surprise to him.

And the man m the broad brimmed hat was Professor J.F. Dobie, visiting professor of American

McWhite awarded the three traceable survivors with the American DFC ribbon and pilot's wings.

history at Cambridge University during 1943-1944. He was present when Tom was christened.

One of the first deeds he performed after arriving in England in October, 1943 was to go to Thetford and help the 388th Bombardment Group present a commemorative plaque to the town's citizens.

It now remains for someone to tell us how long Tom continued the fight. For some weeks after the Posen mission he stood on Beccles airfield while repairs were carried out. Then, one day, he disappeared.

In December 1943, while in London, Professor Dobie met by chance the Red Cross man of the 388th Bombardment Group. He was told that the aircraft had just completed its 20th sortie, 'not shot up much, all its crew sound and believing in Tom Paine.'

Whatever was the aircraft's final fate let us not forget that 18th century Tom Paine demanded not mere toleration among peoples and nations but a positive recognition that differences are beneficial and creative. The State, he recognised, might be entitled to punish acts. It could never, however, have the right to prosecute or penalise opinions And would not the crew of that crippled bomber be proud to echo some other words of Tom Paine:

Robert McWhite, American DFC, at Ellough airfield, with (left to right) Mrs Maureen Skeels (the former Miss Elliott), Mr Norman Dodd and the author, the only traceable children of McWhite's ground loop on 11th April 1944.
Photo: Courtesy Eastern Daily Press.

"When it can be said by any country in the world, 'My poor are happy: neither ignorance nor distress is to be found among them: my jails are empty of prisoners, my streets of beggars; the aged are not in want; the taxes are not oppressive: the rational world is my friend, because I am the friend of happiness.' When these things can be said, then may that country boast of its constitution and its government."

Footnote: This is one of the longest-running Second World War stories I know. What happened in 1944 was, the author at once marked the incident by executing a miniature water-colour depicting the B-17F 'Tom Paine', tail-up, pulling off the dangerous ground loop, watched, when the dust had died down, by two P-47 Thunderbolt fighters that, far out in the North Sea, had guided the battered plane to the East Anglian coast by hand-signals because of the bomber's wrecked radio. When, in the article, co-Pilot Copeland stated "It was only through the valiant efforts of the First-Pilot and Engineer we made it back to England", he was referring to 2nd-Lt Robert B. McWhite, who won the American DFC for the feat, and Flight-Engineer, T/Sgt Donald F. Winn. At the same time as he guessed height and speed with a wrecked instrument panel, McWhite, whose wounded co-pilot had been replaced by Winn, was suddenly confronted by people ahead of him. Some of the running figures turned out to be children, and one of them, then of Beccles and now of Wimbledon, London, noted the 'Tom Paine' incident in a 1946 essay at the Sir John Leman School, Beccles, which earned him 17/20 marks and rare teacher's praise. In the 'Eastern Daily Press' of 2nd April 1962, he polished the essay into an article. Seen in America, the story rallied the scattered crew of 'Tom Paine', and afterwards some of them kept in touch with Mr Elliott. All are now dead, except McWhite. Finally, in 2002, McWhite and some of his family visited Beccles airfield, home of Rain Air (Beccles) Ltd, and Duxford where they received a royal welcome. And then, in 2003, the author was invited to stay with the McWhites in America. Throughout his stay McWhite flew the Union Flag alongside his Stars and Stripes. Now that flag is back in England. For, at a brief gathering at Beccles Flying Club in 2005, Mr Rainer Forster and pilot John Maclead, who in 2002 flew McWhite over the Suffolk coast in his Piper Cub, dressed in American colours, accepted the flag. Also present at the handing over was Miss Elliott of Beccles who in 1944 was one of the running children involved. Mr Norman E. Dodd, of Hall Farm, Worlingham, Suffolk, the third traceable child survivor of the incident, was unable to be present. Interestingly, all three in 2002 were presented with replica pilot's wings and the ribbon of the American DFC by McWhite "for being involved". It has been suggested to Mr Forster that the Union Flag be flown on every 11 April, to mark McWhite's landing in 1944, and on occasions when stray American airmen visit Beccles airfield. Interestingly, when staying with the McWhite's at Wayzata, Minnesota, I was taken on a surprise visit to the local Chapter of the Eighth Air Force Historical Society, where I met several grown-up children of war-time East Anglian marriages. As it was the 60th anniversary of Eighth Air Force Week (8-14 October 1943), the local Chapter shared their birthday cake with me. Asked for more information on this organisation, Mr Roger A. Freeman, the British historian on the Eighth, told me: "The Eighth Air Force Historical Society is the veterans' organisation and was formed in the early 1970s. It once had 20,000 members but is less than half that number now. Your card is one of several local Chapters in different parts of the USA who have regular meetings. The main organisation has a reunion once a year (in 2005 it will be in Washington, DC.)"

The author (left) on a visit with Tom Paine's captain, Robert McWhite, to the 388th Bomb Group's museum at Knettishall, Norfolk.

Photo: Courtesy Roger Copeland

English Village Characters

THIRTY or so years ago my native East Anglia still held a good few characters in the twilight of their lives who had been born in the latter half of the 19th century. Seemingly unchanged by the vicissitudes of war and peace, many of them remained strongly independent to the end, but it is doubtful if many of today's 50-year-olds (my generation), if they live to the year AD2000, will be such sturdy originals.

It was in the years soon after World War II ended that I started to take photographs and record details of local characters in Suffolk and Norfolk, although from childhood I could remember others from the middle 1930s, including a couple who lived in a barn outside Beccles, their means of transport being an old tricycle.

In the late 1940s, according to notes I made at the time, I spent a curious morning with three old widows at Halesworth. They were living in William Cary's almshouses built in the 17th century to accommodate "12 poor widows". At the time of my visit the almshouses had been surveyed and condemned as unfit for habitation. Fortunately the building proper was reprieved for architectural reasons. During my visit I noted "there are 12 rooms . . . but today only three widows survive. Mrs Eliza Wright is 86. She has lived at Halesworth for 70 years with the remaining 16 years in the almshouses. Mrs J. Harper is her neighbour. Miss A.M. Croft, who will be 72 in December, lives at the east end of the building. She is a staunch believer in the gospel and once lectured in Hyde Park. Their ancient grant of two-shillings and sixpence a week and free coal ceased some time ago. The lighting is very primitive

On a spring morning in 1948, John Arthur Lee, 'gentleman of the road', near Needham Market, Suffolk.

and water has to be obtained outside. The widows have little contact with the outside world. Wood bark seems to be the main fuel. The widow I photographed asked me if I would care to share her lunch".

On a spring morning in 1948, while cycling near Needham Market, I came up with one John Arthur Lee, gentleman of the road, with whom I shared my egg sandwiches. He was born, he told me, in 1893 but was not a native of Suffolk. I wrote of him: "Listing to port under his load of chattels like a badly trimmed windjammer, his stick rhythmically flicking the grass verge, John Arthur Lee strode away, helped, it seemed, by a sea breeze that drove his faded coat tails before him. Where he was off to, I know not . . ."

One wonders, so long afterwards, if John Arthur Lee is still alive, for if he is he'd be turning 90. Anyway, I took several snaps of him with my box camera, forgetting in the excitement to adjust for portraiture, but the one of him by the gate, head tilted to the sky, gives a good impression of the weather-beaten face at peace with the countryside.

On Sunday, 24th June 1956, I met a proud spinster at Drinkstone whose half-derelict cottage and old Suffolk garden caught my eye. A well-worn path, entered through a wooden gate, took me to the door, slightly ajar. I knocked. There was no answer. I knocked again, for I felt sure there was life inside.

"Who's there?", asked a woman's voice.

I explained that I wanted permission to photograph the cottage and garden.

"Are you on foot or horse?", asked the same voice.

Then, hesitatingly, the owner of the voice half showed herself round the door. She was, I learnt, Miss Elizabeth Mayes, who for over 50 years had

In the late 1940s, three old widows were visited in William Cary's almshouses at Halesworth, Suffolk.

One of the Cross brothers at Walberswick.

George Baldry worked on 13 different 'perpetual-motion models'.

lived in the same 17th-century cottage, having been born in the neighbouring village of Rattlesden "over 80 years ago". At first, Miss Mayes, who remembered Drinkstone in the days when it was mostly common-land, did not quite appreciate what my camera did. When, however, she understood the nature of my visit, she reminded me that it was Sunday and that, if photographed, she wished to be 'dressed in accordance with the day'. But she had no intention, just then, of being photographed.

Not long after the war ended in 1945 we made a number of houseboat trips to the Norfolk Broads to visit places much neglected during hostilities. It was on one of these expeditions up the *Bure*, when river craft were few and far between, that I came on Arthur "Chink" Sturman, of Salhouse, who worked the ferry punt at Horning. Then in his 70s, and a well-known local character, he told me some hearty tales of days-gone-by on river and marsh. I see from correspondence I afterwards had with the then

landlord of the Horning "Ferry Inn" in 1949, in order to confirm some points, that "Chink" was still in their employment working the ferry. The letter went on: "He will be 75 next September. He has been working here intermittently since he was 19-years old. He has six sons whose names are Rusty, Water Rat, Fresh Air, Peewit Cruiser and Autocrat". What apt names for lads of river and marsh !

A thing about many of these worthies was that their dwellings and their workshops were highly individualistic. At Walberswick, Suffolk, where I knew the famous Cross brothers, Robert and Ernest who worked the rowing boat ferry after the war, their cosy shelter on the Walberswick side of the *Blyth* would today be snapped up in its entirety by a museum because it was a repository of beach finds. Both brothers, at different times, showed me their little treasures.

Similarly, at Slaughden, near Aldeburgh, in the 1950s, I photographed a splendid row of mariners' huts belonging to respected local names like Cable, Wood and Ward. Jerry Wood, who occupied one of the sheds, was Alfred George Henry Wood who knew the Tennyson boys, Julian and Penrose, both killed in World War II, whose local experiences were so ably described for the first time in 1939 by Julian Tennyson in his book *Suffolk Scene*, a rare find in bookshops today.

On 21st June 1955, I went to see George Baldry, then in his 90th year, at his home at the Mill House, Ditchingham, near Bungay – the man whose auto-biographical book *The Rabbit Skin Cap*, edited by the late Lilias Rider Haggard and illustrated by the late Edward Seago, first appeared in late 1939. I knew that George Baldry was not so active but hoped that he would co-operate and let me take pictures. In this I was completely successful and the photographs form some of the best I have taken of East Anglian characters.

The Cross brothers' old ferry hut at Walberswick.

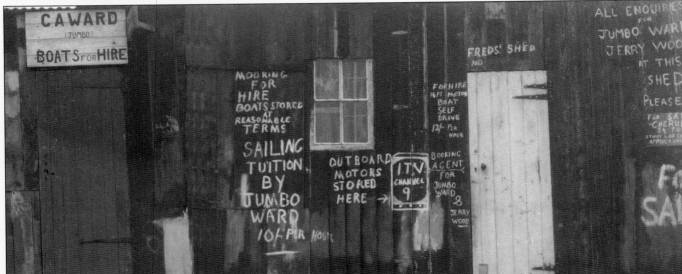

The highly-decorated huts of J.W. Cable, A. 'Jerry' Wood and C.A. 'Jumbo' Ward, which were a feature of Slaughden Quay, south of Aldeburgh, in the early 1950s.

George Baldry's house, and his marvellous workshops packed with tools by the *Waveney*, were completely demolished not long after my visit when the old man moved into a council bungalow. They had been home to him for over 80 years. It was in the workshops round the Mill House that George worked on 13 different perpetual-motion models. In the end he wrote: "He who would build, or endeavour to build, a machine that will maintain its motion forever, without any outward force or power, must first of all seek for a power that is retained within itself. The man or woman who discovers the secret will change the world. I have sought high and low all through my life to find it – and I have failed".

George Baldry, who told me he was "born on 26th November, three minutes to seven pm, 1865", whose world for nearly all his life was Bungay Common and round about, died in February, 1958, aged 93. It was a wintry day when I put some flowers on the old

man's grave and remembered how throughout his life he had loved the sound of Bungay bells chiming over the Common.

But George was not the only East Anglian character I saw slip away as the world entered the Space Age. There were people whose names just now slip my memory but whose pictures were taken by me in the late 1940s and early 1950s. I remember going to Sotterley, near Beccles, at harvest time not long after the war to photograph a bearded farm worker – he was in his 90th year – working a reaper-binder which, by means of sails, swept the cut grain on to a moving canvas platform. I remember, too, visiting Wangford and Henham in the early 1950s to photograph a devoted couple, by then quite old, who had served the Stradbroke family of Suffolk for many years. They appeared hand-in-hand in the winter sunshine from their lodge home, frail-looking but determined to be photographed. The old lady had a particularly care-worn but lovely face.

My tale would not be complete without mention of Francis Howlett, of Turnpike Farm, Shadingfield, near Beccles, who regarded his 300-year-old barn as a kind of cathedral – a place of peace, warmth, rural smells, friendly waggon-shapes and tangled harness. When he died 20 or so years ago, aged 77, a neighbour wrote to his family: "He lived close to the earth and had a simple faith – belief in the seed-time and the harvest, a love and understanding of Nature, a love of children, his fellow-men and animals that only a true country man can understand".

So it came about that, when they buried this Suffolk farmer at Weston, I saw flowers arranged on the coffin in the shape of a cock-pheasant. It was his wish, and no one objected to the idea, that the shot gun he had carried all his farming days should be buried with him. Such a burial was reminder that, while the modern world could attempt to stamp on tradition, some aspects showed a determination to survive regardless. Certainly from the record point of view it was very interesting to witness in the 20th century, when Man was preparing to reach the moon, an East Anglian buried in the ancient warrior tradition – with his hunting weapon.

Working an old-fashioned reaper/binder at Sotterley, near Beccles, in the late 1940s.

A Henham, Suffolk, couple seen hand-in-hand in the winter sunshine by their lodge home, frail-looking, but determined to be photographed.

Knights of the Gulf Air

AS I write (10 January 1991) the shadow of President Saddam Hussein's cruel transgression in Kuwait, which has stirred the community of nations to unite against him, takes world attention.

At the same time the Ministry of Defence has issued rules for reporting war news from the Gulf and the release of information at home. Such steps on this scale have not been necessary since the 1939-45 War.

So, only a few days into 1991 from the 50th anniversary commemoration of the Battle of Britain, 1940, the RAF is once again very much to the fore with several squadrons in position in the Gulf area, with more likely to follow.

Already, it seems, many people have forgotten how long back it was last year that Saddam set himself up as, it now appears, a world dictator.

Certainly, in my view, Hussein's war-like postulations in the summer greatly reduced the British public's opportunity of settling down to remember more peacefully the sacrifices and the achievements of the RAF in 1940, particularly in defence of London.

In fact, it is now thought in some quarters – and I quote from a Christmas card note I received from a well-known Suffolk aviation artist – that "most newspapers and TV bungled a great opportunity" in not making more of the very grand RAF flypast of 168 aircraft over London on 15 September, which was declared the last ever flypast of that size.

I, too, sensed that more could have been made of the Palace salute that turned thousands of eyes skywards as the RAF squadrons, in tight formations,

BATTLE OF BRITAIN FLYPAST 1940-1990

This is to certify that Mr. Christopher R. Elliott flew
in VC10 No. XV 109 from RAF Brize Norton, Oxfordshire,
on Saturday, September 15, 1990, on the occasion of the
Battle of Britain 50th anniversary flypast over the Palace at noon in which 168 aircraft were involved.

Signed: .... Captain
Wg Cdr OC 10 Sqn

.... Copilot
Flt Lt

.... Air Engineer
ENG

.... Navigator
ALM
NAV

*Due to a faulty door, VC10 C Mk I (No. XV105), of No. 10
Squadron, which was the command plane for the flypast,
was unable to take-off as zero hour approached and Wing
Commander Peter Bingham, Officer Commanding the squadron,
had to transfer to No. XV109. In company with two VC10 K
tankers of No. 101 Squadron, and two Tornado GR1 escorts,
XV109 led the flypast spearhead to London from East Anglia.

Battle of Britain 50th anniversary fly-past, 1990

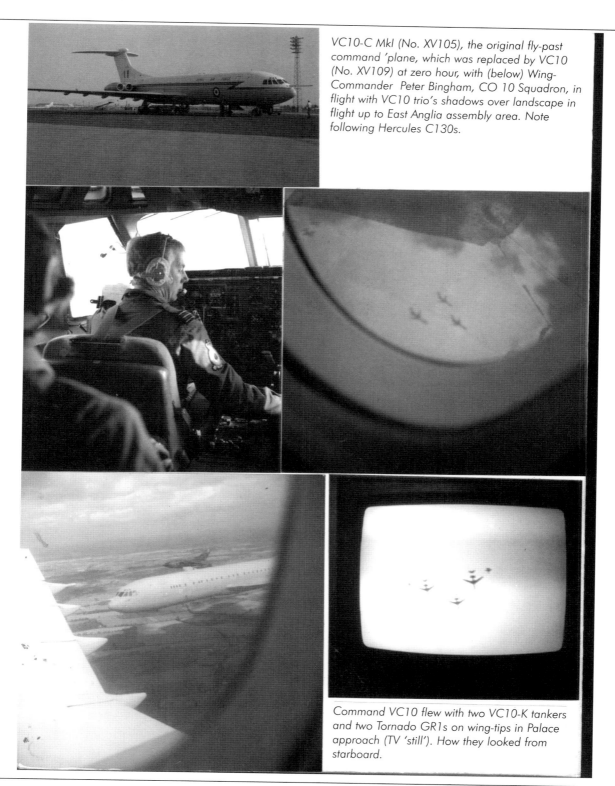

VC10-C MkI (No. XV105), the original fly-past command 'plane, which was replaced by VC10 (No. XV109) at zero hour, with (below) Wing-Commander Peter Bingham, CO 10 Squadron, in flight with VC10 trio's shadows over landscape in flight up to East Anglia assembly area. Note following Hercules C130s.

Command VC10 flew with two VC10-K tankers and two Tornado GR1s on wing-tips in Palace approach (TV 'still'). How they looked from starboard.

streamed in from East Anglia in a column over 18 miles long which, to clear London, took six minutes.

Furthermore, the flypast was mounted with "warlike precision amounting to plus or minus five seconds of the noon setting".

Normally earthbound, it was my privilege as a journalist on 15 September to join the command VC10 jet – the white leader of the formation spearhead of three VC10s – at RAF Brize Norton, Oxfordshire, for the breakfast briefing and mid-morning take-off.

I think the RAF decided to take me – only a handful of journalists flew on 15 September – because, back in the summer, I had attended the first general Press flypast briefing at the Ministry of Defence, in London, then a more technical one at Norwich, and finally the mass briefing of over 350 pilots and navigators at RAF Cranwell, in Lincolnshire, at the end of August. I was certainly interested, and I believe no other journalist sat in for all three sessions which settled the flypast.

As, therefore, so little was made of the flypast on

15 September, as the RAF was already being drawn to the Middle East, perhaps this is the right moment to recall some impressions.

But, first, a reference to the memorable gathering of aircrew at RAF Cranwell.

Dressed in light flying overalls, and sporting squadron badges and other colourful insignia, row upon row of the RAF's best fliers, with a smattering of Americans on exchange postings, sat behind us in the briefing hall.

In two or three glances at them, as they waited for the then Air Officer Commanding No. 11 Group, Air Vice-Marshall W. J. (Bill) Wratten, who has since been promoted to command them in the Gulf, I was reminded of the similarity of the RAF faces artists like Sir William Rothenstein and Eric Kennington painted during the 1939-45 War.

Finally, to please the photographers, a 40-foot aerial platform on the airfield at Cranwell enabled the 350-plus aircrew, tightly packed, to be photographed en-masse making, I dare say, the last grand photograph of such a big assembly of RAF fliers from so many squadrons, many of whom, of course, are now in the Gulf and in our thoughts.

Several colleagues, who believed they would be taken aloft on 15 September, have since asked me what it was like to fly on such a special day.

I give the following extracts from my notes of the two-hour flight which covered over 600 miles.

"Soon after 10 o'clock we were taken to VC10 (XV105), the command 'plane, but after settling aboard with Wing-Commander Peter Bingham, Officer Commanding 10 Squadron, and his crew a passenger door, which failed to lock, caused a hasty transfer to the spare VC10 (XV109).

"As take-off time was now critical, because of the switch, we taxied at a fair pace. . . .

"It was a sunny morning, with some light cloud, and as we gained height, and the pair of VC10 tankers joined us, I noticed the trio's ground shadows and those of the following Hercules C130s under our port wing.

"The course of the heavy aircraft was by way of Upper Heyford, Cranfield, Bedford, Cambridge, Stradishall, Wattisham and Ipswich into the holding area over Bentwaters and Woodbridge, in Suffolk, and seawards with altogether three circuits to enable the other formations to get into position behind us.

"A submarine-type periscope in the rear or our VC10 enabled a view to be obtained of how some of the following aircraft, including the big Hercules and Nimrods, looked.

"Finally, as the formations fell in behind us from their holding area over The Wash and north Norfolk, two Tornado GR1s took up position on the tankers' wing tips as 'live' escorts for the final critical run down to London from the Southwold, Suffolk, entry point, starting at about 11.35 am.

"All other air-traffic over the south east was halted as the huge aerial column, by temporary government statute, had complete right of way.

"All wing-spans added up in our formation: the three VC10s and pair of fighters spanned a total of 146 feet by 3 x 46 feet by 2 – well over 530 feet, when the separating distances were allowed!

"However, the big spearhead formation clung together nicely, riding the air-currents in unison, for the entire run south and turn for the final salute over RAF Abingdon's Battle of Britain "At Home" display in Berkshire.

"Our approach to London was roughly by way of Ipswich, Colchester, Chelmsford and Stapleford where, well below and ahead of us, but very difficult to spot because of their camouflage, we joined up with five Spitfires and two Hurricanes in their Essex holding area. Thus, for a short time, they rightly took over the lead position for the final run into London.

"The view from the flight deck of the command VC10 as east London hove in sight, was of series of distant, scattered, high buildings, the familiar *Thames* and, finally Trafalgar `Square, the Mall and Buckingham Palace.

"The heavy aircraft turned to starboard to cross west London once the Palace salute was over. The faster following formations went on some distance south of London to rejoin us some minutes later when, as described, we were heading for RAF Abingdon.

"At a little past 12.30pm we landed back at RAF Brize Norton having led over 160 'planes in what was understood to be the RAF's last ever mass flypast of that scale.

"Back in London by tea-time and I was able to see on TV what I couldn't see during the flight: how our VC10 trio looked from the ground at the head of the aerial armada."

Now, as I have already said, the scene has changed to possible war with some of the RAF squadrons you watched pass over from the ground, and which I couldn't see from my perch, at operational readiness in the Gulf.

The flypast itself was an experience but, most of all, I have a favourable, lasting impression of the 350-odd 'Knights of the Air' I saw under that quiet Lincolnshire afternoon sky back in the summer.

Sizing Up Dear John

WHEN horse-boy-cum-ploughman John Larter passed the fence by my mother's Suffolk cottage, bound for his vegetable plot, he sometimes called out to the ninety-year old, "Are you alright?"

And when, sometimes, she needed to tell him she'd baked a loaf of bread or made an apple pie for him to collect from atop the gate post, he nearly always answered the 'phone by saying, "Hello, can I help you?"

Now John, who was born at Dennington in High Suffolk, a place associated with Henry V's horsemen of the Battle of Agincourt, has died at the age of 77.

It so happened that when his funeral took place I was visiting my mother. I was able to represent her. I got up early that summer morning, after hearing a distant cuckoo (25th June), and cut some fresh roses and sweet-peas. I inscribed on the farewell card: 'Mr Larter from Mrs E (Hammets Cottage) and CE with happy memories of many chats.' Somehow or other, all on its own, the posy travelled in the hearse with the half-dozen family wreaths.

These chats, which, as far as I was concerned, had taken place on occasional evenings in local pubs when I was in Suffolk, usually revolved around farm horses because John, who was no writer but loved talking, came of a line of countrymen who grew up with horses.

Indeed, they were, if only in memory, so much part of his life that often in general conversation he digressed so that it was difficult to tell if he meant a neighbour or one of his horses!

Anyway, before I went to the parish church, I walked round by the path to John's plot. The two little sheds – in one he used to sit for long periods puffing his pipe – were locked. Then it was time to walk up old Church Street past John's little cottage.

John's relations, as it turned out, were numerous and it seemed, too, that he had a lot of friends from round about. Sadly, the vicar seemed unaware of his long association with horses, which was a pity, as some of his involved tales of horse-handling, ploughing, sowing, harvesting, carting and threshing were ready-made parables.

One, I remember, went back a long way in his life for I gathered that when he was a toddler at Dennington his father, looking to the future, "let me wander under stabled plough horses to see if they stayed calm." Apparently they did.

Robert Bloomfield, Suffolk's nature poet, who lived between 1766 and 1823, and as a small boy at Sapiston, near Ixworth, did his first day's work on a farm there, spoke of John's tred in *The Farmer's Boy:*

> With smiling brow the ploughman cleaves his way
> Draws his fresh parallels, and, wid'ning still
> Treds slow the heavy dale, or climbs the hill
> Strong on the wing his busy followers play
> Where writhing earth-worms meet th' unwelcome day
> 'Till all is changed, and hill and level down
> Assume a livery of sober brown
> Again disturb'd, when Giles with wearying strides
> From ridge to ridge the ponderous harrow guides
> His heels deep sinking every step he goes
> 'Till dirt adhesive loads his clouted shoes.

I wondered, as the church service progressed and thoughts went through my mind of some of Bloomfield's lines, what John used to think about as

he puffed his pipe – he smoked St Bruno my mother believed – in one of the shacks? Sometimes, if the wind was right, one could smell the pipe in her garden.

"Mr Larter's up there", I'd tell her.

After the church service, we trooped to the local cemetery, some distance away, and after the blessing saw John lowered into the brown earth he knew so well.

Leaving the cemetery in twos and threes, the family met for a lunch-time snack at one of their homes.

During the afternoon, as I sat in my mother's garden, listening to the turtle-doves cooing, odd people trooped past the fence. Later we learned from a neighbour that these were some of John's relatives sizing up the countryman's plot in the way only country people do as a form of homage, quite without envy. Some of the men's voices could have been John talking.

"Fancy that, so this was dear John's plot," they would have said.

The evening after his funeral was calm and warm, the lowering sun lingered a while beyond still, towering clouds brooding over the West Suffolk landscape, and when night finally came, and only then, I was able to feel that John Larter, countryman, had plodded by for the last time.

"Are you alright?"

John Larter's favourite garden shack was the one on the left.

John Larter's way out of the 'tunnel' on to his treasured plot.

The engravings – some of 30 – are from Robert Bloomfield's 1857 edition of The Farmer's Boy (Sampson Low) with engraved gold cover and gold-edged pages.

East Coast Smacksmen and The U-Boat War

THE deep, wide Atlantic Ocean, covering an area of about 30 million square miles, has in two world wars seen submarine warfare on a savage scale. So, surprisingly, has the shallow North Sea, covering an area of some 190,000 square miles, but that was 50 years ago.

Regular challengers of the Flanders' Flotilla of German submarines were mostly East Anglian smacksmen. For the destruction of many of their number off Lowestoft and Cromer, beginning on a large scale in 1915, led them to accept with alacrity a scheme whereby armed decoy smacks fished with ordinary vessels.

In the late summer of 1915, too, enemy submarines sowed over 300 mines off Lowestoft alone. Drastic counter-measures were therefore necessary to combat the submarine menace although, at the start of the First World War, the Germans did not immediately appreciate the importance of the submarine as a mine-layer.

But first, however, it is interesting to reflect on the damage that enemy submarines alone inflicted on this country's fishing fleets, sail and steam, in the First World War. German submarines sank, mostly by gunfire and time-bombs (torpedoes were reserved for bigger targets), 578 fishing craft and 98 fisher-folk perished. Mines sank 63 other fishing boats and this more sudden method of extinction took 322 lives. Enemy cruisers and destroyers, particularly active at the start of hostilities, took a further 34 fishing vessels resulting in a toll of 49 lives.

At the other end of the scale – the enemy's end – 178 submarines were lost by Germany and her confederates on war cruises during the First World War. And the North Sea, as we shall soon see, is the grave of many of them.

Soon after the declaration of war in August 1914, unarmed fishing boats in home-waters came under fire from enemy submarines. By the end of that month, too, the enemy had laid 600 mines off the east coast alone. As our fishing fleets were important food providers for this country, there was, perhaps, some military justification for total war, but gradually, as the fishermen toughened to, and the Admiralty harkened to, the peril, the struggle between our smacks and enemy submarines became an organised business.

Tenacity, on our side, was the order. For instance, off Barrs Head, Outer Hebrides, an armed trawler

Lowestoft-born Skipper T.A. Crisp, VC, DSC, RNR, who died fighting an enemy submarine in the North Sea in 1917. His son, Tom, was with him in the smack 'Nelson' at the time

Photo: Courtesy Imperial War Museum

once fought an enemy submarine – the *U41* – for eight hours. The outcome, however, was inconclusive.

Now for the turning point in the battle of the North Sea. Imperial War Museum records show that in August 1915 four Lowestoft smacks – the *G.&E.* (first holder of the official £1000 prize for a confirmed submarine sinking and later renamed *I'll Try* and then *Nelson, Inverlyon, Pet* and *Teesia* – were each fitted with a concealed 3-pounder gun. That month the *Inverlyon* – she fell to an enemy submarine in February 1917 – shelled and sunk *UB4* (Ober-Leutnant zur See K. Gross) "off Smith's Knoll Spar Buoy, Yarmouth".

The Admiralty-chartered fishing vessels performed many tasks. Some fished for enemy submarines with mined nets. One submarine – the *UC77* – got caught in nets so she had to go ahead and astern to free herself. The *UC77* reported, on another occasion, that dummy lighthouses had been spotted along the East Anglian coast. Their purpose was to confuse submarines over landmarks when entering the channels between sandbanks for the purpose of mine-laying.

The mined-nets of the armed smack *Cheerio*, working with the *Hobby Hawk* (alias *Telesia* and killer of several enemy submarines), led to the destruction of the *UC3* (O/L G. Kreysern) in April 1916. She was detected by hydrophone, then an innovation, and this acoustic 'sighting' is thought to have been the first case of the apparatus being used to successfully detect an enemy submarine. Hitherto the only means of detection had been through the presence of gulls over a particular area of sea – at

Mine-layer 'UC5', typical of the small submarines of the Flanders' Flotilla which fought the smacks of the east coast in the First World War　　　　Photo: Courtesy Imperial War Museum

least, that is the story I have had from Great War fisherman.

The cunning smacksmen, as I have already indicated, embarked on all kinds of 'red herrings' under the direction of the Royal Navy. Sometimes the smacks – their sails doing no work for they had been given engines – towed half-submerged submarines which, when required, cast-off and torpedoed the foe – often a very surprised foe. One enemy submarine, caught in the act of sinking a little Dutch steamer in October 1917, received a torpedo from British submarine *E45* 'east of Lowestoft'.

Several rammings, deliberate and accidental, took place in the North Sea. In January 1916, for example, Lowestoft's *Acacia*, when challenged by an enemy submarine, turned on it in darkness but missed it "by only a few feet". For this furious charge, which caused the submarine to submerge and flee, Skipper J. Crooks and crew of four received an Admiralty award of £50 and a letter of appreciation.

Seven months earlier – in July 1915 – *UC2* (O/L K. Mey) had been accidentally run-down by the coaster *Cottingham,* of 513 tons "off Yarmouth". When the submarine – the Flanders' Flotilla was composed of small submarines of about 90ft in length – was raised, she was found to be carrying 12 mines. Here was important evidence. For about this time the Germans began to use submarines on a grand scale for mine-laying.

Fishing boat casualties, as I have said, were severe in the First World War, but often crews were allowed to abandon ship before their vessels were shelled or blown up by means of time-bombs – the casualty figure of 98 for 578 boats sunk by submarines suggests this. But when an armed-smack met a submarine the tradition was a fight to the bitter end.

Such was the case with the *Nelson* (alias *G.&R.* and *I'll Try*) on the afternoon of 15th August 1917. Skipper T.A. Crisp, DSC, RNR, who was born at Lowestoft, was down below packing fish. He came up on deck, saw an object on the horizon, and sent for his glasses. Then with a flash, the German submarine opened fire with its 4.1-gun at long range, closing as she did so. Skipper Crisp, working fast, cleared the decks for action just as a shell struck the *Nelson* below the waterline.

At the enemy's seventh shell Skipper Crisp was hit in the side, the shell passing through the deck and out through the smack's side. As the gun-layer went to his aid, Skipper Crisp's son, Tom, took the tiller.

"It's all right, boy; do your best", Skipper Crisp told his son. Then, as he lay dying, he ordered a carrier pigeon to be freed with the message: "*Nelson* attacked. Skipper killed. Send assistance at once".

Five rounds were now left to the gunner of the smack. But even if he had been left with 50 rounds it would have made no difference: the submarine's 4.1-gun – a new gun at the time – easily outclassed their little 3-pounder. Skipper Crisp, still in command, then had the confidential ship's papers cast overboard and gave – one can imagine with great reluctance – the order to abandon *Nelson*.

Then, says the official record, Skipper Crisp told his son: "Tom, I'm done; throw me overboard". But Skipper Crisp, wounded beyond description, could not be moved. . . . Then the survivors rowed away into the dusk in their tiny dinghy. A pair of old trousers and a large piece of oilskin were fastened to two oars to attract attention, but it was two days before they were picked up.

The London Gazette of 2nd November 1917, listed three RNR Victoria Cross citations. Lowestoft, whose sons had endured such punishment, was moved to learn that one – posthumous – was for Skipper Crisp of the *Nelson* for his devotion and gallantry when so sorely wounded. His son, too, was not forgotten: he got the DSM for carrying out his father's orders.

But the sea took only part of Skippers' Crisp's life. For in the 1920s the *Nelson's* stern portion, I was surprised to learn from Edgar March's book, *Sailing Trawler's,* was trawled up "40 miles ENE of Lowestoft". A piece of the vessel's transit rail, marked *G.&E.,* confirmed this. For the *Nelson,* it will be remembered, was alias *G.&E.,* and *I'll Try,* a smack of resolution in the best traditions of her famous name.

Backyard Flying

NEWS in June 1985 that 'make-it-at-home' aero enthusiasts were lining up to back a new British light aircraft the Super-2 (the kit cost £14,750), even before it gained its full permit to fly, reminds me of the flurry there was when I was a boy in the mid-1930s when the country was swept by Henri Mignet's Flying Flea craze, press reports predicting "A pilot in three hours – 5000 flying light 'planes by next year".

My father, ex-RFC and a Suffolk engineer who was behind a number of early wireless patents, was taken aback by Flying Flea fatalities. So he set to work building a powered, propeller-driven aeroplane roundabout in our garden in Fair Close, Beccles, which, had the war not taken his time on other things, might have progressed as a harnessed and very cheap backyard trainer.

His vision in 1936-37, as I remember it, was for the aeroplane roundabout to have a counter-boom arrangement, using weights on wires, which, when the joy-stick and rudder-bar were operated, would cause the gondola to rise up and down and to bank to some extent.

The Beccles aeroplane roundabout, which began to take shape in 1937, was first of all anchored rather insecurely and both the concrete block in the ground and the vertical steel-post failed during early rotation tests, causing the writer and the gondola to belly-land with great realism.

Also, after my father had spent many hours in the garden workshop shaping and smoothing a small

During the Second World War thousands of airmen received their early flying-training on Tiger Moths. Here a flying training school gets into a day's flying.

sycamore propeller of the right pitch from the rough, the 1-hp air-cooled petrol-engined gondola, during engine running tests, lifted off its trestles, smashing the high-revving propeller into kindling.

Anyway, from these setback, which caused no one any injury, emerged the novel aeroplane roundabout which kept us amused until we were well into our 'teens.

Because flying in the 1930s in just about any form was of enormous public appeal, Gaumont British News, of Wardour Street, London W1, came in 1938 to make a film about the aeroplane roundabout which was shown throughout the country.

The racy commentator, who could just as well have been reporting the start of the great Mildenhall Air Race of 1934 four years before, described the starting procedure – but not quite. When, at the first crank or two – swinging the 23-in. prop was done through a cycle chain to a sprocket just behind the airscrew – the engine refused to fire, the Gaumont man, on seeing the pilot's blushing temper rising, declared: "Looks as if the engine's cold but the pilot's hot!"

Newspapers and magazines in this country and abroad – even in Hitler's Germany where the Luftwaffe was rising – published pictures of the aeroplane-roundabout. One photograph of us at full throttle concluded a pictorial history of flight, starting in 1500 with Da Vinci's ornithopter and ending with us, which appeared in the *News Chronicle* of 5 January 1939. That was an honour, we thought.

On the same date, amid tales of death, torture and blackmail, the *Daily Mirror*, which was a newspaper we were not allowed to see as young children, used a spread of pictures of the aeroplane-roundabout, warning that "These pictures are going to cause a spot of bother for fathers with ambitious play-boys".

Young children loved dressing-up for a spin on the roundabout.

MAKING THE ROUND TRIP

These pictures are going to cause a spot of bother for fathers with ambitious play-boys.

Clad in snug flying kit, Maureen and Christopher Elliott are setting out on a joy flip . . . in their garden at Beccles (Suffolk).

Christopher starts the 1 h.p. engine that drives the wooden propellor of the gondola their father, Mr. Maurice Elliott, has built for them (top picture).

Then, away they go, round and round on a boom attached to a post set in concrete (picture on right).

These pictures are going to cause a spot of bother for fathers with ambitious play-boys. Clad in snug flying kit, Maureen and Christopher Elliott are setting out on a joy-flip . . . in their garden at Beccles (Suffolk). Christopher starts the 1-hp engine that drives the wooden propeller of the gondola their father, Mr Maurice Elliott, has built for them (top picture). Then away they go, round and round on a boom attached to a post set in concrete (picture on right).

In the United States, as on the continent, there was widespread interest in the Beccles demonstration of Britain's air power. An American magazine, depicting us whirling round the garden, engagingly entitled the photograph "On the tight little isle". Nine months later war was declared, the first Blenheim raids set out from Suffolk airfields, and England herself became the tight little isle.

For safety reasons the high-revving wooden propeller was enclosed in a sealed cowling with wire netting air vents front and back. Soon after 'take-off' the snappy little engine (I think my father got it new for 21-shillings (£1.5p) from someone's bankrupt stock in London) spun the contraption up to 30mph or so that, from a distance, the steel pot – an adapted steam drifter's propeller shaft – visibly flexed when measured against a distant, fixed object.

As the war progressed, and we watched developments in *Flight*, we tried all kinds of experiments. For slowing down, a large flap-like door hinged down under the gondola, while later aeronautical advances gave us the idea of trying a small drogue parachute (still preserved), from a British anti-aircraft air-mine, as an air-brake.

For realism in hot weather, a garden hose-spray hung from a nearby apple tree, which the gondola sometimes chafed as daring pilots banked steeply, to give us the effect of battling through tropical rain.

A well placed bonfire, catching the engine's powerful slipstream which lifted ladies' skirts yards

Builder (left) and young pilot of the Beccles contraption.

back, could be blown up into an inferno and, when we felt like potential VC winners, we'd hurtle through the flames and smoke until our faces were a dirty brown. Realistic ground explosions, which resembled the 1945 atomic bomb puffs, resulted from letting off piles of cordite from discarded .50-calibre machine gun ammunition we found around American airfields.

Yet, in the long history of the aeroplane-roundabout, starting in earnest in 1938, and reaching into the post-war years, no one was ever hurt in any of the stunts which mostly took place with no adults in sight. Missiles yes, were sometimes aimed at the speeding gondola, but water-filled toy balloons, containing a spot of cochineal to make scarlet 'wounds', did no-one any harm on bursting like flak!

A good few RAF and USAAF friends – some weighing 12 stone – tried the aeroplane roundabout after Wellingtons and Liberators.

By the end of the 1940s, its gantry in need of a coat of paint, the contraption was tethered, its engine wrapped in an old waterproof coat, at the back of our old home in Fair Close. On dismantling, the engine was given to a man at Sudbury, Suffolk, while the gondola's little propeller, stamped with two Union Jack transfers, joined my serious collection of aviation artefacts.

Did Beccles pioneer the idea of backyard flying?

Well, in 1980 Group Captain S. Wroath, who was familiar with test flying at AAEE, Martlesham Heath, Suffolk, between 1935-39, told me: "Before World War II, when gliding was popular in German and Poland, they had gliders suspended on a gallows-type framework high on the mountains to give the youth of those countries a feel for flying. Seems as though your father was thinking along the same lines".

More recently, in connection with early aviation in East Yorkshire, I learned that between the wars there was "an aeroplane on the top of one of Hull's stores". The 'plane was mounted on a universal joint and was free to fly round the roof in circles. Its propeller gave enough lift to balance and control the aircraft.

Using modern materials, I am sure there is a future for a more sophisticated version of our aeroplane-roundabout of the 1930s as an introduction to flying.

A close-up of the contraption: swinging the 23 inch wooden propeller was done through a cycle chain and crank to a sprocket just behind the airscrew.

Photo: Courtesy Fox Photos

157

Junkers Captain Who Was Too Bold

MY home town of Beccles, Suffolk, witnessed the end of a Junkers 88 bomber of 11KG77 on 1 April 1941, after it had set out from its base at Rheims, France, on an armed reconnaissance against North Sea shipping. Its interception was copy-book style.

Beccles, however, was not to know until the late 1960s that one of the pilots concerned in its destruction was famous in RAF Fighter Command. My preliminary account first appeared in the *Eastern Daily Press* in 1968, and, as so often happens with articles, it turned up some unpublished impressions.

The most interesting of the letters came from Mr Alfred H. Warminger, of Bracondale, Norwich, who gave the following details from his 257 (Burma) Squadron log book: "Intercepted Junkers 88 over Great Yarmouth being chased by a section of 242 (Canadian) Squadron. Pilot Officer G. North and I managed to cut its retreat off from the sea. It then dived towards a cloud layer but was caught in time by 242 and shot down by cannon fire".

Pilot Officer North and Sergeant Warminger had taken off from RAF Coltishall, while 242 Squadron which Douglas Bader, the legless fighter ace, had led in the Battle of Britain, had sent a section from RAF Martlesham Heath.

Sergent Pilot Alfred H. Warminger (third right) with fellow sergent pilots.
Photo: Courtesy A. H. Warminger

Mr Warminger, in subsequent correspondence, supplied a sketch of the local interception as he remembered it, adding: "When we were 'scrambled' from Coltishall after a report of an unidentified aircraft approaching the Norfolk coast, Pilot Officer North and I were sceptical of it being a bandit. We were even more sceptical when finding a clear sky over the approaches.

"On sighting the aircraft 2000ft or so higher and coming in, our first reaction was one of caution: Bristol Blenheims looked remarkably like Junkers 88s from head-on and at that time were engaged in

Firemen at the crater at Henstead, Suffolk, of the Junkers 88 brought down by RAF fighters on April 1, 1941.
Photo: Courtesy Ford Jenkins

anti-shipping strikes off the Dutch and German coasts.

"The bandit had no doubt about our nationality, however, and immediately dived to increase speed, at the same time turning on to a south-west heading to cross directly overhead. Although climbing as hard as our Merlins would let us, we were still a good 1000ft below when it passed overhead. I vividly remember seeing the two black crosses under the wings, dispelling any lingering doubts as to its identity, but standing literally on my tail with the Hurricane almost on the stall I just could not get my sights on the raider.

"An enemy gunner gave me a short burst for good measure and then the Junkers, in a shallow dive, streamed off in the direction of Beccles. We were directed by the controller on the R/T to climb up and turn south, thus cutting off his seaward retreat as 242 Squadron were in a favourable position to effect a second interception.

"A few seconds later, I saw the 242 section we knew were about dive down on to the tail of the enemy aircraft just before it reached the sanctuary of a cloud layer. We then heard the satisfactory outcome on the radio. Although a little disappointed at losing it to our rivals in 242, we felt well satisfied with the outcome.

"I would say the captain of the Junkers was a brave, but foolish man to press on with his reconnaissance at a relatively low height with a wide clear sky on the approaches and over the East Coast", concluded Mr Warminger.

What did the interception look like to the pilots of 242 Squadron section?

Flying Officer R.D. Grassick, who was flying a Hurricane equipped with the usual eight .303 machine guns, said that as they attacked black smoke came from both engines.

The Junkers 88 then jettisoned four bombs, and county ARP records show that two HE bombs fell on Frost's Meadow, Lowestoft, west of Yarmouth Road, and two more on an allotment alongside Gorleston Road, Oulton Broad.

Flying Officer Grassick shortly afterwards saw the raider "burning quite fiercely" on the marshes by Basey Fisher Farm, Henstead, three-quarters of a mile west north-west of Henstead Church. On landing back at Martlesham Heath, he found one bullet hole in his starboard wing and aileron.

When, in 1941, the *Beccles and Bungay Journal* published a censored report a few days later describing the local raider's end, it said that the Junkers fell to "a squadron-leader who was taken prisoner by the Germans when he was shot down over Dunkirk in May 1940 but managed to escape".

Asked to elaborate in the 1950s on the pilot's

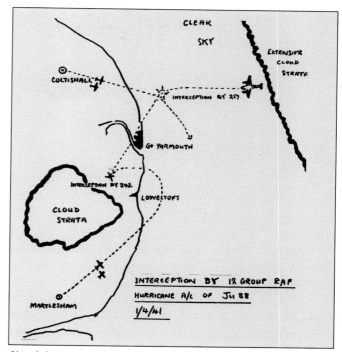

Sketch by Mr. Alfred H. Warminger of how he saw the interception of the Junkers 88 on April 1, 1941.

identity, the old Air Ministry supplied this snippet: "On 1 April 1941, a Hurricane . . . piloted by Squadron-Leader Wilfred P.F. Treacy, of 242 Squadron . . . while on patrol between 17.10 and 17.50 hours, engaged and destroyed a Junkers 88 near Lowestoft."

Famous for his daylight escape from an enemy PoW column with Air Marshal Sir Basil Embry at Desvres on 29 May 1940, and mentioned in books like Embry's *Wingless Victory* and Wing Commander Ira Jones' *Tiger Squadron*, Squadron-Leader Treacy, who was flying a special Hurricane armed with four 20mm cannon-guns of great destructive power, reported that he first saw the Junkers 88 north of Lowestoft in clear air "circling above two fighters".

The squadron leader noted: "Over Lowestoft, a long burst was given at 15 deflection. Bursts were observed along side of fuselage. Starboard engine disintegrated and flame was seen in the aircraft. Two members of the crew baled out and aircraft dived vertically, hitting ground near Beccles".

The first member of the crew – he was a 21 year old officer wearing the Iron Cross – was captured by Police Constable H. Mann, of Worlingham, who saw the parachutist descending.

PC Mann reported: "I ran up the field and caught him just as he was picking himself up. . . . He had no weapon and gave me no trouble". PC Mann then drove the German, whose right-hand was badly burned, to Beccles police station where, as was customary with captured German airmen, he was put in a cell to await a military escort.

The other survivor did not land so kindly. His parachute took him to a desolate area of marsh and trees behind Musk Hall Farm, Worlingham, and this was the reason why Squadron-Leader Treacy, making tight tree-top circles, hung around in case the German made off into the woods.

It was at this stage that I was allowed up from the air raid shelter and, with dozens of other people, raced over the railway footbridge leading to Beccles Common.

To the left, as described, was the slowly circling Hurricane with the then unusual long cannon barrels protruding from its wings. Flown very skilfully, just above stalling speed, and so low the pilot's helmeted face was clearly seen in the cockpit.

What we did not then know was that as the second German touched down, he was dragged through several deep drains before he could release his parachute He then waited for his captors to arrive, but they appeared on the opposite side of a particularly wide and deep drain. The German, quite reasonably, refused to cross, so the men made a detour and approached him from behind. An eye-witness noted: "He was then kicked into the drain and dragged out on the other side".

As soldiers, it was reported in the local press at the time, took charge of one prisoner, it seems probable that the ashen-faced figure I saw seated in a Bren gun carrier crossing Beccles Common, against the stream of spectators, was the German who was somewhat roughly handled. Then the cannon-armed Hurricane, which was circling round, waggled its wings and flew off in the direction of the smoke-pall at Henstead.

Members of the local fire service were soon at the

marsh scene and flooded the crater, made by the Junkers, which was 40ft across.

I remember my father quietly telling a colleague, but to my acute hearing that, when he reached the crash scene, he saw a soldier in possession of a ring from one of the two airmen who perished with the Junkers.

A day or two after the incident soldiers billeted in my street at Beccles, who were guarding the wreckage, brought me some large parts of the Junkers. Among the items was a buckled underwing bomb rack, which was also too cumbersome to keep, but I preserved one of the streamlined egg-shaped bomb-steadying pegs, of which four went to a rack, and various number-plates.

In 1942, when I again visited the site, a primitive cross was noticed under a tree bordering the marshes. Later, it disappeared with no doubt a proper interment in Henstead churchyard.

Today the huge crater made by the Junkers, which must have been unable to get rid of all its bombs while trying to fly on one engine, has been filled in. An engine, it was said, was never recovered at the scene, but this was possibly because, as Squadron-Leader Treacy described, one engine disintegrated on being struck by cannon shells. Local people at the time, of course, would not have known this.

When, in the course of my 1942 visit, I used a grappling-hook in the water-filled crater, pulling up some fuselage pieces, one big portion was painted black and had been roughly sanded to reduce searchlight reflection – a method sometimes used on RAF and USAAF planes for night operations.

Footnote: The Lowestoft War Museum holds a number of artifacts from this Junkers 88, including, according to Bob Collis, aviation researcher, of Oulton Broad, Suffolk, "the label from a wine bottle with a picture of a train crossing a river bridge at Rudesheim-on-Rhine". The wine bottle label and other items were recovered "from the adjacent ditch at this site".

As for Treacy's escape back to England in 1941, which has often been wrongly described by writers, Leslie Hunt, aviation writer, of Leigh-on-Sea, Essex, told me in 1968 that he'd given a close look at escape and evasion records – over 3000 – and found the following statement by Treacy: "I eventually managed to get hold of an Irish passport and went to live as a civilian in an hotel in the town (Marseilles). I managed to get an identity card, my visa de sortie and my visa for Portugal. I left Marseilles 22nd January 1941. I left Lisbon by air 30th January, arriving Chivenor (Barnstaple), where I was first questioned by the authorities." On 20th April 1941 Treacy lost his life off the south east coast when, in a sharp turn, an accompanying Hurricane collided with his machine. He is thought to be buried in the Pas de Calais.

Left: A Junkers 88 passing a dump of mixed HE bombs at its airfield.
Photo: Courtesy MOD

Deserter's Flight

AN unusual visitor to Suffolk on 15th May 1944, just before 7pm, was a Messerschmitt 109G-12, a dual-seater trainer version of the famous German fighter, flown by Luftwaffe deserter Karl Wimberger, aged 25, who had flown the 400 miles from Zerbst, near Innsbruck, in just under two hours.

American Lt. Robert L. Harper's sketch of how the deserter's Messerschmitt 109G-12 may have looked before the crash-landing.

Bearing the markings 22DG+NR, and possibly equipped with long-range fuel tank in the pupil's cockpit behind the pilot, the 'plane 'apparently brushed through tree-tops' before crash-landing on Herringfleet Hill, near Lowestoft, after crossing the coast at Hopton unobserved. Landing heavily on its belly, the machine broke into three parts – engine, wings and fuselage – and when the author visited the scene soon after, the distorted fuselage markings were entered in his notebook as 20GD+NK.

The pilot, who broke his leg in the landing, was wearing a light flying-helmet and overalls over his German Air Force uniform. When told where he was, Wimberger said "Good". The deserter carried documents, possibly to do with the German jet programme, and he wished to be of assistance to the British authorities.

Next day he was taken to a RAF hospital at Lingfield, Surrey, by 146 Ambulance Brigade, Lowestoft. Bob Collis, aviation researcher, of Oulton Broad, Lowestoft, after the war was able to obtain a series of superb drawings of the Messerschmitt 109G-12 on the ground and in flight which were sketched at the time by Lt. Robert L. Harper, Assistant Group S-2, 448th Bomb Group, Seething, Norfolk, whose photographs, films and drawings were later confiscated by RAF Intelligence!

Relics from the deserter's Messerschmitt 109G-12.

Madingley's Sentinel Windmill

OVERLOOKING Cambridge cemetery at Madingley, the only American military cemetery of World War II in the British Isles, is an English post-mill. But, like the hundreds of American service men and a few women buried on the hill, the mill is not a native of Cambridgeshire.

When did American burials start at Madingley? The ritual started in December 1943, on the north slope of a hill where, on a clear day, Ely Cathedral, 14 miles distant, is visible.

Two years' later Major General Carl Spaatz, 8th USAAF commander, said to Lord Trenchard, the RAF's first Chief of the Air Staff, that he would not rest until "a fitting monument to the dead airmen of both nations rose on American soil".

Lord Trenchard, however, replied: "No, this is where we must have it. England was their base." So the American chapel in St. Paul's Cathedral was dedicated in the presence of the Queen and the then vice-president of the United States, Mr Richard Nixon, in 1958.

The growth of the Cambridge cemetery in the heart of British 'bomber country' is, therefore, most appropriate for, among other things, it was in 1945 that the Mayor of Cambridge handed a casket containing a scroll of freedom to Major General William E. Kepner in honour of the 8th Air Force – some 300,000 men and women

And what of the windmill on Madingley hill? Well, for two or three centuries a mill stood there but, as the thousands of English windmills – post, tower and

Lord Trenchard (1873-1956): from the original oil painting by Sir Oswald Birley in the RAF Club, London.

smock types – declined, so did this one until, in about 1909, it collapsed.

Then, in 1927, Mr Ambrose Harding inherited the estate of Madingley and came to live at Madingley Hall. It was after this that the new owner told local carpenter Mr C.J. Ison, who was doing work about the place, of his long-cherished dream of "restoring a windmill to Madingley".

In the early 1930s, remembering Mr Harding's ambition, Mr Ison discovered that the derelict Ellington post mill, in Huntingdonshire, had no local admirers. So it came about, in 1935, that Mr Ison negotiated its purchase for Mr Harding – for just £25!

The 3811 or more burials at Cambridge American Military Cemetery and Memorial, Madingley, are arranged in quarter circles whose wide sweep across the green lawns is best appreciated from the mall near the memorial.

Mr. Ison and just a few men he employed, it appears, went over to Ellington and in a matter of months, working at odd times, took the mill apart. In the late summer of that year the essentials were conveyed by builder's lorry to Madingley but the brick roundhouse at Ellington was left standing.

It is said that Mr Ison was challenged by visitors at Madingley about his ability to rebuild the parts into a new post-mill, and even his backer, Mr Harding, wondered if his dream would mature. But after examining the sails of another windmill, in order to understand how they were constructed, Mr Ison, who wasn't a millwright by trade, succeeded in making Madingley's sails in his workshop and put them up in a week.

After Madingley post-mill was rebuilt from the Ellington pieces a plate was fixed inside marking the completion. According to Freda Derrick in *A Trinity of Craftsmen* (Chapman and Hall, 1950), a lad who had worked with Mr Ison on his Herculean task afterwards inscribed in pencil on the lintel of the round-house what must have been the Madingley carpenter's secret motto: "What man has done, man can do."

Today, however, Madingley windmill, known to so many Americans on pilgrimages to the cemetery, is no longer in the hands of the Harding family. But there is a good chance that, with the coming into being of the Historic Buildings and Monuments Commission for England and more resources for caring for windmills, necessary restoration work on it may become a regular happening.

It was Arthur Mee in his *Cambridgeshire: The Country of the Fens* (Hodder and Stoughton 1939) who said of Madingley: "Its name brings up a vision to every Cambridge man, and not to them alone, for who can forget the view from this wooded hill of the towers and spires of Cambridge rising from the trees against the background of the Gog Magog Hills?"

Well may Rupert Brooke ask:

> *Is sunset still a golden sea*
> *From Haslingfield to Madingley?*

Above: Madingley American Cemetery. When this photograph was taken in 1947 the Madingley burial site looked more like a Flanders' war cemetery. The post mill (left), which was removed from Ellington, Huntingdonshire, in the middle 1930s and rebuilt, still overlooks the American graves.

Left: Here they lived: well preserved Nissen huts at old 8th USAAF airfields are now few and far between. This example at great Ashfield, Suffolk, home of the 385th Bomb Group, was looking poorly in the 1960s.

Wren Who Flew High

TWO years ago, as he was applying the finishing touches to a Christmas card for inclusion in the RAF Benevolent Fund's selection, A.E. 'Chris' Wren died suddenly from a heart attack.

The card was finished by his son, pilot instructor Squadron Leader Chris Wren. The design, featuring an airborne Santa Claus, was also on the front cover of the Winter 1982 issue of *Air Mail*.

Artist and journalist Chris Wren will always be remembered for his work, going back to the Second World War, when the RAF recognised and welcomed his method of helping aircraft identification by turning types of aircraft, friend and foe, into human and sometimes animal manifestations. This aspect of his art was continued with enormous success during the post-war years.

As we all know, he was a regular contributor to *Air Mail* from 1975.

I first met Chris in March 1957 when I boarded a Comet of 216 Squadron, RAF Lyneham . It was to be a one-day pioneer flight for members of the press to Malta and back, marking the jet transport's introduction into RAF service following the costly series of accidents to the civilian version which required much forensic work at the RAE, Farnborough.

In the course of our resounding bound to the Mediterranean and back at 42,000ft and 520mph, I wandered up to the pilots' cabin. There, seated in the captain's seat with a cup of coffee balanced above the instrument panel, I found Chris sketching the second pilot, Flt Lt C. Ellis, at the controls. I snapped him in the act.

It was said that he made history on the flight by being the first cartoonist to sketch the crew of an RAF aircraft eight miles above the earth.

Afterwards, I sent snaps around to other well-known journalists on the flight. (They included the late Ronald Walker, *Daily Express* air correspondent, who wrote 'Flight to Victory' in 1941, and the late Noel Monks, *Daily Mail*, who wrote *Squadrons Up* in 1940). There was a general vote that 'A wren at such a height' should be published in the house magazine of The de Havilland Aircraft Co Ltd, of Hatfield. And so it was.

For some years after the epic England-Malta-England flight, achieved between breakfast and tea, I kept in touch with Chris Wren and often gave him ideas for cartoons for which he was grateful.

Once, however, I overstepped the mark. This arose when it occurred to me that the flak-jacket of the Second World War, which was manufactured by a British company founded in the 1700s and was sometimes worn by American bomber crews, might have been a more acceptable piece of attire if it had been hinged like a lavatory seat!

Having been sent pictures of aviators so dressed, seated and standing, Chris Wren wrote in 1959: "I'm afraid that your idea about the lavatory seat would not get past the editorial blue pencil. 'Y' and 'Z' (mentioning two aviation journals of the time) have an embargo on sex, sin and sanitation, although I manage to get under their guard from time to time.

'Your delicious idea would need to have the photographs published and I know they would never get by. However, I award you Wren's commendation, which entitles you to put W.C. after your name, an appropriate decoration in this context".

Everything Chris Wren did was done artistically.

Comet Captain S/Ldr. W. Harris, AFC, at the controls of RAF Comet XK699 during the 1957 flight to Malta and back.

RAF Comet XK699 at Luqa Airfield, Malta, after its high speed flight on the morning of March 18, 1957

It was said in 1957 that A. E. 'Chris' Wren, who became aviation's best-loved caricaturist and who died in 1982, made history on the Comet flight that year by being the first cartoonist to sketch the crew of an RAF aircraft eight miles above the earth. Here he is shown sketching from the captain's seat the second pilot, Flt. Lt. C. Ellis.

Second pilot Flt. Lt. C. Ellis – without and with his mike – as Chris Wren saw him at 42,000 fet. and 520 m.p.h.

What Chris Wren saw of the earth as he sketched the second pilot at 42,000 ft.

Noel Monks standing for exercise.

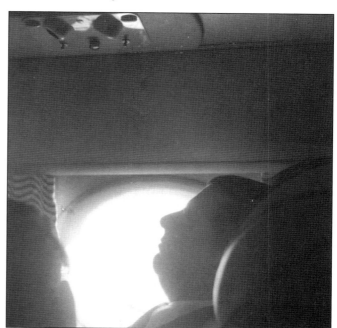

Ronald Walker asleep on the outward flight.

Christopher Elliott seated on ancient cannon salvaged from Valetta Harbour. Time: midday, March 18, 1957.

Daily Express asleep? Of course not! Commented Ronald Walker: "Your picture of me, thank goodness, was cancelled out by the one on the newsreels, which shows me awake and working."

So when in March 1959 he moved from Richmond to Worcester Park, Surrey, he sent to all his contacts a picturesque 'Change of Wresidence' postcard depicting a cocky little wren beating it to the new roost followed by the tools of his trade – pens, ink, typewriter and camera.

Incidentally, there are several legends about the wren. But the most applicable to our Comet sketching, I always think, is the one concerning the smaller golden-crested wren and how he became the king of all birds.

The story tells how the birds of the forest, field and seashore met and the wise old owl decided that the crown should be awarded to the bird which reached the highest altitude in a flight test.

All flew off, believing they had a chance, but eventually only the golden eagle was left soaring. Not being content with his victory, he went up until he reached the limit of his strength, then proclaimed himself king of all birds.

But no sooner had he done this than there was a movement among the feathers of his back, and a tiny wren, which had been hiding there, slipped out and fluttered up a few feet higher than the eagle.

Thus the wren, the smallest British bird, became king of birdland. And so, I suppose, did Christopher Wren become king in his own right when he sketched the crew of an RAF aircraft eight miles above the earth.

Tramps' Folly

A real crash: during an air-display at RAF Wattisham, Suffolk, on 17th September 1955, the author took this graphic picture from the control tower as crash crews, including a running medical officer (left) raced to a much-broken Chipmunk trainer which the spectators had been led to believe had been 'stolen' by two tramps. Flying blind, as their heads could not be seen in the cockpit, the pair of RAF pilots accidentally stalled and, as depicted, landed so heavily that the fixed undercarriage collapsed. The author, unaware that among the spectators were senior staff of the *East Anglian Daily Times,* was reprimanded for reporting the tramps' act as – well, all part of the act!

Dr Emerson's Priceless Treasures

WHEN I heard in March that Christie's South Kensington were selling a selection of photographs of East Anglian life and scenery by the renowned photographer Dr Peter Henry Emerson (1856-1936), who is classed with other Broadland photographers like George Christopher Davies and John Payne Jennings, I naturally went along.

An active photographer in Norfolk and Suffolk, and the author, among other books of *Pictures of East Anglian Life* (1888), I was first drawn to him in the 1950s when a fisherman friend at Southwold, Suffolk, gave me an old eel spear, rather like a trident, which later I learned had been the subject of a photograph by "a well known photographer of a fisherman and a boy eeling near the town." The picture, said my informant, had been taken "over sixty years ago".

Inquiries revealed that Emerson, who was born in Cuba, and educated at Cambridge, had Southwold connections and that just such a photograph appeared as Plate XVII (eel-picking in Suffolk waters) in his *Pictures of East Anglian Life.*

Close scrutiny of Emerson's photograph by a librarian, coupled with detailed features of the eel spear, perhaps a little thinned with use, pretty well confirmed that it was the very one or, if not, an identical example made by the same Southwold blacksmith, as eel spears were localised products with distinct features.

What was beyond doubt was that Emerson did use a fisherman and a boy as models for such a picture. So the grounds for the association are sound. Anyway, I have the particular eel spear as evidence today, knowing that the smithy who made it was thought to have been William Blowers, of Southwold, and that, according to the donor, local fishermen for certain like William Herrington, Benjamin Winter and William Tooke used it over a great many years. Of the three, a Herrington or a Winter could have been the model fisherman – perhaps grandfather or father.

In looking at Emerson's *Pictures of East Anglian Life* just before the sale I found he devoted two chapters to Southwold's Blackshore, the *River Blyth*, and eeling (illustrated), as I have said, with the man and the boy babbing.

What Christie's offered at their sale was a selection of Emerson's works, including such well known titles as *Life and Landscape on the Norfolk Broads, Pictures of East Anglian Life, Wild Life on a Tidal Water, On English Lagoons* and *Marsh Leaves,* all of which were published between 1886, when he moved to

In the second edition of G. Christopher Davies' book Norfolk Broads and Rivers, published in 1884, steel engravings of his photographs were used. Here wherries are waiting for the tide at Cantley.

Southwold and started to collaborate with the East Anglian painter T.F. Goodall, and 1895. All were illustrated with either platinum prints or photogravure plates.

Emerson, who admired Crome and Constable, may be regarded as the father of naturalism in photography. He rejected Victorian sentimentality and strove to portray nature "as it really was".

All his works were printed in limited editions only and the plates destroyed after publication. Thus the rare copies which come to auction are highly sought after. Prices at the recent sale included *Life and Landscape on the Norfolk Broads* (£13,000), which was acquired by a Toronto, Canada, source, *Marsh Leaves* (£2,600) and *Pictures of East Anglian Life* (£700). As far as is known, *Life and Landscape* was a limited edition, only 25 fine and 175 ordinary copies being printed.

As for photographer G. Christopher Davies, who first came to Norfolk in 1871 when he was 22-years-old and died in 1922, he became clerk to Norfolk County Council in 1906 and owner of Burnt Fen Broad. He was dubbed "the man who found the Broads", and one of his admirers was the Great Yarmouth naturalist, Arthur Patterson, who also wrote extensively about the Broads.

In the 1960s, in a South Wimbledon junk shop, I acquired for 5p a second-hand copy of the 1884 edition of his book *Norfolk Broads and Rivers,* which in those days cost 14 shillings (70p).

The book, when it first appeared in 1883, seems to have been a great success for next year's second edition – the edition I picked up – has steel engravings of his camera work instead of photographs, suggesting a considerably larger run

Emerson's Southwold study of eel-babbing. The particular eel-spear is claimed to be in the writer's possession.

than the first, for the copper autogravures were restricted to about three-thousand impressions.

Like Emerson, Davies was interested in eel spearing, noting: "Eel spearing is quite an athletic occupation, as well as one requiring much skill and knowledge of the habits of eels. There are two kinds of spears in use in different parts of the Broad district.

"The one in use on the *Yare and Bure* is the 'pick', formed of four broad serrated blades or tines spread out like a fan; and "The one in use on the Yare and Bure is the 'pick', formed of four broad 5errated blades or tines, spread out like a fan, and the eels get wedged between these. The spear in use on the *Ant and Thurne* is the dart, and is made with a cross-piece, with barbed spikes set in it like the teeth of a rake.

"The mode of using both is the same. They are mounted at the end of a long slender pole or shaft, by which they can be thrust into the mud. These thrusts are not made at random; but the 'pickers' watch for the bubbles which denote the presence of an eel in the mud, and they aim accordingly."

As for photographer John Payne Jennings, whose family probably came from Market Harborough, Leicestershire, he was drawn to the Broads by Great Eastern Railway Company commissions for pictures for railway-carriage compartments.

Later many of his photographs appeared in book form, one being *Sun Pictures of the Norfolk Broads*, published in 1891 by Jarrolds. Working from premises at Ashstead, in Surrey, Jennings died in 1923.

From Emerson's book Life and Landscape on the Norfolk Broads, 1886, containing forty plates, which in March, 1985, fetched £13,000 at a London auction. The cutter is returning with bundles of the common bullrush which had many uses in Norfolk in those days.

The Porcupine's Nail Brought to Life

ENGLISHMEN being great hoarders, it was no surprise long ago when I found in an old family chest a six-inch-long iron nail marked with a pink ticket "Souvenir – From the Battleship *Porcupine* — War of 1812 – 'We have met the enemy and they are ours'."

Irritatingly, no one could throw any more light on the nail's history but my paternal grandfather, who died at Beccles, Suffolk, in 1939, was supposed to have acquired it.

Anyway, years went by until, in 1950 I approached the National Maritime Museum, Greenwich, who stated: "How a relic from the United States warship *Porcupine* comes to be in this country is a mystery, but you may find some clues in *A History of the United States Navy from 1775-1901* by E.S. Maclay. This was issued in an enlarged edition in three volumes by Appleton and Co. of New York in 1901.

"*Porcupine's* commander in the Anglo-American war of 1812 was Oliver Hazard Perry, who earned rapid promotion for his part during hostilities, reaching the rank of captain in 1813."

From elsewhere came a reminder that it was Sir Philip Vere Broke, of Broke Hall, Nacton, near Ipswich, Suffolk, who as commander of the *Shannon* of 24 guns, sunk off Boston, Massachusetts, in 15 minutes on 1st June 1813 the more powerful *Chesapeake* of 49 guns.

In the action Sir Philip, who had captained the *Shannon* since 1806, was wounded by a blow from the but end of a musket which bared open his skull, and also by a cut from a broad-sword.

On his return to Suffolk he was created a Baronet, had much plate presented to him, and was offered the command of one of the new ships built to match the large American vessels but had to decline for health reasons.

Curiously, it was Sir Philip's victory over the *Chesapeake* which caused Perry, about to launch a new ship, to christen it *Lawrence* in memory of the *Chesapeake's* dead captain. Indeed, Sir Philip's victory must have been a powerful influence in making the Americans on the Great Lakes, almost at the moment of defeat, turn the tables and capture the British squadron on 28th September.

Maclay's history, as the National Maritime Museum forecast, soon revealed *Porcupine's* part and the nail's association with acts of chivalry which demonstrated the blood-ties between the American and British sailors.

To begin with, on the night of 12th August 1813, two American schooners in Lake Erie were captured by a party of 75 British seamen in nine boats. The *Porcupine,* however, beat off her assailants

On 10th September, we know, Perry's squadron consisted of, among other ships "the schooner *Porcupine,* Midshipman George Senate, one long 32-pounder."

At 10 o'clock in the morning the American vessels got underway and stood out to sea, while hundreds of soldiers and civilians with anxious faces lined the shores of the lake to watch the battle.

Maclay's history goes on: "The surviving officers from the different English vessels now began to arrive alongside of the *Lawrence.* One by one they stepped over the gangway and cast a wondering glance at the destruction and butchery they had caused and the great sufferings the Americans had endured.

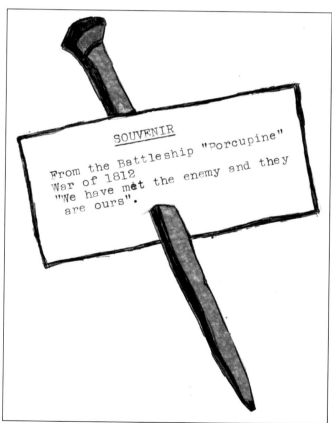

Nail from the American Porcupine of the Anglo-American War of 1812 when British prisoners were treated with great courtesy by their victors.

Then, carefully picking their way over the bodies of the slain, they went aft, where Perry in quiet dignity stood to receive them. As each one presented his sword the American commander bade him retain it.

"Immediately on receiving the surrender Perry wrote with a pencil on the back of an old letter, using his cap for a desk, his famous dispatch: "We have met the enemy and they are ours – two ships, two brigs, one schooner and one sloop, which he sent to General William Henry Harrison by Midshipman Dulany Forrest."

All the British prisoners who were not wounded were put on board the *Porcupine* and later landed at *Cannon River*. The conduct of Perry was magnanimous, every kindness being shown to the wounded and prisoners, and it made a deep impression in his favour on all who were witnesses He showed himself as humane towards the fallen as he had shown himself brave in battle.

The commander of the *Porcupine* was equally kind. He ordered food and grog to be served to the British prisoners when they went on board, "which was at an unseasonable hour, and was quite unexpected, it being but the dictates of his humanity."

By the victory the British were compelled to evacuate Detroit and Michigan, and Perry conveyed 1200 troops up *Lake Erie* and took possession of Malden. A few days later he reoccupied Detroit in conjunction with the army, so that what had been lost by the land forces in 1812 was recovered by the navy in 1813.

Congress voted a total of $225,000 to the captors of the British squadron as prize money, Perry and Master Commandant Jesse D. Elliott each receiving $7140, besides which Congress voted Perry an additional $5000.

The Anglo-American War of 1812 was caused by the disruption of American trade through Britain's stranglehold on the continent by sea blockade, and a continuous series of annoyances due to the boarding of American ships by naval parties in their search for deserters.

Apparently, the *Chesapeake's* flag, hauled down in Boston Bay in 1813 by one of the *Shannon's* officers, was auctioned in London on 21st January 1908, and the conquest "was carried on by an American gentleman and an English dealer, the latter prevailed at £850 and the flag was knocked down amid cheers at that figure."

After the auction, I understand, there was a tug-of-war as to which side of the Atlantic should hold the flag. I have no knowledge at the time of writing as to the end of the battle.

But the circumstances of the acquisition of *Porcupine's* nail, which baffled the National Maritime Museum in 1950, trailed on until a year or two ago when, by chance, I mentioned its existence to an uncle who had spent most of his life in America.

He said: "The battle you speak of was fought just sixty miles west of Cleveland, 'victory' is commemorated by a rather lovely column on one of the Catawba Islands. Your grandfather was present in 1912 for the dedication of the monument – don't ask me why. Just a little junket, I suppose."

So it seems that the 'little junket', if that is what he went on, gave me the chance to acquire the nail. In seeking a sound reason for my grandfather's presence at the centenary celebrations, the only justification I can suggest is that we know that on 2nd October 1813, Master Commandant Elliott "ascended Lake Erie's Thames with the *Scorpion*, the *Porcupine* and the *Tigress*. "I suppose it was a kind of victory show."

Perhaps grandfather had a bee in his bonnet that Jesse Elliott was somehow related but I don't for one moment think he was. I expect grandfather acquired the nail during his American visit. Beyond that it is a matter of conjecture.

Sea battles and storms have wrecked many vessels in the North Sea over the centuries. This old boot vamp (c.1600-1800), seen by a museum dealing wth footwear, was considered of special interest because "the neat initials F-HGI, with the little triangle ends, are based on a style of lettering which begins about the last quarter of the 16th century . . .". The vamp was found on the Suffolk coast after the Great Flood of 1953, and may have been re-used as a hanging receptacle to put trifles in.

Coach Trips Lead to Several Trails

FOR most long distance coach passengers there isn't much to say or talk about and quite a few fall asleep on the tedious motorway rides in and out of London.

However, on two trips in recent weeks between London and Bury St Edmunds, and vice-versa, I have stumbled on interesting passengers with contrasting stories.

Those chance companions turned out to be the grown-up daughter of one of Britain's best known animal authors – she lives at Barnes, Surrey – and an interesting Rumanian-born man now settled near Diss.

First, the lady passenger. What happened was that, as the lady got on the coach at its new scheduled stop by Bury St Edmunds public library, I was able to give her additional guidance on a matter she had raised with the driver.

Henry Williamson created the otter Tarka.

As the coach sped out of the town, London-bound, she exchanged further words with me, the point being that, when she said she had been to see her elderly mother at Bungay, I simply added that I was a native of nearby Beccles.

Asked if Bungay was her birthplace, the lady explained: "No, I grew up at Stiffkey, in Norfolk, in a derelict farm."

So, on hearing this, my thoughts turned to a number of Stiffkey recollections – to the churchman there who, between the wars, got himself into trouble and into the press, to the 71-year-old Duchess of Bedford, the airwoman who, in 1937, crashed in the sea off Stiffkey in her Gypsy Moth in a snowstorm, and to the fact that in the 1930s, Henry Williamson, who wrote *Tarka the Otter*(1927) which won him the Hawthornden Prize, afterwards settled there from the West Country and wrote *The Story of a Norfolk Farm* (1941).

As the possibility of a Williamson connection formulated in my mind, my travelling companion pre-judged my thoughts by seconds and explained that her father – she was one of six children – was indeed the daughter of *Tarka's* creator.

In fact, she had nursed him at the time of his last illness and was with him when he died in August 1977.

Amazed at the way the thinking coincided, I told the lady that from a photograph I remembered of Henry Williamson, her father, in *The Sunday Times*, way back in the 1950s, she was incredibly like him. She agreed.

The rest of the chat drifted to other literary figures and, so far as East Anglia was concerned, we found common ground – Adrian Bell, Lilias Rider Haggard (who collaborated with Henry Williamson in writing *Norfolk Life)*, old George Baldry who was the enduring subject of *The Rabbit Skin Cap* book of 1939, Edward Seago, the painter, who lived at Ludham, Norfolk, and also wrote several books, and so on.

Alas, almost all the subjects we mentioned had passed on.

The other interesting coach passenger I met in the course of using the same route, but this time from the London-end, was a Rumanian-born businessman who lived north of Diss.

He told me that after the war he married First Officer Maureen Adela Chase Dunlop, who was a woman pilot of the Air Transport Auxiliary, long remembered for the work they did in ferrying British and American 'planes from factories to squadrons.

Did he, I wondered, remember the epic long-range bombing raid from North African bases in 1943 when a big force of Liberator bombers, the majority on detachment from 8th USAAF groups then settling in the Diss area, hit the Ploesti oil refineries at great cost at low-level on a round trip of 2400 miles?

Yes, he did, and he was, in fact, a witness at the receiving end.

Furthermore, as many Rumanians were not ill-disposed to their attackers, he met some of the Americans as they were rounded-up, 54 of the bombers failing to return.

Interestingly, he recalled seeing some of the airmen prisoners obtain shaving kits from the local chemist's shop, for the majority were very weary.

Parting company at Bury St Edmunds, the Rumanian traveller invited me to an interesting evening lecture he gave about his country's history at the Linnean Society of London in Burlington House, Piccadilly.

So, it seems to me, long-distance coach rides needn't always be as dull as the featureless motorways tend to make them.

What's certain, unless a conversation is struck, one can never be quite sure who the person is alongside you.

How England Lost Her Railings

With historians of all grades spending more and more time investigating war records at the Public Record Office, Kew, when is one of them going to compile an official history of the war-time government drive for scrap metal between 1939 and '45?

Apparently, railings, gates, bollards, fencing, regardless of historic value, were "severed in pursuance of Regulation 50B of the Defence General Regulations, 1939".

What was more, declared a notice signed by a Mr E.J.R. Edwards for and on behalf of the Commissioners of HM Works and Public Buildings, London, in July 1942, it was hoped that this material would be surrendered in the national interest, free of payment, but those wishing to claim compensation could obtain a special form from their local authority.

However, it appears that particulars of "fixtures severed or to be severed" were floating around in early September 1941, but the government for months had been allowing private firms to collect such scrap from all over the UK without, it seems, a proper record being kept.

As a result of this so-called patriotic drive to produce armaments (much of the material was unsuitable for use by the three services), post-war England grew up with the idea that property demarcation lines — walls and wooden fences — were a thing of the past.

Interestingly, I have the official paperwork for the taking of our fine wrought-iron railings at Beccles, Suffolk, but my father, who was an engineer, was never satisfied with the government statement that the "fixtures . . . or the materials . . . are required by the Commissioners in the interests of the defence of the realm or the efficient prosecution of the war, or for maintaining supplies and services essential to the life of the community."

As, of course, many fixtures, especially fine railings, were secretly removed by owners and hidden or "destroyed during the night's raid" what is the legal position now, should a member of the public discover buried remnants of the faulty Regulation 50B?

What is certain from enquiries I have made, is that some thriving scrap-firms after the war were built entirely on the mishandling by the government of the Regulation.

King Raedwald – Idol Steps

POOR KING RAEDWALD, whose death occurred AD624/5 and whose possessions (a body was not then detected) are associated with the great Anglo-Saxon ship burial unearthed in 1939 at Sutton Hoo, near Woodbridge, Suffolk, has been accused of allowing a half christian and a half pagan household.

When, many years ago, I read of this, I thought of him as a bit of a lad, but, on referring to some history notes I compiled in Suffolk in the late 1940s, I am now more inclined to see his purpose in the 7th century of allowing such a mixture of cults while living so grandly.

My story starts at Campsea Ash, by the abbey ruins, not far from Raedwald's alleged palace at Rendlesham and close by the upper reaches of the *River Deben,* which, back in his day, probably bore his longship cenotaph to Sutton Hoo.

In May, 1949, while on an inquisitive cycle ride, I noticed among architectural fragments in a newly-built wall there an old 'spectacles' stone which may be relevant to the Sutton Hoo Research Committee's present probings into the King's habits.

When I showed the photograph I had taken to the late Mr J. Wickes, of Newton Green, near Sudbury, who was serving on the council of the Suffolk Institute of Archaeology and History, he suggested that the stone at Campsea Ash "may have been carved to represent the 'spectacles' often found on prehistoric zodiac tablets".

Mr Wickes, who encouraged youngsters by his own enthusiasm on all matters to do with history, referred me to Comyns Beaumont's book *The Riddle of Prehistoric Britain.*

On the subject of such 'spectacles', the author stated: "They have been found frequently on amulets, rocks, wall paintings and early British coins, usually in conjunction with the spiral emblem to the course of a cometary body.

"In such connection it is regarded as the symbolis-action of a split or twin comet one that fell in two main bodies . . .

"The 'bridge', which links the two circles, may indicate a luminous link or connection. between the two separated bodies."

A brief note on the Campsea Ash 'spectacles' stone find was published in the *East Anglian Magazine* of December 1952.

Now the late prolific writer. W.A.Dutt, in a fascinating little booklet entitled *The Ancient Mark-stones of East Anglia: Their Origin and Folklore* (Flood, Lowestoft, Lowestoft 1926), which I acquired at

The curious 'spectacles' stone spotted at Campsea Ash, near Wickham Market, Suffolk, in 1949, with a possible pagan worship connection.

Ipswich in the 1950s, came nearer to explaining a pagan link.

To start with, the booklet reiterated the well-established fact that many early British churches (a good few in East Anglia) were erected on the sites previously occupied by pagan temples and idols.

It appears that Pope Gregory (AD590-604), who in AD597 sent Bishop Augustine to Britain and to the Isle of Thanet, Kent, in writing to the Abbot Mellitus in AD601 (about 25 years before Raedwald died), commanded him to tell Augustine that "I have, upon mature deliberation on the affair of the English, determined . . . that the temple of the idols in that nation ought not to be destroyed; but let the idols that are in them be destroyed . . .

"For if these temples be well built, it is requisite that they be converted from the worship of devils to the worship of the true God; that the nation seeing that their temples are not destroyed may remove error from their hearts, and knowing and adoring the true God may the more faithfully resort to the places to which they have been accustomed".

How wrong, then, we have been in modern times, when developing our towns and cities, to demolish not only unwanted churches but splendid old taverns – the meeting places and anchorages of families and friends for generations. Pope Gregory's command of AD601 was, in the light of 7th century conditions, just right and workable with missionaries so widely scattered in hostile communities. The shock of rapid change was cushioned.

Interestingly, W.A. Dutt observed in his 1926 booklet: "In Britain . . . Pagan temples were probably very far less numerous than sacred sites on which stones or wooden idols were worshiped . . . indeed, some writers have held that the stones themselves were the temples often referred to".

So, in looking for a substantial temple at Rendlesham, should not today's researchers allow for the fact that perhaps there never was a building, as such, but more likely a stone or stones.

While various interpretations were placed on Pope Gregory's long range advice, King Canute (c.994-1035), many years later, found it necessary to forbid the "barbarous worship of stones, trees, fountains, and of the heavenly bodies".

'Historical and archaeological evidence point to the fact that in many instances, the early Christian priests not only consecrated Pagan temples to the worship of the true God, but also permitted the "stones which were worshiped" to remain on the sites, "be embedded in the walls" or placed on the altars of churches, or made symbolic of the new faith by "carving or otherwise marking on them the sacred Cross".

The Venerable Bede, whose fame rests on his *Historia Ecclesiastica*, one of the main authorities for the history of England down to AD 731. recorded that the inhabitants of Northumbria, to which the Kingdom of East Anglia had special ties, even after they had accepted christianity, "shrunk from incurring the hostility of the old deities by destroying their temples".

W.A. Dutt. who lived at Carlton Colville, near Lowestoft, and was writing long before the discovery of the Sutton Hoo ship in 1939, added: "King Raedwald of East Anglia is said to have kept two altars in the temple in which he worshiped, one for the worship of the grim idol for his forefathers, and the other for that of the true God".

While an isolated find, the Campsea Ash 'spectacles' of 1949 may, as the late Mr Wickes suggested to me, be linked in some way to those far-off pagan days when, not far away, it is alleged that King Raedwald, a descendant of Uffa by which nearby Ufford takes its name, enjoyed the best of two worlds, partly because his queen liked black magic.

What troubles me, however, is that Campsey Ash Abbey by Abbey Farm, by all accounts, was founded in the 12th century for – well, Augustinian nuns and not monks! Perhaps the stone relic was secreted until modern times at Campsey Ash as King Canute, only a hundred or so years before the local abbey was built, had warned that he wasn't putting up with, among other things, shapes like heavenly bodies associated with pagan worship.

It would be interesting to have some public discussion on surviving local evidence of mark-stones in Suffolk.

The quiet upper reaches of the River Deben at Campsey Ash as the author found the scenery in 1949.

The Little Blitz

IN the early 1950s, when I attended funerals in West Suffolk as a local newspaper reporter, there used to be several temporary wooden crosses marking the graves of German airmen killed on raids over this country in world war two.

Two, I recall, were at Cavendish and Glemsford – the graves respectively of Oberfeldwebel C. Mayer and Observer W. Szyska who died on the night of 21/22 March 1944, when their Junkers 88 crashed at Cavendish. The two Luftwaffe airmen belonged to the phase of raids known as the 'Little Blitz' which ran from January to April, 1944, as the Germans, hopefully, prepared to switch to pilotless V-weapon bombardment in order to prevent the expected Allied invasion of the continent.

Using elaborate pathfinder techniques, the Little Blitz tested Germany's only World War II heavy bomber, the controversial Heinkel 177 or the Greif (Griffin), with a wing-span of some 103 feet, and with its four engines geared and accommodated in two engine cowlings driving very large propellers with a sweep of some 14 feet.

One of these giants – it broke in two – fell at Wolsey Farm, Yoxford, and Parkgate Farm, Kelsale, in Suffolk, on the night of 22 February; another fell on the night of 19 April at Cole End, Saffron Walden, Essex.

It was during the night of 21 March 1944, and a Junkers 88 had crashed at Cavendish. On the same night a personal diary of great intelligence interest was retrieved from the remains of another crashed aircraft showing it to be a Junkers 188, a more advanced version of the old 88.

The German diary, which was the subject of detailed treatment in a then secret Air Ministry weekly intelligence summary as a warning to RAF crews about carrying such records on operational flights, covered the period 21 January to 21 March 1944, in great detail.

The diary (6 February) described a party – the officers' ranks and names were listed – at which four fliers consumed "eight bottles of white Bordeaux and champagne and then about forty liqueurs".

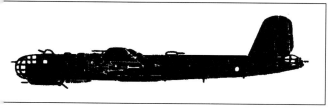

The Heinkel 177 was a heavily armed heavy bomber with four engines geared into two engine cowlings.

This Junkers 88 crash landed on the beach at Weybourne, Norfolk, on May 3, 1941.

Incredibly, the diary went on: "Very tight, but all under control in the presence of the gentlemen of the artillery and their ladies. Played the piano. Just got the train. Then I felt worse than ever I did in my life. Into bed like a sack, snoring like a horse."

Over England (20 February) the diary recorded "the devil's own flak over the target" – then, short of fuel, the crew landed back to a welcome of cognac followed by a meal of "broth, roast potatoes, roast meat and red cabbage, lemonade . . ."

Night raiding (14 March), the diarist was over East Anglia – "Then came the crazy approach. First out to sea on the Norwich-Rotterdam level; from there in the direction of Cambridge; then turning-point to London . . . One night-fighter between Cambridge and London. Amazingly powerful searchlights and ground marking for night-fighters in the northern area of the approach, ie. Cambridge – Ipswich – Norwich. Colossal rocket-flak over the target . . ."

The same weekly intelligence summary referred to the fact that between 23 February and 2 March 1944, three Heinkel 177s had been shot down over Britain and a technical assessment of the wreckage was being undertaken by the Royal Aircraft Establishment, Farnborough.

In the London attack on 13 February, it was stated that, out of a force of thirty Heinkel 177s waiting at Rheine airfield, technical troubles, etc., led to only four reaching the target.

Furthermore, on the 13 February raid, the Gruppenkommandeur, of all people, it was learned from prisoners at interrogation, had "found himself over Norwich, turned back and was only reminded that he still had his bombs on board after he had crossed the Dutch coast". These he "dumped in the Zuyder Zee" before making for base.

The story about the Heinkel 177 at Cole End, Saffron Walden, which had crossed the coast just north of Orfordness, is very interesting and is

The smashed tail unit of the Suffolk Heinkel 177. The position held a 20mm hand-operated cannon. Gefr Emil Imm, the gunner concerned, had an incredible escape when the tail landed at Kelsale.

based on information obtained direct in the 1960s from a native of the area, Mr Ben Auger, who was being questioned about Little Walden airfield's wartime history. Four of the crew of six escaped by parachute.

Mr Auger told me: "As far as I can remember it was just after dawn – about 6am on 20 April 1944 – that I looked out of the window and on the horizon near a wood saw what looked like a white object in the field . . . At the end of the field there is a ditch with a high hedge. As I stepped over the ditch, and pulled myself up by the hedge, keeping an eye on what I later discovered was a parachute, a German airman jumped up and stuck a gun towards my chest.

"He said something that I couldn't understand. We remained like that, without speaking, for some minutes. I then said: 'You are German. You can understand what I am saying. Throw down your gun.' With that he stepped back, muttering, and then threw his weapon towards me. I picked it up and put it in my pocket . . . I took him to the farm of Mr P. Wiseman, the police were told, and the prisoner and gun were handed over.

"As we walked towards Mr Wiseman's farm – and this is the interesting thing – the German took a cigarette tin out of his pocket and placed it in the hedge with some care. Later, at the direction of the police, I returned to the scene to help find the other

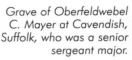

Grave of Oberfeldwebel C. Mayer at Cavendish, Suffolk, who was a senior sergeant major.

airmen. I picked up the cigarette tin – a Piccadilly tin – and placed it on my mantelpiece at home.

"A day or two later I was questioned about anything I had seen or picked up where the German had held me up. It never dawned on me that the cigarette tin was of any significance, since it stood facing us on the mantelpiece. Two or three further visits followed, made by different men and finally I was told there would be nothing to fear if I owned up to having picked up something. I then remembered the Piccadilly tin, and the man said: 'That's it, that's all we want'."

Mr. Auger could offer no explanation in the 1960s as to why the tin was wanted. My feeling is that, from experience, we had come to know that secret information – perhaps navigation or target – was being secreted in the most unlikely places.

After all, who would have been suspicious of an apparently empty tin of English cigarettes on home ground? The intelligence men of 1944 must have known what they were looking for when they questioned Mr. Auger after the crash of the raider with the fuselage markings 6N + AK.

Footnote: The Junkers 88 of the story was shot-down in flames by Mosquito nightfighter pilot Squadron-Leader Nigel Bunting, of 488 Squadron, who on 13/14th July 1943, five miles off Felixstowe, Suffolk, "shot down the first Messerschmitt 410 destroyed over the UK".

In giving these facts, Bob Collis, aviation researcher of Oulton Broad, Suffolk, told me: "The crew of the Junkers 88 were the longest-serving crew in 111/KG30, having spent some time at Aalborg as instructors during 1942/43. Pilot Obfw C. Mayer was on his 182nd sortie, while one of the two survivors, Fw Karl-Heinz Elmhorst, who after the war visited the area, was on his 117th sortie." The death-dive was at a steep angle and the raider made a 14ft-deep crater.

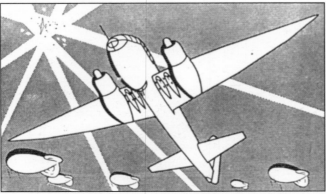

The big engine nacelles were the outstanding feature of the new Junkers 188.

A Suffolk Village
TWENTY YEARS AGO

IT IS over twenty years ago, when my children were quite young, that I went back to my native Suffolk for a holiday in high summer in a quiet hamlet not many miles from Eye, ancient stronghold of the Romans, the Saxons and the Normans.

In those days the local blacksmith's forge was still being worked in the village. How the children loved the sound of the wheezing bellows and the sight of little sparks, like shooting stars, curving up the sooty flue.

In those days, too, an old man in the village kept white rabbits in the corner of his garden – and soon small pink noses, all of a twitch, were touching bigger noses, all of a twitch.

There was also a village shop with a single window – a window which, in those days, seemed to contain all the little things children liked and could afford.

It was during that holiday, which we all enjoyed, that I was shown in our host's thatched house a child's country-made chair, c1675, which I gathered had an interesting history.

The stout little chair had come from an Elizabethan house at Yaxley, a village not far away, when the contents were sold. As my host explained: "It stood in the bedroom of the lady of the house for many a long day and no one ever moved it – not even the maid. It was said the lady of the house had ghostly visitors. For when she was alive a spectre coach and four horses sometimes swept up the drive and, halting outside the porch, appeared to discharge a young man into the arms of a passionate young woman.

"The visitation must have brought something because the lady of the house always left the big iron gate to the drive open so as not to impede the coach's arrival."

Was the child's chair, I wonder, part of the legend? My host never committed himself.

Towards the end of our stay the nights became hotter and once, for air, I looked out of the open window in the dead of night. All was still – absolutely still – save for faint plops outside which puzzled me.

Inside, the roughly-made chair with its ghostly associations stood vaguely by our daughter Anne's cot. The thatched house across the road, with its substantial chimney, just hid the rising moon. A fine diaphanous cloud belt lay between earth and sky but there was no heavenly movement – only a faint lunar light.

I thought of the fox that lived down the road by the

Anne testing the Yaxley ghost chair.

little brick bridge, untouched by the villagers, because, as far as I could make out, it left their chickens alone. I remembered, too, that the village was founded by two Saxon brothers in the seventh century.

It seemed to me, as I stood by the window, that the deep silence, unknown in restless London, was the elusive gulf between their day and ours. For what else could such a silence possibly signify?

Then, far above the sleeping village, came the distant sound of a Javelin night-fighter, now a museum piece, skimming the midnight veil in search of – what? Its note faded and left me with a graver problem: what were those incessant plops?

A day or two later I decided that they, too, were of aerial origin The plops were sycamore seeds, their tiny blades twirling, dropping into hedges and striking fences in an effort to regenerate.

But the history of the child's chair, with its ghostly associations, still intrigues me and my host tells me it is still where I saw it over twenty years ago.

In my local library Jane Toller's book *Country Furniture* provided a little more light: "There were many more chairs made for country children than for those living in towns. The reason is obvious. In the country almost any handyman, given the wood and the tools, could make a chair for a child. In the town it had to be the cabinet-maker who doubtless would make a little master-piece, but at considerable cost".

However, I'm sure the chair I know couldn't be matched, as I feel it is related in some way to the Yaxley legend of the spectre-coach and the passionate young woman in the porch. I wonder what manner of hands made the little chair?

Arnhem: The Rescue Bid

THE Battle of Arnhem, fought 30 years ago, in which the British 1st Airborne Division and the Polish 1st Independent Parachute Brigade were involved, and the equally hard fighting of the 82nd and the 101st American Airborne Divisions at Nijmegen and Eindhoven, will long be remembered. A number of smaller specialist units also took part.

Major
J. D. Grafton

The first huge movement of troops by air took place on 17 September 1944, and the aerial armada, which carried the British element, flew on an easterly course out over the Suffolk coast in the region of Aldeburgh and Orfordness. Other crossing points, particularly for the Americans, were the Essex and Kent coasts, straight across the English Channel, on a leg to Eindhoven. Over 4300 aircraft, including about 500 gliders, were involved.

The operation, code name "Market Garden", which had as one of its prime objectives the reduction of V-2 rocket sites ranged on London, ended after some days with the withdrawal of the survivors of the attack.

After the Arnhem affair – I was 15 at the time – a Major J.D. Grafton came to lecture to munition workers in the Suffolk town where I lived as, I understood, he had been in the relief force that actually succeeded in reaching the encircled airborne troops – but too late. He personally carried to them secret withdrawal plans.

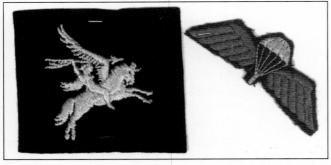

A press report of the time said of Major Grafton and his men – he left me a signed salutation and found from somewhere a parachute badge for my collection – that throughout daylight on 25 September men of the 43rd (Wessex) Division had fought in scattered groups in a confused hand-to-hand battle.

The report went on to state: "It was during this time that Major Grafton . . . called over the radio for our own guns to put a concentration down on his

A Dutch boy attending a Polish soldier's grave at Oosterbeek cemetery on August 28, 1946.

own map reference. German tanks had infiltrated right into the area".

A year or two later – in 1946 – I was one of a party of Suffolk children exchanged with Dutch children, who had been through the mill, who stayed in Holland for two or three weeks. It was during this visit that I left the school party and went to Arnhem. The day was 28 August 1946.

I wrote afterwards: "At Lichtenbeek the first signs of battle were noticed: gaps in the pine wood pointing to shell damage. A village green sporting a solitary German anti-tank gun.

"From Arnhem railway station we made our way

The 1946 Sir John Leman School, Beccles, expedition to Holland at Parkstone Quay, Harwich, before their departure.

Blasted St. Walburgerskerk, Arnhem.

Glider recognition shapes of the Hamilcar Mk. 1 (top) and the Horsa Mk. 2 (bottom)

to the centre of the town. Damage was not too bad: only a solitary house here and there and marks of small arms fire on the walls at corners.

"About a mile from Arnhem bridge, however, we saw the first real signs of battle. There was the burnt out shell of St. Walburgerskerk, not far from the great Neder Rijn bridge, where I found a piece of hand-painted window glass among the rubble. It was here, I got the impression from my Dutch friend, that airborne troops sheltered in the last hours.

"Trees and bushes flourished on the mounds of rubble. Working on one mound were Dutch women with baskets but their progress, without proper tools, seemed very slow.

"We learned from a Dutchman, who was in charge of traffic over the new bridge which replaced the Neder Rijn bridge-span cast on the left bank of the river, how all the buildings round about were destroyed.

In the warehouses by the bridge stubborn airborne soldiers on the roofs and in the gutters refused to give in to the Germans in the streets below. Demolition charges were therefore used by the enemy to blow up the buildings and, said my informant, 400 Red Devils were killed or wounded. He told us of other happenings, too. . . . Here I photographed a crushed Jeep just found under the rubble.

Guide Jan Kammenga

"For our journey to the cemetery at Oosterbeek we boarded the only Dutch bus available – an old Army lorry. A walk at the end of our bus ride took us through pleasant tree-lined streets. On one corner we noticed a house had been hit by a shell. The occupants must have left in a hurry, or been killed, for the rooms contained upturned chairs, personal effects, and bullet holes were everywhere.

"Then we were by the edge of Oosterbeek cemetery dominated in its centre by the Union Jack. Here we saw Dutch children, some quite poor, tending the graves or waiting to plant flowers on new graves in a corner. One boy I photographed asked for a snap to be sent to him and it led, in the end, to a friendly exchange of letters to his family and to the next-of-kin."

It was clear, from talking to Dutchmen at Arnhem in 1946, that they believed at the start of the landings on 17 September that we had come to stay. Loyal Dutchmen boldly pointed out members of the Nationaal Socialistische Beweging (Dutch quislings) to our troops who, however, could only question and

Allied fighters straffed steel railway carriages carrying German reinforcements into Arnhem, and railway sidings, in 1946, contained hundreds of damaged wagons.

Near Arnhem's famous bridge in 1946 a wrecked Jeep was dug out.

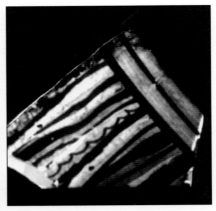

Piece of ancient hand painted window glass which was found in 1946 among rubble in the ruins of St. Walburgerskerk, Arnhem.

release as the battle situation worsened. Dutchmen who co-operated, believing deliverance was at hand, were at once singled out for harsh treatment by the returning Germans and local quislings.

Of the woods I walked in, so that my Dutch guide could show me the old trenches, craters and scarred trees, I did not find them at rest. Soon a Dutch soldier confronted us and told my friend that exhumations were in progress in collapsed trenches near by. We turned away and I knew for certain that the Arnhem woods, in 1946, were not ready to receive sightseers.

Indeed, at that point, I felt homesick, for I had

never been abroad before, and that, I dare say, was how many young soldiers, not much older, must have felt in those same woods in 1944. But for them, if it wasn't to be captivity or death, the only way home was across the river.

The press cutting about Major Grafton jolts one into remembering how the survivors of the 1st Airborne Division did it: "To guide them Bofors guns fired two lanes of tracer continuously throughout the night across the river . . . But of the 250 men of the Dorsets who crossed to save the airborne troops only some got back that night. Some swam, others crossed in boats. Another 50, little groups who swam or floated across on logs, bit by bit found their own painful way back".

One who made the river crossing in a boat brought back a German officer's leather map-case, complete with crayons and whistle, which reached me many years after. Inside it I found the officer's shoulder-pip. It looked very much as if the soldier who brought it back wanted to show, although the 1st Airborne Division had been forced to retire in disarray, that they had met the enemy at close quarters and had done their utmost to hold the line.

I was glad that I stopped by at Arnhem all those years ago when I should have been with the school party in the Hague looking round art galleries.

Footnote: No fewer than five VCs were won at Arnhem in September 1944. While general information-packs about Arnhem have from time to time been issued, lots of people are unaware that Allied forces in the airborne assault suffered more casualties than in the invasion of Normandy earlier in 1944. In the nine days of the bitter struggle combined losses – in airborne and ground forces in killed and wounded and missing – amounted to more than 17,000. British casualties were the highest – 13,226. Equally, the Dutch civilian population suffered many deaths. Finally, it was not until 14th/15th April 1945, that the British 49th (West Riding) Division "captured Arnhem, Holland" as American forces entered from another direction.

Contrasting with the author's school-trip to Holland in 1946, and unauthorised outing to Arnhem, the Royal British Legion's 2005/06 'Guided Battlefield Tours for Schools', supervised by Legion guides, sounds a super opportunity for youngsters to take advantage of the Arnhem package-tour.

Newly made graves of airborne troops at Oosterbeek cemetery as they appeared on August 28, 1946.

Fiery Death of L48
A SURVIVOR

COINCIDENTALLY, as the 70th anniversary of the shooting down at Theberton, near Leiston, on 16/17 June 1917, of the German super zeppelin L48 approached, a vigilant book person living near Bury St. Edmunds sent to me for my airship records a rather scarce copy of Rolf Marben's *Zeppelin Adventures* (John Hamilton) which was published, I'd guess, in the early 1920s.

The book contained in 26 chapters the stories of the experiences of zeppelin crews, mostly operating over England, from the German point of view. It was a goldmine of information. Sure enough, the L48, which was over 600 feet long, had a whole chapter and, as the German angle is so little known to East Anglians after all these years, the following extracts are worth giving.

To begin with, only two of the crew of the L48, which descended on fire, stern-first, survived the ordeal.

So Marben's book recalls that after 1918 he found one of them, Chief Artificer Engineer Heinz Ellerkamm, running a public house at the corner of Schlachterstrasse near St. Michael's Church, Hamburg.

When the L48 left Nordholz at noon on 16 June, Commander Franz Eichler, who was in charge of her, was accompanied by Captain Victor Schutze, Commodore of the North Sea Airship Division.

Heinz Ellerkamm recalled that it was a lovely day as the six zeppelins flew for a couple of hours in one long line, steering due west, across the North Sea.

Pictured on the River Alde a few hours after the destruction of the L48 are Second Lt Frank D. Holder (hand on tiller), the victor, and Capt. W. Walden Hammond, the photographer who took the aerial shots of the crashed zeppelin.

Then, at about 4pm, the squadron dispersed in order to get into position for forming a ring around London. At about midnight the L48 crossed the coast near Harwich.

Soon after 1am, having carried out a successful attack on its objective, the L48 was put about for home. It had "escaped untouched out of the hellish fire of the defences".

A wireless message from Nordholz told the L48's commander that there was a south-west wind blowing at 4000 metres "which will push us along nicely".

But the instruction to drop down to 4000 metres proved fatal as it was just about as high as local fighters could reach at that time.

Royal Flying Corps' pilot Saundby's impression of how the L48 looked over the Suffolk coast as he climbed in his D.H. 2 biplane. In the distance, right, is another zeppelin which, on seeing the L48 burst into flames, flew home. This must have been the L42.

Royal Flying Corps' pilot Saundby's impression of the blazing L48 as it headed toward Theberton, scattering metal and fabric pieces.

Aerial view of the crashed L48 showing much ground-activity. It is clear that the zeppelin fell stern-first.

June 14th
22nd Flight. Pilot F.D. Holder F.E. 2000ft 35 mins
flew over to take official records of
the Zepp Z48, brought down by Holder
a few hours earlier ie 3-26 A.M.

Captain W. Walden Hammond's diary extract (he flew over the smoking remains of the L48 at dawn) giving the credit for its destruction to Lieutenant F.D. Holder.

Ellerkamm described in the book how he was dressed in a heavy fur overcoat and huge felt overshoes, checking the benzine supply with the thermometer at minus 30 degrees, when he heard in the distance the faint rattle of machine guns.

"Suddenly", he said, "I saw tiny blue flames appear in the fifth and sixth bags aft. Then followed a mighty explosion, and a couple of seconds afterwards the L48 burst into flames".

Ellerkamm went on: "I can still see the rigger racing through the gangway to the control car. Behind and in front of me were flames – bright red flames that danced about. I knew that nothing I could do now would be any use . . .

"Slowly the ship dipped by the stern. Then there came a sudden jerk, and the L48 shot downwards. Stern foremost she crashed down into the depths.

"I had a hard job to hold on to one of the girders in the side gangway . . . all around me the flames were dancing and already they were beginning to lick at my fur overcoat . . .

"There was one pillar of fire that was over 200 metres high, and the gas bags were burning away like mad . . .

"The ship's specific weight was 16,000 kilo-

grammes, so we weren't falling or crashing any more, we were just whizzing through the air like a streak of lightning.

"The draught was driving the flames to port. I was in the starboard side walk, but all the same I felt the heat through my leggings. I tried to beat out the flames on my fur coat but a sleeve caught fire . . .

"At last I saw a pale gleam of light below me. A lighthouse, perhaps? Were we over land or sea? Suddenly the ship's stern crashed to pieces with a fearful din . . .

"The shock of the crash must have torn some of my muscles and taken the wind out of my body; I was panting in short gasps . . .

"The benzine and oil tanks had burst. Behind me oil was running about like liquid fire. My fur coat was burning on my back. I was imprisoned in a cage, the bars of which were a glowing, red-hot mass. When I made up my mind to get out of the cage, it was just about the last second in which I could have done so!

"Another girder gave way in front of me and left a gap. I crawled along the ground and felt grass. I crept forward. Behind me was a mass of burning oil. I rolled over two or three times in the grass.

"Then I found myself in the open air. Three metres away from the burning debris I collapsed exhausted. I can still see the meadow, with horses and a wild duck flying overhead in the dawn.

"Then I heard the drone of a Sopwith 'plane, I saw the horses galloping away madly, scared by the flames of the L48. Then an Englishman came running across the field, wearing only a shirt and trousers . . .

"I was sent to a prison camp. My fiancé, Gretel, and my parents received news that I was dead. Some weeks elapsed before I was able to send them word that I still lived.

"Only after several years did I learn that, in addition to myself, Lieutenant S. Mieth, the officer of the watch, was saved". So concluded Ellerkamm's story.

While I knew a little of the story of the L48 as a boy in the 1930s, my father more than once taking me to the quiet Theberton churchyard where, in those days, the L48 dead were buried, I did not write about this zeppelin until 1951 – when a full-length article appeared in the now defunct *East Anglian Magazine*. In it I included eyewitness accounts gathered at Theberton in 1950 and, following

Between the two world wars 16 of L48's crew were interred in Theberton churchyard.

Exquisite gold-pendant containing a piece of tinted anti-searchlight glass from the L48's command gondola. The gold surround may be associated with a piece of regalia taken from the wreck.

publication, there was an energetic response from readers with new information. At that time the record was still not quite straight as to who actually shot down the L48 and I said so in the story.

However, the late Air Marshal Sir Robert Saundby, who was one of the pilots who climbed to intercept from the experimental air station at Orfordness on the Suffolk coast, told me in 1970 that, because they weren't really part of the recognised fighter defences, the powers-that-be did their best to tilt the credit to Lieutenant L.P. Watkins of 37 Squadron, Goldhanger, Essex, who was up on 'official' patrol.

It was interesting, then, to find Rolf Marben's book reproducing something like the impression I had obtained at Theberton in 1950, that a pilot involved in the L48's destruction did, in fact, touch down by the glowing wreck lightly dressed.

Many years later, while researching for my book *Aeronauts and Aviators*, which appeared in 1971, I received extensive help from the late Mrs Anne Hammond, aged 80, of Aldringham, whose husband, the late Captain W. Walden Hammond, the photographer, formed the photographic flight in the RFC at Orfordness in 1916.

Finally, near the end of her life, Mrs Hammond presented my then young daughter with a gold pendant of exquisite design, stating that the tiny gold frame held a piece of anti-searchlight tinted glass from L48's command car.

She never, however, explained the exact origin of the gold surround and decoration holding the glass fragment, but could it have been from the melted gold decoration, legend claims to this day, was found at Holly Tree Farm and possibly shared by the pilots concerned for jewellery for their ladies?

Mrs Hammond also turned up, for my perusal, her husband's diary of his Orfordness/Martlesham flying days in which he related how, at dawn on 17 June 1917, he circled the smoking wreck in an FE.2b piloted by Second-Lieutenant Frank D. Holder, MC, who was the L48's victor.

Captain Hammond, who was a very capable photographer, took a number of aerial pictures of the busy scene, the wreck being surrounded by a ring of armed soldiers.

In 1950, when I visited Theberton to talk to people who remembered the downfall of the L84, whose fearful flare-like descent lit up much of East Anglia for two or three minutes, a substantial portion of the zeppelin hung in the church porch.

Numerous souvenirs – some very elaborate – were fashioned from the duralumin girders and something like a small industry sprung up in the Leiston area making a variety of artefacts.

Over the years I have been given an Iron Cross-shaped piece stamped with the date of the crash, and in a London bric-a-brac shop 20 years ago, I obtained a very nice girder portion inscribed from the L48. It is true, I believe, that Germans have visited Theberton over many years seeking relics to take back to a zeppelin museum in the Nordholz area of Germany.

It is fitting to end this tale with yet another extract from Rolf Marben's *Zeppelin Adventures,* for the book tells of the experiences of the crew of the L42 which flew with the L48 on the same night mission.

"Now we are crossing the North Sea again. Dawn begins to break in the heaven. Suddenly we realise the enemy's swift aeroplanes are pursuing us . . .

"Then we catch sight of a German airship to southward of us. It seems to be travelling over the land, and its silhouette is sharply outlined against the clear sky.

"But suddenly an English aeroplane comes into view above the ship; we can see it quite plainly without our glasses. We hold our breath . . .

"Suddenly the airship becomes a bright, red glowing mass. Then a flame darts out of its envelope. The first thin wisp of smoke curls in the air; then the

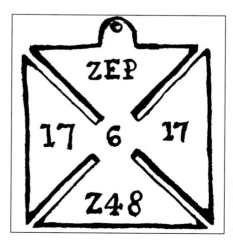

Roughly-made aluminium pendant from the L48 destroyed at Theberton, Suffolk, in 1917.

In 1950 Theberton Church, Suffolk, where in those days the dead of the L48 were buried, displayed a large piece of framework from the zeppelin.

stern dips, and the zeppelin plunges earthwards. It is a meteor hissing down from the sky.

"We of the L42 are not exactly timid folk. But our faces are pale as death. The men at the controls have hard work to keep their hold on the wheels.

"Perhaps three – perhaps five minutes is the duration of the airship's death dive. When she was about 1000 metres off the ground, I thought I saw one or two comrades – little black specks in the sky – jump out of the blazing torch . . .

"The ship was the L48. The comrades who manned her were on their 13th voyage to England. But we came safely home that day".

The L42's final observation of the last minute of the L48's flight fits in with an unpublished picture I hold, taken by an amateur photographer in 1917, of the body of one of the crew who, as described, leapt without a parachute. Like Heinz J. Ellerkamm, who survived, he was dressed in a heavy fur overcoat and huge felt overshoes.

Footnote: The Autumn 2002 issue of *Dirigible*, the journal of the Airship Heritage Trust, published a list of British and German rigid airship relics in UK museums. Earlier, the Summer 2001 number of *Dirigible* listed British airship artifacts held by the RAF Museum, Hendon.

Airmen and Their Ladies

At the time of the shooting-down of the L48, Martlesham Heath and Orfordness air-stations had living round them the families of officers and men. The social life of the officers was conspicuous for the picnic outings round about. This series of pictures, provided by an officer's wife, show aspects of one such outing, the subjects all being dressed in their Sunday-best. They seemed to be able to brew-up tea as they settled among the ferns of Butley Priory, near Orfordness.

Photos: Courtesy Anne Hammond

An Egyptian Puss Who Taught Me A Thing Or Two

IN 1968, I recall, the supposed mummy of an Egyptian royal baby, Princess Moutemhit buried some 3000 years ago with her mother, Queen Makeri, was shown by an X-ray picture to be – well, that of a monkey.

Then, in 1986, the 1900-year-old mummy of a still-born baby, 18-inches long and bound in cloth and bitumen wrappings, was the subject of a paid-for X-ray at the Private Patient Plan Medical Centre, in London, before being offered by Sotheby's for £6500.

Anyway, when I was a young journalist in West Suffolk in the early 1950s, an Egyptian mummified cat was sold at Boardman and Oliver's sale-yard at Sudbury for 5p, the buyer being a local woman "because no-one else appeared to be concerned about the cat's future".

The story is as follows and, to top the lot, I had the mummy X-rayed in 1955 on the National Health for nothing! The excellently preserved specimen, with its X-ray film, is with me as I write

It was in June, 1955, while collecting corn and cattle prices at the local market, that I heard about the cat but the purchaser, when approached two days later, believed it had been put out for the dustman. But on looking in her yard she found the mummy on the ground behind the dustbin.

The cat-mummy – it was acquired by a family governess on a trip to Egypt – measures 10-inches long and the wrappings remain to this day

20th century British cat (left) alongside an Egyptian statue of about 600 BC. While the scale is not true, the cats of ancient Egypt were much smaller.

undisturbed. However, as I have explained, it was X-rayed over 30-years ago, mainly to find out if it had a charm of some kind, probably a carab beetle, in its mouth. A black, unidentified object was spotted near the cat's throat and there appeared to be pins among the bandages. A brown bituminous pigment was the sealing agent.

Mummies of cats, certainly a century ago, were found in very large numbers, particularly at Bubastis in the Nile Delta, the site of the cat-goddess, Bastet. As a rule they are not earlier than the XXII-dynasty (c.950BC). Method of preservation was normally in linen bandages enclosed in pots rather, I imagine, like our English field-clay drainage pipes.

A British Museum expert, who saw the X-ray film, commented: "The modern Egyptian cat, which is clearly descended from Pharaonic times, seems to be rather smaller than the average western cat but I cannot judge whether or not the specimen is fully grown. Also uncertain is the interpretation of the black object at the neck. Cat-figures are sometimes shown with the Udjat-eye suspended on a necklace. It is just possible that this is the explanation in the present case.

In 1951 it seems that only one skull of an Egyptian mummified cat was in the British Museum. Later, it seems, a box of bones of 192 such cats was discovered in the vaults of one of our national museums and a lecture resulted.

It appears, from tomb paintings, that the cat called Bubastis was domesticated in Egypt as far back as the days of Darius and Nebuchadnezzer. The painting showed "rather long-eared animals, ginger-coloured, with long dark-ringed tail". Two Theban paintings depicted cats sitting on chairs. One, which wore a collar, was gnawing a bone. Another picture showed a "long-faced" cat balanced on a papyrus stem presumably, it was suggested, in the role of a retriever on an Egyptian hunting expedition.

While it is clear that cats were sacred to the ancient Egyptians, in the 19th century they certainly were not, for they were collected in their thousands and shipped abroad as fertiliser

It is known, for example, that Messrs Treventon, of Liverpool, received between 1870 and 1880 a consignment of 19 tons of "embalmed cats" for use as manure. The cargo contained no less than 180,000 specimens of the feline species, supposed to have

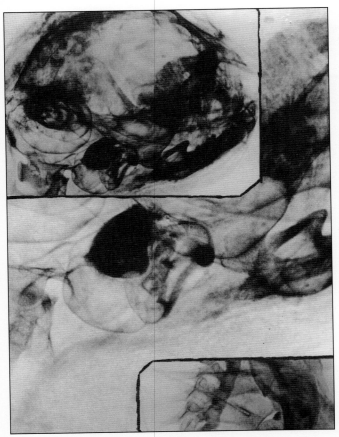

Close-up details of the X-ray: head, black object at the neck, and pinning evidence.

been buried about 2000BC in a subterranean cemetery about 100 miles from Cairo into which "an Egyptian fellah was accidentally precipitated". The cats were found laid out in rows, one on top of the other, and all duly embalmed as though dead Egyptian notables.

According to the late Mr Basil Brown, of Rickinghall, near Diss, who found the Sutton Hoo ship near Woodbridge Suffolk, in 1939 and provided the note about the Liverpool consignment of ancient cats, they were bought in Egypt by the company at 70s. 9d. per ton. He associated the shipment of cats with a small c.1870 glass case he possessed containing "some Egyptian cat relics and an old newspaper cutting, believed to be from *The Times*, from which the details were taken".

As field-walking today is now very widespread, with many claims being made which I, as an amateur, have disputed with museum curators, ebullient archaeologists should remember, when they come to place an Egyptian settlement in the middle of England, that more than likely the "object" leading to the claim owed its arrival to mummified cats being spread on the land. After all, my specimen could hide a scarab beetle or a Udjat-eye under its wrappings.

Indeed, in my wanderings in East Anglia over many years, I can recall an occasion in the late 1940s at Halesworth, Suffolk, when I was shown several Egyptian artefacts about which there was no satisfactory evidence of where they had come from. However, with regard to my Sudbury cat, it was possible in 1955 to trace the circumstances, including the family, and I am satisfied how my specimen reached England.

Needless to say, I like cats, and when we had a new cat presented to us in 1985, as Halley's Comet hove in sight, she was named Halley after the astronomer and her kittens Jupiter, Saturn, Edmond (the astronomer's christian name) and Newton (after his friend, Sir Isaac Newton, the scientist).

Newton, I am pleased say, is still with us with Halley his mother. Writers, poets and artists throughout time have been inspired by the feline presence.

In 1905 Lytton Strachey wrote in a poem "The Cat":

> *Miraculous puss! As o'er your fur*
> *I trail a negligible hand*
> *And gaze into your gazing eyes,*
> *And wonder in a demi-dream*
> *What mystery it is that lies*
> *Behind those slits that glare and gleam . .*

A modern cat meditates behind net curtains on a spring day.

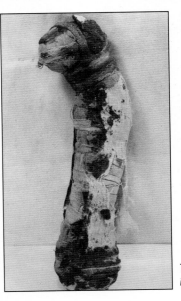

The Sudbury cat mummy in its cloth wrappings.

Lifeboat Saved Wartime Author
TRAGIC STORY OF A FIGHTER PILOT

THE *Sunday Telegraph* has made much play of the 'hitherto secret romance' between the late Pilot Officer Richard Hillary, who wrote the Battle of Britain best-seller *The Last Enemy*, and the beautiful Mary Booker, 22 years his senior, during 1942.

But the literary world owes it all to the Royal National Lifeboat Institution – for it was one of their lifeboats which, by chance, found the young RAF fighter pilot as he slowly lost consciousness in the sea off Thanet after his flaming descent.

It was on 3rd September 1940, while flying from RAF Hornchurch, Essex – which is now a housing estate – that Hillary's Spitfire of 603 (City of Edinburgh) Squadron was hit and set on fire at 12,000 feet.

Before he could escape from the cramped cockpit, the searing heat ravaged his face, but his parachute pack escaped serious damage and dropped him in the sea seven miles north-east of Reculver, on the Kent side of the Thames.

As he floated in the sea, nearly unconscious, he thought he was done. But the motor lifeboat J.B. Proudfoot, on temporary duty at Margate came out of the morning haze and dragged him aboard.

Meanwhile, because of the pilot's grave burns, another boat was asked to wireless for medical help to be in readiness ashore.

Richard Hillary's parachute-pack escaped serious fire damage and landed him in the sea seven miles north-east of Reculver, on the Kent side of The Thames.
Photo: Courtesy Michael Hillary

...old photograph of the motor lifeboat J.B. Proudfoot, which ...so had sails, which rescued Pilot Officer Richard Hillary off ...argate, Kent.
Photo: Courtesy RNLI

Only later did the crew find that the gravely burned figure they had rescued was none other than the great-great-great-great nephew of the founder of the lifeboat service in 1824, Sir William Hillary.

What is certain, too, is that, as the nearly-lifeless figure lay sprawled on the deck, the crew had no idea that their 'catch' would write a book of world-wide appeal.

So we find the pilot's father, the late Mr Michael Hillary, writing shortly afterwards to the lifeboat secretary at Margate: "I am told that my son, Pilot Officer Hillary, who is now in Margate hospital, was rescued by the Margate lifeboat and I want to express the heartfelt thanks of my wife and myself to the coxswain and his crew for returning him to us.

"It would surely have afforded my ancestor, who founded the lifeboat service, the liveliest satisfaction to know that his own kith and kin are numbered among those who have benefited by its wonderful works."

It was in 1955, while organising a small Battle of Britain exhibition at Sudbury, in Suffolk, for the local RAFA branch, that I thought it would add interest if I could get hold of the original manuscript of *The Last Enemy*.

Finding the pilot's father living in Seymour Place, London, I wrote to him and he replied: "On opening the parcel labelled 'Manuscript of *The Last Enemy*' I find that the manuscript is typed.

Royal National Life=boat Institution.

Report of Service on the _____3rd_____ day of _____September_____ 1940

LIFE-BOAT _J B Proudfoot Relif_ stationed at _____Margate_____

Case of the _____"British Airman"_____ of _____Hounshurst._____

Please give here an ACCOUNT OF THE SERVICE from the time of receiving first news of vessel in distress to Life-boat's return to Station.

(If convenient the account may be typewritten on a separate sheet.)

About 10-15 am a Telephone message was received by the Coxswain from the Coastguard Station saying a Parachutist was down in the sea 7 miles NE Reculver. The Lifeboat was at once launched & proceeded to the position given a very extensive search was made visibility being bad and at 11-45 am the airman was found 3½ miles NNW of Reculvers. He was very badly burned, (most of his clothes having caught fire) & on the point of collapse having been in the sea over an hour. He was at once taken aboard & with the help of the Hon. Sec. bandaged & made comfortable owing to his state, the Hon Sec administered Brandy occasionally with wonderful results. The Lifeboat was then approached by a Speed Boat from Sheerness & the Hon Sec asked them to Radio a message to Margate for an Ambulance, & after a journey at full speed the Lifeboat arrived at the Stone Pier at 1pm & the Airman handed over to the Doctor and officials awaiting

NOTE.—It is particularly requested that all the following questions be answered and full Information given.

Questions.		Answers.
1. Type, Name, and Port of Vessel?	1.	
2. Name of Master, and name and address of Owner?	2.	
3. Number of Persons on board?	3.	

The Royal National Lifeboat Institution's official log of Richard Hillary's rescue. It is preserved today at their headquarters at Poole, Dorset. During the Battle of Britain, 1940, their lifeboats were busy.

"Richard dictated the whole of the book to Frieda Levine in Eddie Warburg's office in New York – but I know that at one time I had a lot of written manuscript.

"I cannot, for the life of me, put my hand on it now. and I fear it may have been either lent and not returned or destroyed. As time is getting short I am sending the typed manuscript under registered cover. I know I can depend upon you to take every care of it."

Most of the manuscript, as Mr Hillary predicted, was type-written but the corrections in ink, he believed, were in his son's hand.

Ten years later, while probing for further information about Pilot Officer Hillary, his father invited me to tea and showed me Eric Kennington's portrait, which he later bequeathed to the National Portrait Gallery, of his airman son after Sir Archibald McIndoe's skilled surgery to his face, hanging over the mantelpiece.

Subsequently Kennington painted another picture – he called it 'The Heart of England'– as a gift to the pilot's mother in which the artist tried to capture "something of the spirit of the young officer's sacrifice".

In the picture – it is very moving – Richard Hillar[y] is shown leaving the sea-girt shores of England on hi[s] last journey. As he passes, his head is turned toward[s] his beloved country.

The bandaged head and hands are signs of h[is] suffering. From his right-hand falls a red rose on th[e] green land. The coast is East Anglia. To the east th[e] dawn breaks.

Mr Hillary, who had a spare coloured-repro[-] duction of 'The Heart of England', gave me a copy[.]

Asked why, like the numerous portraits of oth[er] RAF pilots painted by Eric Kennington, that of h[is] son was not included in the artist's book *Drawing t[he] RAF*, which was published in 1942, Mr Hilla[ry] explained:

"The probable explanation why Richard's portra[it] is not in the book is that he ordered and paid for [it] himself so that he could keep it."

This portrait, there is little doubt, played a[n] important part in the young pilot's return to life for [it] is recorded that, on seeing the finished pictur[e] Richard Hillary commented: "I've got a face".

In 1969, in connection with further inquirie[s] Mr Hillary told me: "After my wife's accide[nt] towards the end of 1966 I reduced our flat

Eric Kennington's portrait of Richard Hillary as his burned face healed.

Photo: Courtesy Michael Hillary

In Eric Kennington's painting "The Heart of England", bandaged Pilot Officer Richard Hillary, author of The Last Enemy, who was saved by the Margate, Kent, lifeboat during the Battle of Britain, drops a red rose over the south-east coast.

Photo: Courtesy Michael Hillary

Seymour Place to a sales basis and never intended to return to it.

"As part of the process I packed all the Richard Hillary material in a case and sent it to the chairman of the Richard Hillary Trust, to which I have bequeathed this material.

"The case is now at Churchill, Oxford, and I suppose will never be opened unless reference to some of the papers in the dim future should become necessary."

Did the RNLI, who have preserved the lifeboat incident reports relating to Richard Hillary's rescue in 1940, see anything of the pilot after his recovery?

Mr Patrick Howarth, an author himself and the RNLI's public relation officer for many years, told me in 1965: "A member or this staff tells me she distinctly remembers meeting Richard Hillary and his mother when they came to our depot at Borehamwood, which was the headquarters of the institution during the war".

Sadly, on 7th January 1943, while flying in wintry conditions at night from a Berwickshire airfield – he was desperate to return as a flier – Richard Hillary's Blenheim hurtled to the ground and exploded, killing him and his navigator. Fire followed.

But an official letter was already in circulation saying that he was unfit to fly, his badly burned hands causing him great pain, for in the searing heat of his 1940 dive he had put both hands to his eyes as at first the cockpit hood stuck.

Afterwards, Richard Hillary's ashes were scattered from a 'plane off Margate where, three years before, he had been pulled from the sea, courtesy of the RNLI, to write *The Last Enemy*.

As for Richard Hillary's two or three courtships, which were very moving, Lovat Dickson, the well known publisher, who died last year and with whom I had correspondence in 1953, quoted some of the Hillary/Booker letters in his penetrating study, *Richard Hillary*, which Macmillan's who first put out *The Last Enemy* in 1942, published in 1950.

Footnote: While Richard Hillary, in the minds of many, was one of the earliest RAF pilots to suffer severe burns in the Battle of Britain, Flying Officer (later Squadron Leader) Alan G. Page, of 56 Squadron, was quite as badly burned on 12th August 1940, when his Hurricane crashed in flames two miles off Epple Bay, not far from Hillary's bale-out. Landing in the sea by parachute, Page was picked up by a tender and transferred to the Margate, Kent, lifeboat that had saved Hillary's life. Page needed medical attention for two years, and underwent plastic surgery at Queen Victoria Hospital, East Grinstead. He was a founder-member of the Guinea Pig Club. Page, who returned to flying, was again severely hurt, and fractured his back. Recovering, he was by 1945 a test pilot. While Hillary and Page fell into the sea, and no doubt obtained some immediate benefit from the salt-water on their burns, Squadron Leader Thomas P. Gleave, of 253 Squadron, who suffered grievous burns on 31st August 1940, when his Hurricane was shot down in flames near Biggin Hill, Kent, parachuted over land. He later described the incident in *I Had a Row with a German*. Recovering after treatment at the East Grinstead hospital, he became vice-president of the Guinea Pig Club, with the title of Chief Guinea Pig. He retired as a Group Captain.

In Search of Little Worlingham

HARDLY a day goes by without news from abroad of large numbers of people being killed by unbridled revolution or natural catastrophe. Sometimes there isn't even time to hide the dead from the eyes of the living.

But nearer home, as we rush about our daily labours, a bit of local history suddenly comes to light to remind us of those who have trod the lanes before us and are now no more. Indeed, if one is sensitive to the past, the pressure of the gnarled hand of time on one's shoulders may be felt . . .

It was with surprise that I found in the early summer of last year, while visiting All Saints' churchyard, at Worlingham, a simple white tombstone inscribed:

> Here Lie The Mortal Remains
> Of 23 Parishioners
> Of
> St. Peter's Parish
> Worlingham Parva
> Re-interred 1981

As I looked at the stone, I remembered reading in the press a brief reference to ancient skeletons found in the Worlingham area and wondering what span of time they represented.

So, finding some of the inhabitants of pre-Domesday Book Worlingham safely marked in this christian way, I approached Beccles Library and Lowestoft Central Library for guidance.

According to the *Beccles and Bungay Journal* of 20th June 1980, the finds were made by Eastern Gas Board contractors almost opposite the *Three Horseshoes* public house. I knew the fields from boyhood walks, but I never suspected they held secrets of a lost civilisation.

A study of the skeletons, said the report, showed them to be "a mixture of both sexes and all ages, from children through to old age". What seemed to be certain was that, lying on an east-west line, most with their heads facing west, and being found with no ornaments, the remains were those of christians.

The Rector of Worlingham, the Rev. Geoffrey Johnson, was convinced the discovery was "the churchyard of the former Worlingham St. Peter, or Worlingham Parva". It was he who strongly advocated the re-interment of the scattered remains.

Support for Mr Johnson's theory – that the site marked the centre of Little Worlingham – came from the late Miss Janet Hadenham, a local historian, who believed that masonry unearthed by ploughing near the *Three Horseshoes* pointed to forgotten Worlingham Parva.

Erected at Worlingham, near Beccles, in the early 1980s to commemorate the remains of 23 parishioners of the first village of Worlingham found during trenching, the tombstone is a good sign at a time when so many churchyards are neglected with few graves visited.

Finally, the *Beccles and Bungay Journal* of 3rd Jul 1981, reported the reinterment at All Saint churchyard Worlingham, on St. Peter's Day (29t June), of the remains of those people who had bee found at North Cove by the "remains of a smal round-towered church".

The report described how the remains wer preserved in "a sturdy burial chest" and, following simple service, lowered into the new grave by beare Mr Aubrey Forman, chairman of Worlingham paris council, Mr Alan Muttitt, Mr Harry Clutter chairman of the Beccles Historical Society, and M Reg Moore, a church councillor.

Still guided by helpful librarians, I was told that tl *Lowestoft Archaeological and Local History Socie Annual Report*, Vol. 13, 1980-81 had written up tl discovery in detail.

There was, I found, a listing in the study of tl

small bronze, pottery and lead finds, including some coins, of Roman, Saxo-Norman, and Medieval origin, but they were not, in my opinion significant, although the local archaeologists concerned felt there was "sufficient evidence to indicate substantial occupation of the site in the early second and fourth centuries". The lost church with "round tower and apse" was "indicative of origins . . . in the 10th to 12th century".

The conclusion to the dental examination of the skeletal remains uncovered at North Cove observed: "The amount of attrition gives a very good indication of the coarseness of the diet and it would appear that this probably contained a considerable amount of grit . . . One skull was found with an edge to edge bite and one got the impression from several of the mandibles that this was by no means the only one . . .

"Not infrequently one finds medieval stone or wooden carvings in churches depicting tooth-ache. Having studied these jaws, one realises that it must have been a far from infrequent experience!"

Not long after I had satisfied my curiosity over the lost village of Worlingham, a thoughtful friend sent me a cutting from the *Beccles and Bungay Journal* of 1st October 1982, describing how All Saint's Church was carrying out repairs to part of its 17th-century red brick road wall at a cost "nearly 90 times greater than the whole wall cost to build three hundred years ago".

In fact, when the wall was completed in 1686, a bill was sent to the church for £23 12s.6d. Today's bill is likely to be £2,000 to prevent the Elizabethan wall from collapsing!

So the Worlingham of today, pounded by an endless stream of lorries, is determined to keep a gentle hold on the past.

This fact was confirmed once-and-for-all when, on looking at the new tombstone marking the resting place of the village's 23 unknown parishioners, I heard the shrill voices of small children. Then two or three came skipping through the churchyard from the nearby infants' school, bound for home and tea.

I thought: if parts of the rest of the world can't manage to achieve much Worlingham proves that it is old enough, and wise enough, to cater for the living and the dead as if they were one great mortal family.

Delft's Craftswomen

Obtaining a lift aboard a scrapmetal coaster bound for Holland in the 1950s from Great Yarmouth, Norfolk, the author visited the famous Delft pottery, founded in 1653, and was able to photograph a potter and an artist at work.

191

Frugal Outpost of Prayer

AMONG my East Anglian artifacts is a nice fragment of 17th-century green glazed tile which I retrieved in 1953 from a pile of debris mixed with several unexploded 25-pounder shells near the lonely chapel of Minsmere associated with St. Mary's Abbey, Leiston, Suffolk, the area having been a war-time bombing range.

So I write this time on a further aspect of East Anglia's fascinating contribution to the growth of christianity resulting from the endeavours of 7th-century missionaries like St. Fursey, St. Felix and St. Botolph.

In this connection it is interesting to recall that around the British Isles, often on exposed coastal sites like Minsmere, are a number of small, ruined, chapels of great antiquity which were once occupied by hermit-like men and women in the name of God.

That Northumbria had a very important link with Sutton Hoo, Suffolk, now the subject of a 10-year investigation, becomes clearer when one finds that Ebb's Nook hermitage chapel, south of Bamburgh and near Beadnell harbour, had a believed-association with St. Ebba, step-daughter of 7th-century King Ethelfrith of Northumbria. Interestingly, St. Ebba is said to have had a link with the community of nuns at Ely whose minster is the cathedral church of the Fens.

Signs of her chilly cell, typical of these lonely chapels standing as 'powerful examples of the juxtaposition of the spiritual and the elemental' in the growth of christianity, may still be seen in Northumberland.

In the vale of Minsmere, even after rough treatment through shelling, the building within its ancient walls of a concrete pillbox against invasion in 1940, and centuries of neglect, the chapel remains,

The double-fronted 14th century crucifix noted at Leiston Abbey, Suffolk, in 1950. It was probably designed to stand at a cross-roads.

even now, are considerable. But, as a comparison o[f] my picture will show, the chapel's defined shape o[f] the first 10 or so years of this century has all but gone[.]

B. Granville Baker, who lived at Beccles, Suffolk[,] when I was a boy there in the 1930s, said in his boo[k] *Blithe Waters: Sheaves out of Suffolk* (Heath Cranton[,] 1931):

"With all the beauty of this vale of Minsmere, it lie[s] very much exposed to the nor'east wind, and that, i[t] seems, is why the Canons of St. Mary's Abbey . . [.] removed from their first abode to the more sheltere[d] spot where you may still see the majestic ruins of thei[r] old home.

"The original monastery, as erected by Sir Ranul[f] de Glanville in 1182, was not totally abandone[d] when the new buildings were completed in 1362[;] indeed, they were inhabited until the Dissolution, b[y] such members of the fraternity as desired to live i[n] strictest seclusion . . . There remains nothing, bu[t] the shell of a chapel to mark the first settlement o[f] these Praemonstratensians . . .".

W.A. Dutt in *The Norfolk and Suffolk Coast* (T[.] Fisher Unwin, 1909) noted that John Grene, one o[f] the abbots of Leiston, relinquished the abbacy i[n] order to become an anchorite "at the Chapel of S[t.] Mary in the old monastery by the sea". That was i[n] the year 1531.

And James Bird of Earl Stonham and Yoxfor[d,] Suffolk, in his mysterious poem in five cantos calle[d] *The Vale of Slaughden* (C. Baldwin, 1819), touchin[g] the Suffolk coast, wrote "By Druid's cave, or cell [of] Anchorite". Was he, I wonder, thinking of the chap[el] at Minsmere?

In his book *Minsmere, Portrait of a Bird Reser[ve]*

Under lowering storm clouds driven by a nor' east wind is how the writer saw remote Minsmere chapel in 1953. The slightly elevated site above the marsh level is apparent. When the photographer reached the ruins the figure (left) had vanished . . .

Side elevation of the old Minsmere chapel in Suffolk in 1953. The gun port of the 1940 concrete pill-box is visible to the right of the structure.

The white canons of Minsmere knew the chapel when it had dignity. Here is how it looked in the 1930s.

(Hutchinson, 1978) Herbert Axell explained the chapel's demise: "But geological history was too late for the monks of Minsmere Level. At the time of the Abbey's founding, in the late 12th century, the estuary which flowed past its walls was broad; its waters spread at will at flood-tide and lapped around the chapel mound. For many years, successions of monks laboured to build earth embankments to protect their building's ill-chosen site and to gain land for agriculture but the position finally proved to be untenable.

"After widespread floods had occurred in this part of Suffolk's coast in 1347, a new abbey was erected by Robert de Ufford on high land to the west and the monks transferred there. Grassy banks can still be seen meandering around the Level and one of the longest, attributed to the abbey's workers, makes it possible to maintain water in the marshland of Minsmere Bird Reserve".

The Praemonstratensian order took its name from the locality called Premontre, near Laon, France, the date of the foundation by St. Norbert being 1119.

M.R. James in *Suffolk and Norfolk* (Dent, 1930) observed: "These White Canons, as they were called, had 34 houses in England, and of these Leiston, the only one in Suffolk, was perhaps the most considerable in our district, Norfolk had three."

In 1950 I was shown, and was able to photograph, at Leiston Abbey an ancient Brittany granite crucifix of the 14th-century, then badly overgrown, marking the site of the high altar. The peculiar double-fronted carving suggested 'that it was designed to stand at a crossroads'.

It was interesting to find the crucifix and to remember that, in its heyday, the present Leiston Abbey site and the less-known chapel at Minsmere all heard the chants of pious men upholding the teachings of Suffolk's 7th-century missionaries.

What Floods Leave

The Great Freeze of 1947, followed by severe flooding in some parts of East Anglia, often due to ice floes in many rivers, led to this houseboat being left stranded on the quay by the River Waveney at Beccles, Suffolk. The whole of the Waveney Valley was inundated for days.

Battle of Britain
HOW IT WAS NOT FOUGHT

THERE is nothing about this airfield – RAF Potsworth, Kent – which makes me think that the Battle of Britain is on. A skylark soars high in the summer sky against a backcloth of drifting vapour trails: the dogfight is too high for mortal ears. Haycocks dot the landing strip, which, due to unfilled craters, has shrunk to tightrope-like proportions .

Will the gallant RAF pilots, battling with the Luftwaffe, get down safely without tipping on to their noses? The truth of the matter is that the entire squadron, except those ordered to 'scramble', went on strike at 1400 hours today.

In the roofless canteen the airmen, some wearing civilian clothes, are having a long lunch. The menu is officer-class, for, in addition to pinching their lunch, the airmen have commandeered the officers' crockery.

Flight mechanics, armourers, wireless mechanics, instrument repairers, clerks, cooks and butchers are all happily tucking in. There's an air of bravado about the place.

On the canteen notice-board someone has pinned a copy of Hitler's 'A Last Appeal to Reason' propaganda leaflet, based on his speech before the Reichstag on 19th July 1940. One paragraph, specially marked, declares of Field Marshal Hermann Goering: "As Commander of the German Air Force he has so far in the course of the war contributed to the creation of the pre-requisites for the final victory. His merits are unique."

When I ask a dozing armourer how a journalist is expected to interpret such egotistical rubbish, he says with a yawn: "Well, if he doesn't win we shall. Just wait, my old beauty, for the fun and games in 20 minutes' time when the officers are coming in short of juice. Just you wait."

With that the armourer, who is unshaven, wags a nicotine-coated finger at the vapour trails and, with a quick change of finger plan, indicates his contempt for them, the solitary skylark and the blue expanse of sky

In dispersal pens nearby are several reserve Spitfires and, for the first time, I feel secure. But wait a moment. The Spitfires, by jove, are without propellers, the rudders have been removed, the port wheels have been removed, and the port wings are jacked up.

Girlish laughter emanates from a sunken water tank: the Waafs are splashing like young seals under the hot sun.

Farmer Rapier's flarepath.

Suddenly the stillness is disturbed by the snarl of Daimler Benz engines. Three Messerschmitt 109s sweep across RAF Potsworth – without firing a shot – and end up by doing an 'upward Charlie' over the far side.

But what do I see in the distance? I see two or three aircraft-hands dancing round a burning effigy of the CO dressed up in the squadron-leader's best uniform. They are banging off red and green Verey lights in all directions. One aircraft-hand, sitting cross-legged on the ground, is playing an accordion. The sight is fantastic.

Down come the trio again, their red-painted cowlings flashing in the sun, and I adjust my tin hat and close my eyes. However, not a gun fires. But that is not surprising. The Army came out in sympathy at 1400 hours without asking the reason.

The leading Messerschmitt suddenly flicks on to its back and, to my amazement, flies inverted through the wide-open doors of No 1 hangar. He rejoins his two comrades and makes off in a south-easterly direction.

I hope and pray that the wildcat strike will be called off. Fifteen minutes hence will see the squadron overhead – a dozen Spitfires with 96

gunports black with cordite smoke, all short of fuel and with nowhere to land.

As I ponder on the situation, wondering whether to telephone Fighter Command or my newspaper, I catch sight of a parachute coming down. The aviator, whoever he is, is pulling on the lines and is making for the aerodrome.

He lands with a thump, only 50 yards from me, and is slightly winded. Then he rises, rolls up his parachute, places his revolver on the bundle, and heads towards me. But he is German. I haven't a clue what to do and dash for the canteen.

"There's a Jerry down outside," I scream.

By then the canteen is in a jolly state, for the key has been found to the bar. Waafs, now dry and dressed from their splash in the tank, are dancing on the tables. A gramophone is playing. There is even a trace of cigar smoke.

The German airman strides into the canteen, clicks his heels and in perfect English orders egg and chips. He gets his order and resplendent in his Luftwaffe peaked cap and overalls, plus his empty Luger holster, takes a seat.

A bottle of tomato sauce and a salt-cellar are shoved his way without invitation. He nods. The meal over he rises, bows and makes for the guardroom.

"Hauptmann Emil Heinrich wishes to surrender," he tells the duty corporal.

"Not today," says the corporal. "No, not today, old matey. We're on strike. The riggers complain that your 20mm Oerlikons are no longer making the neat, round holes of the smaller Mausers."

The German looks surprised, nods and walks over to the CO's parked Magister. He checks the petrol tank, looks at the oil and starts the engine. He then takes off across the adjoining stubble field. As things turn out Hauptmann Heinrich is back in the Pas de Calais for tea.

By now I am speechless – or nearly.

I make for the pilots' duty hut, guided by the sound of a ringing telephone. Sitting by it, his head on the desk, is the adjutant.

I pick up the telephone and announce smartly: "RAF Potsworth."

"This is Farmer Rapier," says the caller, "and I'm tellin' you that the pheasants are restless and that means Huns in five minutes."

I explain to Farmer Rapier, in as few words as possible the state of play at RAF Potsworth. I check my watch as I speak.

"They've had trouble down there before," explains Farmer Rapier, "and when that happens I always drive my old Austin up on to our muck-heap, point her bonnet to the sky and switch on the headlamps. Then the squadron takes my longest stubble field."

Dancing around a burning effigy of the CO . . .

"Expect the squadron overhead in five minutes," I snap.

I take the CO's car and make for Farmer Rapier's field. Behind me RAF Potsworth is under heavy attack, just as the pheasants predicted, and I think of the canteen . . .

Farmer Rapier, bless him, is already on the muck-heap, headlamps pointing to the vanishing vapour trails. The first Spitfires of – – Squadron are coming in. One pilot, obviously the CO, taxis in with great gusto and for a moment I am proud.

"Get anything?" I yell above the din.

"Not a sausage," shouts the CO. "Hadn't been up three minutes before we got a radio message about the strike. I called up the others and we decided to strike in sympathy. We've been circling Brighton pier ever since.

Woodhenge at Arminghall

While Stonehenge, Wiltshire, one of English Heritage's most important and popular ancient monuments, has in recent times attracted a great deal of publicity in connection with steps to prevent a pop festival on the site, and quasi-religious groups from holding their midsummer day ceremony, many people forget that East Anglia, short of easy stone supplies, possesses one or two Woodhenge monuments of great antiquity.

What are the facts?

Well, in 1929, Wing Commander Gilbert S.M. Insall, VC, was flying over Arminghall and Trowse Newton, south of Norwich, when he noticed and photographed eight dark patches within a broad ring like a horse-shoe and a narrower outer ring.

A ground-reconnaissance of the site revealed an oak temple (35-centuries old), around which chieftains of the Bronze Age were buried in barrows. Excavations proved the outer circle to have a diameter of 262-ft, and the middle area (reached by a gravel causeway across a gap in the inner ditch) to be 87-ft across.

The dark patches on the airman's photographs were the clues to where eight oak posts – tree trunks as high as 20-ft – were set up, each of them being three feet across, and cleverly charred at the base for better preservation before being buried to a depth of seven feet.

The earlier Bronze Age people were mostly nomadic farmers, but, after about 1000BC, they became more settled and made much greater use of metal.

During the Bronze Age "some wealthy chieftains migrated into West Norfolk from the Salisbury Plain area", their bell-barrows being found at Weasenham and Rushford, Norfolk.

But while Wing Commander Insall, who died in 1972 at the age of 77, did well to single out the site south of Norwich, the late W.A. Dutt, East Anglian author, noted three years before in *The Ancient Mark-Stones of East Anglia* (Flood, Lowestoft) that the absence in Norfolk and Suffolk of "imposing megalithic remains such as circles, dolmens and menhirs must not be taken as proof that the pre-historic inhabitants of this part of the country never participated in the particular religious rites with which many megaliths, and especially the standing stones, were originally associated.

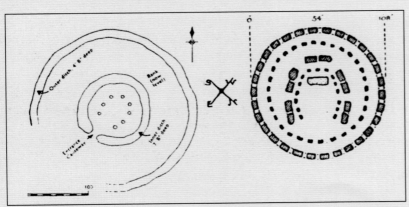

Dutt, puzzled by the then absence of such evidence, advised the reader to "seek for evidence of the use of such substitutes as were most readily accessible during the period or periods in question". Idols and symbols of wood as well as stone, he pointed out, were worshipped at that time, or associated with the places.

The henge monument at Arminghall as seen from the air (left) and Stonehenge as it was (right) in its heyday.
Note the similarity of the shapes of the wood and stone structures respectively.

Tragic Case of William Smith

MR. WILLIAM SMITH lived in the village of Wangford, near Southwold, in the early part of this century. He was headmaster of Henham and Wangford schools and he held that position for 30 years. He was a popular man and well respected.

Then, on 4th November 1914, at the age of 57, he was found dead with his throat cut. He was lying in a shed at the rear of his residence.

What was the reason for this tragedy? The simple answer is that William Smith died as a result of village gossip, of idle tittle-tattle, nothing more.

The first world-war was then three months old and rumours were started on the flimsiest of foundations, sometimes on no foundations at all. But before we come to the rumour that caused the death of William Smith let us consider a few simple facts.

He had been born in the market town of Okehampton, Devon, on 23rd July 1862 and his family had lived in the same house for 'five or six generations.' When he was 20 he went from his native village to Culham College and spent about a year there. That was in 1882-3 and in 1884 he became a schoolmaster at Henham and Wangford.

He took a leading part in the life of the two villages – religious and social as well as educational. In order to supervise his scholars during the time that they were not supposed to be under his care (presumably in the holidays) he established the system of school gardens in the county and this later became the basis of the national scheme. He was also largely responsible for damming the little *River Wang* to provide a bathing place and here he taught his pupils to swim. Viscount Dunwich was one of those who, as a boy, benefited from William Smith's swimming instruction.

A few years before the start of World War I William Smith visited Germany. His son, Alec, was staying there at Aix-la-Chapelle (better known as Aachen) learning the language, and when he fell ill William Smith went out to bring him home. There was nothing very criminal in that. This was the only occasion that William Smith ever left England. Later, two German girls went to stay with the Smith family at Wangford. There was nothing very criminal in that either.

But then came the war and on 2nd November 1914 the postman delivered to William Smith a typewritten notice. It was a lengthy document and it was read in full to the county coroner, Mr A.F. Vulliamy, at the inquest.

'Whereas,' it said, 'by the Defence of the Realm Act, 1914, His Majesty has power during the continuance of the present war to issue regulations for securing the public safety and the Defence of the Realm, subject to and in accordance with that Act, and whereas by the Defence of the Realm Regulations, 1914, it is ordered by Regulation 24a as follows:

'Whereby the behaviour of any person is such as to give reasonable grounds for suspecting that he has acted or is acting or is about to act in a manner prejudicial to the public safety or the safety of the realm, the competent naval or military authority may by order direct him to cease to reside in any area (specified in the order) within or in the neighbourhood of a defended harbour or area and any person to whom an order relates shall within such time specified in the order leave the area specified in the order, having first reported his proposed residence to the competent naval or military authority, and shall not again reside in that area without a permit for the purpose from that authority;

'And whereas an order dated 30th October 1914 has been made by the competent authority under the

Henham and Wangford School. Here William Smith was headmaster for 30 years.

Mr. Smith with some of his pupils and, on the left, the two fraüleins. The photograph was taken sometime before 1914.

within regulations, you, your wife, and family (if any) are hereby required to cease to reside in the county of Suffolk, or in any proclaimed or prohibited area, and to report your departure to the police before you leave and your arrival to the police at the place to which you go.

'Dated the 31st day of October 1914.

'J.G. Mayne, Capt.

'Chief Constable of East Suffolk.'

Subsequently there had been written on this notice:

'Will leave this prohibited area of Suffolk on Friday, 6 November 1914,

J.G. Mayne C.C., (Capt.),

East Suffolk, 3/11/14'.

THE inquest was held on 6th November 1914. The coroner asked a trusted witness if she knew of anything in Mr Smith's life to justify a demand that he should leave the district. She replied: 'He was loyal to the country, I will stake my honour.'

William Smith's widow told how her husband had been found 'lying in the hay shed of the stables.' The rumour that her daughter was married to a German, she said, was false.

The hearing was long and complicated and towards the end of it Lady Stradbroke asked permission to read a letter from her husband, Colonel the Earl of Stradbroke, CVO, CB, ADC, who was absent with the colours.

'I have just heard with the utmost horror about poor Mr. Smith,' said the letter. 'It is too dreadful to think that his death should have been caused by those who had occasion to be very grateful to him . . . I do not think he can be replaced as an influence for the spiritual and general welfare of the village.

'I often said of Wangford that great harm was always being done by tittle-tattle. I never thought such a tragedy would be enacted as now has taken place. These males and females (one cannot use the words men and women) who have maligned Smith and set about tales concerning him must know in their own hearts that they are in reality just as much his murderers as if they had drawn the knife across his throat with their cowardly fingers . . .'

The coroner remarked that he had had cases where tittle-tattle had done great mischief.

Mr H. Lyon, barrister, who represented the family, said: 'But tittle-tattle ought not to cause a notice like that.'

At this stage the inquest was adjourned until 13th November 1914. In the meantime the funeral at Wangford church was attended by a very large gathering. It is recorded that the 'one thought uppermost in the minds of many was regret that they had been unable to do something to show their confidence in Mr Smith and thus to save his life.'

The funeral procession was met at the border of the two parishes by the school children, each carrying a bunch of white chrysanthemums, and later they deposited their flowers on the coffin. Mr Smith's son, who was in Guatemala, Central America, could not get home in time but other members of the family were present. On the following Sunday many tributes to Mr Smith's work were paid in the churches of the neighbourhood.

At the resumed inquest, the coroner and the jury pressed Capt. Mayne to disclose the nature of the allegation that had been made against Mr Smith. Capt. Mayne said that he could not reply to any question put to him with the object of 'eliciting information as to the nature or substance of confidential or privileged documents, or as to the grounds for the order made by the competent military authority and served on the late Mr Smith by the police to leave temporarily the proclaimed area under the Defence of the Realm Act.' As a Chief Constable of one of the eastern coastal counties, he said, it was his duty to enforce the legislation laid down by the government.

Mr Smith, stated Capt. Mayne, had never been accused of being a German or of carrying on espionage. 'Speaking at this moment for myself,' he continued, 'I believe he was guilty only of injudicious behaviour and utterances. But that would not necessarily justify the withdrawal of the order, having regard to the special times in which we live and to all the circumstances.'

The jury retired and after long absence returned to give their verdict: 'The deceased committed suicide whilst of unsound mind, caused by false reports against his patriotism.' And they asked that their fees should be given to the war-wounded at Henham Hall Hospital, for whom Mr Smith had been organising a concert at the time of his death.

After the inquest, Mrs Smith, the widow, went away to stay with relatives. On her return to Wangford, still overcome with grief, she too committed suicide.

A suggestion not made at the inquest that Mr Smith had had liaison with enemy zeppelins can be ruled out as false, for there was no zeppelin activity over any part of England in 1914, though a few reconnaissances by naval airships took place over the North Sea in December of that year.

About the same time that Mr Smith was putting an end to his life there was a rumour in the Chelmsford district of Essex that a spy had been caught but the man turned out to be a harmless labourer. After examining some of the evidence that was made public at the time I am convinced that William Smith was a harmless schoolmaster.

Souvenirs Fortify Remembrance

BEING a non-combatant, I have to be careful what I say about ex-service men and women, but what I am now sure of is that, left on their own with the best will in the world, they are not always the best people to advocate remembrance issues.

But need I apologise for being a non-combatant when, all added up, only a small percentage of soldiers, sailors and airmen of all the world's fighting services in World War II actually saw action or came close to death?

I say this because, beginning in 1940, at the age of 11, I had been taken to the bedside of my dying soldier cousin in a Norfolk hospital, the victim of a German mine explosion; had narrowly escaped death when straddled by bombs in a Suffolk town, was to see enemy and friendly 'planes in the sky on their last legs, see airmen fall to their deaths on candled-parachutes, see dead bodies at 'plane wrecks, and in 1944 and early 1945 have opportunities to be present at East Anglian airfields to see the start and finish of bombing and escort missions.

At home I had an ex-RFC/RAF father, who had been a pupil-pilot in World War I, an engine-fitter brother in the RAF, an ATS sister teaching radar, and an American cousin, on my father's side, an engineer with the 8th USAAF in England.

These ingredients, mixed together, helped to forge the remembrance streak in me. So as World War II ended in 1945, I went up to London armed with a box-camera to catch Squadron Leader J.K. McGrath, who flew Hurricanes with 601 Squadron in 1940, leading some of the "few" to a special Battle of Britain thanksgiving service in Westminster Abbey on 16 September. At the same time similar services were held throughout the country.

On that Sunday afternoon 25 RAF squadrons, led by Group Captain Douglas Bader, the legless fighter pilot, soared over London and much of southern England. I watched them go over.

When the writer was 16 he went to London with a box-camera and got this picture of Squadron Leader J. K. McGrath about to enter Westminster Abbey on September 15, 1945, when the first peace time Battle of Britain service took place with some of the 'Few' present.

It was the beginning of a long annual remembrance ritual for me, for my brother, on leaving RAF Halton in the early summer of 1940, joined 66 Squadron and 421 Flight (later 91 Squadron) and saw action throughout the Battle of Britain (10 July to 31 October).

But when the war ended in Europe in May 1945, my thoughts were far away in North Borneo, East Indies, for my brother, captured after surviving the Battle of Malaya and the Battle of Java, had been taken to Sandakan prisoner-of-war camp on the north-east coast, and it was rumoured that all the prisoners had been marched into the interior.

In October 1945 the following telegram was received by my parents: "Deeply regret to inform you that your son, LAC Donald V. Elliott, is reported to have died while a PoW in Japanese hands on 17 March 1945. The Air Council express their profound sympathy . . .".

As the old Air Ministry were never able to tell us another word about my brother's fate, I carried out an investigation by correspondence and by 1955 had compiled *In the Shadow of Kinabalu*, the reserve copy

"One wonders if, in another 50 years' time, he will still be looking out from that spot and that people . . . will be so interested in him and what the 1940 sacrifices meant to civilisation?'

of which was, on 18 March 2002, presented to the Imperial War Museum, London.

In it I recalled how, by cross-questioning North Borneo headmen through European district officers, I finally found evidence of his possessions.

The marching of hundreds of Australian and British prisoners held at Sandakan into the interior of North Borneo, starting in early 1945, was one of the worst PoW happenings in the Far East war with the Japanese.

Some of the prisoners of the hostile journey did, in fact, reach Ranau, at the foot of Mt Kinabalu, but hundreds died en-route, or had to be shot, some of them by their comrades because a few of the Japanese guards, being christian, could not bring themselves to execute hospital cases who hadn't the strength to carry on. With the prisoners, died a number of Japanese guards who, like the prisoners, were short of food and medical supplies.

Because of the British government's unwillingness after 1945 to try to establish the fate of, for example, several hundred RAF prisoners, next-of-kin were left with no idea of where their loved ones rested.

So, in the 1990s, a few families, who hadn't forgotten the wicked Sandakan/Ranau death-marches, banded together to form a remembrance group who met once a year in London for a service at the RAF church of St Clement Danes and a lunch.

These gatherings led to an exchange of feelings, which had never been possible to express since 1945, and it is interesting to note, were the catalyst for the correspondence between two of the families involved – one senior, the other junior referred to later in this article .

In the case of my RAF brother, it was true that, by 1955, I had a good idea of what his fate had been.

The Sudbury branch of the RAFA in the early 1950s presented the author (extreme left) with Wings of War for staging Battle of Britain exhibitions in their aid. *Photo: Courtesy R. A. Burn*

But over the years that followed, my daughter, Anne Wincott, wanted to know more about what happened in 1945 to the uncle she never met. A short poem she compiled, marking her feelings, appeared in an Australian publication on the Sandakan outrage. Then, in the 1990s, we both journied separately to North Borneo to follow the prisoners' route, which covered about 155 miles.

Finally, in August 2004, Anne Wincott produced a longer poem, entitled *The Walk*, the last verse of which ran:

> I see you, there.
> Look! you have come at last
> You've found me.
> You remember me.
> There's hope, the tears come rolling down.
> Not of pain but of joy.
> Oh, little Brother, I am here!
> I am not lost – after all!

Marking the 96th Bomb Group's association with Snetterton Heath airfield, Norfolk, nearby Quidenham Church has a stained glass window and chapel dedicated to lost bomber crews who flew from there.

Mr Donald Freeman, of Dickleburgh, Norfolk, who lost his RAF brother, Phil, at the same camp, on reading Anne Wincott's second poem, had this to say:

"It is a privilege that you felt the desire to share such intimate thoughts about your uncle with me. No, it did not upset me, it might have done at one time, but thank God I now seem to have burnt up all my anguish and most of my bitterness with it. I have travelled a very similar road in my thoughts as the one you describe so emotionally . . . and it is right for you to put these thoughts onto paper, it is all part of the healing process.

"There is that well-known saying 'To know all is to understand all, and to understand all is to forgive all' but, of course, that is something we shall never know, but writing and talking and sharing our thoughts with others, all helps. I know to my cost that brooding in isolation is a very bad thing. I went through years of bitterness, and whenever I passed a showroom of Japanese cars I would get this urge to daub the windows with graffiti! I used to get recurring dreams that my brother had returned but was kept locked away in a room by his wife, isolated because he was mad. In my dreams I would occasionally catch a glimpse of him as he was hastened away – no one ever spoke of it. So, yes, I do understand, and, of course, it was all a result of not knowing.

"You are obviously the child of a father who has mourned a dearly loved, lost brother, you have had to live with and listen to his grief from your earliest days, it is little wonder that you have absorbed something of this. Then, of course, there is this feeling that the more we grieve the more we are honouring their memory – in the absence of anything else, it is all we can do.

"So how did I come to terms with my sorrow? Well, I have Bunny Warren, RAF, to thank for that, from out of the blue, 10 years ago, he came into my life. A friend of my brother in Malaya, himself a prisoner-of-war, there are times when I can convince myself that my brother sent him! The many others who were introduced to me and through him . . . writing to them, talking to them . . . we nearly all felt alike. Then, finally making the journey to Sandakan and on to Labuan . . . for me to kneel by his graveside was almost like a reunion. I had this overwhelming feeling that he had laid there waiting for someone to visit him and it brought a great sense of peace to me.

"Of course, your family's grief is all the greater because of the added uncertainty of where your uncle died, that is why I was so pleased to find yor poem ending on a note of optimism. You know, my mother always maintained that before the telegram arrived announcing Phil's death (which, incidentally, was two months after the war had ended) that she knew he had died because he walked into her room one afternoon whilst she was lying down, and spoken to her. Some would say she was dreaming, but she believed (she was a very rational person) and I believe it too.

"I have often thought that whilst in captivity, your uncle and my brother must have spent a great deal of time together . . . both were ex-Halton boys, coming from the same county and he sharing my name! We have a much younger brother, who was but three years of age when Phil was posted to Singapore in August '39. When I visited Sandakan, he sent a poppy with the simple message 'to the brother I never knew.' Two years later I wrote the life story of 'My Big Brother Phil' and sent it to him for his birthday. It contains a poem that I wrote when I was in Sandakan and that, too, ends on an optimistic note."

As if to signify 'mission completed', the few

The principal window in the Church of St Michael All Angels, Sandakan, honouring the PoWs and their wartime helpers.
Courtesy: Sandakan Memorial Window Project.

surviving next-of-kin of the North Borneo mass murder were able to contribute to the unveiling in April 2005, of a number of stained-glass windows in the Church of St Michael and All Angels, Sandakan.

The four British representatives at the unveiling were Peter Lee (RAF), who with a number of other officers was in August, 1943, transferred from Sandakan to Kuching PoW camp, also in Borneo; Steve Mockridge, whose father LAC Leslie Mockridge was, in 1943, also moved to Kuching, and survived, dying in England in 2000; Hazel Braund, niece of AC Benjamin Hughes, who died as late as 11th July 1945, at the final Ranau jungle camp close to Mt Kinabalu, and her friend Sue Street.

The centrepiece of the chapel is a finely-crafted,

altar-like Table of Honour, with polished granite top, on which are inscribed the words: *For there are deeds which should not pass away. And names that must not be forgotten.*

Over the granite top is a glass case, containing the Roll of Honour, inscribed with the names of all the Sandakan PoWs, and local people who died or helped them, and the Book of Special Remembrance, containing the names of all donors, along with the names of people they are jointly or individually honouring, and any special inscription. Each week, a new page is turned.

So when Ronald Blythe wrote *Private Words: Letters and Diaries from the Second World War* (Viking 1991), which in 1993 was produced by Penguin, he told of the search and the impact it had on me.

Now for remembrance and the way a disciple can turn war trophies and souvenirs into talking pieces.

Interestingly, as far back as 1916, when scientist Sir Oliver Lodge (1851-1940), who had a special interest in physical and psychical research, published *Raymond or Life and Death* (Methuen), telling of happenings after his son's battlefield death in action, he observed: "It may sound superstitious, but it is a matter of actual experience, that some sensitives have intuitive perception, of an unfamiliar kind, concerning the history and personal associations of relics or fragments of personal belongings. The faculty is called psychometry; and it is no more intelligible, although no less well-evidenced, than the possibly allied faculty of dowsing or so-called water-divining".

Naturally, then, my family's various connections with the fighting services over two world wars have generated a lot of souvenirs, my brother's technique during the Battle of Britain being a case full every time he came home on leave! His many letters, too, often written under fire, often discussed in advance what was on the way for what he dubbed 'our' museum.

When World War II ended – and, of course, I was busy collecting in East Anglia from incidents I witnessed – I had quite a big collection, which remains intact, and in the early 1950s, when I worked as a young reporter at Sudbury, Suffolk, the local branch of the RAFA, who made me a 'Friend' member, appreciated the three or four Battle of Britain exhibitions I put on for them getting, at the same time, support from RAF and USAF stations in the area.

Subsequently, when I settled in London, I continued to stage exhibitions, sometimes to assist the local ATC, and at one period the Imperial War Museum, London, felt justified in taking some of the relics on loan for display in three or four cabinets over a year or two.

As Sir Oliver Lodge said in his 1916 book, relics tend to draw attention in mysterious ways, and I can think of several instances where some item or other has brought me grateful thanks and lasting friendship from the airman it was linked with.

For instance, when the late Group Captain Tom Gleave's 1940 Hurricane, very melted, was found in a Kent wood in the 1960s, and pieces reached me, this famous Guinea Pig, who was the author of *I Had A Row With A German* (Macmillan, 1941), drew me into his circle.

Collecting goes hand-in-hand with keeping in touch with the present. So when the 50th anniversary Battle of Britain fly-past took place over the Palace on 15 September 1990, I was taken aboard the VC-10 command jet at short notice for the rounding up over East Anglia of over 160 'planes. It was an experience I will always remember and, I am told, it is unlikely that the RAF will ever mount such a big fly-past again. The spearhead was formidable: three VC-10s, including two tankers in vee-formation, with two outriding live Tornado escorts.

On this occasion I was able to help Mr John R. Gillies, of Cheshunt, Herts, whose father, F/Lt Ken Gillies, aged 26, of 66 Squadron, went missing from RAF Gravesend, Kent, in October 1940. Days later, following storms, the pilot's body came ashore at Covehithe, on the Suffolk coast, at a spot where we often played as children in the middle 1930s.

Mr Gillies request? To carry a photograph of his father – Mr Gillies was born a month after his father's death – and have it signed by the leader's captain on landing back at RAF Brize Norton, Oxford.

Finally, it was possible for me to attend the unveiling by the Queen Mother at Capel-le-Ferne, near Dover, on 9 July 1993, of the Battle of Britain Memorial in the shape of a seated young pilot looking out over the English Channel.

One wonders if, in another 50 years' time, he will still be looking out from that spot and that people, as now, will be so interested in him and what the 1940 sacrifices meant to civilisation?

Sudbury Tail-Gunner
THE BRAVERY OF CORPORAL LILLIE

THE market town of Sudbury, in West Suffolk, learned with pride in 1940 that a local lad, Corporal William G. Lillie, RAF, had been awarded one of the Second World War's first DFMs for the part he played as rear-gunner of a Short Sunderland flying-boat in a fierce battle with six Junkers 88s off the Norwegian coast.

In the heavily outnumbered fight, which took place on 3rd April 1940, young Lillie, who served with 204 Squadron stationed in the Shetlands, shot down one of the attackers and damaged another so that it had to make a forced-landing n Norway.

Corporal Lillie's pilot took the giant flying-boat – it had a wing-span of over 112ft – down within 100ft of the sea to safeguard himself against attack from below, which was his blind spot, and subsequent hull damage.

As four of the German bombers dived on Sunderland N9046 from the rear, the flying-boat dived to 1500ft enabling Corporal Lillie, whose turret housed four .303 machine-guns, to open fire.

The leading Junkers 88 turned, stalled, and spun flaming into the sea. Another, damaged, flew away for a crash-landing in Norway where its crew set it on fire.

While all this was going on, two more of the attackers tried to bomb the Sunderland from above but the second-pilot, "his head out of the top of the cockpit", shouted instructions which enabled the captain to take evasive action!

The Sunderland and its crew of 11, thanks to a combination of excellent gunnery and airmanship, returned safely, although the flying-boat was badly damaged.

In the 1950s, Mr Geoffrey R. Diaper, who in those days was honorary secretary of the Sudbury branch of

Corporal William G. Lillie, who was one of the first DFMs of the Second World War, pictured standing on the cowling of one of his Sunderland's port engines.
Photo: Courtesy G. Diaper.

the RAF Association, told me that he attended SS Gregory's and Peter's Church School with young Lillie some years before the last war.

Mr Diaper said: "William Lillie, who lived in Girling Street, Sudbury, used to run straight down the house passage-way and across the road into school – the nearest pupil but almost always the last to school! A large photograph of him hung in the school during the war."

Corporal Lillie, whose gallant action defending the Sunderland was depicted by an unknown war artist soon after the 1940 engagement, did not live long after the six-to-one air-battle; he was reported missing on 21st July 1940, off Trondheim, Norway.

Footnote: In 2005 it was learned that Sudbury, Lillie's home-town, wished to honour him with a street named after him. His medals were expected to be accepted for display by the Duxford Imperial War Museum, Cambridgeshire.

The Short Sunderland flying-boat had a wing-span of 112ft.
Photo: Courtesy Flight.

Last of the Norwich Raiders

SOON after the war ended 40 years ago, the county authorities published reports on war incidents in their areas which, when added together, form a kind of Domesday book of those hectic times.

For example, the then Chief Constable of Norfolk (Captain S.H. Van Neck) reported that 20 German planes were brought down in his area of jurisdiction – at Terrington, Welney, East Walton, Starston, Porlingland, Gillingham, Ashby St Mary, Cley, Sharrington, Salthouse, Sheringham (two), Waxham, Somerton, off Hemsby, off Caister, Fring, Ovington, Scoulton and Narford.

The crews were either killed or captured, and 35 of the 141 bodies, washed ashore along the Norfolk coast between 1939 and 1945, were mostly members of the Luftwaffe.

R.H. Mottram in his booklet *Assault Upon Norwich: The Official Account of the Air Raids on the City*, the profits of which were distributed among local charities that assisted during and after the raids, observed: "Three more minor raids occurred, but that of 6 November 1943, appears to be the last (manned) attack on the city".

That November night is remembered by many Beccles, Suffolk, people because, towards midnight, a Dornier 217 bomber of III/KG2 from Gilze Rigen, Holland, bound for Norwich had its slender fuselage severed four or five feet ahead of its twin tails through a direct hit from an AA shell at about 6000 feet, fired by the Burgh Castle battery, which must have been operating as a mobile unit at the time.

Severely crippled, and with the disadvantage of only a few thousand feet, the forward part of the Dornier carrying four men started its top heavy plunge. Only one man, believed to be the lower rear gunner, managed to overcome the centrifugal force and get out in time. On falling near a small barn and

An escaping Dornier 217 from one of the Norwich raids lost this hatch cover over Redisham, south of Beccles, where it was found next day and carefully preserved.

trees at Winston Hall Farm, Gillingham, its main bomb load blew up, fire followed and a bullock shed and two stacks close by were burnt out.

The crash, within sight of Beccles, caused activity in the streets and I remember the sound of running feet, voices and a whistle being blown.

Next day, having got details of the location, I was off on my cycle to Gillingham, before breakfast, and found the Dornier's tail in a field near a cottage on the right of the Gillingham-Raveningham road.

The tail, which was unguarded, was upside down, its twin swastikas bold and clear, but the tangle of wires – some coloured red – hanging out of the severed fuselage made me cautious about touching

Last manned raid . . . Dornier 217 bomber.

204

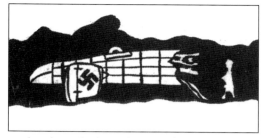

Last manned raid . . . As the author saw the severed rail of the Gillingham Dornier 217 of 1943.

anything, a narrow escape from injury at the scene of another enemy crash in 1942 being the reason.

The tail-wheel was extended a little from its retracted position, and I noticed that the Gillingham Dornier was not fitted with the very novel umbrella-type diving brake at the extremity of the fuselage which the magazine *Flight*, in an article about the Dornier 217, had mentioned in 1942. A day or two later some 8th USAAF personnel in a truck arrived in the field and, using screw-drivers, tried unsuccessfully to punch out the swastikas as souvenirs.

Over at Winston Hall Farm, where the main body of the aircraft fell, technical officers were looking for intelligence among the wreckage, half of which was badly burnt, including the main wing centre-section, which was tossed against a tree.

On the Monday or Tuesday following the crash, I returned to the scene after school. By then, Belgian troops were guarding the wreckage and, as the November rain continued and the wind blew, they retired to a shelter.

I was thus able to potter about the site in the failing light and I noticed, among things, that the Dornier was carrying a large quantity of 'duppel' anti-radar metal strips which the RAF called 'window' and the USAAF 'chaff'. I picked up a number of cockpit instrument faces and a distorted Luftwaffe belt-buckle portion embodying an oak leaf motif.

Sensitive cannon and machine-gun ammunition, much of it still belted, was scattered everywhere. The rear half of the bomb bay, I noticed, was intact and contained a complete incendiary bomb container of the AB500 type packed with unexploded bombs. A good length of the fuselage, with unit and German cross markings visible, somehow escaped the force of the main explosion.

The crew member who escaped from the Dornier was 22-year-old Unteroffizier Kork who, on landing by parachute, made his way to the house of Mr Harry Goddard, a horseman, in a shocked state. Although unable to converse in English beyond the word "machine", the airman pointed to the glow of his burning plane. Mr Goddard took him down the lane and handed him over to a member of the National Fire Service. The fireman, in turn, passed the prisoner to Sergeant Douglas Kiddle, a member of the local Home Guard, who was preparing to leave the scene.

The sergeant and the German then started out on foot for Beccles in the moonlight, and were met en route by Inspector William Bryant and a police constable who had set off towards Gillingham on being advised that the prisoner was on his way.

The German was handed over at Beccles police station soon after 12.30am on 7 November, it being noticed that, in spite of his hurried exit from the plunging Dornier, he was fully dressed in flying kit, carried a Verey-light signal-pistol, his cap, a whistle on a cord and a compass on a leather strap.

His more personal possessions included his metal identity disc, an identity card in a case, a small card giving the exact aircraft type (Dornier 217K-4), a packet of 'Overstolz' cigarettes – and an empty matchbox. He gave the names of his dead comrades as Leutnant Wulfhorst, Gefreiter Geyer and Gefreiter Komp.

Mr Gerald Lawson, senior officer in the Special Constabulary at Beccles in 1943, and for many years editor of the *Beccles and Bungay Journal*, wrote after the war: "I remember vividly how the Dornier went down to earth like a ball of fire . . . It was a spectacular sight. The explosion was colossal and some windows on The Walk, Beccles, were smashed by the blast".

In 1967 Mr C.E. Sayer, of Stockton, who was in the Home Guard at the time, told me that in 1944 a Verey-light signal-pistol from the Gillingham Dornier was found in Stockton Woods, and handed to the

Searchlights over Norwich Cathedral.

authorities. Other contents from the spinning 'plane must have been scattered over a wide area.

Most interesting, however, was the information that the survivor who had shown concern for his comrades when he reached Mr Goddard's house, had in the 1960s visited their graves in Gillingham churchyard. There was reason to believe the German had settled down to live in Wales.

For many years after the Dornier crash, a half section of an AB500 type incendiary bomb-container was used as a flower tub in the car park of the old Black Boy Inn at Stockton. As Mr Sayer thought that "about 3000 small incendiaries" fell around his home on the night of 6/7 November 1943, it was possible that the burning Dornier across the fields was afterwards bombed by Luftwaffe colleagues in mistake for – well, Norwich!

Footnote: Aviation researcher Bob Collis of Oulton Broad, Suffolk, was, in 2005, able to fill in gaps in the history of this crash, the nineteenth of twenty German raiders to crash in Norfolk in the Second World War. Apparently the raider was engaged by the majority of gun-sites in the Great Yarmouth/Lowestoft ground defence area, and illuminated by Coltshall searchlights. The flak came from 3.7in guns, which expended 275 rounds, and "at 9500ft a flash was seen among the shell-bursts and the enemy aircraft lost height." The shell strike tore the tail off the Dornier. Apart from survivor Uffz Alwin Kork, the crew-member who settled in Wales and afterwards made "several vists to Gillingham" to pay respects to his dead comrades, the only other public remembrance of the 1943 incident is the preservation in the Tolhouse Museum, Great Yarmouth, of a complete propeller blade from the bomber.

Suitably inscribed, it was presented to the borough by the 63rd AA Brigade, and the war diary of the 172 (Mixed) HA Regt, RA, logged the shooting down of the Dornier. In *Private Words: Letters and Diaries from the Second World War* (Viking/Penguin Group, 1991), Ronald Blythe allowed me to record: "It was against this background of desolation . . . that one of the Belgian guards . . . came up to me and caused me to find no words. For he had in his hand a surprise. It was a brown human eye. So I left the scene and the brown eye for ever."

When Norwich Built Planes

Photos: Courtesy Boulton and Paul Ltd

While the Luftwaffe made an attack on Boulton and Paul Ltd, of Norwich, early in the Battle of Brtain, 1940, it was possible that they believed the works were still making aircraft. But aircraft production at Norwich finally ended in August 1936, with the transfer of that plant to Wolverhampton, Staffordshire.

Certainly, in the busy days between the two world wars, the company's skilled design team at Norwich were responsible for a number of advanced 'planes which, at the tme, didn't fit wth the Air Minsitry's somewhat old-fashioned conception of what the modern RAF might need.

One design was the 1927 Boulton Paul P.31 Bittern twin-engined fighter. Prototype J7937, shown here, carried a pair of Lewis guns mounted in barbettes – a very advanced armament arrangement – in bulges each side of the nose. The gus could be incined from zero to 45-degrees in elevation and could fire upwards at hostile aircraft. The Luftwaffe used such a surprise technique against RAF Bomber Command at night.

Codeword 'Cromwell'

"It would be possible to write almost indefinitely of the many things, large and small, which combined in the summer of 1940 to give life in the UK a flavour which distinguished that brief period from all the rest of British history" – from Peter Fleming's book, *Invasion 1940*, published in 1957.

O N THE EVENING of Saturday, 7th September 1940, after an urgent meeting in London of service chiefs, with the Prime Minister, Mr Winston Churchill, in the chair, the invasion code-word 'Cromwell' was flashed to troops along the south and east coasts. It had been decided that, all things considered, there was reason to believe that the German Army, backed up by the German Navy and the German Air Force, was about to assault the shores of England.

It was indeed a dramatic moment in our long history but, although I lived through it as a child, I cannot pin down that particular date as being of any significance. Certainly no mention of the alarm was made in the press next day. Skillfully the young were shielded from the truth.

On 5th September my brother, whose fighter squadron had gone in a hurry from Coltishall RAF Station, Norfolk, to an airfield south of London on 3rd September, wrote a vivid letter telling of the desperate situation with no hangars left standing, its Spitfires shot to pieces, and with several pilots missing.

However, let's go back a little to May 1940. I remember the road blocks which were set up in the Beccles area following the evacuation from Dunkirk. We were stopped one evening on the Beccles-Norwich road at Gillingham, Norfolk, just past the old smithy, by a group of sullen soldiers who wanted

On March 6, 1944, Beccles Home Guard members of No. 5 Platoon, Ingate Iron Works, Beccles, used a horse to haul their Smith gun and limber into action at Shipmeadow. Then, in 1975, Capt. Mainwaring of Dad's Army fame was depicted riding a white horse with, as at Shipmeadow, his men round him!

to see my father's papers. The trunk of an oak or elm was drawn half across the road.

Meanwhile, what kind of preparations had the Germans made for the landing? They had gone ahead with the preparation of countless documents based on the work of a small army of spies, geologists and cartographers who must have spent some time in Britain in the 1930s. The British invasion dossier included British survey maps on which was over-printed in red, purple and other colours a vast amount of military information (my East Anglia map, dated August 1941, is a good example). An elaborate index went with the maps.

A place suitable for the possible accommodation of horses was marked by the symbol of a horse's head in red . . . a munition factory was marked by the symbol of a gun . . . a brewery by the symbol of a glass of beer

Just a few miles away from Beccles, at Covehithe, the coastline from 1940 was protected by these tubular steel anti-invasion fences pictured as they looked in 1947. Corrosion and gales, however, left these brooding stubs (above) as seen at Walberswick, looking towards Dunwich, after the East Coast floods of 1953.

In the years when our Country

was in mortal danger

John William Bull

who served 14 May 1940 – 31 December 1944

gave generously of his time and

powers to make himself ready

for her defence by force of arms

and with his life if need be.

George R.I.

THE HOME GUARD

With the threat of invasion gone, the Home Guard throughout the UK lay down its arms on December 31, 1944. Each member received a certificate signed by King George VI.

. . . . flour mills, windmills (possible observation posts), signal boxes, railway stations, police stations and so on were all noted.

The preparations for the occupation of East Anglia were vast and it is known that some factories were specially pin-pointed for the use of the invading army – for instance, the engineering and shell- making plant of Elliott & Garrood Ltd, Beccles, because of its heavy lifting gear, was to be used for tank repairs.

And what if the Germans had landed? I have no doubt that, with the country at such a pitch of readiness, the troops and the local volunteers would have fallen on the enemy with fanatical zest. All kinds of weapons, old and new, would have been brought

into use; and countrymen everywhere, including poachers, who had been issued with a special type of shot-gun cartridge containing half-a- dozen large balls, would have done their duty.

The civilian population received much guidance from the Government in the form of invasion pamphlets. My example – it was distributed in the Beccles area – was headed 'Beating the INVADER', was signed by Mr Churchill, and bore a code showing that 14,050,800 copies were printed.

If the enemy had got a foothold, what would have happened in East Anglia? It is a fact – a public fact – that arrangements were made whereby picked members in each community, who were only known to the Chief Constable of the county area, were selected for subversive activities. This meant, for example, that the Beccles team would not have been known to anyone at Lowestoft or Bungay. There were several hidden arms and petrol dumps in the Beccles area. I still have preserved hand-made duplicate keys for one of the secret dumps of those far-off days.

Stanley Firmin, in his book, *They Came To Spy,* which came out just after the war, said that a 'big country house in Norfolk had been ear-marked to become German Headquarters for the invasion army'.

Did we care much about restricting what we published in the months leading up to the war? Apparently not. A classic example of this can be found in the Suffolk County Handbook and Official Directory for 1939 where, with the approval of the government of the time, scientists and principal officers working at the Bawdsey Research Station, near Woodbridge, the Aeroplane and Armament Experimental Establishment, Martlesham Heath, and the Marine Aircraft Experimental Establishment, Felixstowe, were listed together with their scientific qualifications. It was thus possible, from the scientific qualifications alone, to guess the pattern of research at these establishments. It meant, too, that these men were quartered in the vicinity and that this was a direct invitation, in my view, for casual family helps to infiltrate into households where doubtless 'homework' existed in desks.

Spies! How that word got around as the

Pair of rough brass keys made at Beccles in 1940 for a secret cache of Home Guard arms.

Loyal countrymen everywhere, including poachers, were issued with a special type of shot gun cartridge containing half-a-dozen large lead balls.

government called on the fishermen and others of England to go to Dunkirk between 26th May and 3rd June 1940. In May – it was at 1.15pm in the afternoon of 30th May – the RNLI was asked to send at once to Dover as many of its lifeboats as possible for the evacuation operation – the greatest evacuation operation in history. The first of these boats to leave their stations were the *Abdy Beauclerk* and the *Lucy Lavers* of Aldeburgh, Suffolk. Great Yarmouth and Gorleston responded . . . and so did Lowestoft . . . so did Southwold and so on round the coast.

It was said that at Fritton Lake, Suffolk, possibly because of some geological freak, it was possible to hear the distant roar of the Dunkirk guns in the quiet of the evening. Once or twice I was taken over there to listen in the evening but I could not tell whether the pounding I heard was that of distant guns or of my own heart. Certainly, on one of those evenings at Fritton, I heard the nightingale and then the owl – and then twilight came. My father said: 'You will never forget what you have just heard'. I have the sounds clearly in my mind – the sounds of light and darkness.

Spies again! What steps did the authorities take to combat the situation? The all-powerful Regulation 18B was put into operation whereby everyone under suspicion was put into the bag. It caused the Prime Minister, Mr Winston Churchill, arch defender of these islands, to protest at the wholesale arrests and the unwillingness of the authorities to tolerate any expressions of opinion that deviated from the patriotic.

One of Mr Churchill's notes to the Home Secretary said: "I should like to have my opinion put on record that this sentence (of five years' penal servitude on Miss Elsie Orrin for saying to two

Well known at Worlingham, near Beccles, was this privately owned armoured car used by the Home Guard.

Photo: Courtesy George Dodd

soldiers that Hitler was a good ruler, a better man than Mr Churchill) is far too heavy for expressions of opinion, however pernicious, which are not accompanied by conspiracy. Nothing in the internal state of the country justifies such unreasonable and unnatural severity. I consider such excessive action defeats its own ends."

How were people caught in the 18B net? It seems that plain-clothes men came down from London with information provided by the Special Branch and by Military Intelligence. At least, that is how the story goes, but it seems likely that less dependable sources helped to ensnare people.

Arrests, in some cases, rested on such scanty evidence as what the suspects read and the organisations to which they belonged – or had belonged in carefree days at university or elsewhere. Post office workers were questioned about the nature of mail received by suspects over many years. Newsagents – and some I know never read anything else but the *Daily Mirror* – were asked to pass judgment on highly intelligent and sensitive

The Home Guard of 1940 did not die when the war ended in 1945. It was revived in the BBC-TV series "Dad's Army" under the watchful eye of Capt. Mainwaring (Arthur Lowe).

Photo: Courtesy Imperial War Museum

The observation post guarding a Beccles works was put up in 1939, as a temporary spotters' post, but survived until 1945. In November, 1940, while an observer was in the crow's nest, it survived being straddled by two of 10 bombs dropped by a dawn low-level attacker.

customers whom they no more knew than the leader page of *The Times*. Much of the prying, furthermore, was done without the knowledge of the county police. For I know personally that the arrest of several men and women in East Anglia was hotly opposed by local police inspectors who were willing to stake their right-hand that the people concerned were in reality 'safe'. But all protests were overruled as the purge got into its stride. Many painful scenes resulted.

In my 18B file for East Anglia, which I built up without referring to official sources between 1946 and 1957, is an amusing story of how, when an old radio cabinet was taken to be a radio transmitter, it was broken open to reveal – well, two bottles of beer and two glasses. But the beer had been made in Scotland.

Interrogator: 'Why are you drinking beer from Scotland?'

Suspect: 'Because I have just been to Scotland on holiday.'

Interrogator: 'Why did you go to Scotland?'

Suspect: 'Because I wanted a holiday.'

Interrogator: 'Did you speak to anyone?'

Suspect: 'Why, yes, my wife.'

Interrogator: '. . .'

Was 18B necessary in the light of events? Well, I have read many books about the German occupation of Europe and I am firmly convinced that it was the right decision for a limited period in 1940. However, in the heat of the moment the application of 18B had the stamp of Nazism about it. By the end of 1940 a large number of those detained under the regulation were ready for release. Unfortunately there was no machinery for redress and to this day those who fell into the net have no written pardon. Libraries and papers seized at the time were never returned.

Such were the times. For the children of East Anglia they were years of excitement and anxiety. But the moment I remember most was at Fritton at Dunkirk time –

I heard the nightingale and then the owl – and then twilight came.

Top: Observer Watling (left), a retired sub-mariner, with the author, in 1941, visiting the control caravan under the observation post guarding a Beccles factory.

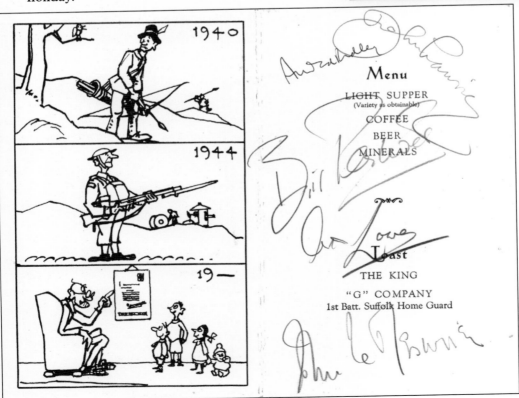

Left: When No. 5 Platoon, 'G' Company, 1st Batt. Suffolk Home Guard, held their stand-down supper at Beccles, Suffolk, on December 9, 1944, they produced this humorous menu card – later autographed by some of the leading players in "Dad's Army".

Polly's Boots and Sailor Brothers

THE Riches family, from whom Mary Ann (Polly) Elliott (born 1865) came, originated at Bungay, where her father, James Riches, was a shoemaker or snob, the original meaning of snob being cobbler's mate or boy. At that time – the middle 1850s – there were certainly a number of shoemakers in the town.

About the 1870s James Riches moved his business and family to Ravensmeer, Beccles, where he set up his workshop. Although not a churchman, he was a good raconteur on religious topics as an example, and it is said that local dignitaries, including the rector of Beccles, 'liked calling in to converse with him.' Certainly he was skilled in his trade and made boots and shoes from scratch.

Married, with a family of five (three girls and two boys), some of the children on coming to Beccles went to the National School, Ravensmeer, founded in 1868, where Polly, who later married my grandfather, Alexander Elliott, the Beccles engineer, was remembered as a bright child.

For her ninth birthday, and in the closing months of his life, her father gave her a novel surprise: she woke up on the great day with the boots he had made for her tied to her plaits so that, on lifting her head, she was tugged into the happy realisation!

When Polly was about 11 her mother, who was by then a widow, was taken ill and the girl didn't turn up for school. When her teacher made inquiries it was found that she had elected to remain at home to care for her mother.

Polly's two brothers, William and James, were Royal Navy reservists and both were in the Battle of Jutland (31 May-1 June 1916), James being struck on the head and hurt by falling super-structure caused by a German shell.

William at that time was a chief petty officer aboard Sir John Jellicoe's flagship of a force consisting (in addition to Sir David Beatty's ships), of '24 battleships and three battle cruisers, eight old armoured cruisers, 26 light cruisers and 78 destroyers'. William was based at Portsmouth; James was with the Harwich, Essex, flotilla.

Interestingly, William, years before, had done service in the Far East, being in the international force which quelled the Boxer Uprising of 1900. It appears that 'William brought back from this service a figure of a warrior mounted on a horse'. The figure, damaged, is still in my possession but its place in the

As for Polly – well, she went to America in 1916 with some of her children but, like so many people do who have deep roots, she returned to her native area and died at Beccles in 1931.

family – it was always safe-guarded in successive house moves – was never understood until the Boxer connection was explained. It is thought that the equestrian figure was 'looted' at the time in Peking.

The Boxers were members of a Chinese society, more or less secret in its organisation and aims, but generally professing a fervent nationalism, hatred of 'foreign devils,' and loyalty to the reigning dynasty. In 1900 the Boxers marched on Peking and besieged the legations for two months, but on 14 August the city was occupied by the troops of the allied European powers and the uprising was suppressed.

There's no doubt that the Boxer Uprising caused world-wide interest, since all the legations were attacked, and *The Illustrated London News* for the months July-December 1900, gave extensive coverage, drawings and photographs included, to the fighting.

Proudly their issue for 25 August declared: 'The Allies have reached Peking at last, and the legations are safe. Beyond that definite message, much is mere rumour . . .'.

So William, the sailor, must have had lively stories to tell on his return. Certainly the press of the time indicated that the countries affected by the rebellion saw to it that their representatives on-the-spot took steps to indemnify their losses by seizing local treasures. Thus the horseman, whose presence in the family was a mystery for so long, may have been William's little piece of booty for his mantelpiece.

Various expert London sources in 1982 passed

conflicting opinions on William's mounted horseman.

Christie's, who like people to call in with their treasures, believed it was 'certainly Chinese' and, although the reason for the disjointed rider was explained, were prepared to say that the hollow body of the horse 'suggests its use as an incense burner'!

The 'Museum of Mankind', after examining the group, passed me on to the British Museum's oriental department who identified the lead(?) figure as 'mass produced late 19th century (Victorian) depicting a Japanese warrior' with manifestations of detail embracing 'several centuries'. What was more, 'it certainly wouldn't have come from temple if, indeed, it was found in Peking'.

Such, then, were the levels of opinion reached in my inquiries into William's piece of loot.

It appears that, at some stage during his overseas service, William's wife died at Portsmouth, without word reaching him for some time, and when he returned he was 'unable to trace his daughter Ruby, who may have been adopted by a family called Wright'.

Keeping on a little cottage at Beccles for his eventual retirement, so like a sailor, William came home some time after Jutland but did not report back to his ship. He was no doubt apprehended by the Navy for this desertion, if that is what it amounted to, but was then retired, probably on account of his long service. He remained, as from earlier times, a reserved man; his brother James, on the other hand, was a boisterous fellow who liked evening gossip on the Public Hall corner with his pals. He married into the Paddle family of Beccles who ran a fish-and-chip shop.

Doubtless both sailors, as they grew old at Beccles, liked the sound of the fine peal of bells of St. Michael's Church 'carried far up the Waveney valley and far inland by the nor'est wind from over the sea'.

As for Polly – well, she went to America in 1916 with some of her children but, like so many people do who have deep roots, she returned to her native area and died at Beccles in 1931.

Such are the many facets, some sad, some happy, of the ordinary families of England who for centuries have been the salt of the earth in peace and war. The web they weave never fails to fascinate me and no two families are quite alike – from the cradle to the grave.

Footnote: The fastening of the girl's boots to her plaits, while she was asleep, may have a Swedish association. For Jenny Paschall and Ron Lyon, in *Hatches, Matches and Dispatches: Birth, Marriage and Burial Around the World* (Harper Collins, 1997) observed: "Traditionally in Sweden the bride would go through the entire wedding ceremony with her shoes untied, then proceed to her honeymoon chamber, go to bed and consummate her marriage, still wearing the untied shoes. She would sleep with the shoes dangling on her feet, hoping that they would fall off by themselves during the night, an indication that she would bear children as easily as she removed her shoes."

East Coast Devastation

After the Great Flood of 1953, which affected the East Coast of England, familiar scenes turned to desolation. This view, taken from Walberswick, Suffolk, side of the River Blyth where the steam ferry used to have its berth, shows on the Southwold bank a stranded vessel high and dry. A damp haze hides distant Southwold.

Anne's Challenge to the Luftwaffe

WHEN Bruce Robertson, the aviation expert, compiled *Epics of Aviation Archaeology* (Patrick Stephens, 1978) he asked me to contribute a chapter on "Abandoned American Bases of Eastern England".

In that chapter I briefly described how, in 1954, the former Miss Anne Haywood, of Wetherden, near Stowmarket, took me round decaying Great Ashfield airfield to show me some of the artwork she did on buildings for the 385th Bomb Group. But her main art contribution, it turned out, was done on B-17 Fortress noses and soon word had spread to other 8th Air Force groups.

Beginning in 1943, she was soon in demand at the base, and on 10 December 1943, Lt-Col Elliott Vandevanter, Jr, the group commander, asked the Ministry of Labour, Bury St Edmunds, to give her an extension as "she has been rendering very valuable service in this Command . . . with certain essential work in lettering and painting designs on the B-17s at this station".

It was back in 1953, while on a visit to an American Air Force unit at RAF Wethersfield, Essex, that I met Capt. Charles M. Guyler, ex-385th Bomb Group, who first told me of the local artist, now Mrs Anne Haywood-Gordon, living in Oxfordshire, who decorated their aircraft.

Finally, when I traced her, Mrs Gordon, who in September 1976, returned to Great Ashfield with the 385th Bomb Group Association, said: "I am most surprised that anyone, so long after, should remember my work at Great Ashfield. Yes, with Col. Vendevanter's permission, I was responsible for painting the pet names on nearly all the Great Ashfield Fortresses, the leather flying-jackets of most of the crews and, I suppose, nearly all the interior murals in the mess rooms. A Fortress, bearing my name, went to Nazi targets on 100 occasions with out a single engine failure".

How did Mrs Gordon, then in her late teens, become unofficial artist to one of the 8th Air Force's first Fortress groups? Mrs Gordon, it seems, felt she had to do some kind of voluntary work, so she joined the Red Cross, but only to serve coffee to the men. A Yale undergraduate, who was the mess officer, heard about her artistic talents, and told her: You're just the person we need. You must decorate our mess".

But Mrs Gordon's official work, as she was often

Anne Haywood in 1954 looking at the faded badge on the gable end of the mess at Great Ashfield. It is to be compared with the war time view of the same mess shown below.

told by her superiors, was the issue of coffee to returning crews. However, much to the irritation of her more domesticated colleagues, she spent "most of the time on the line painting the Fortresses with names like 'Back to the Sack', 'Mr Lucky', 'Powerful Katrinka' and "Dragon Lady'."

'Powerful Katrinka', piloted by Capt. Guyler, lost two engines as a result of enemy fire, but he managed to fly half way home before 'ditching' in the North Sea. Hardly had the captain got back before Mrs Gordon, palette in hand, had the name 'Powerful Katrinka' painted on his new B17. The Luftwaffe, however, knew about Great Ashfield and dropped a

HEADQUARTERS
ARMY AIR FORCES STATION 155
A. P. O. 634

A-A-3

10 December 1943

014

Ministry of Labor
Bury St. Edmunds

Dear Sirs:

Request is hereby made for the deferment of Miss
Anne Haywood, Thedwards, Wetherden, for a period of three
weeks. She is at present employed in the American Red
Cross Aero Club, Gt. Ashfield.

In addition to Miss Haywood's duties in the Club,
she has been rendering very valuable service in this
Command, in that she has been assisting with certain
essential work in lettering and painting designs on the
B-17's at this station.

Any consideration given to this request will be
appreciated.

Sincerely,

E. VANDEVANTER, JR.
Lt. Col., Air Corps
Commanding

A copy of Lt. Col. Elliott Vandervanter's 1943 letter to the Ministry of Labour, Bury St. Edmunds, telling of Miss Anne Haywood's contribution to the group's war effort.

bomb on one of the hangars, blowing 'Powerful Katrinka' to pieces.

Despite the veiled resentment among her colleagues, Mrs Gordon, who was too young to appreciate that it mattered very much, continued her work, and the base colonel, to clear the air, declared that, as such, she was "a great morale-booster".

"Talking of pet names," Mrs Gordon continued, "a flier would tell me that he had had a dream in which he saw a crocodile, and the alligator had the ears of a donkey, the claws of a witch's cat and the head of the Devil himself. Would I interpret the 'message' and paint it on the nose of his Fortress?"

A London publisher once suggested to Mrs Gordon that she should write a book about her Great Ashfield experiences. "I haven't the time to write it myself", she explained, "but perhaps one day I shall dictate it to someone. I'd really like to do the illustrations for it, that is certain".

Almost every day, particularly in 1943 and early 1944, when the Luftwaffe fought strongly, the group suffered losses. Sometimes, after going down over enemy territory, airmen managed to return to Great Ashfield, as did a Middle Westerner, who arrived back "dressed like a Spaniard and a 'Cor Blimey' chap".

There was the oldish-looking aviator, too, who on returning from a mission, used to go straight to the mess piano and play Debussy's 'Clair Du Lune'. He played it many times because, at the beginning, he was lucky, and then one day Mrs Gordon missed the familiar tune. His 'plane failed to reach the Suffolk coast. Later, when Mrs Gordon had almost forgotten him, she suddenly heard the strains of 'Clair Du Lune'. There, seated at the same piano, wearing a battered cap, was the airman – he had escaped from a Nazi PoW camp. Next day, with a new parachute

In September, 1976, when 385th Bomb Group veterans returned to their old airfield at Great Ashfield, Suffolk, some of them signed a famous photograph of one of their G in square B-17 Fortresses landing with wounded aboard.

and same old rakish, defiant cap, he faced the Luftwaffe again.

There was competition for her art among the Fortress groups in the 4th Combat Wing, 3rd Air Division, and once, when Mrs Gordon, without the knowledge of her home airfield, took her palette to the 447th Bomb Group, Rattlesden, Suffolk, she was told: "Anne, you're a first-class traitor."

While Mrs Gordon worked for the 385th, her sister, Jean, toiled for the Red Cross at Mendlesham, Suffolk, where the 34th Bomb Group, also operating Fortresses, was stationed. She was a great organiser and 'miles above' her sister in that respect. "My sister tolerated no nonsense," said Mrs Gordon, "and I think the base personnel respected her as much as they did their colonel."

When clothing and boots were destroyed before the departure or the 34th for America in 1945, her sister saw the fire and, rushing over to the startled Americans, declared: "You wicked men. What will the natives think?" The Americans appreciated her point, the fire alarm was sounded, and the base fire engine saved the rest.

Mrs Gordon remembered the remarkable escape of a six-foot Texan tail-gunner who, trapped in his tiny compartment which had been severed from the main fuselage, fell to the ground over Holland – and lived. A loyal Dutch blacksmith managed to extract him from what would otherwise have been the gunner's twisted metal coffin. Although suffering some internal injuries, the airman lived to tell the tale.

There was the sensitive ball-turret gunner who, just before a mission, confessed to Mrs Gordon that he did not know how he would stand up to the test. A word of encouragement from the young artist did the trick, and the gunner who in the evenings was "unable to mix and laugh with the others", went to his 'plane unafraid.

Mrs Gordon saw the signs of battle fatigue, such as the occasion when an airman, tripping over four chairs in crossing the mess room, broke down and said he could not carry on. Once a sergeant, who earlier on had seen some of the crew of a stricken Fortress drop into the propellers of another bomber, went berserk. Rushing to the bar Mrs Gordon called for a bottle of whisky and allowed the troubled aviator to drink himself to a state of collapse.

When the target was 'Big B' – Berlin – everyone felt anxious because, in Mrs Gordon's words, it was "a terrible target beset with wall after wall of AA guns". But although she was able to mix freely with the aviators, she had to observe certain rules, such as the ban on riding in the base bus. If she had work to do on the hardstands, where the 'planes were parked,

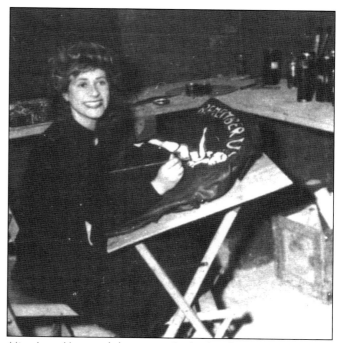

Miss Anne Haywood decorating the leather flying jacket of a crew member belonging to the 385the Bomb group, Great Ashfield, in 1943. The design, apparently showing a "flying lady", was inscribed "Remember Us". Miss Haywood is shown working in her base studio 45 years ago.

then a military Jeep took her out and brought her back. She had to dress in a formal style while painting.

There were many parties at Great Ashfield, but perhaps the most memorable was the 'hundredth mission' celebration. Mrs Gordon and the other Red Cross workers, however, saw little of the celebration, which was an all-male affair, but she understood that "nearly everyone enjoyed themselves so much that after midnight they were running about the airfield on all fours".

Mrs Gordon, in the course of her varied duties at Great Ashfield, shared the worries and triumphs of the airmen, but never knew the name of a target before a mission although 'Big B' was sometimes mentioned when Berlin was to be bombed. But in any case it showed on the fliers' faces and that was enough for the girl with the palette. Neither did the airmen allow her to decorate their 'planes to denote targets, raids, and Nazi 'planes destroyed.

"Once," said Mrs Gordon, "through no fault of the pilot and co-pilot, three labourers were accidentally decapitated on the airfield. When three little bowler hats appeared, with the other silhouettes, below the cockpit, the English workers naturally protested and the symbols were erased."

It was not until the 385th Bomb Group had made two trips on 6 June 1944, that Mrs Gordon knew that the long-awaited day – D-day – had arrived. She remembers it very clearly because "you seem to see so much sky in Suffolk, and that sunny day, with, I believe, the sergeants of the 'Wolf Squadron', we watched the aerial-armadas come and go against a back-cloth of soft blue sky."

Mrs Gordon was at the airfield when the Fortresses left for America in July 1945. There was the overweight mess sergeant, for instance, who was so large that, fearing he would be unable to escape through the hatch in the event of an emergency, had to be sent home by sea!

So it came about on 2 November 1954 that Mrs Gordon showed me faded examples of her work at the airfield. In the wrecked officers' lounge, she pointed to a list of targets still readable on the wall,

and over the entrance to the Red Cross Club, "where I was supposed to issue cups of coffee", the base crest, much weathered.

"Sometimes," she confesses, standing among the debris, "I go back to the airfield to see how much, in the interval, has disappeared.

Now, with over 30 years gone by since we looked at a more intact Great Ashfield, there is almost nothing of her war-time handiwork left to see. But in Germany, perhaps, there is the old Luftwaffe fighter veteran with a piece of her Fortress-nose-art hanging over his mantelpiece – Anne's punch from Suffolk.

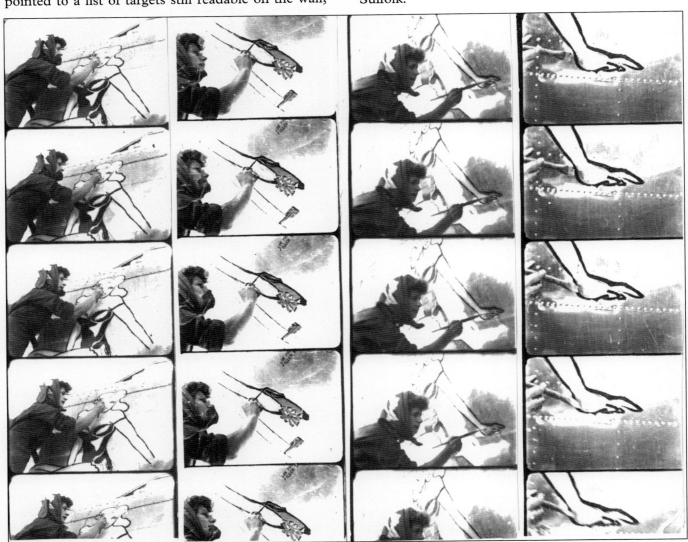

The kind of American bomber nose art that tickled Luftwaffe fighter ace Heinz Knoke during the war being applied by the then Miss Anne Haywood, of Wetherden, near Stowmarket, Suffolk, to a B-17 Flying Fortress of the 385th Bomb Group, Great Ashfield, in late 1944. The sequence of frames were taken from an unofficial film made of her at work – work which on December 10, 1943, led to Lt. Col. Elliott Vanderwanter, Jr., the group commander, writing a confidential letter to Bury St. Edmunds Labour Exchange. In it he referred to Miss Haywood's "essential work in lettering and painting designs on the B-17s at this station".

How Suffolk Artist Made the Luftwaffe Smile

A WORLD WAR II Luftwaffe fighter ace, Heinz Knoke, of West Germany, who was shot down and wounded five times in combat, has written to the newsletter of the 390th Bomb Group Memorial Air Museum, Parham Airfield, near Framlingham, Suffolk, declaring that, after reading one of the quarterly articles describing how a Suffolk girl painted pet names on local B-17 Flying Fortresses during the war, "I think it would have been better to make war just with Anne's paint pots!"

The bomber-artist was the former Miss Anne Haywood of Wetherden, near Stowmarket, Suffolk, now Mrs Anne Haywood-Gordon, of Nettlebed, Oxfordshire, who was 'employed' by the 385th Bomb Group, Great Ashfield, Suffolk, decorating their aircraft, leather flying-jackets and airfield buildings.

Heinz Knoke, in a letter sending one of his own paintings of his Messerschmitt fighter group diving on Fortresses of the 390th Bomb Group from Parham, comments: "I very much enjoyed reading the different reports. Very amusing is the story of Anne who challenged the Luftwaffe with her paint pots. Some of her paint pots seem to have hit me – please give her my best compliments and tell her that her paintings were very popular on our side. I think it would have been better to make war just with Anne's paint pots!

"I enclose . . . a photograph of the result of my paint pot. It is an oil-painting which I painted at the beginning of this year for the officers' club of the

German fighter ace Heinz Knocke in 1943.

Luftwaffe at Jever airfield, which was my base during the years 1941-43 and from where I flew most of my missions. It shows a typical dogfight situation – the meeting of Me.109s with B-17s as I saw it, many times.

"Since my retirement last year, I have been painting again, and, besides that, I have been studying philosophy and literature at University which will keep me busy for the next few years. There is an old German saying: *Rasten heisst rosten* (Reposing means rusting). I hope that, with painting and learning, it will keep me going for a fairly long time before I join my old brothers-in-arms, playing cards upstairs at Petrus", adds Heinz Knoke.

Reporting the amusing exchange, the latest newsletter of the 390th Bomb Group repeats the declaration in their journal by a former RAF Bomber Command chaplain, Evelyn Dunford, RAFVR, 1941-46, that "Those who do the fighting, rarely do the hating."

When Heinz Knoke's book *I Flew for the Fuhrer*, appeared in the 1950s he noted for 4th February 1943, that "from early morning we have been standing by (at Jever airfield) ready for take-off in case of an alert. Our radio-direction finders report heavy concentrations of enemy aircraft (allied 'planes assembling) over the Great Yarmouth area."

Later that month Heinz Knoke, who logged over 2000 flights as a Me.109 pilot, claiming in the process 52 allied aircraft, said he felt "just in the

Mrs Anne Haywood-Gordon at Great Ashfield in 1976 when 385th veterans visited their old airfield.

The kind of American bomber nose-art that tickled Luftwaffe fighter ace Heinz Knoke during the war being applied by the then Miss Anne Haywood, of Wetherden, near Stowmarket, Suffolk, to a B-17 Flying Fortress of the 385th Bomb Group, Great Ashfield, in late 1944. The sequence of frames were taken from an unofficial film made of her at work – work which on 10th December 1943, led to Lt.-Col. Elliott Vandevanter, jr., the group commander, writing a confidential letter to Bury St. Edmunds Labour Exchange. In it he referred to Miss Haywood's "essential work in lettering and painting designs on the B-17s at this station".

The likes of 'Roundtrip Jack', painted by the former Miss Anne Haywood in the course of war-time work in Suffolk for the 385th Bomb Group, Great Ashfield, amused Luftwaffe pilots as they swept in to attack

mood for a good scrap" but "over Great Yarmouth everything is quiet as yet."

It is understood that the 385th Bomb Group Association, who last visited Great Ashfield in force in 1976, are returning this August 1988 when, no doubt, Mrs Haywood-Gordon will be there as she was 12 years ago.

Footnote: In recent years the Suffolk artist, who amused American and German airmen alike with her aircraft nose-art, has demonstrated to youngsters how she did this work during the 1939-1945 war.

The great Ashfield airfield artist at work on a jolly-looking figure holding a pistol.

Dated 1942, this drawing was early evidence of the girl's airfield recording of daily life. Airmen everywhere found time for prayer.

Japanese Swords
SEARCH FOR LOST WAR TROPHIES

AN interesting exercise in international relations took place in the middle 1930s when the *Royal British Legion Journal* published the results of a suggestion from a German source that soldiers' battlefield souvenirs – watches, letters, bibles, paybooks, etc – be returned to their owners or next of kin.

The appeal led to a parcel of souvenirs taken by Germans from British soldiers during World War I being delivered in 1935 to Haig House, London, by returning members of the Legion Delegation to German Ex-Service Men.

In a subsequent article in the *Journal* every known clue to ownership of the various articles was given in the hope that families would be reunited with possessions. A follow-up article – the sequel – showed that in many cases the items were returned and were greatly appreciated by those receiving them.

After World War II, as far as is known, no similar steps were taken to interest American, British, German and Japanese ex-servicemen in returning battlefield souvenirs with the friendship aspect in view.

But in the early 1970s it was learned, for instance, that so many swords were taken from the Japanese in World War II that the trend was for the Japanese to buy swords on the Western market and return them to their own country.

Apparently the record sum paid for a sword at auction in the West in the early 1970s was £6000, but a rich Japanese had been known to 'pay anything up to £60,000 for an ancient masterpiece'.

More recently the *Journal* learned that the Japanese were once again interested in the recovery from British and American sources of swords obtained from Far Eastern battlefields 1941-1945.

So for owners of Japanese swords – particularly the more elaborate ones – the rewards could be very large. But the average sword taken by British soldiers was a fairly primitive weapon in a scabbard worth much less.

It is known that a colonel in 1945 was ordered by

In early 1945, as the Japanese Air Force increased its suicide attacks on Allied aircraft carriers, many of the pilots carried short ceremonial swords. Here an attacking plane is hit and destroyed by AA-fire from an American carrier. Photo: Courtesy US Navy

Admiral Lord Louis Mountbatten's HQ to go to Sumatra to select, with the help of Japanese army interpreters, 'ten out of thousands of the best swords'. These were later presented by Lord Mountbatten, Supreme Allied Commander, SEAC, to his principal officers.

The Japanese interpreted the histories and told the colonel that the reason "some of the swords seemed short for the scabbards was that they had been worn away with centuries of cleaning and sharpening".

When the colonel responsible for selecting the prize swords had to return to India by air, the Japanese sword he had won in the Burma campaign – it was "a real beauty", complete with purple silk cords and tassels – was never forwarded to him. But he knew that it had belonged to one of the ancient families of Japan and their battle achievements were engraved around the hilt.

Lower ranks, however, were sometimes honoured with Japanese swords. Following the re-entry into Singapore of British forces on 5th September 1945, a member of the ATS was given a Japanese warrant officer's sword equivalent to her company sergeant major's rank. Accompanying it was a certificate authorising ownership and printed card stating:

'Japanese Officer's Sword, Surrendered 1945, presented by Admiral the Lord Louis Mountbatten, Supreme Allied Commander South East Asia.'

When asked about the colonel's expedition in search of the best Japanese swords, Lord Mountbatten, who had one in his possession, commented in 1969: "It is perfectly true that I decided to give some of the best swords to senior Allied officers in staff appointments who would not normally have had swords surrendered to them, but who were clearly entitled to them".

While Lord Mountbatten had no idea whether there was more than one mission to search for Japanese swords, he did not think very many were actually presented to senior officers.

However, the ATS informant said of her acquisition: "Almost every officer and many warrant officers who were sufficiently 'in' were given one".

It is said that the subject of the Japanese sword, with its continuous history of some 1500 years, is a vast one. The names of over 12,000 swordsmiths and 3000-makers of sword furniture are known and recorded.

So it is plain to see why the Japanese are now so keen to re-acquire some of the more elaborate swords which fell into Allied hands in 1945.

Would you return (or sell) yours if it had a pedigree and a wealthy Japanese knocked at your door? For in July it was reported that the Japanese were once again in the UK looking for ancestors' swords.

Prayer flag, whose original owner's name is on the flag, wished him 'everlasting success in war'; the sword belonged to a 'lower rank'. The prayer flag was acquired by a colonel between Toungoo and Pegu, Burma, May/ July, 1945; the sword was presented to an ATS company sergeant major with appropriate certification while on Admiral Lord Louis Mountbatten's HQ in Singapore in 1946.

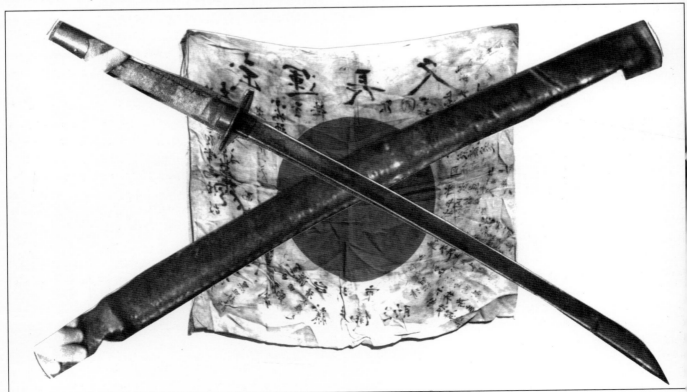

USAAF – Early Books

FROM time to time references are made to current books about the 8th and 9th Air Forces without, it seems, enough regard for what has appeared on the subject almost since the first groups settled in England in 1942.

I wonder how many remember *American Flyers In England* (Hutchinson, 1943) by Majors John M. Redding and Harold I. Leyshon about the early B-17 and B-24 groups

The book, which is well illustrated, carries a foreword by the late Lt.-General Ira C. Eaker, the 8th's commander at the time, who noted: "To an observer or a reporter, the vantage point is important. It is also important to his audience. . . . The book was written by these two officers in their own time after long hours of official duty . . .".

Then, in 1947, came Bert Stiles' *Serenade To The Big Bird* based on his time with the 91st Bomb Group, Bassingbourn, Cambridgeshire.

In 1948, when B-29 Superfortresses came into RAF Scampton, Lincolnshire, I was sent there as a young reporter and at a subsequent RAFA dinner met their commander, Col. John B. Henry, former C.O. of the 339th Fighter Group, Fowlmere, Cambridgeshire

Young Bert Stiles who wrote Seranade To The Big Bird.

Last year (1990) on a social visit to the Chequers Inn, Fowlmere, I learned from the visitors' book that he had visited for a memorial unveiling in September 1986, as a Major General (retd).

Writing to him in San Antonio, Texas, reminding him of the 1948 encounter, General Henry threw some new light on author Bert Stiles who was lost over Hanover on 26 November 1944.

He told me: "One day in late October of 1944 Bert Stiles came to my office at Fowlmere and appealed to me to take him on as a fighter pilot. He stated that he had completed 35 missions (full tour) in bombers with the 91st and was highly desirous of combat flying in P-51 Mustangs.

Major General John B. Henry as a colonel in England in 1948.

"Our base being the nearest to Bassingbourn, it seemed a logical place to start. I was hesitant, but his pleasing personality, enthusiasm and serious intent won me over and I took the action to get him assigned to the 339th . . . as the only B-17 pilot that the 339th took in . . . ".

For airfield atmosphere – mission parties and girl friends – I know of no better book than Julius Horwitz's novel *Can I Get There By Candlelight* (Andre Deutsch, 1964).

A member of the 8th Air Force, Horwitz nearly gives the location of his base when he notes: " 'The party's building up', he said. 'Two civilians from Stowmarket almost took a B-17 up. They said they wanted to end the war'."

And the title? Well, I worked out from a 1890s book that it refers to a local game "because it is essentially a Suffolk name (if not Ipswich) because of the distance to London".

Periphery books, in which there are many 8th Air Force connotations, include *A Letter From Grosvenor Square: An Account Of A Stewardship* by war-time Ambassador John G. Winant (Hodder and Stoughton, 1947).

Writing from 3 Grosvenor Square, London W3, he notes that the flat (No. 30) he had occupied for the war years was significant.

It was at the flat that General Eaker told Ambassador Winant that his son, John, who was a pilot with the 390th Bomb Group, Framlingham, Suffolk, was missing on a Fortress raid.

It was at the flat, too, that Tommy Hitchcock and

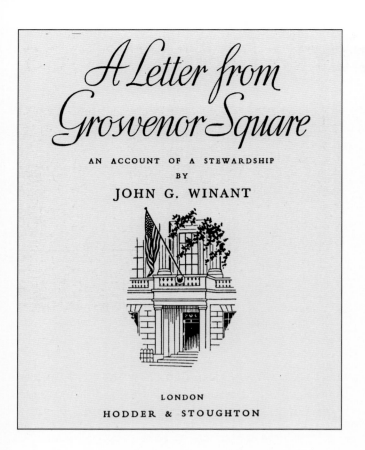

A Letter from
Grosvenor Square

AN ACCOUNT OF A STEWARDSHIP
BY
JOHN G. WINANT

LONDON
HODDER & STOUGHTON

Ambassador Winant "worked on the plans for the long-distance P-51, and here that I was notified he had been killed on an experimental flight".

Then there is J. Frank Dobie's *A Texan In England* (Hammond and Hammond, 1944) based on the author's period as Professor of American History, Cambridge University, 1943-1944.

The book mentions that in late 1943 at Thetford, Norfolk, Professor Dobie was involved in ceremonies marking the birthplace of Thomas Paine (1737 - 1809).

One event he attended was the naming at Knettishall, Suffolk, of the 388th Bomb Group's B-17 *Tom Paine – Tyranny, Like Hell, is not easily Conquered!*

With other youngsters I saw 'Tom Paine' force-land at Beccles airfield, Suffolk, on 11 April 1944, after a remarkable near-solo flight home from a distant Baltic target.

As for magazine articles about the 8th Air Force after its withdrawal from Eastern England in early 1946 – well, there weren't many general ones for some years. It seems likely, then, that my "American Battlefield" article in the now defunct *East Anglian Magazine* of May 1950, was an early tribute to their three-year occupation.

All these titles are mostly now out of print but might turn up in second-hand book shops or at local jumble sales.

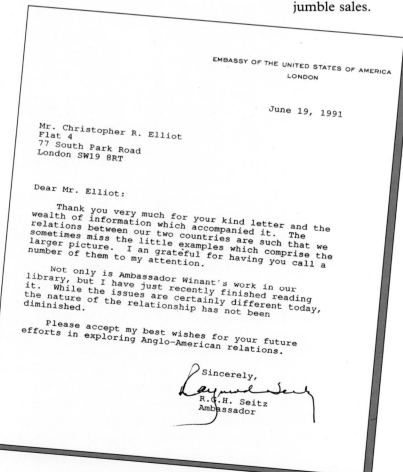

EMBASSY OF THE UNITED STATES OF AMERICA
LONDON

June 19, 1991

Mr. Christopher R. Elliot
Flat 4
77 South Park Road
London SW19 8RT

Dear Mr. Elliot:

Thank you very much for your kind letter and the wealth of information which accompanied it. The relations between our two countries are such that we sometimes miss the little examples which comprise the larger picture. I am grateful for having you call a number of them to my attention.

Not only is Ambassador Winant's work in our library, but I have just recently finished reading it. While the issues are certainly different today, the nature of the relationship has not been diminished.

Please accept my best wishes for your future efforts in exploring Anglo-American relations.

Sincerely,

R.G.H. Seitz
Ambassador

American Invasion – Memories

IN January 1942 – twenty-five years ago this month – the first American servicemen landed in Britain. Their coming – two million were to follow – had a profound effect on our village and city life.

Soon the heavy concentration of 8th and 9th USAAF bomber and fighter bases in East Anglia brought thousands of young American servicemen in contact with East Anglians, many of whom hitherto had only a film-goer's appreciation of Americans and their way of life.

Some East Anglians, who troubled to get to know them away from the bars, found to their great surprise, that a good few Americans had English names, and that some had better connections with the Puritan 'family' of John Winthrop, of Groton, Suffolk, who set sail with other local men and women for the New World in 1629, than they themselves could claim – even after scraping the barrel!

For my part I had a cousin from Ohio in the 8th Air Force and, later in the war, a cousin living at Ipswich, Suffolk, married an American stationed at Wattisham, and now lives in Pennsylvania. Hundreds, if not thousands, of other East Anglian families have similar links. In fact, Allan A. Michie, the well-known American journalist and commentator of the war years, told me after the war that some 50,000 Americans, mostly 8th Air Force men, married British girls.

Are the Americans of today very different from those we knew when, 25 years ago, we first met them on their English bicycles sailing through our lanes, their feet on the handlebars, or struggling, perhaps in a wounded condition, to release themselves from parachutes caught in our trees?

The best spontaneous judgement I heard passed on this point was as a guest of my American cousin

Cousin Molly Baker, of Ipswich, married Private First-Class Kenneth B. Payne, 8th Air Force, and in 1945 went to live in Pennsylvania.
Photo: Courtesy 'US Steel News'

in the famous American Red Cross Rainbow Corner, now demolished, at the corner of Shaftesbury Avenue and Windmill Street, Piccadilly, where there was a notice over the main entrance that said: *Through These Portals Pass America's Finest.*

As I prepared to put my notebook away an American Air Force officer, with a wound-patch over his right eye, put his hand on my shoulder and said: "Son, that may be true. It all depends on who's the judge, but I reckon that it would be true to say – and you can put it in your notebook – that we are no better and no worse than our fathers who came over in the First Great War. We certainly ain't angels."

Memories, generally, are very short. I wonder, therefore, how many people are aware that Major-General William E. Kepner, last commanding General of the 8th Air Force, was given the first non-British Honorary Freedom of Norwich. On behalf of the 8th he received from the Mayor of Cambridge a casket containing the Scroll of Freedom for his entire force – some 300,000 men and women.

Also Bedford, in whose prison John Bunyan wrote *Pilgrim's Progress*, bestowed the Honorary Freedom on Major-General Howard M. Turner, commanding General of the original 1st Air Division of the 8th.

Elsewhere there are several tangible monuments to the 8th Air Force's three-year association with the Eastern Counties. At Norwich, for example, the city can be proud of the American Room at the Central Library – a memorial to the 2nd Air Division based in Norfolk. On the main Norwich-Ipswich road, close to the old base of the 34th Bombardment Group at Mendlesham, there was unveiled in 1949, a fine memorial showing the head and shoulders of a pilot framed in the cockpit of a Flying Fortress. Then there is the beautiful memorial window in the old church at

American cousin Edward Miller, of Ohio, who was an engineer in the 8th USAAF, pictured in England in October 1944.
Photo: Courtesy USAAF

Major-General William E. Kepner, last comanding General of the 8th Air Force, was given the first British Honorary Freedom of Norwich.

Quidenham, Norfolk, in memory of the dead of the 96th Bombardment Group from Snetterton Heath.

In other directions there must be many people at Diss who remember the doctors and nurses of the US Army 65th General Hospital, where many flak-wound cases were treated, the service being so good that wounded airmen were often on the operating-table by the same evening. It was at this hospital near Diss, I believe, that American surgeons once removed a foreign body from an airman's heart – and the patient lived.

At least two good books by East Anglian-based USAAF authors emerged from the three-year occupation – *Suffolk Summer*, by John T. Appleby, in 1948, the proceeds of which were given towards the upkeep of a memorial garden in the abbey grounds at Bury St. Edmunds, and *Here We Are Together*, by Robert S. Arbib, jnr, a little earlier in 1946.

Many of the more outstanding groups published elaborate histories a year or two after their return home. Published in limited editions, they are now very rare and expensive, some histories being priced as high as 20-guineas. On the other hand, several groups, before they left this country, had booklets printed locally, and in the 1950s I was able to round up a number of stray copies from various printers.

American airmen operating from our bases, mostly in Eastern counties, paid a high price – over 41,000 men dead and over 6000 aircraft lost. Many of these airmen, whom we knew when they were alive, are buried on a hill in the Cambridge American Military Cemetery just off the Cambridge-Bedford road.

> *I only know that you may lie*
> *Day long and watch the Cambridge sky*
> FROM RUPERT BROOKE'S
> 'THE OLD VICARAGE, GRANTCHESTER'

Footnote: One of the best providers of American fighter and bomber histories, particularly in relation to the 8th USAAF, is East Anglia Books, Station Road, Elsenham, Bishops Stortford, Herts CM22 6LG. Interestingly, John T. Appleby's *Suffolk Summer*, which was first published in 1948, had by 1980 been reprinted eight times.

A number of paintings were done by British artist Frank Beresford of scenes in the 65th General Hospital, US Army, near Diss. Here an American nurse is shown taking the pulse of a patient named 'George' who had been badly shot-up. Eventually he recovered and was sent back to the States.

Airfield children formed part of British artist Roy Diggens' 'Those darn kids again' depicting them talking to American servicemen by a P-38 Lightning fighter. Photo: Courtesy RAF Museum

Long Runways – Concrete Partnerships

EARLY this month (1983) it was announced that the USAF is to open all but one of its six major British bases to the public in the summer.

Thus RAF Mildenhall, headquarters of American's Third Air Force, will be opening its doors on 28/29 May, and RAF Lakenheath, home of the 48th Tactical Fighter Wing, will be visited on 2/3 July by many people from far beyond the confines of East Anglia.

Apart from the war years, when East Anglians regularly saw the old USAF flying daily 2000 bombers and fighters overhead without so much as a spent cartridge-case hitting anyone on the head, the RAF and the USAF are not, of course, very likely to assemble such huge formations again, as a single aircraft now represents the protective punch-plus of a 2000-strong strike-force of the war years.

So the airmanship required is greater than ever and the forthcoming air displays will confirm that this is the case.

Looking back to the early post-war years, when I was a cub reporter on a Lincolnshire weekly newspaper, it's hardly possible to believe that when I was sent to RAF Scampton on 18 July 1948, to report the arrival of the USAF B-29 Superfortresses (some out of mothballs from the Tokyo raids of 1944-45, as the Berlin Blockade started, it marked America's return for all the years since.

But between 1945 and 1948 America's General Carl Spaatz, one time commander of the 8th USAF

Major General Carl Spaatz looked for longer runways.
Photo: Courtesy USAAF

and Britain's Air Marshall Sir Arthur Tedder were always concerned about "the fully-armed Soviet military force that stood ready in the East while the West disbanded."

Correctly, these two very experienced airmen believed that not many years on Eastern England would have to accommodate long-range B-29s but not a single British airfield was equipped to handle them.

To correct this, they decided 'informally' that the RAF would prepare four bases – just in case – to receive B-29s.

So when the Berlin Blockade came about in 1948 their decision proved correct and it was, in fact, the Labour Government under Prime Minister Clement

Old Pacific B-29 Superfortress "Hongchow", out of mothballs, parked at RAF Scampton, Lincolnshire, soon after the arrival of the 28th Bomb Group in July, 1948, as the Berlin Blockade developed.

After their long flight to RAF Scampton, Lincolnshire, some of the B-29 crews relaxed playing cards.

The author with one of the Shepherd's Grove F-86 Sabre jet pilots. Lt. Ray E. Roestel was a school teacher by profession.

Attlee who invited the first of many United States military units.

The first B-29 into Scampton, which saw Guy Gibson's Lancasters go out via Southwold to attack the German dams by night in 1943, was flown by the CO of 28th Bomb Group, Col. John B. Henry, who told me he had been in the 8th Air Force.

Amusingly, the old *Illustrated* for 14 August 1948, quoted one of the ex-8th airmen (other B-29s of the force went into Marham and Lakenheath) as saying: "I'll never forget the time I was asked to go shooting with Lord . . . I hadn't seen a pheasant before, and they warned me on no account to shoot a hen. You've guessed it, the first bird I shot was a hen. But they asked me to come again . . ."

Next encounter I had with an American unit strengthening our guard was when I was reporting for a newspaper in West Suffolk. On 27th August 1951, the first 25 'smoking' F-86 Sabre jet-fighters arrived at RAF Shepherd's Grove, near Bury St. Edmunds. This was the first time that a foreign power had shared with the RAF the actual air defence of Great Britain

The pilots comprised "a substantial contingent of America's former 'weekend' airmen, flying the fastest jet-fighters in service with the Allied air forces" at the time.

I spoke to some of the pilots of the 116th Fighter Interceptor Squadron, 81st Fighter Interceptor Wing,

A line-up of some of the Shepherd's Grove F-86 Sabre jets on September 24, 1951.

A crashing F-84 Thunderjet belonging to the 20th Fighter-Bomber Wing, Wethersfield, Essex, set fire to cottages and a barn as Assington, near Sudbury, on July 14, 1954. Its pilot, Capt. Robert Fair escaped by parachute.

F-86 Sabre jet showing its paces at Armed Forces Day, May 15, 1954, at Bentwaters base in Suffolk.

getting them to give me their World War II units, and two of them, it turned out, were with us between 1943 and 1945 in such famous units as the 4th Fighter Group, Debden, Essex, and the 357th Fighter Group, Leiston.

Two of their number, one day, gave me a private display at Sudbury and one nearly clipped the spire of St. Peter's Church! Their daring stunts for me had another twist when, climbing away to fly back to Shepherd's Grove, one lost a long-range tank filler cap and streamed white vapour all the way home!

Interestingly, during my six years as a reporter in West Suffolk, I had contact with RAF Wattisham and

met, during that time, Major Howard N. Tanner, USAF, a veteran from the U S 5th Air Force in Korea, who commanded 257 (Burma) Squadron of the RAF under the Anglo-American exchange scheme. The squadron flew Gloster Meteor and Hawker Hunter jets during the Major's term, which ended in 1955.

So the cross-pollination of the RAF and the USAF has been going on for all these years and what one does the other most certainly understands by day or by night.

No wonder, then, that the two air forces are the envy of the rest of the world, including the Soviet Union, whose long-range reconnaissance aircraft are publicly known to regularly survey the north-east coast of Britain.

During the Cold War the RAF and the Soviet Air Force photographed each others' aircraft off the East Coast. 12 Squadron tested their prying cameras by making slight changes to the fox faces on their own planes. Soviet comment was then looked for in their military press.

Photo: Courtesy Ministry of defence

Storm Dogs of Suffolk
FACT OR FICTION?

STORMS, fires, frosts and other unusual natural occurrences, such as meteors, eclipses and comets, are occasionally described in old parish registers.

What is certain is that the terrible fire at York Minister in July 1984, attributed to a bolt of lightning, which destroyed seven-hundred years of history in the south transept, will go down in the minster's archives for researchers to rediscover in the centuries to come.

Nearer home, however, lightning in the 16th century at Bungay and Blythburgh, Suffolk, caused damage to two churches, killed people, and left legends of 'black dogs' rushing among the congregations.

The date of the two Suffolk manifestations was Sunday, 4th August 1577, and even today enlightened thought on what actually was seen, and why, isn't in complete agreement.

Let's take the Bungay tempest first: it vented itself on good St. Mary's Church to such a degree that today the black dog and a streak of lightning form a Bungay sign.

Chronicler Fleming said the Bungay storm consisted of *"rain violently falling, fearful flashes of lightning and terrible cracks of thunder, which came with such unwanted force and power, that to the perceiving of the people . . . the church did as it were quake and stagger, which struck into the hearts of those that were present, such a sore and sodain feare,* *that they were in a manner robbed of their right wits."*

It was in the heat of the disturbance that what appeared to take the form of a black hound, believed by some to be the devil, ran down the body of the church at great speed.

Incredibly, as the dog form passed between two kneeling members of the congregation, it *"wrung the necks of them both at one instant clene backward, in so much that even at a moment where they kneeled, they strangely died."*

But Bungay's spectre dog hadn't finished with the congregation. Remaining as a hound, as it appeared to the eye witnesses, it attacked another man.

This time the beast, if that's what it was, *"gave him such a gripe on the back, that therewith all he was presently withdrawn together and shrunk up as it were a piece of leather scorched in a hot fire . . . The albeit he was in so strange a taking, dyed not, but as it is thought is yet alive: which thing is marvellous in the eyes of men, and offered much matter of amasing the mind."*

While all this was happening, the church clerk, who was gallantly clearing the gutter of the church, presumably to allow the flood water from the roof to escape more easily, was "smitten down" by a violent clap of thunder, fell many feet, but survived without injury.

Meanwhile, the curate "comforted the people" until the storm was gone. The lightning bolts, if that's

When lightning struck churches at Bungay and Blythburgh, in Suffolk, on Sunday, August 4, 1577, there were black dog manifestations which are remembered to this day

what they were, left marks on the stones and church door "which are marvellously renten and torne, ye marks as it were of his clawes and talans".

At Blythburgh, a few miles from Bungay, a thunderstorm struck about the same time – between nine and ten in the morning – and it, too, vented itself on church property while the congregation were at prayer. Its target was the beautiful church, high above the flatness of the marshes of the *River Blyth*, which has close associations with St. Felix, a man of peace, who came preaching christianity in East Anglia in the 7th century.

Chronicler Holinshed, describing the Blythburgh incident, said *"a strange and terrible tempest of lightning and thunder strake through the wall of the same church into the ground almost a yard deepe, drave downe all the people on that side above twentie persons, then renting the wall up to the venstre, cleft the doore, and returning to the steeple, rent the timber, brake the chimes, and fled towards Bongie . . . The people that were striken downe were found groueling more than halfe an houre after . . ."*.

The death toll at Blythburgh, as far as I can ascertain, was three – two men and a boy – while other people were scorched.

What, I wonder, was the true nature of the hounds seen at Bungay and Blythburgh in the same storm? I expect, in both cases, shaggy dogs accompanying worshippers broke free and, in the weird half-light that some believed marked the end of civilisation

The dog notice spotted at Blythburgh Church, Suffolk, in the 1950s.

in Suffolk, appeared to be part of the fiery visitations.

If the beasts, as I suspect, wore heavy iron collars, perhaps with flailing chains, it is possible that the lightning sparked around them, thus giving the impression to the frightened congregations that they were the originators of the ungodly din and destruction.

Curiously, in the 1950s, while visiting Holy Trinity Church. Blythburgh, I spotted the following notice pinned to the door, signed by the vicar and two churchwardens; "Owing to regrettable incidents we are obliged to give notice that, in no circumstances whatever, can dogs be allowed inside the church."

And at Bungay some people still recite:

> *All down the church in midst of fire*
> *The hellish monster flew:*
> *And passing onward to the choir*
> *He many people slew.*

Storm clouds in the making.

A Bure Ferryman
TWILIGHT MEMORIES

IN NORFOLK between the wars slab-sided ferries capable of carrying farm wagons, farmers' gigs, cattle and the like were essential in Broadland as bridges, as now, were few and far between.

I see in an old RAC county road map and gazetteer for Norfolk and Suffolk, published between the wars, that these long-established ferries operated from well before 6am and ran until as late as 10pm, in all weathers. In those days cars crossed for 1s, motor-cycles for 6d, and these charges were inclusive of all the passengers.

In the old days, too, some marsh farmers used to swim their herds of cattle across the rivers, thus names remain like *Runham Swim* and *Mautby Swim*. Wild West-like, the bellowing animals must have presented a frightening sight as they made for the opposite bank.

But when, as the war ended in 1945, we once again set out for the *Norfolk Broads*, this time in the little Beccles-based cabin cruiser *Dart* (W232), to explore rivers and inns, some of which had gone to sleep since 1939, we found only one or two ferries still in use and some were no more than punts.

The most memorable ferryman I met during the August 1946 holiday was Arthur 'Chink' Sturman, then in his early seventies, of Salhouse, who worked the ferry punt across the *Bure* at Horning, by the inn.

The evening we talked, I see from notes still preserved, was thundery, gnats were about, and Chink, who was wearing a kind of trilby hat with a little fan of jay's feathers in the band, was clearing reeds from the Horning bank for house-boat berths.

Asked about his river background, for all evidence pointed to Chink being Horning's character, he revealed he had six sons named, believe it or not, Rusty, Water Rat, Fresh Air, Peewit, Cruiser and Autocrat.

This information I must have doubted at the time for in August, 1949, I wrote to the then landlord of Horning Ferry Inn asking for verification. Back came word that it was so and that Chink did indeed give his sons those Broadland names.

What was more, the landlord added: "Chink is still in our employment working the ferry. He will be 75 next September. He's been working here intermittently since he was 19 years old".

Sometimes just a rowing-boat ferry was the only means of bridging a river crossing.

Horning's veteran ferry man, Arthur 'Chink' Sturman, performed his duty under a changing Norfolk sky and in all weathers.

Now, if Chink were still alive, he'd be around 107.

The Horning ferryman, I see from photographs taken at the time, co-operated for two or three. One shows him working the punt in the fading light of that August day, at a time when the rivers of Norfolk could still be sailed for long periods without sighting other vessels.

What many of today's holiday-makers calling at Horning won't know is that, just at closing time on the night of 26th April 1941, a German bomber, pursued by an RAF night-fighter, dropped a stick of 112-lb bombs across the river.

Of the 15 bombs released, four fell on the crowded inn, including one on the old pontoon ferry, 10 fell on the Woodbastwick side of the *Bure*, and one dropped in the river itself.

Twenty-one people died in the attack, with many others injured; and Charles F. Carrodus, one-time yachting correspondent of the *Eastern Daily Press*, who just after the war edited that rare little book *A Norfolk Village In War-Time: 1939-1945* (H. Clarke & Co., London), believed the pontoon ferry was "still out of action nearly four years later".

In my copy of Walter Jerrold's book *Norwich and The Broads* (Blackie), illustrated with pictures by E.W. Haslehurst, there is a coloured plate of the Horning Ferry Inn crossing-point pre-war when, on the Woodbastwick side, there stood a pretty wrought iron sign with a bell with which to summon the ferryman.

J. Wentworth Day's 1951 book *Broadland*

Adventure (*Country Life*) gives a fairly full account of the state of the county's ferries.

Stokesby and Horning ferries, he noted, were both memories. On the *Yare*, Buckenham and Surlingham ferries had gone. Only the ferry pontoon at Reedham remained.

And I see from car (3s.) and passenger (3d.) tickets pasted inside the cover of my copy of Christopher Davies' 1884 edition of *Norfolk Broads And Rivers* that I last used Reedham ferry in 1964. Interestingly, just as at Horning, the spot had been a ferry crossing for hundreds of years – Reedham, certainly, since "around the 15th century".

Perhaps there is still time for the brewers to develop the following suggestion made by J. Wentworth Day in his *Broadland Adventure*: "In most cases the ferry operated from the front of an Inn. When you wanted to call the ferry on the opposite bank you jangled a brass bell dangling from a gaunt wooden post. The inn door opened, out came the ferryman, you were ferried across and there was the welcome of the inn. What could be more human, more to the point? The brewers kept up the ferry and the ferry passengers very largely kept up the inn. The brewers should wake up and restore the ferries . . .".

So the late Arthur 'Chink' Sturman, of Salhouse, who couldn't get to work, or home again, without using Horning ferry, performed an ancient and honourable service in his day.

Snap Judgements

THE early history of photography is adorned with lavish names such as Joseph Nicéphore Niepce and Louis Mandé Daguerre. As early as 1835, Fox Talbot sensitised paper with silver nitrate, fixed negatives with common salt, and produced positive prints. Another pioneer, Sir John Herschel, used hypo (hyposulphite of soda) as his fixing agent, and is said to have invented the term 'photograph'.

These men could hardly have foreseen the enormity of the photographic industry today. Never in the history of photography have so many people possessed cameras, and never have so many prints, colour and black-and-white, been mass-produced so quickly. By the time you have read this article, millions of pictures will have been taken across the world.

However, no one can convince me that taking many photographs of one subject, as a lot of professionals and amateurs do, is the way to improve one's eye for composition.

Far more of a discipline, surely, is the idea of clicking the shutter just once or twice and still getting a picture that is pleasing. With a few exceptions, all the hundreds of pictures I have taken since the mid-1940s have depicted no more and no less than I expected or desired.

In some respects, my approach to photography is old-fashioned. It was not until the early 1980s that I first tried colour photography after years of restricting myself to plain black-and-white! Even now, I believe colour photographs – mine and others' – have a prettiness which hide composition faults black-and-white cannot conceal.

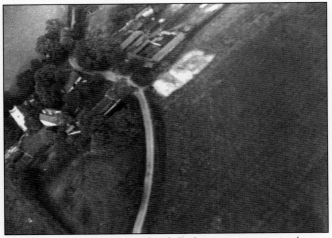

An old box-camera, acquired with Typhoo tea coupons in the 1930s, got this urgent evening aerial photograph of Borley Rectory, Essex, which was often written up as "The most haunted house in England". Destroyed by fire in 1939, the original rectory was, it is claimed, troubled by "several ghosts", including a poltergeist, although there is now doubt.

The author (left), with no one present to operate his camera, uses a mirror for a self-snap image, while the young ape (right) handles an old plate camera with apparent dexterity. Which only goes to show that photography is getting easier. But how stands picture composition as digital cameras take over?

I have never been one for anything but the most essential equipment, and that goes for darkroom equipment as well. I started photography as a teenager using my father's all-metal 1920s Ensign box-type, which produced 2¼ inch x 3¼ inch negatives. When the civilian ban on the use of cameras was lifted at the war's end, I took over his smart German Rolleicord IIA (2¼inch-square negatives). Surprisingly, that same veteran Rolleicord is still going strong, producing photographs of publication standard.

I have taken photographs at all hours of the day and night, in all kinds of weather, on land, at sea, and from the air. Even after all these years, I still find my best subjects in the English countryside – weather scenes, village people, and rural architecture.

When I started taking photographs, film was in short supply, so economy was a discipline I had to learn. This was well illustrated during a short holiday at Ipswich in May 1949. The Rolleicord was with my father on an American visit, so I was left with the simple Ensign. Wonderful spring weather coaxed me into a Suffolk cycle ride and from two 120-roll films I produced 16 saleable exposures for such publications as *Country Life* and *The Field*.

It was a performance I have yet to repeat – I put it down to a combination of fine weather and artistic inspiration. What I sensed I wanted to photograph turned out exactly as planned.

Darkroom? If you are ever caught without one there are, of course, many places to go. In the Grimsby of the late 1940s, when I worked for the old *Grimsby News* and lived in a boarding house in dockland, I frequently used my landlady's wardrobe for developing films by hand in a tray! "Mrs.

Golden eternity: a remarkable sunset at Hales, Norfolk, in the 1950s.

Grimshaw", the cry used to be on completion of the job, "I'll be out of your bedroom in five minutes".

When I started to dabble in photography at Beccles, Suffolk, my darkroom was a blacked-out gardener's shed without a light trap at the door. This

When the Suffolk Association of Architects staged an exhibition of photographs at the Festival of Britain/Aldeburgh Festival, June 1951, "to show some of the riches of the historical architecture of the county", the author was the most junior of the eight photographers invited to exhibit. His 1948 picture was of decaying Westhall post-mill, near Halesworth, Suffolk, now gone.

meant that once inside, you could not leave until development was completed. On one occasion, a sudden drop in winter temperature and a lack of ready hot water left me with a panchromatic film that would not clear.

This situation called for initiative, so I was surprised when the film cleared to negative shapes without any chemical damage. A medical friend, himself an experienced photographer, on hearing of the steps I took, commented: "Well done, old chap, I wouldn't have thought of that solution. It speaks well for a healthy bladder, and an alert mind!"

Even when a vital piece of the camera goes missing, there is always a way out. In the 1960s, a Cockney friend took me to see an intact wartime air force headquarters building in Essex. We arrived at the abandoned airfield without a flash unit and my guide commented: "The building's a huge blockhouse without a window of any kind. We are on a wasted journey."

Years before, however, tired of flash bulbs that misfired, I had developed torch photography, using a tripod-mounted camera loaded with panchromatic film, opening the shutter wide for one to three minutes, and waving a torch uniformly over the subject from a position behind the camera.

This was the technique I used in the totally dark headquarters. Two of my torch photographs eventually appeared in *Flight International* to help illustrate an article on airfield archaeology.

No one need feel lost with inferior equipment, despite relentless advertising proclaiming various 'unique' features which will take you to the very peak of perfection.

In the early 1950s, for example, a speedy aerial picture was needed of the site of Borley rectory in Essex, which was periodically written up as 'the most haunted house in England'. There was no professional photographer on hand for the evening assignment, so I took my aunt's box camera, which she had acquired with Typhoo tea coupons years before, and flew out from Ipswich Airport in an old ex-army plane.

We found Borley in the evening light, and I told the pilot what I wanted him to do. We approached from the west with the sun behind us and made only one pass, as there was only one piece of cut film in the camera! It turned out to be a passable single negative.

Enjoy your photography, but don't forget the artistic side. Don't snap a whole film on a single subject when, with a little care, you can embrace half a dozen others.

One of several dawn pictures taken of Blyth Waters, Suffolk, in 2003 using a hand-held box camera. Vistages were successfully photographed as early as 3.30 am.

Distant Blythburgh Church seen from the old Halesworth/ Southwold railway track which saw its last train in 1929

Mr W. H. Garwood, the Ashwellthorpe, Norfolk, wheelwright, working on wheel spokes in 1948.

Pony and trap at Brockdish, Norfolk, in the late 1940s.

Shoeing a horse at the smithy at Holton, near Halesworth, Suffolk, in 1947.

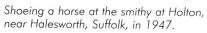

Duck and drinking horse at Mettingham, Suffolk, in the 1950s.

Political Correctness

AS the Conservative Party disintegrated at the end of 1997, shedding its rusty nuts and bolts (and much else) all over the place, I ran into a spate of politically correct (PC) situations which left me smarting but, as always, cocky.

I feel, for the good of the country, I should now reveal what I dare about these alarming encounters.

The first arose when, wishing to quickly consult three specialist books at one of our national museums in London, I was informed by a female member of the staff, in the course of a telephone conversation, that I would have to wait two months "as we are putting our reference library on the computer".

I was astonished at the forecast,. and made noises to that effect.

Not to be outdone, I tried again within minutes, but was again rebuffed by a female voice.

I grunted my displeasure.

Finally, I asked to speak to the museum's director, who turned out to be away, and was landed with the deputy director who, like his female colleagues, took the same stand.

By then very heated, I told him that I intended to write to the director as I thought a delay of two months far too long when I knew they sometimes made exceptions.

When I wrote to the director, himself no chicken, I related how his staff had been united in holding me back two months.

His letter to me on headed notepaper, indicating that a member of the Royal Family was their patron, explained at length how stretched the museum was for funds and so on.

Rounding off his two-page letter, the director then took me to task for the way, he alleged, I had spoken to his staff on the telephone. He, on behalf of his staff, who appeared to run a kind of co-operative, had no hesitation in banning me from their reference library.

On learning this, I decided to appeal for clemency via the museum's royal patron, but the Buckingham Palace equerry concerned replied that, having raised my letter with his employer, I simply had to take the punishment like a man!

Next demonstration of PC (political correctness) gone mad occurred when I revisited an East End pub which, years ago, I used to frequent near my office at lunchtime when it was a friendly place.

On buying half-a-pint of Guiness and a packet of plain crisps, I retired, as I used to, to a shelf corner, where I wanted to write something or other, but was almost immediately accosted by a small woman who wanted to know, above the din, my business in the pub! I was flabbergasted.

Taking her for a common prostitute, and her oblique question about my presence a veiled way of introducing herself, I bellowed "Be off, wench" as would have been uttered on that very spot 300 years ago in a similar situation.

Furious at my words, she screamed for the pub's strong man who, confronting me with folded, hairy arms and feet apart, ordered me to abandon my drink and crisps and leave the premises.

Not to be outdone, for the treatment seemed illogical, I resolutely stood my ground (I am quite a little fellow) and demanded *all* my money back before leaving.

By then, half the darkened pub's clientele had closed round me, some in shirt sleeves, hoping for a sight of a 67-year-old taking on the chucker-out whose face showed his dislike for my daring confrontation.

Then, as I went out, there was a cry of "You silly old fool, this is a strippers' pub and you pay for all you see".

But I was not to retreat so easily without firing a parting shot: I turned on the crowd, many of whom were local business men who should have been back at their jobs by 3pm, and made a Churchillian V-sign which could, because of the way I arranged my fingers, have been mistaken for something else . . .!

Outside, quite dazed by the swiftness with which my intended lunch-break had been so quickly terminated, I decided to find the nearest police station to ask if pub strippers had the right to eject

---

Quangos

JUST before the fashion of political correctness took hold, England was forced in the 1980s to recognise Quangos, which were quasi non-governmental organisations. But these organisations were, according to the *Daily Telegraph* of 24th January 1993, 'cuddly toys' compared with their successors of the 1990s – the Sefras, or self-financing regulatory agencies.

A Sefra is a semi-autonomous body, set up under statute or hived-off from the Civil Service, which has the power to impose regulations on businesses or other forms of activity; to pay its own way by charging fees for compulsory registration or licensing; or to, in many cases, charge fees for inspections; to impose penalties for non-compliance (fines, closure, withdrawal of licence); to act in effect as its own arbiter (there is usually no appeal to law against its decisions).

Furthermore, local authorities are being forced to take on Sefra characteristics to make up revenue deficits, by imposing an ever-increasing range of charges for everything from planning and building control to the licensing of sex shops.

law-abiding citizens who didn't want to see their naked bodies.

But the privatised clerk on duty, who was not a proper police officer, was flummoxed, saying that all he could do was to report my treatment to "a higher authority".

Quite exhausted by the all-round stupidity, I walked out of the police station, only to be nearly knocked down by a barrow-boy in a fast car carrying a load of netted onions!

The effect of my third PC (political correctness) transgression was even more alarming for, as a result of it, I have every reason – and we are well into 1997 – to believe that I am now marked down as an international trouble-maker without, it seems, the right to appeal! How this came about is quite ridiculous.

Having received the usual NHS check reminder from my dentist of many years, I went along, but found he had gone abroad and his practise was in the hands of a man from the East who was set on going 'private'.

As the dentist, who was wearing tribal head-gear, turned his searchlight on my mouth, temporarily dazzling me, he spoke gravely of 'tartar evidence', which I did not consider very important, and I remarked that "Often it's better to leave alone the incrustation in an old kettle or you might pierce the bottom. After all, the mounted Tartar nomads of long ago were a right lot of piercers . . .".

Apparently this upset my dentist who, taking the kettle and tartar remarks out of context, summarily dismissed me from his NHS list!

Dazed, I staggered from his couch, picking up my coat, scarf, umbrella and papers as I did so, and squeaked that I would ask his receptionist as I went out, for the name of a replacement NHS dentist.

"You will do nothing of the kind," bellowed the man from the East, "for you are a trespasser and I want you off my premises at once, never to return".

However, as I did with the pub chucker-out, I stood my English ground: I presented myself to the foreign receptionist who, unbeknown to me, had already been alerted on the dentist's mobile 'phone that I was trespassing, and she, too, ordered me to quit.

But I dug in. Several of the dentist's female staff mustered in the vicinity, and one short, darkly-tanned woman, put out a 999-call to the police as if I were a rampant rapist!

While, in my London borough, I sometimes have to hang around for the police to appear, when I witness something or other, their response to the dentist's SOS was almost instantaneous. For up the stairs dashed a pair, one tall and one short, their radio chatter like something from a TV crime thriller.

Talking to the tall officer, away from me, the darkly-tanned woman sealed my fate, without allowing me to speak, and when the tall officer insisted that we were all Europeans by law, I remarked: "You're not. You, like me, are a form of Anglo-Saxon".

This appeared too much for the law-abiding officer and he made a move to get me. All he got, however, was my scarf, umbrella and papers as I went down the stairs at the double where outside on the pavement, as my neighbours went by, my belongings were handed back to me by the pair of helmeted officers!

Wondering why no proper written details were recorded by the police on the spot, and anxious to discover if it had all been done electronically, I went round to the local police station to find out.

As happened when I consulted the police about the way I had been thrown out of an East End pub, I was dealt with by a privatised clerk, and I objected. Meanwhile, the officers who had 'arrested' me, were seen at the back of the office, fiddling with a computer, and it seemed to me as if they were looking up my past, if any.

Eventually, however, a senior officer, who had been called from his desk, confronted me but could give me no clue as to how the call-out would be recorded on the international police network.

Thus, it seems, I could be marked down as an international trouble-maker and, if I needed to visit the dentist's native land, I could be stopped from entry.

Well, with the new Labour government all set to defend the little man and woman against life's oppressive pin-pricks, what can be done to clear me on these three counts? Unless one is blessed with a good sense of humour, as I am, these types of occurrences, particular to the older generation, could be very upsetting.

Footnote: There is no doubt about it, political correctness is a form of instant mental terrorism, the aim of which is to stifle free speech between sensible people of all races. It must be routed from society. A law report in *The Times* of 28th July 1999, headed 'Freedom to be offensive defended by court', stated: "Free speech included not only the inoffensive, but also the irritating, the contentious, the eccentric, the heretical, the unwelcome, and the provocative, as long as such speech did not tend to provoke violence." An independent observer commented on the museum ban: "It does seem, reading between the lines, that your letter to the director, which was flippant but harmless, sparked tension at a time when the computer logging was in progress – apparently under-funded and under-staffed. It seems odd that, if some members of the museum staff were upset by the tone of your telephone conversations, none testified when you asked the director for written evidence. It does seem, too, that the director and his senior staff (employees), from the very outset, acted as judge and jury. In the circumstances, you have every right to contest them to the bitter end".

Appendices

A Bure Ferryman – *Suffolk Fair (April 1983)*

Aeronautical Archaeologist – *Air-Britain (April 1967)*

Ambassador in Armour – *Sussex Life (September 1965)*

American Invasion: Memories – *Eastern Daily Press*

An Egyptian Puss Who Taught Me A Thing or Two – *East Anglian Magazine (March 1956)*

Anne's Challenge to the Luftwaffe – *390th Bomb Group Memorial Journal (September 1987)*

Apprentice to Battle – *East Anglian Magazine (July 1969)*

Arnhem: The Rescue Bid – *The Royal British Legion Journal (September 1974)*

Arthur H. Patterson – *East Anglian Magazine (January 1974)*

A Suffolk Village – *Norfolk Fair (July 1984)*

Backyard Flying – *Norfolk Fair (1985)*

Battle of Britain: How it Was Not Fought – *Air Mail (Autumn 1974)*

Beowulf – *East Anglia Monthly (August 1985)*

Billingshurst to Billingsgate – *(Source uncertain)*

Breath of the Jets – *Ipswich Mercury Series (4th October 1968)*

Brig.-General Frederick W. Castle: The Last Flight – *(Source uncertain)*

Built of English Oak – *The Story of the Lifeboat (1973)*

Churchill – The Aviator – *Ipswich Mercury Series (16th April 1971)*

Coach Trips Lead to Several Trails – *Bury St Edmunds Midweek (1987)*

Codeword 'Cromwell' – *East Anglian Magazine (September 1968)*

Confessions of a Cub Reporter – *East Anglia Monthly (September 1984)*

Country Diaries – *Everything Has A Value (October 1980)*

Deserter's Flight – *(Source uncertain)*

Digging for the Hidden Past – *Radiography News (July 1988)*

Digging Up Passmore – *Popular Archaeology (February 1985)*

Dr Emerson's Priceless Treasures – *East Anglia Monthly (August 1985)*

Dunkirk Survivors: Tea & Cakes – *Beccles & Bungay Journal (15th June 1980)*

Dunkirk: the East Coast Connection – *East Anglia Monthly (March 1984)*

East Anglian 'Magpie' (*East Anglian Magazine (October 1969)*

East Anglian Ties with America – *East Anglia Monthly (August 1984)*

East Coast Smacksmen & The U-Boat War – *Sea Breezes (April 1966)*

English Village Characters – *This England (Spring 1983)*

Face to Face with Tom Paine – *East Anglian Magazine (June 1963)*

Farewell Hazelwood Cottage – *East Anglia Monthly (December 1985)*

Fiery Death of the L48: A Survivor – *East Anglian Daily Times (11th June 1987)*

First Man to Fly the North Sea – *The Scots Magazine (July 1964)*

Flying Moles: Beware! – *The Bury Leader (27th September 1988)*

Foreword

Frugal Outpost of Prayer – *East Anglia Monthly (October 1985)*

George Crabbe: Bi-Centenary – *Norfolk Fair (April 1985)*

Glider 'Bashers' 1945 – *Air Cadet News (February 1983)*

High-Jinks at Hawkinge *(Source uncertain)*

How Bomb Disposal Sergeant Proved He Was Loved – *The Royal Engineers Journal (December 2003)*

How England Lost Her Railings – *Country Life (17th September 1992)*

How Suffolk Artist Made Luftwaffe Smile – *(Source uncertain)*

How the US Navy Came to Greenwich – *The American (February 24th 1989)*

In Praise of Trees – *East Anglia Monthly (November 1985)*

In Saintly Footsteps – *East Anglia Monthly (June 1985)*

In Search of Little Worlingham – *Suffolk Fair (May 1983)*

In the Wake of East Anglia's Treasure Ships – *Treasure Hunting (January 1984)*

Japanese Swords (Lost War-Booty) – *The Royal British Legion Journal (September 1979)*

Jets & East Anglia – *The American (5th April 1986)*

Junkers Captain – *Norfolk Fair (July 1985)*

King Raedwald: Idol Footsteps – *Norfolk Fair (June 1985)*

Knights of the Gulf Air – *(Source uncertain)*

Last of the Norwich Raiders – *Norfolk Fair (October 1985)*

Lifeboat Saved Wartime Author – *Thanet Extra (20th May 1988)*

Literary Days at Colchester – *East Anglia Monthly (May 1985)*

Little Chapters in the Making

Long Runways – Concrete Partnerships – *Bury Mid-Week Extra (19th April 1983)*

Madingley's Sentinel Windmill – *East Anglia Monthly (August 1984)*

Master's Tools & Goods – *East Anglian Daily Times (27th October 1970)*

Mr Prickles – *Eastern Daily Press (29th December 1966)*

Nelson: Not Forgotten – *East Anglia Monthly* (December 1984)

Night Under a Wold Sky – *Lincolnshire Life* (Sepember 1990)

Norfolk House & D-Day – *The American* (9th March 1984)

Old Cannon Bollards – *The City Recorder* (7th August 1986)

Political Correctness – *(Source uncertain)*

Polly's Boots and Sailor Brothers – *Norfolk Fair* (November 1982)

Primrose's Painful Transition – *East Anglia Monthly* (March 1985)

Radio – Ahead of His Time – *East Anglian Daily Times* (11th June 1987)

Sir Alfred's Letter – *East Anglia Monthly* (April 1985)

Sizing Up Dear John – *The Suffolk Sage* (February/March 1994)

Snap Judgements – *Radiography News* (April 1988)

Southwold Fishermen – *Norfolk Fair* (September 1985)

Southwold Re-Visited – *Suffolk Mercury Series* (4th March 1983)

Souvenirs Fortify Remembrance – *(Source uncertain)*

Storm Dogs of Suffolk – *Suffolk Fair* (January 1985)

Sudbury Tail-Gunner – *Norfolk Fair* (August 1985)

Suffolk Farm Accounts – *Norfolk Fair* (September 1984)

Suffolk Names in Stone – *Norfolk Fair* (May 1984)

Sutton Hoo & Beowulf – *Norfolk Fair* (July 1984)

The Cat & Custard Pot – *(Source uncertain)*

The Gypsies – *East Anglian Magazine* (October 1965)

The Lady with Unseeing Eyes – *Beccles and Bungay Journal* (1st January 1971)

The Little Blitz – *East Anglia Monthly* (October 1984)

The Tennyson Brothers – *Norfolk Fair* (September 1985)

The Porcupine's Nail Brought to LIfe – *East Anglia Monthly* (September 1985)

The White Mouse Worked Here – *The Chelsea News* (28th August 1970)

Tragic Case of William Smith – *East Anglian Magazine* (March 1954)

USAAF (Early Books) – *390th Bomb Group Memorial Journal* (March 1985)

Vapour Trails *(Source uncertain)*

Vintage Model Planes – *Everything Has A Value* (April 1981)

Walberswick's Patriotic Film-Maker – *East Anglian Magazine* (June 1982)

War Poets with Suffolk Links (Abbey Honour) – *Norfolk Fair* (September 1985)

When Windmills Were Dashed to the Ground – *East Anglia Monthly* (June 1984)

Woodhenge at Arminghall – *(Source uncertain)*

Wren Who Flew High – *Air Mail* (Winter 1984)

Notes